M000074507

Reclaiming Gender:
Transgressive Identities in
Modern Ireland

Edited by
Marilyn Cohen and Nancy J. Curtin

St. Martin's Press
New York

ISBN 0-312-21337-9

Library of Congress Cataloging-in-Publication Data
Reclaiming gender:transgressive identities in modern Ireland/
   edited by Marilyn Cohen and Nancy J. Curtin.
      p.   cm.
   Includes bibliographical references and index.
   ISBN 0-312-21337-9(cloth)
      1. Gender identity—Ireland   2. Sex role—Ireland.   3. Identity
(Psychology)—Ireland.   I. Cohen, Marilyn.   II. Curtin, Nancy J.
HQ1075.5.I73R43   1999
305.3'09415—dc21   99–23512
                                                                CIP

Design by Letra Libre, Inc.

First edition: November, 1999
10   9   8   7   6   5   4   3   2   1

Contents

Contributors

GORDON BIGELOW is Assistant Professor of English at Rhodes College.

ANGELA BOURKE is Statutory Lecturer of Modern Irish and Director of the M.Phil. Program in Irish Studies at the National University of Ireland, Dublin.

JOANNA BOURKE is Reader in History at Birkbeck College, University of London.

ANNE BYRNE is Lecturer in the Department of Political Science and Sociology at the National University of Ireland, Galway.

MARILYN COHEN is Assistant Professor of Anthropology at Montclair State University.

KATHRYN CONRAD is Assistant Professor of English at the University of Kansas.

NANCY J. CURTIN is Professor of History at Fordham University.

JANE GRAY is Lecturer in the Department of Sociology at the National University of Ireland, Maynooth.

RUTH-ANN M. HARRIS is Adjunct Professor of History and Irish Studies at Boston College.

MARY J. HICKMAN is Reader in European Studies and Director of the Irish Studies Centre, University of North London.

WILLIAM F. KELLEHER is Assistant Professor of Anthropology at the University of Illinois.

VERA KREILKAMP is Professor of English at Pine Manor College.

JOAN VINCENT is Professor Emeritus of Anthropology at Barnard College, Columbia University.

BRONWEN WALTER is senior Lecturer in Geography at Anglia Polytechnic University.

HEATHER ZWICKER is Associate Professor of English at the University of Alberta, Canada.

Introduction

Reclaiming Gender: An Agenda for Irish Studies ▣

Marilyn Cohen and Nancy J. Curtin

A s recently as ten years ago, when the editors of this volume were dotting the i's and crossing the t's of their finely polished dissertations and sending out the usual stack of job letters, prospective employers typically assumed that the simple absence of a Y chromosome was grounds for expecting the candidate to teach Women's Studies. After all, pressure in the United States had been building up for twenty years to include more women's courses in the curriculum. Outside of such strongholds as Brown, Wisconsin, and Rutgers, provision for academic training was still the exception rather than the rule in the top-tiered universities, and even more exceptional in the tiers below. Women's Studies was, or so it was presumed, a subject only of interest to women. Only women would want to take such courses, and only women would care to teach them.

The academic ghetto to which Women's Studies was relegated may have been splendid in some places, and there is no doubt that those who inhabited it or associated with it took full advantage of institutional marginalization. Not only did they produce an impressive body of scholarship interrogating the role of women in history, society, and culture, and the sex/gender systems shaping that role, but they also promoted equally impressive organizational supports, like the Berkshire Conference on the History of Women and the National Women's Studies Association. Marginalization within colleges and universities, and even within departments, necessitated interdisciplinary dialogue and association. The subject itself, "woman," required such dialogue, and that dialogue helped to push the subject from the margins toward the center of a variety of academic discourses, where the tools and assumptions of feminist analysis have become increasingly common.

A consideration of developments within Women's Studies offers another way of charting this push toward the center (and it is still a push, for many road blocks still bar paths to the center). Much of the impetus behind the formation of the hundreds of programs in the United States and elsewhere came from early second-wave feminist coalitions of students and scholars seeking redress for the exclusion of women from the curriculum. The first task was the recovery of a women-centered past and culture—women's history, women's literature, women's art and music—a project that carried with it the suggestion of an essentialist feminism that rationalized the ghettoization and isolation of Women's Studies. But at the same time, feminist scholars began attacking essentialist and reified notions of the female and exploring the cultural construct of gender. As feminists sought to foreground that which had been hidden from history, they came to problematize, as opposed to simply rationalize, the production and reproduction of sex-gender systems, or the cultural construct of gender. Just as the social and cultural category of "woman" could not be considered in isolation from the sex/gender system that shaped the category, neither could systems of social structure be completely understood in isolation from the gendered division of labor upon which they were founded.[1] Furthermore, understanding sex/gender systems and the political, social, and cultural hierarchies they spawned required a critical reconstitution of the social meaning of "man." Women's Studies thus emerged as both an identity-based program and a site for the interrogation of all forms of social and cultural identity. And that interrogation required dipping into anthropology, history, psychology, biology, literature, law, and more.

Consider another widely presumed identity-based academic project—Irish Studies—marginalized, sometimes richly and gloriously so, in its academic centers, often Catholic universities eager to project their Catholic identity through ethnic association. Once again the presumption is that only the ethnic Irish are interested in Irish Studies, and only the ethnic Irish, or better, the Irish themselves, are essentially qualified to teach it. The mere possession of an Irish surname can establish an instructor's credentials to teach a survey course in Irish history. It's feel-good history anyway, with courses attuned to massaging ethnic sensibilities, but Irish history, or Irish Studies, is so exceptionalist, and so peculiar, as to be not very useful for scholars in other fields.

While scholars based in Irish Studies welcome such institutional support (it provides employment, after all), as well as the attention of the ethnic community and the enthusiasm of students in their over-subscribed classes, the failure of their work to penetrate other fields and disciplines has been a source of perplexing frustration. Splendid ghettoization has supported fine scholarship, yet European and even British historians feel no necessity to keep abreast of Irish historiographical developments, which, so it is assumed, chart a unique experience that can contribute little in the way of illuminating more generalized historical experiences. Irish literature has been more fortunate in having a few canonized writers up its green sleeve, fare tokens out of the ghetto. Just as a similar disregard and marginalization helped to transform the particularist Women's Studies into the more universal Gender Studies, so we hope Irish Studies will push its way toward the mainstream of academic discourses. This book seeks to serve both mainstreaming enterprises, bringing gender to the central questions of Irish Studies, and Irish Studies to the central questions in Gender Studies.

We hope to "reclaim" gender as a central tool of analysis from those who still regard it as synonymous with Women's Studies. This is not to say we don't applaud the growing number of publications illustrating the agency of women in Irish history and culture that have been published over the last two decades.[2] We sympathize but must take issue with an agenda for Irish women's history set forth in a 1992 article in *Irish Historical Studies* by Margaret MacCurtain, Mary O'Dowd, and Maria Luddy.[3] The authors acknowledge that in much of Europe and North America the emphasis in academic inquiry has shifted from a preoccupation with identity-based scholarship—women's history, women's experiences, women's participation in the state and the economy, and women's relation to culture in general—to gender analysis. But they caution against the application of this shift to Irish scholarship. Their reasons are two-fold: first, while replacing women with gender was supposed to lead to incorporation of women into the mainstream of historical writing, that hasn't happened, and will probably not happen in the near future; and second, the empirical reconstruction of women's lives and experiences must precede gender analysis, and that empirical project, the authors claim, has a long way to go. We agree with the importance of uncovering empirical evidence relating to women's lives, and many of the chapters in this book contribute to this project. However, we question the empiricist assumptions often lurking just beneath the surface of this project, which presume that facts about women's lives speak for themselves. MacCurtain, O'Dowd, and Luddy are probably correct that, dress it up as you will as gender history or women's history, the subject will still have considerable difficulty in permeating the work of a male historical establishment that persists in regarding sex/gender systems as either natural or inevitable, and therefore in no need of interrogation. The agenda for Irish women's history calls upon us to challenge these expectations, and write the history of Irish women the way we want to—an historiographical enterprise running parallel to mainstream history, and justified by its own intrinsic value rather than the judgments of the establishment.

We like the attitude. But we take issue with this insistence on placing the recovery project of women's history as the necessary first ontological step. A more comprehensive theoretical analysis of gender reveals the limiting empiricism of Irish scholarship, particularly in history and the social sciences. We maintain that placing gender at the center of the feminist agenda is essential to advancing both feminist scholarship and praxis. Feminists and queer activists, committed to the political and social consequences of their academic work, have long held that the realization of gender equality and justice will not emerge from a one-sided concern with women or from a one-dimensional hegemonic construct of masculinity. Gender equity also depends on understanding or deconstructing and reformulating oppressive masculinities.

The female subjects in Irish women's history have been fit into received historical categories, periods, and paradigms without examining the extent to which these have emerged from the normative experience of men. Rather than questioning the narrative foundations of mainstream scholarship, women's history has tended to insert women as missing subjects, usually separately, into these narratives. Such a perspective not only overlooks the social construction of masculinity but also cannot address how women can be part of analyses that present human experience as exemplified by the lives of men—wars, revolutions, and state building, for example. Rather than integrated into its processes, women are often isolated as a special and separate topic of history. Such isolation de-emphasizes the symbiotic social construction of masculinities and femininities as well as the transformative and transgressive dynamics within gendered systems of power and social organization.

It is to redress the lopsided attention placed on women in Gender Studies that this collection emphasizes the varieties of Irish masculinity. Nancy J. Curtin illustrates the theoretical crux of postcolonial critics— the intersection of gender and imperialism—as she explores the gendered civic subject. A self-immolating republican masculinity emerged in the 1790s and endured through the twentieth century, providing legitimization for persistent anti-colonial resistance. Vera Kreilkamp continues the saga, mapping out this reactive binary in several middle-brow texts of post-Independence fiction that pitted virile and virtuous republican man against a sexually dysfunctional landed and colonial elite. The assertion of "manhood" as a strategy of colonial resistance in the contemporary period is illustrated by anthropologist William Kelleher, whose ethnographic research probes workers' gendered identities on the shopfloor of a northern Irish glassworks factory. But lest the boys have the last word, Heather Zwicker explores contemporary republican women's critique of what we might well call the Irish republican masculine mystique.

An outgrowth of highlighting the interdependence of cultural constructs of masculinity and femininity is the exposure of a tenacious conceptual binary posed between public and private domains, with men occupying the former social space and women the latter. Thus men's history focuses on the state, while women's history focuses on the home. This conception has had significant consequences for the analysis of social life, especially the political and the economic. Recent scholarship has revealed the widespread reluctance among American economists in the formative years of that academic discipline to consider women, children, or the family as appropriate subjects for economic analysis.[4] A woman's unpaid labor in the home, which reproduced her family on a daily basis, was morally important but economically unproductive. One consequence is the persistent underreporting of women's occupations in the census, a problem addressed by Jane Gray, who in this volume creatively attempts resolution by formulating her own means to measure and access the importance of handspinning to the pre-Famine Irish economy. The founding fathers of political economy and their neoclassical successors both reproduced the gendered binary of men as rational self-interested agents and women as moral and altruistic. The reluctance to view women's unwaged work as productive was partially overcome, though closely contained, by the new home economics movement. As Gordon Bigelow demonstrates in his chapter on Asenath Nicholson, it was more acceptable for women than for men to apply economics to women's sphere, especially within the feminine parameters of domestic economy.

Yet, as so many of the chapters in this volume demonstrate, gender permeates the ordering of political, economic, and family life and cultural consciousness, and hence destablilizes such easy artificial demarcations. Connections between familism, its concomitant heteronormative definitions of gender and roles (see the chapters by Anne Byrne and Kathryn Conrad), and broader developments at the political and economic levels in Ireland continuously weave throughout the fabric of these chapters. Feminists have long argued that the family or private domain is no less political than the public, and further, as Byrne and Conrad show here, the private has been aggressively colonized by the public in Ireland. Familist ideology is, after all, as many of our contributors remind us, enshrined in Article 41 of the Irish Constitution. The public/private binary is further challenged by Joan Vincent, who argues in her analysis of the Land War in the Irish northwest that men and women engaged in Land League agitation because family interests were at stake. Appeals to men "through their womenfolk" were not simply attempts to appeal to an essentialist, public, political masculinity, but rather reflect the interdependence between public and private at the level of quotidian life. Joanna Bourke also confronts the public/private dichotomy directly by examining the construction of an acceptable Irish masculinity within the "private" domain of the home.

We hope this book will accomplish three goals that inform both its structure and content. First, we seek to advance Irish Studies in general by showing how its practitioners are engaging topics and theoretical matters of interest to scholars in other fields who often dismiss Ireland and things Irish as particularist and parochial. Second, we want to stimulate critical interdisciplinary dialogue within Irish Studies. And finally, we expect to advance Gender Studies by demonstrating the illuminating qualities and centrality of gender analysis when applied to mainstream historical and theoretical concerns.

Feminist scholars have long emphasized that the connections and continuities existing in knowledge and real life are falsely compartmentalized within academic disciplines. In Irish Studies, the move toward interdisciplinarity has been sluggish; we are organized in multidisciplinary organizations, but rather than promoting dialogue and exchange, we more or less tolerantly take turns. For the most part, disciplinary boundaries have few crossers. Part of the explanation, of course, is that Ireland has been grossly undertheoretized. For the past several decades or so a particularist empiricism has been at war with an equally particularist and uncritical romantic metanarrative based on nationalism. But increasingly many Irish Studies scholars are responding to new theoretical and interdisciplinary challenges such as postcolonialism, feminism, and cultural studies, mostly because they find these challenges intrinsically interesting and useful. Such boundary crossing promises to breach some of the ghetto walls, permitting more Irish Studies scholars to see out, but more important, permitting other scholars to see in.

Interdisciplinarity has been defined in a variety ways, but it involves more than just raiding other disciplines to analyze an issue or problem. It is an approach that integrates disciplines by creating new organizing concepts, methodologies, skills, and epistemologies. Feminist scholars have been path breakers in attempts to formulate an authentic interdisciplinarity.[5] In Irish Studies, where such discourse has only just emerged, a handful of scholars, some of whom are represented here, are grappling with these issues.[6]

This book approaches interdisciplinarity in a preliminary manner. We define interdisciplinarity as receptivity to theoretical and methodological approaches from outside the boundaries of disciplinary protocols. The volume's multidisciplinary contributors are drawn from history, anthropology, sociology, literary and cultural studies, and geography. For the most part, they engage in dialogue from their own disciplinary enclaves. But it is this dialogue that is the first step toward interdisciplinarity. Thus we witness interdisciplinary exchange in the organization of this book, divided into four broad themes, with each theme addressed from representatives of different disciplines. Integrative methodological and theoretical approaches that demonstrate an efficacious interdisciplinarity are demonstrated here by Bigelow, Vincent, Marilyn Cohen, and Gray, and by the only example of interdisciplinary collaboration in this volume (aside from this introduction), Mary. J. Hickman and Bronwen Walter.

It is significant that social scientists (both in this book and generally) are taking the lead in offering authentic interdisciplinary analyses, especially since part of the explanation for the slow advancement of interdisciplinarity among social scientists in the Irish academy is the century-long domination of structural/functionalism—a theoretical paradigm antithetical to history and emphasizing functional interdependence at the expense of conflict. Recent analyses of gender in Irish society by social scientists have challenged functionalism to address the depth of inequality existing between men and women in the past and present. They have begun to explore the theoretical intersections between gender, class, and ethnic/religious stratification revealing the complexity and instability of Irish gender identities as they are constructed and reconstructed across cultural space and historical time.

As postcolonialism and neo-marxism, inherently interdisciplinary theoretical paradigms, continue to permeate literary studies, we anticipate a further and welcomed erosion of disciplinary boundaries and the creation of more space for interdisciplinary engagement. In this book, for example, Angela Bourke's opening chapter addresses the gendered monolithic construction of stories and "tradition" in ways that reinforced nineteenth-century Catholic and patriarchal norms institutionalized in the church, the state, and the educational system. Orderly linear narratives by men were privileged through print at the expense of "uncentralized, polysemic, contradictory" oral narratives where the "silenced alternative cosmologies" of women and children were voiced. Conrad transcends the traditional disciplinary confines of English department protocols and expands the concept of "text" to a larger politicized concept of "information" and the security requirements of the Northern Irish state. Both these expanded concepts of "information" and "tradition" lead us to consider the ways in which disciplines such as feminist literary criticism have integrated the concept of culture, once the quintessential concept of anthropology.[7]

Part I of this book sets the theoretical tone by identifying recurrent gender binaries and the persistent implications of these in such basic articulations as tradition and narrative, citizenship, the state, and familism. Part II explores the construction and reproduction of Irish maculinities from the cottage to the Big House to the factory floor. The erasure of the female from economic discourse constitutes a major theme in the chapters included in Part III, shedding new light on political economy as theory, history, and domestic strategies of survival. The last section, Part IV, broadens Byrne's notion of "difficult identities," focusing more specifically on the local construction of gender and the transgressive subject by examining the agency of Irish people, in historically-specific contexts, renegotiating restrictive class, gender, and ethnic identities and relations.

In all sections, emphasis has been given to the voices of Irish subjects under scrutiny. This reflects in part a growing impatience with the dense, distancing, impersonal tone of so much scholarly analysis. The chapters here, laden with stories, experiences and voices, address a broader concern with resolving the apparent contradiction between compelling accessible narratives and rigorous but often inaccessible analysis. As feminists in search of women's literary traditions have pointed out, resolving the contradictions among analysis, writing, and praxis is of particular relevance.

While gender inequality permeates the social life of modern Ireland, south and north, there is a new consciousness of how the omnirelevance of gender symbolism is reflected in both scholarship and activism. Ireland today is still characterized by gender asymmetry, but this privileging of the male is being modified in significant ways by more inclusive, pluralist and feminist ideologies and politics, exemplified by the emergence and impact of the "women's coalition" in the north. We hope this book makes a contribution to these movements at the concrete and abstract levels by offering problem-focused research and analysis informed by feminist consciousness and inspired by the desire that people understand, explain, and change inequitable distributions of power.

NOTES

1. See, e.g., Gayle Rubin, "The Traffic in Women: Notes on the 'Political Economy' of Sex," in Rayna Reiter, ed., *Toward an Anthropology of Women* (New York: Monthly Review Press, 1975), 157–210.
2. For a discussion of recent works on gender in Ireland, see Laura Lyons, "The State of Gender in Irish Studies: A Review Essay," *Eire-Ireland* 32–3 (Winter 1997/Spring-Summer 1998): 236–60.
3. Margaret MacCurtain, Mary O'Dowd, and Maria Luddy, "An Agenda for Women's History in Ireland, 1500–1900," *Irish Historical Studies* 28 (May 1992): 1–37.

4. See, e.g., Nancy Folbre, "The 'Sphere of Women' in Early-Twentieth Century Economics," in *Gender and American Social Science: The Formative Years,* ed. Helene Silverman (Princeton: Princeton University Press, 1998), 35–60.

5. See the special issue "Disciplining Feminism? The Future of Women's Studies," *Feminist Studies* 24 (Summer, 1998) for a thorough treatment of these and other issues relating to interdisciplinarity.

6. For a discussion of the interdisciplinary impulse in Irish Studies, see Marilyn Cohen, "Beyond Boundaries: Toward an Interdisciplinary Irish Studies," *Eire-Ireland* 31 (Spring/Summer 1996): 137–62.

7. This kind of theoretical hybridity has been slower to penetrate the discipline and practice of Irish history, which, with certain important exceptions, has been dominated by empiricism and the tendency to see the sources as transparent reflections of social reality. Occupying one of the most traditional and privileged enclaves in the academy, historians in general and Irish historians in particular have not been required to earn legitimacy by seeking out innovative theoretical paradigms and epistemologies. See Nancy J. Curtin, "'Varieties of Irishness': Historical Revisionism, Irish Style," *Journal of British Studies* 35 (April 1996): 195–219.

Gender Ideologies

Chapter One

Irish Stories of Weather, Time, and Gender: Saint Brigid ▓

Angela Bourke

Brigid, said to have lived in the sixth century, is honored by the Christian churches and by folklore as the chief female saint of Ireland. Catholic devotion to her was revived and standardized in the nineteenth century, and she was offered to generations of schoolchildren as the very model of all that was most desirable in Irish womanhood. Brigid's is one of the longest entries in the monumental nine-volume *Lives of the Irish Saints,* published in the late nineteenth century by Canon John O'Hanlon.[1] Her cult had a nationalist dimension too, for medieval references to her as *Maire na nGael* ("The Mary of the Irish") and *ala Maire* ("another Mary") allowed commentators to single her out as embodying values and a version of femininity that they could present as uniquely Irish. One parish priest in County Clare was reported to have preached every year between 1893 and 1923 on the life of St. Brigid as a true model for Irish women.[2] Churches, orphanages, convents, schools, hospitals—and girl children—were named after her, and when Irish women emigrated in their thousands and took up jobs as domestic servants in Britain and North America, so many of them were called Bridget (as the name was then usually spelled), that "Biddy" came to be the common term used to refer to them. Recent scholarship emphasizes the extent to which the medieval figure of the Christian saint was constructed on the foundation of an earlier goddess cult,[3] but the Catholic tradition of late nineteenth- and early twentieth-century Ireland downplayed this connection. Stories about Brigid featured prominently in the school reading books of the newly independent Irish state. Statues and images, ubiquitous in churches, schools, hospitals and other public buildings until the 1960s, and still to be seen in many of them, showed the saint dressed in a brown and white habit, such as nuns wore in nineteenth-century Ireland. In her hand she held a model of the church she is said to have founded in Kildare. She was often accompanied by a cow.

Many of the themes and images associated with Brigid in Canon O'Hanlon's *Lives of the Irish Saints* and in the cultural prescriptions of the emerging Irish State were derived from medieval hagiography—the lives of the saint written in Latin and Old Irish from the seventh century onward—but the oral tradition current in many parts of Ireland was another important source for these writers. They constructed a consistent figure of Brigid as a beautiful and modest virgin, kind and generous, working wonders of food production and hospitality, healing the sick and performing miracles by her innocence and sanctity, excelling above all at dairying and domestic tasks.

One of the most common of the stories that appeared in schoolbooks is found in both medieval and oral sources. It tells of Brigid's coming in out of the rain after herding sheep, and hanging her wet cloak on a sunbeam to dry. This cloak also features in the legend of how she obtained land to build her church: having persuaded the local king to give her as much as her cloak would cover, she laid it on the ground, whereupon it spread to cover the many acres of the Curragh of Kildare. Another narrative tells us that Brigid was pursued by a man who wanted to marry her on account of her great beauty, and who had the support of her father and brothers. She did not wish to marry. (Pious literature says that she wanted to enter a convent and devote her life to God, but we can equally well read the story as saying she preferred an autonomous life in a community of women). When her brother remarked that such a beautiful eye as hers ought to lie on a pillow beside a man, she plucked out the eye, whereupon her suitor gave up, her family relented, and she became a nun. Later, when her virginity was no longer in danger, the eye was miraculously restored.[4]

This sort of didactic consistency and standardization is not the norm in oral tradition; rather, it represents the appropriation of oral storytelling by dominant interests through writing. Oral tradition, by its nature, is various, uncentralized, polysemic and often contradictory, but the versions of oral tradition adopted by Irish churchmen and educationalists in the nineteenth and twentieth centuries appeared to speak with one, extremely conservative, voice. Ireland was by no means unique in this. As Ernest Gellner remarks, "Nationalism usually conquers in the name of a putative folk culture. Its symbolism is drawn from the healthy, pristine, vigorous life of the peasants."[5] Outside the operetta-like representations of sturdy peasant culture favored by those in power, however, oral tradition lives on, as people continue to observe practices and tell stories that have meaning for them. The manuscript archive of the Irish Folklore Collection (IFC) at the National University of Ireland, Dublin, is a rich repository of legends and observances relating to Brigid. The vernacular tradition that predates the nineteenth-century revival of devotion associates her with certain areas more than with others. Brigid is supposed to have come from County Louth, where Faughart, in the hills north of Dundalk, is marked as her birthplace. Her main church foundation is in Kildare, but parts of Connacht also claim her as their own, and dozens of places around the country are called "Kilbride," from *Cill Bhríde* ("Brigid's Church"). A famous holy well at Liscannor, near the Cliffs of Moher in County Clare, is only one of an immense number of wells where Brigid is invoked for help with problems ranging from eye trouble to infertility.

Much of the material now in the IFC was collected by the then Irish Folklore Commission in the ordinary course of recording stories and traditions, but in 1942, the commission sent a questionnaire to hundreds of enthusiastic informants around the country, asking for information about Brigid: stories of her life, and traditions relating to her feast day or to wells and other places associated with her. Three hundred and eighty-five replies were received: some 30,000 manuscript pages, which now comprise nine large bound volumes in the archive.

It is not surprising to find among the questionnaire replies some material that is clearly influenced by devotional literature, such as this verse from Ennis, Co. Clare:

> O dear St. Brigid of the Gael
> Flower of the emerald sod
> Over all our Irish hearts prevail
> And keep us close to God.[6]

The stories favored by revivalists also appear, as informants tell of the spiritual beliefs and practices of their own lives, but these manuscripts also contain a wealth of material that clearly owes little or nothing to the piety of the pulpit or the print media. Kevin Danaher's writings on calendar custom have drawn on this "other" material to show how stories and traditions relating to St. Brigid's Day mark the beginning of the agricultural year, while Séamas Ó Catháin's 1995 monograph focuses on connections between Celtic and Nordic traditions, and a possible link with the bear cult.[7] The present essay is concerned with how the figure of Brigid articulates ideas about weather, time, and gender in oral tradition, in ways that reflect a division of the year into dark and light halves, and of the world into male and female spheres (or hemispheres).

Brigid's stories illustrate how a symmetrical model that has the potential to validate equality and partnership between the masculine and the feminine, or between women and men in society, has been skewed in such a way as to privilege the masculine, all in the name of "tradition." Some of these stories also offer the possibility that the symmetry and balance of that model can be recovered, by attempting to hear oral narratives on their own terms, free from the preconceptions induced by print, and with a more pluralist sense of the word tradition. Resistance to dominant interests may be found in the very varied voices of living tradition, usually in those genres least privileged by the metropolitan mass media. By listening to these forms of oral tradition, or by reading in the margins and between the lines of transcribed text, we can sometimes discover narratives that have been repressed or largely silenced: ones in which alternative patterns of cosmology and ways of looking at the world and at human relations have been encoded.[8]

Long before the coming of Christianity, *Brigit* was the name of a powerful goddess. The Latin and Irish lives of the saints show considerable continuity with the cult of this goddess, associated with fertility and with fire. Other medieval references to the saint (and to secular characters with similar names), contain stories that bulge uncomfortably beyond the contours of the dominant hagiographic discourse, hinting at narratives that have been repressed in the construction of the official one.

Several references suggest that in medieval Ireland, calling Brigid *Maire na nGael*, "the Mary of the Irish," was taken to be more than metaphor. The seventh-century Ultán of Ardbraccan is named as author of a description of her as *in chroíb co mbláthaib, in máthir Ísu:* "the flowery branch, the mother of Jesus," while another poet, Broccán, described her a little later as *máthair mo rurech; ba hoenmáthair Maicc Ríg Máir:* "mother of my king; only mother of the great King's Son." This embarrassingly unorthodox portrayal of a Christian virgin was later glossed by someone who only succeeded in making matters worse. He explained that the line meant *ba hoen de matribus Christi Brigit:* a macaronic in Irish and Latin that translates "Brigid was one of the mothers of Christ."[9] It recalls a more modern Breton tradition that names three shrines of St. Anne, stating that these three Annes were the "three grandmothers of Our Saviour."[10] Celtic mothergoddesses were often found in triple form; like Anne, Brigid has carried some of their characteristics into Christian tradition.

The medieval story of Brigid's birth marks her clearly as a (literally) liminal figure, for she was born on a doorstep—neither indoors nor out—and at dawn—neither by night nor by day. Maria Tymoczko has drawn attention to the way the cult of the Celtic mother-goddesses is localized in liminal zones, suggesting that this enables them to embody a totality expressed in duality and paradox.[11] We shall see that the figure of Brigid, par-

ticularly in the less privileged genres of oral tradition, expresses just such a
preoccupation with paradox.

The oral tradition of Ireland is rich in religious narratives. The vast majority of the population is Catholic, but for some two hundred years, from
the enactment of the first penal laws passed against Catholic ecclesiastics in
the late seventeenth century[12] until after the Famine of the middle of the
nineteenth, religious education was conducted unofficially, and for the
most part orally. Themes and images long abandoned by the European
church of the Counter-Reformation were current, and in some places still
are, in the oral poetry and narratives of the Irish-speaking tradition. Until
Catholic Emancipation in 1829, Catholics had only few and rudimentary
church buildings. The practice of religion was therefore centered on the
home rather than the church, and the oral transmission of religious tradition was mostly the responsibility of older women.[13]

Margaret MacCurtain has written about the transition, following the
great Famine, from "a populist, peasant-based native style [of spirituality]
towards a more disciplined and churchly [town-based] observance. . . ."
She continues:

> After the Famine, particularly during the period of Cardinal Paul Cullen's
> ministry as archbishop of Dublin (1852–78), the Catholic Church gained as-
> cendancy over the minds of its flock. Devotions, more precisely "imported"
> devotions, became the familiar vehicle of prayer for the church-goer. . . .
> The black-covered prayer book appeared, a sign of rising literacy. An an-
> thology of prayers for all occasions, it was packed with invocations to con-
> tinental saints. . . .
> By the death of Cardinal Cullen in 1878, the fundamental changes in
> Irish society, which made its general tone more "bourgeois," had taken
> place. For the Catholic population the dominant spirituality sprang from the
> middle class. It was town-based and centered on the "chapel." Convent
> schools for girls reflected these trends [with an emphasis on] French culture,
> including the spoken language, in girls' boarding schools in Ireland.[14]

When Canon O'Hanlon published his *Lives of the Irish Saints,* the first
volume of which appeared in 1875, Irish Catholicism was a bastion of
conservative respectability. His portrayal of native saints like Brigid laid
heavy emphasis on those virtues most common among European saints
and most acceptable to bourgeois society. One of his sources was the oral
tradition, rich in stories of the saints associated with particular places and
accounts of popular celebrations in their honor, but he selected only those
aspects of folk tradition that suited his agenda. Meanwhile, unwritten and
unknown outside their local communities, stories and practices of other
kinds lived on.

The Folklore of Ireland Society was founded in 1926, and was succeeded, with government support, by the Irish Folklore Commission in
1935. Like Finland and some other emerging nations, Ireland was setting
seriously about the task of cultural decolonization by investing heavily in
the reprivileging of native tradition. A group of talented and dedicated
scholars and administrators set about collecting and archiving folklore in
Irish and English. Essays were written comparing the finest storytellers
to Homer, and writers of fiction were encouraged to emulate the style
and matter of oral storytelling. To the national agenda of fostering con-
tinental-style Catholic piety was added one of celebrating the nobility
and intellectual majesty of native traditions.[15] The longest stories, told
usually by older men in any given community, beginning and ending
with long formulaic flourishes, and featuring kings, giants, and plenty of
fighting, were the ones most sought after. These hero-tales and international folktales are magnificent examples of oral verbal art, but for the
new nation-state they had the additional advantage of escapism: the
virtues they advocated were simple and heroic, the characters uncomplicated. One woman storyteller, Peig Sayers, of the Great Blasket Island,
County Kerry (1873–1958), was singled out for praise and publication,
but in general, women's traditions, children's folklore, the obscene or Ra-
belaisian, and those genres not usually featured in public performance
got much less coverage than full-length folktales, and were less often celebrated in print.[16]

This process of enlisting the people's traditions on behalf of dominant
interests has been placed in a wider context of colonialism by Carol
Coulter:

> The secular nationalism which first attracted the young intellectuals of the
> colonies was quickly combined with a rediscovery of and a reassertion of
> pride in the native culture, which was often homogenised and idealised in
> the process, its more conservative aspects enhanced . . . [as the] . . . emerg-
> ing new elite . . . consolidated a new state perpetuating the inequalities of
> the old.
>
>   This demanded the creation of an ideology to justify the new *status quo*.
> The native culture, inherently uncentralised, further fragmented by years of
> foreign domination, is given an artificial centralisation and cohesion to serve
> the conservative needs of the new rulers. The diverse, chaotic and often sub-
> versive aspects of the indigenous culture are purged in the name of a new
> "national" culture, inculcated by the education system, and combined with
> a new version of history to justify the new status quo. Usually the religion
> of the mass of the people is pressed into service to assist in this role. This
> proves a potent instrument for social control, especially the oppression of
> women.[17]

The selection of Brigid as a model for Irish girls and women was an example of just this sort of cultural programming. Fortunately, however, the Irish Folklore Commission was more concerned with description than with prescription: the manuscripts of the IFC contain images of Brigid that are indeed diverse, chaotic, and even subversive. Most of them seem to owe their survival to connections with calendar custom, or with practices carried out in particular places; such genres would have been less likely than more formal genres of storytelling to come into conflict with prescribed narratives.

Brigid's feast-day was formerly much more than a church celebration. It falls on 1 February, one of the four cross-quarter days in the Irish calendar, the others being *Bealtaine* (Mayday—1 May), the first day of summer, *Lughnasa,* (1 August), the beginning of harvest, and *Samhain* (1 November), the day after Hallowe'en and the beginning of winter. These days fall midway between the solstices and equinoxes, dividing the year in four according to a solar calendar. The seasons they delimit do not correspond to those known in North America or in most of the western world, which expects spring to begin on 21 March, not on 1 February, but in the mild maritime climates and northern latitudes of Ireland (and Scotland, Wales, and Brittany), where day-length, rather than temperature, is what dramatically distinguishes summer from winter, they make sense. In an agricultural society that for centuries did without clocks, calendars, and almanacs, the cross-quarter days were the points around which time was organized.

Brigid's day is the only one of the cross-quarter day festivals to have become a Christian feast. In early sources it is called *Imbolc,* a name which does not survive in modern Irish and which has been etymologized in various ways over the centuries. *Imbolc* appears to have had particular associations with lactation in animals, and with motherhood. In its Christian expression it comes one day before Candlemas, a feast of the Virgin Mary.

All four cross-quarter days are accompanied by a wealth of traditional sayings, stories, and practices, and clearly preserve an ancient division of the year, primarily into light and dark halves, and secondarily into quarters. Winter—from November to the beginning of May—was the season for storytelling and teaching, for indoor activities and community consolidation, while summer was the time for the outdoor activities involved in farming and in interacting with other communities. Nerys Thomas Patterson has written about the complex system of social connections imbricated in the celebration and marking of the cross-quarter days in a medieval pastoral society, while Máire MacNéill demonstrated brilliantly in 1962 how much of that system still persisted in contemporary practice, narrative, and thought.[18]

Samhain and *Bealtaine* are characterized by a perception that the door between this world and the otherworld stands dangerously open as the seasons change. Those dates are marked as much by fear and precaution as by celebration, with many stories of fairy intrusions into human life. The first days of February and August, on the other hand, mark halfway points in human work and husbandry. Both come at the end of periods of hunger, and both are celebrated with special meals. Unlike the better-known festivals that divide the year in half, *Lughnasa* and Brigid's day are personified, and therefore gendered, as male and female, for *Lughnasa* is the festival of the young god Lugh.

Halves and wholes constitute an insistent theme in the stories of Brigid and her day. This is expressed sometimes very explicitly, sometimes implicitly, and often includes the paradox that something whole in itself may also be half of something larger.[19] In the case of Brigid, a binary quality is expressed repeatedly, which seems to have at its most basic a mnemonic function in the organization of the calendar: a warning that although spring is beginning, winter is only half over, coupled with a reassurance that if half the winter's supplies remain in storage, there will be enough to last until new food and fuel become available.

Like the story of her hanging her wet cloak on a sunbeam, much of Brigid's tradition deals with weather. Medieval and modern sources alike credit her with calming storms, halting wind and rain. A common tradition about Brigid's day recalls the American groundhog day: the hedgehog emerges from his winter sleep on the first day of February, but if he can see his own shadow, he declares that winter is only half over, and goes back to sleep.[20] The hedgehog would see his shadow only on a bright, sunny day, which at that time of year in Ireland would be crisp and cold. A February day without shadows, on the other hand, might be very mild, signaling the beginning of new growth. Here we have an example of weather-and-time lore expressed in paradox. Other traditions (found also in Wales, Scotland, and Brittany), state that on Brigid's day, a household should still have half its turf and half its hay: half of the winter stores of fuel and fodder should remain, if they are to last the winter. On the first day of February the ground is ready for breaking, in preparation for spring sowing; the days become longer by the length of a rooster's step; the birds choose their mates. "Half the lock is taken off the birds' throats on St. Brigid's day, we are told, so on that date they begin to sing.

The reiteration of ideas about halves and wholes is particularly striking when Brigid is set against Patrick, the male patron saint of Ireland, whose feast day comes six weeks after hers, on 17 March. On that day, close to the solstice, the second half of the birds' throats would be unlocked. On Brigid's day you can throw away half the candle; on St Patrick's day you can throw away the whole thing, as the season of artificial light is over. Brigid said she would dry half the road; Patrick said he would dry all of it; Brigid put one foot in the water and took the chill out of it (in Irish one foot is *leathchois*—literally half a foot—the expression used to denote one of a pair); Patrick put both feet in and warmed the water properly. There is a misogynistic turn to these sayings that depict Patrick as upstaging Brigid again and again, and imply that she only half-does things. Why should this be?

We have no direct evidence that 1 February was associated with the goddess Brigid in pre-Christian times, but it seems very likely that it was. Brigid, female saint or deity, presides over this festival, while Lugh, young and brilliant male deity of pre-Christian Ireland, owns the feast called after him, *Lughnasa,* at the opposite point in the calendar, on 1 August. Pádraig O Riain has shown how traditions of the god Lugh were woven into the life-stories of several saints, although Lugh was never Christianized under his own name, as Brigid was. Máire Mac Néill has demonstrated that in much oral tradition and local practice, Lugh has given way to Patrick, greatest hero of the Irish Christian pantheon.[21] It seems likely then that the comparison between Brigid and Patrick that is made in so many sayings and anecdotes may derive from an earlier tradition of contrasting Brigid and Lugh. Comparison with Patrick in weatherlore is invariably unfavorable to Brigid, given Patrick's position in the middle of the Irish spring, while Brigid remains ambiguously on its boundary with winter. Comparison with Lugh would have been more balanced—if only because of the symmetry of their positions in the calendar. Brigid's feast marks the beginning of spring sowing, Lugh's the beginning of harvest, exactly six months later.

Such a symmetrical opposition would well express the division of labor in the farm families of rural Ireland in the nineteenth and early twentieth centuries. Men had responsibility for all work beyond the house and farm-yard, and for relations with the wider community, while women took care of the house and yard, of food and light, of the fire on the hearth, and of the production and sale of butter and eggs. Women might do men's work, or men might do women's, when necessary, but numerous stories of fairy intervention in human life show that this was always felt to be a departure from the ideal. The division of labor was not the Victorian relegation of women to a helpless indoor life of economic dependence: rather, at least in its ideal expression in countless sayings and stories, it was a symbiotic relation. This model of work, family and community shows men and women cooperating through the complementary distribution of labor and economic resources: each needed the other, and while a man earned money by selling his labor or his farm animals, a woman's income from butter and eggs could be quite a significant proportion of household earnings, depending on her skill, and was hers to spend or save at her own discretion, according to the needs of the household.[22]

Lugh's is an outdoor festival, celebrated by the whole community's gathering on mountaintops to watch men engage in athletic contests, and to eat wild berries: the first fruit of autumn. It was sometimes called "Men's Sunday."[23] Brigid's day, by contrast, is domestic, clearly gendered feminine, and celebrated in and around the family home by the making of special crosses out of rushes or straw, the baking of a special cake, the recital of special prayers, and preparations for what was understood to be the saint's westward passage through the country on the eve of her feast. I am suggesting here that a theme of halves and wholes, capable of expressing economically and elegantly a whole complex of ideas about weather, time, and gender balance, has been bent out of shape under the influence of patriarchal models perpetrated by the Catholic church on the one hand, and the interests of a patrilocal, patrilinear tenant-farmer class on the other. As Patrick has replaced Lugh in oral tradition, women's contribution to a shared economy has been progressively devalued.

Many writers have remarked on the tendency of western civilization to reduce pairs to unity and to rank complementary opposites as higher and lower: this is seen most blatantly in the use of "man" as the unmarked form to refer to human persons, while "woman" must always be the marked form, a subset contained within the set "man."[24] At point after point in Irish oral tradition, in texts that do not fall within the scope of this chapter but that I have discussed elsewhere, we find expressions of unbearable tension in a world where cows are more important in a marriage contract than the woman being married, and the rights and aspirations of women who view themselves as equal partners in society are infringed upon by the demands of land tenure and inheritance through the male line.[25] In such a world, Brigid, with her resistance to marriage and her skills in food distribution and midwifery, emerges as an ally of women—not so much an ideal to which they should aspire, more a focus of empowering and subversive ideas.

In some parts of Ireland, on the last night of January, straw was placed beside the kitchen fire as a bed for Brigid. On the following day it was woven into crosses—shaped in some areas like swastikas, in others like the Mexican Eye of God—which were then placed in the thatch to preserve the house from fire. Stories told in many parts of Ireland describe Brigid as the Virgin Mary's midwife, and in certain areas women hung a piece of cloth, sometimes of a specific color, outdoors overnight, believing that the saint would touch it and give it power afterwards to ease the pain of childbirth. In Galway and Mayo, the cloth could be a piece of red flannel, or in one Mayo account, an article of clothing regularly worn by the family member who did the most dangerous work; in County Clare it might be a blue ribbon, and in Tipperary a black cloth.[26] The cloth was called in Irish *brat Bhríde*, "Brigid's cloak," or sometimes in English, "Brigid's towel." Recent accounts of the practice describe the *brat* as a rag pegged to the clothesline on the night before Brigid's day—a modern, urban manifestation of ancient practice. The *brat* is Brigid's constant attribute and is mentioned in the many accounts of her aid to pregnant and nursing mothers. In some areas, Brigid's cloak is taken to represent the snow, which is rare in Ireland, but can cover the ground in early February. The story of how the cloak was used to measure the land for Brigid's church resembles one told of Dido in the *Aeneid,* when an oxhide was cut into strips in a similar clever bargain, but Brigid's cloak is not cut; it spreads miraculously, while the assertion that the cloak is white and that it *is* the snow gives this account a particular resonance.

In many parts of Ireland, groups of young men or children carried Brigid in effigy from house to house on the last night of January.[27] Men who followed this custom were known as "biddies," or "biddy-boys," as they moved from house to house, disguised and cross-dressed. John Dunne's 1992 novel, Purtock, set in County Kildare, the center of Brigid's medieval tradition, gives a vivid account of these celebrations as carried out by children:

> All morning, while the women made the Biddy Cakes and wove the crosses that would protect the thatch from lightning, we were busy with our patron saint.
>
> Now, mounted on a stick, she is ready, her white dress fat with straw, her head a turnip covered with cotton tresses. There is no whingeing over who should bear Miss Biddy on her journey. Mary Margaret is the most popular girl in the village. Everyone loves her. And she has never loved anyone but me.
>
> Because it is the first wild flower to herald her feast-day, the dandelion is special to Saint Brigid and, so, Mary Margaret's hair is radiant with its yellow suns. She raises Miss Biddy above her head and we set off along the lane, forty voices chanting through the January air:
>
>> Here is Brigid dressed in white
>> Give us a penny for her delight.
>> She is deaf, she is dumb,
>> She cannot talk without a tongue.
>
> All that afternoon, we march from house to house until, as darkness falls, we crowd into Dunnes' yard and count the money for the Pattern.[28]

This view of the patron saint as "Miss Biddy," whose head is made from a turnip, who is deaf and dumb, and "cannot talk without a tongue," is a far cry from the Victorian piety of printed saints' lives, and the statue of the nun with the cow, but Danaher gives similar rhymes in *The Year in Ireland,* and others are to be found in the IFC manuscripts. Their content is quite compatible with a view of Brigid as ugly or mutilated, expressed consistently in the less privileged genres of oral tradition. In recent times, the *Brídeog* or "Miss Biddy" was sometimes a child's doll; more often, and longer ago, however, it was constructed from a churndash—symbol of dairying—or a broom, and the rhymes of the biddy-boys drew attention to its homely origin.

Equally irreverent were sayings like "Put down the dinner: Biddy is gone back." "Back" means westward, and this saying reflected the fact that after 1 February, as days got longer and farm work began again, the frugality of winter could be relaxed. During the very short days of winter, people stayed in bed or by the fire for a good part of each twenty-four hours, conserving energy and saving food. Only two meals a day were eaten and young men in particular complained of hunger. "Welcome Biddy, with the two dinners!" was another expression of enthusiasm for the increased food supply after the beginning of February: significantly, it is expressed in a doubling.

The tradition that Brigid plucked out her eye rather than marry forms part of received wisdom about the saint as celibate—an appeal to what the Catholic hierarchy in the 1920s spoke of as "the virtues characteristic of our race."[29] Oral versions of this story are often homely and intimate, however: very different from the prescriptive elegance of written versions. Here for instance is a narrative recorded in Faughart, County Louth, said to be the birthplace of Brigid. Medieval tradition says that Brigid belonged to the people called *Fotharta,* who occupied this part of Ireland, and that her father was called Dubhthach. Modern Faughart is a remote hill village with stunning views, on the Northern Ireland border, in what was a liminal area long before that border was drawn. There we are told that the saint's name was Brigid Duffy—the modern reflex of Dubhthach.

St Brigid was a very good-lookin' lassie and she was all the time prayin'. She went away to relayse her mother who was a slave. She was a king's daughter. She was follit home be a man on horseback and when she got to the Sthrame [of Faughart], she couldn't run from him no further, an' wint down on her knees in the wather an' tore the eye from her head; the stone where it lit is to be seen an' the track o' the lash o' the man's whip is in the stone as well. An' whin the man seen her, an' her after disfigurin' herself, he didn't know her at all & left her to herself. She brought a blessin' on Faughart ever since. I've heard it's the best grazin' in all Ireland, an' lightnin' never does no harm here.[30]

That account was recorded from a man in his nineties by full-time folklore collector Michael J. Murphy in 1942. Murphy wrote "sthrame" for "stream" and "follit" for "followed," emphasizing the unofficial, unprivileged and local qualities of this storytelling performance, which was clearly not a "performance" at all, in the mass media sense, but rather a private communication of material felt to be true, important, and relevant to the place where it was told.[31] In its reference to Brigid's pursuit by a man on horseback and his use of his whip against her, it recalls numerous accounts of rape and other oppression by landlords, who generally rode horses while the peasantry walked. It also encodes a resistance to and rejection of that oppression. In its references to the fine grazing around Faughart and the place's immunity to lightning, the narrative expresses optimism and a general pride in home.

The Stream of Faughart is a small river that flows through the churchyard and common land of the community and is the scene of popular pilgrimage on or about 1 February, and of visits by the devout at other times. Another version of the story, from the same area, says "She fell on her knees on a stone by the stream at Faughart. . . . She put up her hand and pulled out her eye and flung it away. . . ."[32] Nowadays, along the course of the narrow stream, little plaques mark variously, "the hoof rock," with what looks like the mark of a horseshoe incised in its surface; "the waist rock"— a sort of hourglass shape; "the knee rock," with two hollows side by side, suggesting the marks of very large knees. The religious practices at this site receive a certain measure of support from the local clergy, and a glasshouse has been erected to shelter the outdoor altar where mass is celebrated on special occasions. Clearly, however, the importance of these markers lies in their expression of a purely local, populist tradition whose fundamental position is one of resistance to hegemonic discourses, whether these emanate from colonialist landlords, from the church, or from the state.

"Performance" has been defined "as an activity that generates transformations, as the reintegration of art with what is 'outside' it, an 'opening up' of the 'field.'"[33] The Faughart narratives of Brigid's self-mutilation were certainly performances in these terms. Rituals, such as praying at the various rocks of Brigid's pilgrimage in Faughart, or hanging a piece of cloth on a clothesline overnight and putting it away carefully afterward, are also performed, and it is possible to think of a story that is silently recalled while carrying out these actions as being itself somehow "performed." It is perhaps in just such less-privileged genres as the local story quietly told, or the practices carried out without elaborate explanation, year after year, that we find those stories that most powerfully encode belief and world-view: unlike the art-for-art's-sake "once upon a time" stories, which contain their whole importance in the sound of the storyteller's voice, implicit stories of this sort are less overtly challenging to dominant discourses, and therefore less subject to censorship and standardization.

The story of Brigid's eye is one of the most enduring elements of her biography, but the folk tradition differs from literary accounts in making her acquired ugliness a continuing trait: the eye is not restored. One remarkable story told in Irish tells of Catholic crewmen on a boat captained by a man "who didn't have much religion." They began in desperation to pray to Brigid when overtaken by a terrifying storm at sea. True to her reputation, Brigid calmed the weather—or at least the wind dropped. The captain approached the men, asking them to whom they had been praying.

"To Saint Brigid," they replied.
"Is your saint one-eyed?" he asked, "Because if she is, I saw her sitting on the mast a little while ago."[34]

That the stories of Brigid's mutilation offer another instance of the theme of halves and wholes is shown by the fact that in several oral accounts the eye is not lost: rather, half of Brigid's face becomes ugly, either because one eye swells enormously, or because one of her cheeks becomes pockmarked, burned or otherwise disfigured. Other self-mutilating saints are found in European and Indian tradition, but the story of Brigid's eye differs from those told about them in that while they pluck out both eyes to safeguard their virtue, she removes only one, underlining the Irish insistence on halving.[35] The idea that Brigid is at once a beautiful young maiden and an ugly old (or at least small) woman of course echoes the *puella senilis* theme, and the common juxtaposition of maidens and hags. As a figure with two faces in one, Brigid also recalls the Roman Janus, who looks simultaneously back toward the old year and forward toward the new, as indeed Brigid does in the Irish calendar.

One of the most common stories told in both Irish and English about the feast of 1 February explains why Brigid's day comes before Mary's. This short account from County Cork is very far removed from the portentous telling of the "big" folktales most celebrated in the reception of oral traditions by metropolitan culture, but it manages to present a vivid and memorable image and to express obliquely the embarrassment and resentment women have often felt at the Judeo-Christian custom of "churching"—ritual purification forty days after the birth of a male child. It also conveys a sense of Brigid as a discreet ally of women in these matters.

When the Blessed Virgin was going to be churched, like any woman she felt very shy and St Brigid was with her and St Brigid lit a candle and put it in the tail of her dress, her own dress, and everyone that was there was looking at the candle in the tail of her dress and she was so holy that the candle didn't burn the dress and while they were all looking at St Brigid the Blessed Virgin slipped in to the church and no-one noticed her, and for doing that the Blessed Virgin left St Brigid's day come before her own day, Lá 'le Muire na gCoinneal.[36]

Other versions of this narrative say that Brigid, instead of placing a lighted candle in her skirt, put a harrow—a very large farm implement, fitted with spikes for breaking up the ground in spring—upon her head, and that on each spike she placed a candle, so that she is known as Bríd Boillsge: Brigid the bright or shining one.

Oral traditions are pluralist and polyphonic. Their richness lies in their multiplicity of performers and performances, and in the differences between them. When Irish-American travel agents in the Boston area at the beginning of this century sold tickets to Irish immigrants for visits home, they sometimes also persuaded them to buy phonographs, and recordings of Irish musicians, for which they also happened to be agents. Recordings of Sligo fiddle-player Michael Coleman were suddenly to be found in homes all over Ireland, and on hearing them, many fiddle-players hung up their instruments.

This is the power of the mass medium: once a performance is reproduced in multiple identical copies, on the capitalist model that separates producers from consumers and restricts the means of production to a very few, no individual performance can possibly compete. The playing of a tune for private pleasure, teaching or practice takes second place to the polished public "performance." Regional variations in style or content begin to seem like deviations from a standard, and elements not part of the published version appear as oddities and aberrations.

In the case of Brigid, several forces have been at work to skew the picture presented in oral storytelling. The revitalized Catholic Church in the nineteenth century sought out religious narratives that would be consistent with the interests both of the urban bourgeoisie with its construction of femininity, and of the tenant-farmer class in rural areas who married for dowry. Negative stereotypes imposed during colonization led to a search for images of Irishness with which to counter them. Catholicism was identified as a defining characteristic of the truly Irish man or woman, while a sanitized version of oral tradition was celebrated as a repository of all that was most noble (and by implication most compatible with dominant discourses) in Irish culture.

Basing my analysis on a reprivileging of "minor" genres of storytelling, and considering only a fraction of the available evidence, I have been describing an intellectual model that I believe underlies much of the tradition about Brigid, that most powerful of Irish women saints. Brigid is a figure of the feminine in all its aspects and is characterized by doubleness and binary division, mapped onto a cyclical yearly calendar. As a reminder of the rules of husbandry and the division of labor, she shares that calendar with a male figure, allowing work, time, and space to take on characteristics of gender. Like the delicate cross made of straw or rushes that is Brigid's symbol, this model can represent balance and symmetry, precariously maintained through cyclical movement. But the symmetry contained in the binary dividing of the world is constantly subject to drag and distortion from another model: that of the unbroken male line, along which family names, family land, and family power are carried. This is the model that best fit the dominant discourses of church and state in the late nineteenth and early twentieth centuries, and that best met the needs of print by providing orderly, linear narratives. It is therefore the model that "tradition," that monolithic construct to which politicians and educationalists so often appealed, must be shown to endorse.

Every so often, however, lines do get broken: crises occur, people and animals fall ill, houses catch fire, children are born outside patriarchal structures, or fail to be conceived within them, families disagree, and people die. A circle of consternation opens, and within it, through story and song and performance, the feminine is reasserted. The stories of Brigid, and the rituals performed, however minimally, year after year, tell us about the opening of such circles: the holding open of intellectual spaces within which contradictory ideas may be held simultaneously. They remind us of the importance of such spaces in facilitating change and about the poetic and social resources that oral storytelling has to offer.

NOTES

For access to and permission to quote from material in the Irish Folklore Collection (IFC), I am grateful to Professor Séamas Ó Catháin, head of the Department of Irish Folklore, National University of Ireland, Dublin, and to his predecessor, Professor Bo Almqvist. A version of this paper was delivered as the opening lecture at a symposium on Irish and Native American storytelling at the University of Massachusetts, Amherst, on 2 February 1994. I thank Peggy O'Brien, director of the Five College Irish Studies Program, who organized it, and Joseph Bruchac, Maggi Peirce, Joan Radner, and Trudy Lamb Richmond, who also took part.

1. The first volume appeared in 1875. For a note on O'Hanlon (1821–1905), who as "Lageniensis" also published extensive collections of Irish folklore "according to his whim and facile pen;" see Richard Dorson in Sean O'Sullivan (ed. and trans.), *Folktales of Ireland,* (Chicago: University of Chicago Press, 1960), x.

2. Irish Folklore Collection (IFC) 901: 110.

3. E.g. Kim McCone, *Pagan Past and Christian Present in Early Irish Literature* (Maynooth: An Sagart, 1990); Séamas Ó Catháin, *The Festival of Brigit: Celtic Goddess and Holy Woman* (Dublin: DBA Publications, 1995).

4. This story is found in the fourteenth-century *Leabhar Breac.* Cf. Matthew 5: 28–9, "If thy right eye offend thee . . ."

5. Ernest Gellner, *Nations and Nationalism* (Oxford: Basil Blackwell, 1983), 57. Cf. Gearóid Ó Crualaoich, "The Primacy of Form: A Folk Ideology in de Valera's Politics," in *De Valera and his Times,* ed. J.P. O'Caroll and John A. Murphy (Cork: Cork University Press, 1986), 47–61, and Diarmuid Ó Giolláin, "An Béaloideas agus an Stát," *Béaloideas* 57 (1989): 151–163.

6. IFC 901:57.

7. Kevin Danaher, *The Year in Ireland* (Cork: Mercier, 1972), 13–37; Ó Catháin, *Festival of Brigit.*

8. For coding, see Joan N. Radner, ed., *Feminist Messages: Coding in Women's Folk Culture* (Chicago: University of Illinois Press, 1993).

9. Whitley Stokes and John Strachan, *Thesaurus Paleohibernicus: A Collection of Old-Irish Glosses, Scholia, Prose, and Verse* (1903; Dublin: Dublin Institute for Advanced Studies, 1975), 2:325, 327.

10. From a funeral prayer recorded in Breton in Plozévet by Donatien Laurent, to whom I am indebted for the reference.

11. Maria Tymoczko, "Unity and Duality: A Theoretical Perspective on the Ambivalence of Celtic Goddesses," *Proceedings of the Harvard Celtic Colloquium* 5 (1985): 22–35.

12. Maureen Wall, *The Penal Laws, 1691–1760* (Dundalk: Dundalgan Press, 1976).

13. See Angela Partridge [Bourke], *Caoineadh na dTrí Muire: Téama na Páise i bhFilíocht Bhéil na Gaeilge* (Dublin: An Clóchomhar, 1983).

14. Margaret MacCurtain, "Fullness of Life: Defining Female Spirituality in Twentieth-Century Ireland," in *Women Surviving: Studies in Irish Women's History in the 19th and 20th Centuries,* ed. Maria Luddy and Cliona Murphy (Dublin: Poolbeg, 1990), 234–5. Cf. S. J. Connolly, *Priests and People in Pre-Famine Ireland, 1780–1845* (Dublin: Gill and Macmillan, 1982), ch. 3, "Popular and Official Religion," and Lawrence Taylor, *Occasions of Faith* (Dublin: Lilliput, 1996).

15. See Ó Crualaoich, "Primacy of Form" and Ó Giolláin, "An Bealoideas agus an Stát" for the political dimension of this effort.

16. Cf. Clodagh Brennan Harvey, "Some Irish Women Storytellers and Reflections on the Role of Women in the Storytelling Tradition," *Western Folklore* 48 (April 1989): 109–28: "Some remarks of Cáit O'Sullivan's [An

Bhab Feirtéar] regarding Peig Sayers are particularly suggestive. Cáit found Peig very impressive, commenting that 'there was something in her that would attract you'; but she added that 'there were a lot of women as good as her . . . around'" (123–4). For the furor that followed the publication in 1942 of *The Tailor and Ansty,* Eric Cross's account of one irreverent and un-inhibited storyteller and his wife, see Frank O'Connor's Introduction to the 1964 edition (Cork: Mercier, 1964).

17. Carol Coulter, *The Hidden Tradition: Feminism, Women and Nationalism in Ireland* (Cork: Cork University Press, 1993), 8.

18. Nerys Thomas Patterson, *Cattle Lords and Clansmen: The Social Structure of Early Ireland* (Notre Dame, IN.: Notre Dame University Press, 1994), 118–149; Máire Mac Néill *The Festival of Lughnasa: A Study of the Survival of the Celtic Festival of the Beginning of Harvest* (1962; Dublin: Comhairle Bhéaloideas Éireann, 1982 [1962]).

19. Cf. Ó Catháin, *Festival of Brigit,* 23, n. 111.

20. Ibid., 50, n. 93.

21. Pádraig Ó Riain, "Traces of Lugh in Early Irish Hagiographical Tradition," *Zeitschrift für Celtische Philologie* 36 (1977): 138–156; Mac Néill, *Fesitival of Lughnasa,* 409–417.

22. Cf. Mary Cullen, "Breadwinners and Providers: Women in the Household Economy of Laboring Families 1835–6," in Luddy and Murphy, *Women Surviving,* 85–116.

23. Mac Néill, *Festival at Lughnasa,* 39, 40, 172.

24. See Robert Herzfeld, *Death and the Right Hand,* trans. R. Needham (Glencoe, IL.: Free Press, 1960).

25. Angela Bourke, "More in Anger than in Sorrow: Irish Women's Lament Poetry," in Radner, *Feminist Messages,* 160–182.

26. IFC 902: 11; 903: 6, 51; 901: 56; 130.

27. The doll or effigy was generally known as the *brídeog,* or "biddy." Caoimhín Ó Danachair ("Distribution Patterns in Irish Folk Tradition," *Béaloideas* 33 [1965] 97–113), shows the custom as practiced in almost all parts of Ireland except Ulster and North Leinster (97–101).

28. John Dunne, *Purtock* (Dublin: Anna Livia Press, 1992), 84.

29. Bishops' pastoral, 1927, quoted in Terence Brown, *Ireland: A Social and Cultural History, 1922–1985* (1981; London: Fontana, 1985), 40.

30. IFC 905: 62: Michael J. Murphy from Frank Woods (aged 90–100), Faughart, 1942.

31. Cf. Margaret R. Yocom, "Woman to Woman: Fieldwork and the Private Sphere," in *Women's Folklore, Women's Culture,* ed. Rosan A. Jordan and Susan J. Kalĉik (Philadelphia: University of Pennsylvania Press, 1985), 44–53.

32. IFC 905: 48.

33. Henry Sayre, "Performance," in *Critical Terms for Literary Study,* ed. Frank Lentricchia and Thomas McLaughlin (Chicago: University of Chicago Press, 1990), 103.

34. IFC 906: 6, translated.
35. Henri Gaidoz, "Les Yeux Arrachés," *Mélusine* 3 (1886–87): 300–302; 316–318; 479.
36. IFC 900: 16–17.

Chapter Two

"A Nation of Abortive Men": Gendered Citizenship and Early Irish Republicanism

Nancy J. Curtin

The Society of United Irishmen was founded in 1791 in Belfast and Dublin to promote radical parliamentary reform, Catholic emancipation (or the abolition of all religious disqualifications in civic life), and a union of Catholic and Protestant to achieve them both. Operating as an open, constitutional network of reformers in their early years, and frustrated by government repression and harassment, the United Irishmen adopted explicitly revolutionary aims by 1795. They then called for a democratic, secular republic, severing all connection with Great Britain, and engaged in an alliance with revolutionary France to achieve this separation. The United Irishmen mobilized as a mass-based secret society, moving from its urban, middle-class origins to embrace the lower orders of town and country and infiltrating the armed forces, their goal to make every soldier a citizen, and every citizen a soldier. The radicals claimed a membership of 300,000 such citizen soldiers, the fruit of organizational sophistication and an aggressive propaganda campaign designed to create a popular political culture in Ireland based on the innovative rights of man and the citizen. Internal divisions, inadequate coordination with their ally, republican France, and especially a ruthless counter-revolutionary campaign by Irish loyalists and their British backers contributed to the failure of the rebellion of 1798. But the United Irishmen left a legacy as the first republican nationalists in Ireland, the first link, it is claimed, in the chain that would lead to the Provisional Irish Republican Army of today.

One of the most striking continuities of revolutionary republicanism concerns the gendering of revolutionary imagery and activism. Irish historians who consider the matter at all tend to date the glorification of a hyper-masculine republican identity to the Fenian movement in the 1860s, but I will argue here that the ideal of masculine patriotic self-immolation was relentlessly constructed in the 1790s. Masculinity is integral to certain ideologies of authority and civic subjectivity, whether they are based on chivalric militarism, religious patriarchalism, economic independence, or civility. Each represents a way of justifying the assumption of power by a different class or group. But the construction and assertion of masculine authority requires the symbiotic and reinforcing construction of certain notions of femininity. Revolutionary republican men could not be made without the symmetrical making of revolutionary republican women.

The radical departure of the United Irishmen, like that of the revolutionaries in France, was to sever citizenship from the rights and privileges of property and to expand the definition of the political nation to include everyone. Thus the universality of citizenship implicit in the United Irish project was the prerequisite for the assertion of Ireland and its people as a sovereign nation. Citizenship might be an attribute of one's basic humanity, but this did not preclude differences in the exercise of its rights and responsibilities, especially differences based on gender. Thus, the republicanism espoused by the United Irishmen in the 1790s was at once an inclusive and an exclusive ideology. On the one hand these late eighteenth-century radicals imagined a democratic, secular republic that would confer the obligations and privileges of citizenship to all Irishmen, Catholic and Protestant, rich and poor, native and settler. But on the other hand, the United Irishmen refused to entertain the notion that women should be active members of the civic polity. This did not mean that women had no contribution to make to the republican campaign. Indeed, they served as activists within the United Irish organization and as symbols of an oppressed nation. But women and men's participation was limited by a gender-based division of labor that was implicit in both the classical republican tradition and the emerging liberal paradigm of public and private spheres.[1] The United Irishmen appealed to men and women to conduct themselves with classical republican probity. For both sexes this required subordinating private to public interest. In the male case, this meant active participation in liberating the feminized nation from dishonor. For women exercising citizenship involved republican motherhood, sacrificing husbands, brothers, and sons to the national struggle.

A republican reading of history confirmed for the United Irishmen the necessity for first radical reform and then revolution. The great republican states of the past had fallen because civic virtue was eroded by moral and political corruption. The private interests of citizens, obsessed with wealth and luxury, had taken precedence over the public good. And now this bleak historical record was threatening to repeat itself. Ireland was teetering dangerously on the precipice of despotism. Corruption in government was rampant, and corruption, in classical republican terms, was the cancer that invaded the body politic and brought it to the death agonies of tyranny. The years after the so-called constitutional revolution of 1782 (which established the nominal independence of the Irish parliament) saw only the acceleration and intensification of this disease. The only cure for this affliction was a strong dose of civic virtue. In other words, citizens must act like citizens.

And active citizens must behave like soldiers. Indeed, it was a maxim of classical republican theory that corruption proved to be the death of the good state, the *res publica,* once citizens relinquished their obligation to defend their homeland in arms. The epitome of virtue was the citizen militia, the epitome of corruption the mercenary standing army. When the United Irishmen enrolled hundreds of thousands into a paramilitary organization, they were conferring on their followers the status of citizen, happily combining practice and theory. The right to bear arms, denied to Catholics and subjected to property requirements in eighteenth-century Ireland, must be seen as the widely acknowledged badge of the most active and virtuous citizenship.

The idea of a union of all Irishmen exerting themselves as citizen-soldiers was long rooted in the Volunteer tradition, and owes much to a pervading civic humanist program, which was especially strong in the Enlightenment-steeped Scottish universities that educated the professional elite of Ulster society.[2] The example of the French Revolution transformed the Volunteer tradition in three ways. First, at a general level, by asserting the sovereignty of the people, a nation of citizens, it democratized the civic humanism that was the legacy not only of Irish radicals, but of their opponents as well.[3] Citizenship had hitherto been closely associated with property; only those with a stake in the society should have a say in its government. The liberal nationalism of the French Revolution, however, elided differences in status, class, or confessional allegiance, by proclaiming a sovereign and indivisible people.[4] From indivisible people to United Irishmen was but a short leap, though a momentous one in Ireland, for it required the radicals to discard sectarian suspicions rooted in divergent histories. That this happened was due to the second influence the French Revolution had on Irish radicals, especially Protestant ones. The revolution occurred in a Catholic country and proceeded to abolish not only the established church, but also all disqualifications based on religion. If Catholics in France could act so decisively on behalf of the nation rather than the chapel, could not Irish Catholics do the same? This was one of the key arguments in Theobald Wolfe Tone's widely influential *An argument on behalf of the Catholics of Ireland,* which went far in countering Presbyterian prejudices and so contributed to the formation of the first Society of United Irishmen in Belfast in October 1791.[5]

Having thus embraced an ideology as well as a strategy that united Catholic and Protestant behind radical reform in Ireland, Irish radicals benefited, so to speak, from a third influence of the French Revolution— war. The continental war that erupted in 1792, and that Britain and Ireland entered in early 1793, provided the context for the spiraling of radicalism and counter-revolution that burst at last in 1798. And contemporaries had little doubt that it was an ideological war, whether seen in terms of a conflict between order and anarchy or tyranny and liberty. As an ideological war, it polarized internally as well as externally. The French had their partisans in all the belligerent countries, and certainly the United Irishmen took pride of place among them.

The militarization of Europe, therefore, was mirrored by militarization within Ireland, marking the character of popular politicization in the country. The virtual exclusion of a popular voice in the established political arena of parliament, mediated only through a tepid and elitist whiggism, required a wider arena for popular political engagement. Thus it was that the United Irishmen emerged as an armed body of citizens, claiming for themselves the virtue of the nation. Even if the spell of the Volunteers on the United Irishmen had been weaker, there were few alternative or practical models for their mobilization. This militarized politicization also meant the soldier's ultimate test, patriotic self-immolation on the altar of the nation, would emerge as one of the defining characteristics of Irish republican masculinity, a phenomenon most recently and graphically revealed in the hunger strikes of 1981.

If the citizen-soldier symbolized the obligations of republican citizenship, the rights of citizenship were demonstrated by active and direct participation in the political process, and both tended to exclude women. In one of the most radical reform programs of the eighteenth century, the United Irishmen called for the enfranchisement of all adult males. No serious consideration whatsoever was given to the political rights of women. Nevertheless, the right of Irish*men* to equal representation and a democratic republic government of their own choosing was well supported by a number of Irishwomen, even if they were not invited to participate actively in this government. Certainly the wives and mothers and sisters of many of the radicals strongly adhered to the cause of democratic republicanism, offering to serve the movement in whatever way was required of them. But men, of course, filled the ranks, assumed the leadership, articulated the aims of the movement, and risked arrest, exile, and death for the cause.

Indeed, United Irish claims to full civic competence contingent on gender drew on a range of masculine ideals, providing some over-determination of the chivalric manly impulse, as well as appealing to all elements within the cross-class alliance that characterized the movement.[6] Classical republicanism adapted the aristocratic ideal of manhood as rooted in military service by identifying citizenship with the bearing of arms, allowing paramilitary bodies like the Volunteers and the United Irishmen to claim for themselves masculine virtue.[7] Middle-class men asserted patriarchal claims to represent familial and economic dependents in the public sphere.[8] And Tom Paine and other plebeian democrats appealed to artisanal and working-class pride in productivity and skill in widening the scope of civic competence.[9] Thus militarized and disinterested patriotism, emerging separate spheres ideology, and the possession of productive skills contributed in part to a redefinition of masculinity undertaken by the politically excluded classes of the eighteenth and early nineteenth centuries. Add to this the destabilizing context of the era of the French Revolution, the beginning of that Victorian prelude when elite British males cut their hair, donned trousers, found religion, and generally acquired more respectable bourgeois values to reinvent themselves in opposition to effeminate Frenchmen. And British women retreated into the private sphere to distinguish themselves from both polymorphously perverse Gallic court ladies and Parisian viragos.[10] If the United Irishmen adapted and transformed the dominant civic republican discourse of Georgian England into a liberal, democratic ideology, so too did they adapt prevailing and emerging notions of masculinity by appropriating male virtue to themselves, grounding their claims to political inclusion on reason, justice, and nature.

Republicanism, then, was a manly calling. Hibernia's bold defenders were called upon to protect her honor, to assert themselves in a just and righteous cause, to render filial devotion and husbandly care to their country. But women could also exert themselves as heroines exemplifying republican virtue, reflecting as well a redefinition of femininity that complemented and supported new ideals of masculinity. The role of woman as patriot had a long heritage in the Roman tradition that inspired much of late eighteenth-century republicanism, not just in Ireland, but in America and France as well.[11] Since the fundamental core of republicanism was the subordination of private interest to the public good, Roman women were expected to display their civic virtue by freely giving up their men to the affairs of state and the defense of the country, to ease the choice that men must often make between happy domesticity and public duty.

This proscribed role for women in the state was echoed by Montesquieu as well as Rousseau, who were both concerned that women could seduce men from their civic obligations. Virtuous women must breed, nurture, and finally relinquish good republican men. Men gave their lives, but "Ah," said the poet laureate of the United Irishmen, Dr. William Drennan, "what can woman give but tears."[12]

Real women gave much more than tears to the public cause, serving as active agents in United Irish recruitment, nurturers of prisoners and their families, messengers within the movement, and in general enabling their husbands and brothers to bustle in the world of revolutionary politics by assuming their share of domestic and even business responsibilities.[13] While the United Irishmen wished to confer active citizenship on all adult males, the women of the republic also had their own duties to perform as passive citizens—to favor republican heroes and to raise republican sons, to be the patriot mother or wife who would permit and encourage her menfolk to meet their civic obligations. In a ballad of the period, "The Patriot Mother," a young man faces execution unless he betrays the United Irish movement. His mother, fulfilling her republican role by selflessly championing the public cause, urges her boy to choose death with honor. She will not love a traitor, even if he is her own son. "Dearer, far dearer than ever to me, / My darling you'd be on the brave gallows tree."[14] The same morbid theme is to be found in the poems and ballads celebrating the republicans of 1867 and 1916, affirming the historic, gender-based division of labor that would advance the cause of republican separatism. Virtuous women must be prepared to sacrifice their sons, their husbands, and their brothers to the public good.

> You ladies, true friends to Hibernia,
> The rights of old Erin maintain;
> Futurity, history will mention,
> Your actions of honor and fame,
> The Genius of Ireland defend you.[15]

The United Irishman Charles Hamilton Teeling rejoiced that in terms of "national feeling" the "enthusiasm of the females even exceeded the ardour of the men; in many of the higher circles and in the rustic activities, *that* youth met a cold and forbidding reception from the partner of his choice, who either from apathy or timidity had not yet subscribed to the test of the union [or United Irishmen]."[16] And so the radicals urged women to demonstrate their support for the United Irishmen by donning an array of republican symbols and emblems—cockades, medals, and of course green articles of clothing and accessories. As Drennan put it:

And the triumph of Erin her daughters shall share,
With their full swelling chests, and their fair flowing hair,
Their bosoms heave high for the worthy and brave,
But no coward shall rest on that soft swelling wave.[17]

Mother Erin and her real-life daughters thus were to inspire men to self-sacrifice in the cause of the aggrieved nation. In the ballads and songs of the 1790s, however, the active if minor role of women in the United Irish movement was entirely ignored. One way in which the opponents of the United Irishmen sought to discredit the movement was gleefully to point out the disreputable presence of women in republican public demonstrations. Women in public were vulnerable to the taunt that they were, indeed, public women. Female activism, then, had to be consigned to the private sphere. Thus women were most visible in the United Irish movement, invited in a sense into the public space of politics, as symbols prodding men to perform their national and republican duty. The feminized, maternal nation, Hibernia, Granu, Erin, the Shan van Vocht, by turns a graceful, dignified matron and an old woman summoning her sons to protect and defend her homestead, called upon "the gen'rous sons of Erin, in manly virtue bold" to avenge her wrongs.[18]

Indeed, the liberation of Erin was the test of her sons' manhood. As Drennan put it, "And where Britain made brutes, now let Erin make men."[19] Armed filial devotion to the mother-nation represented, then, a rite of passage to full manhood. "But our brave Irish boys, / Soon let them know we were united men."[20] Ireland was thus represented as both mother and sweetheart, a prod to filial devotion as well as a trophy for the exercise of manly virtue, giving the "family romance" of the Irish nation a steamy incestuous edge.

The imperiled female provided yet another prod to the assertion of masculine chivalry. When the United Irishmen were feeling the full force of the government's counterrevolutionary campaign in 1797 and 1798, radical propagandists recounted only too many examples of the savagery and cruelty of loyalist forces in Ireland. Favored targets of these republican pens were the Orange Order and the government-sponsored and gentry-led yeomanry corps, both zealous supporters of the Protestant Ascendancy. Orangemen and yeomen figured prominently in the government's repressive campaign against the United Irishmen, all too frequently giving credence to the republican propagandists' claim that these loyalists were waging war against the people. In this propaganda the radicals emphasized the dangers posed to Irish womanhood by the marauding and barbarous Orangemen or yeomen. The *Press,* the United Irish organ in Dublin, recounted an Orange rampage near Dungannon, Co. Tyrone, in March 1798.

The loyalists burned down two Catholic chapels before they attacked the house of one Ruddy, a comfortable, peaceful farmer. The Orangemen raped Ruddy's daughter; when he attempted to stop them they killed him with a hatchet. And when they had satisfied their "brutal lust," the Orangemen set fire to Ruddy's farm.[21]

Republican propagandists especially urged Irish soldiers and militiamen to turn against a government that sanctioned such beastly assaults against the honor of their wives, mothers, and sisters. One handbill cited the contradiction between an Irishman serving his majesty "perhaps at the same moment when his aged mother lived to see her daughter violated by a horrid soldiery, who had mingled the ashes of her husband with those of her humble habitation."[22] A poem in the *Press* evokes a similar scene of violated womanhood.

> Crackling blazes pierce the skies,
> Thither waft the victim's cries;
> Vain the virtuous mother's prayers,
> Vain the feeble virgin's tears,
> Cruel lust nor knows to spare
> Virtue mild nor beauty fair.[23]

This notion of Irish women as victims of an unbridled and vengeful loyalism enjoyed a recognizable affinity with feminine allegorical representations of Ireland that figured so prominently in United Irish songs and ballads, especially when the appeal to filial devotion or chivalrous manly exertions fed upon the central theme of rape. Indeed, the Roman tradition of civic virtue and patriotism intersected with this theme of rape in the story of the violation of Lucretia and the consequent abolition of the monarchy. Ireland, the sister kingdom or Swift's "injured lady," had experienced on a national scale a violation of her honor.[24] Furthermore, as metaphor or reality, the assault on Irish women posed an even graver threat, in the eyes of republican men, for her virtue was entrusted to the custodianship of a woman's male protector—her husband or father or brother. To violate a woman was to insult and indeed emasculate her male protector. Republican rhetoric abounded with calls to Irishmen to assert their manhood. The violation of their women was the price Irishmen paid for suppressing their own patriotism and their civic duty. "The fault is thine, degenerate sons, thus long in slavery to be, / Come join your hands, and bravely die, or else renounce fair liberty."[25]

Women existed as metaphors in United Irish propaganda, but men's active involvement in the cause meant that Erin's real-life sons could be elevated as examples of masculine republican virtue, particularly if, as the verse just quoted suggests, they would "bravely die" in the service of "fair liberty." One such widely accessible model of manly behavior was William Orr, the first man to be hanged under the infamous insurrection act for administering an illegal oath. The *Belfast News-Letter* described the Presbyterian Orr as a "respectable farmer and man of property in the neighbourhood of Antrim," about thirty years of age, "remarkably good-looking," a devoted husband, and the father of six young children.[26] This eminently suitable hero seemed to embody the ideal of the sober and industrious farmer, the broad-minded Christian, the loving husband and father—the backbone of rural society. Rustic values were also a primary component of the classical republican tradition, where the ideal citizen derived economic independence and moral ascendancy from tilling the soil. The song "Swain's Awake" combined the roles of simple, virtuous agriculturalist with that of masculine protector.

> We for her forks would wield
> (Weapons of our meadows),
> Bare our breasts, and stand the shield
> Of orphans and of widows.[27]

The numerous encomiums to Orr's manly beauty and heroic virtues in song and poetry recall the ancient legend of Cincinnatus, the great republican hero—a farmer who saved Rome and then returned virtuously to his plow, rejecting power and glory. Cincinnatus, sacrificing his private interest to the public good, had been the ideal incorruptible citizen-soldier of the Roman republic, just as Orr came to symbolize the ideal citizen of an Irish republic, making his death a rallying cry against the government.[28]

Orr also bequeathed a widow and six orphans to the patriot nation. His famous elegy, penned by Drennan and published in the *Press,* focuses on the family trauma of William's judicial murder. His pregnant wife miscarries.

> Oh William, how pale was thy cheek
> Where beauty so lately did dwell;
> When thy true love hung faint on thy neck,
> And thy breast heaved to her—the farewell.
>
> Ah, clay cold her heart with despair,
> And closed were her eyes from thy view,
> All sense had abandoned her ear,
> As abhorring to hear thy adieu.
>
> And the pledge of thy love that she bore
> "Grew suddenly still" in her womb,

> One stir! and it quickened no more,
> And the stroke that stopped life was thy doom.[29]

Republican men give their lives, as Drennan said, while women offered their tears, their children, and their men.

The ultimate assertion of revolutionary masculinity, then, was death in the mother-nation's cause in an exemplary blood sacrifice lauded by successive generations. Drennan imagined the graves of the fallen heroes crying out:

> O, guard our orphans and our wives!
> Like us, make Erin's fate your own,
> Like us, for her yield up your lives.[30]

Or as a later poem on another executed leader, Robert Emmet, put it, he was one "who lived an hero, and who died a man."[31]

Emmet, the ill-fated leader of a Dublin street revolt of 1803, was adopted by later generations as the emblem of self-immolating republican masculinity, thanks largely to his powerfully evocative speech from the dock, the first of many such emotive and self-justifying proclamations.

> I have but one request to ask at my departure from the world. It is the charity of its silence. Let no man write my epitaph; for as no man who knows my motives dare now vindicate them, let not prejudice or ignorance asperse them. Let them rest in obscurity and peace, my memory be left in oblivion and my tomb uninscribed, until other times and other men can do justice to my character. When my country takes her place among the nations of the earth, then, and not until then, let my epitaph be written.[32]

Emmet's tomb remained uninscribed, but his memory hardly rested in oblivion. Emmet's Rising might be regarded as merely a failed pathetic addendum to the more formidable rising of 1798, but it assumed a powerful mythological pull over later republican movements. Emmet came to be remembered, through an evolving and careful tending of the myth, as a Christ-like figure sacrificing himself to redeem the nation from the original sin of conquest, an ideal of republican manhood consciously embraced and reaffirmed by the Rising of 1916. As Patrick Pearse, president of the chimerical republic proclaimed in 1916, observed:

> No failure judged as the world judges these things was ever more complete, more pathetic than Emmet's. And yet he has left us a prouder memory than the men of Brian victorious at Clontarf or of Owen Roe victorious at Benburb. It is the memory of a sacrifice Christ-like in its perfection.[33]

A very secular republican, Emmet was thus transformed by failure into a sacred icon. "Few men have loved their broken and hapless land unto death, merely for example, as Emmet did," a Sinn Féin pamphlet of 1915 proclaimed. "And I think what makes Emmet the most attractive figure in the great army of Irish Nationalists, is that he attempted the impossible, and that his enterprise was doomed to failure from the first."[34]

A sexual division of labor also marked the cult of the martyr in this republican romance with morbidity. Men died and women grieved, and were expected to grieve well. Perhaps second only to the fallen patriot in republican esteem was the widow he left behind. Honored not only for her sacrifice of happy domesticity to the public cause, for giving up her husband to the nation, the widow remained the living reminder that the unquiet graves of the patriot dead placed an obligation on successive generations. One of the most honored widows of the United Irishmen was Matilda Tone, wife of one of the founders of Irish republicanism, Theobald Wolfe Tone, architect of the United Irish alliance with France, who like Orr was sentenced to death for his service in the cause of the nation. Matilda exemplified all the virtues of republican womanhood, a woman who sacrificed a "normal" domesticity and her husband to the patriotic cause.[35] Virtue, as it was understood in the late eighteenth-century, was the cement that sealed the republican partnership that was the marriage of Matilda and Theobald Wolfe Tone. Tone gave himself selflessly to the cause of virtue in government. Matilda's virtue was exercised to the full in enabling him to do so. Their respective roles were determined by their gender. Matilda was honored in the nineteenth century as the widow of a great Irish patriot whose reputation and place in the United Irish pantheon she helped to construct and preserve.[36]

Matilda assumed the custodianship of her husband's memory, zealously protecting his reputation, and delivering him to successive generations through her careful editing of his memoirs and diaries, the stuff that inspired later republicans like Thomas Davis in the 1840s and Patrick Pearse in the early twentieth century. She was hardly unique. Much of what we know about individual United Irishmen comes from the lovingly preserved documents and recollections of their surviving wives and daughters and sisters. They were the chief source of R. R. Madden's monumental series, *The United Irishmen; their lives and times,* the first volumes appearing in the 1840s under the auspices of the United Irish-inspired Young Ireland movement. As patriot wives and mothers, women acquired authority to venture as far as they did in the public sphere, to protect and safeguard their men's sacrifice, a sacrifice that laid obligations on those who survived. Those fierce republican women in the second Dail were, with one exception, the wives and sisters of dead heroes of the struggle for Irish independence. The exception was

Constance Markievicz, herself a veteran of the 1916 rising, second in command at Stephen's Green and an officer in James Connolly's Irish Citizen Army. But every one of those six duly elected women, claiming the right to speak for their martyred kin, remained implacably opposed to the Anglo-Irish Treaty of 1921 that offered something less than the complete independence and national sovereignty of a republic for which their men had died.[37]

Mary McSwiney, sister of one of the first republican hunger strikers during the War of Independence, scoffed at Michael Collins' plea that the only alternative to the treaty was a continuation of war with Great Britain.

> You men that talk need not talk to us about war. It is the women who suffer, it is the women who suffer most the hardships that war brings. You can go out in the excitement of the fight and it brings its own honour and its own glory. We have to sit at home and work in more humble ways, we have to endure the agony, the sunshines, the torture of misery and the privations which war brings, the horror of nightly visitations to our houses and their consequences. It is easier for you than it is for us, but you will not find in Ireland a woman who has suffered who today will talk as the soldiers here today have talked, and I ask the Minister of Defense [Collins], if that is the type of soldier he has, in heaven's name send the women as your officers next time.[38]

The treaty was approved by a narrow vote of 64 to 57. Cumann na Ban, the female auxiliary of the Irish Republican Army, was the first national organization to reject it; by a vote of twenty-four to two the executive committee affirmed their allegiance to that republic that still existed only in the imagination. The decision was ratified later by a Cumann na Ban convention, where 419 voted in favor of the republic, and only 63 for the treaty. Such hostility to the new Free State government was rewarded when the Dail refused to lower the voting age of Irish women from 30 to 21. Like the unquiet graves of the Fenian dead, these widows and bereaved sisters and sweethearts provided a constant and very self-conscious reminder of the unfinished state of the Irish revolution.

Early Irish republicanism was very much a fraternity, a band of brothers engaged in the realization of a liberationist vision of a harmonious, prosperous, and self-governing Ireland. Brotherhood, is, of course, one of the central founding myths of nations. The Irish Republican Brotherhood, or Fenians, established in the 1850s, most directly articulated the fraternal dimension of revolutionary republicanism. The Fenians represent a departure from the United Irishmen, in that they thought of themselves solely as soldiers, warriors in the service of the mythical Finn. No political, economic, or social questions should divert them from their sacred mission to liberate Ireland from British rule. "Let national independence once be reached through manhood's road, the only way it can be reached," Yeats's mentor John O'Leary declared, "and all other blessings will follow as natural results."[39] As a later member of the IRB, Patrick Pearse, put it: "men who have ceased to be men cannot claim the rights of men." But as with the United Irishmen, for the Fenians the test of manhood was self-immolation. "There is a word which should be engraven upon the hearts of all men who struggle for freedom," O'Leary wrote, "and that word is self-sacrifice."[40] The Fenians inhabited a much more homosocial environment than the United Irishmen, the happy band of brother warriors, where the intrusion of the female proved destabilizing. As the soldiers of Finn rather than the sons of Erin, they even masculinized their mythic antecedents.

But what of the sisterhood? Or to put it bluntly, what did women get from their collaboration with men in constructing this gendered republicanism? Unfortunately, the women of the 1790s are generally silent about their own liberationist vision, preferring to let their men speak for them. But there is the rare and perhaps untypical exception. The devoted sister of Henry Joy McCracken, United Irish activist and general of the insurgent forces in County Antrim in June 1798, Mary Ann McCracken was an ardent republican. In her unstinted approval of her brother's revolutionary activities, she did, indeed, play the role of nurturing, patriotic woman. But McCracken took the radicals' notion of the rights of man and the citizen to its logical inclusion—the extension of those rights to women. As she wrote to her incarcerated brother in March 1797, "If we suppose woman was created for a companion for man, she must of course be his equal in understanding, as without equality of mind, there can be no friendship, and without friendship, there can be no happiness in society." Certainly women, as rational creatures, were entitled to realize their full abilities and contribute to the public good under the enlightened government proposed by the United Irishmen. Indeed, as McCracken asserts, women were perhaps more rational then men, "their bodies being more delicately framed and less fit for labor than that of man, does it not naturally follow that they were more peculiarly intended for study." Her brother need only look at the diminutive Theobald Wolfe Tone, acknowledged by both Henry and Mary Ann as a man of genius, for a demonstration of this particular thesis relating size inversely with intelligence. But more seriously, she asked her brother,

> Is it not almost time for the clouds of error and prejudice to disperse and that the female part of the Creation as well as the male should throw off the fetters with which they have been so long mentally bound? . . . There can be no argument produced in favour of the slavery of women that has not been

used in favour of general slavery. . . . I therefore hope that it is reserved for the Irish nation to strike out something new and to shew an example of candour, generosity, and justice superior to any that have gone before them.[41]

Matilda Tone is perhaps more typical of those silent republican women and certainly more representative of the feminine republican ideal of the 1790s. Settling first in France after her husband's death, Matilda enlisted the powerful support of Lucien Bonaparte in forcing the French state to honor its pledge to Tone to provide a pension for his widow. "If the services of Tone were not sufficient to rouse your feelings," Bonaparte implored the French legislature,

> I might mention the independent spirit and firmness of that noble woman, who, on the tomb of her husband . . . mingles, with her sighs, aspirations for the deliverance of Ireland. I would attempt to give you an idea of that Irish spirit which is blended in her countenance, with the expression of grief. Such were those women of Sparta, who, on the return of their countrymen from battle, when, with anxious looks, they ran over the ranks and missed amongst them their sons, their husbands, and their brothers, exclaimed, He died for his country; he died for the Republic.[42]

Matilda was thus seen as the living embodiment of idealized republican femininity. One of the virtues of virtuous women is silence, and Matilda Tone's silence permits the inscription of idealized femininity upon her. The most famous of silent women in early Irish republicanism was Robert Emmet's housekeeper, whose legend undergoes a feminist deconstruction in Pat Murphy's 1984 film *Anne Devlin*.[43] Anne, a committed republican, is arrested with the rest of Emmet's associates. In one scene she is seen walking in the prison yard where she actually confronts Emmet himself. He apologizes to her for getting her into this situation. "What makes you think I did it for you?" she replies. The feminist filmmaker of the 1980s imagines Anne must have had her own reasons, but is no more able to supply them than the feminist historian of the United Irishmen. That many women shared the republican dream is well evidenced by the actions of so many United Irishwomen. But how they envisioned this dream, and the extent to which that vision differed from that of their menfolk, will probably remain a subject of tenuous and imaginative speculation.

The more abundant and voluble voices of republican women in the early twentieth century, however, provide a chorus of liberationist expectations. Certainly after a hundred years, the meaning infused into republican rhetoric had evolved from the emergent liberalism of the United Irishmen to the romantic revolutionary nationalism of Pearse,

tinged with the socialism of James Connolly. And women rode into revolutionary republicanism on both of those currents. By 1900 the mass-
based constitutional nationalism forged by Daniel O'Connell and later
Charles Stewart Parnell firmly occupied the mainstream of Irish political culture. Dependent on the Liberal Party in England to bring in the
long hoped for but rather limited degree of self-government that was
Home Rule, the constitutional nationalists could only bide their time.
Passion and enthusiasm were left to seek out the margins, and around
1900 those margins began to swell with advanced nationalists and cultural nationalists who were excluded from the mainstream. Not surprisingly, women found their way there, as women often do to movements
on the fringes, and found to their delight unprecedented scope for their
activism. The Gaelic League, founded in 1893, fully accepted women in
its ranks, and Constance Markievicz and the Maud Gonne first flew in
advanced nationalist circles in that arena. Highly critical of mainstream
politics, these women, the "new woman" of Ireland, teachers, academics,
actresses, women self-employed in shops and restaurants, founded newspapers and women's political and cultural organizations that openly sym-
pathized with revolutionary republicanism. Socialist and feminist
sympathies abounded in the movement, but as with the Fenians, the
focus was exclusively on separatist nationalism. In 1914 many of these
women formed Cumann na Ban, the women's auxiliary of the republican movement, and about 90 took part in the 1916 Rising.

Republican women were critical of the political feminism emerging
on a parallel track. Irish suffragettes, the republicans claimed, were tacitly
accepting British rule by seeking to include women in the British fran-
chise. Republican women wanted equal rights, but this could only be
achieved, they maintained, after British rule was ended in Ireland. There
can be no free women, they argued, in an enslaved nation. Sexism was a
British import. The constitution of Cumann na Ban proclaimed the aspiration to reclaim "for the women of Ireland the rights that belonged to
them under the old Gaelic civilization, where sex was no bar to citizenship, and where women were free to devote to the service of their country every talent and capacity with which they were endowed; which
rights were stolen from them under British rule."[44] Get rid of British rule,
and you get rid of gender-based inequality.

Yet if the women of 1916 were animated by an egalitarian vision that
went further than that of the women of 1798, or were at least speaking out
more, the roles they performed in their respective republican organizations
were strikingly, depressingly similar. The gender-based division of revolutionary labor persisted. Those ninety women in the Rising were mostly
cooks and nurses. With very few exceptions the women who spoke out

derived their authority as channellers for the voices of the patriot dead. Their faith that gender inequality would follow the British out of Ireland was adversely tested by Eamon DeValera's Constitution of 1937, which among many other things that continue to distress Irish feminists, recognized that "by her life within the home, woman gives the state a support without which the common good cannot be achieved." Here again is the classical republican formulation of female civic virtue, enshrined in the constitution under which Irish men and women live today.

Gender cuts to the very heart of political discourse, the structuring of power and social relations, in early modern Europe, from the patriarchalism of Filmer and other supporters of a rigid social hierarchy and monarchical authority, to the Machiavellian or civic humanist opposition of the female Fortuna with the male Virtu.[45] Gendered citizenship was hardly unique to Ireland; it was implicit in republican movements in France and America, and indeed, in the civic humanist political discourse in England and Scotland from which the United Irishmen drew heavily. In her study of gender and the making of the British working class, *The Struggle for the Breeches,* Anna Clark reminds us that popular ideologies are the results of choices.[46] Thus, the universality implicit in the Enlightenment project and late eighteenth-century democratic republicanism was capable of asserting gender equality. Mary Ann McCracken greeted the new dawn of liberty ushered in by the French Revolution as leading to a bright day of deliverance for all women as well as men.[47] That her brother and his comrades dismissed Mary Ann's aspirations as ridiculous or unnatural indicates their choice to maintain patriarchal privilege while turning the rest of the world upside down. The martial dimension of the classical republicanism from which the United Irishmen imbibed supported that choice. Citizen equals soldier equals man. Yet as liberals, petit-bourgeois individualists, the United Irishmen chose to break from the organic assumptions of an undifferentiated people implicit in republicanism.

Ideologies acquire legitimacy and are deemed worth dying for when they seem to make sense of actual experience. With their extraordinary propagandist acuity the United Irishmen persuasively interpreted the actual felt experience of ascendancy rule and British dominion as a tyranny whose endurance would be worse than death. It debased social relations everywhere, from the Castle to the cabin. The gendering of citizenship provided additional moral authority to republicanism because it accorded with unquestioned gendered social and political practices. As Lynn Hunt has shown, republicanism had to allow for both the overthrow of the father-king and the reconstitution of patriarchal authority in state and society.[48] While the whole range of women's familial roles is presented in United Irish literature and iconography, fatherhood is noted only by its absence—by the widows left bereft by government brutality, by the abrogation of paternal care by Ireland's governors, by John Bull's abuse of his stepchildren, or even by the Hamlet's ghost aspect of Thomas Drennan's influence on his son William.[49]

It is as Erin's sons, but especially as brothers, that the United Irishmen imagined themselves as acting in accord with their adapted rules of masculine chivalry. Drennan had wanted to name the United Irishmen simply "the Brotherhood." Fraternal union among Irishmen of all religious persuasions was a standard theme of United Irish songs and handbills, and indeed, the possession of such unity provided the greatest moral claim to independence. The family drama then consisted of the growing sons claiming their birthright from the tyrant stepfather, and thus passing successfully into full manhood. "Yet Erin falls not, but her sons/ In arms assert their rightful claims."[50]

In this drama the mother occupied a pivotal though passive position that accounts for her ubiquity in republican propaganda and imagery. While Hibernia and Erin might be dismissed as merely standard literary conventions, the appearance of Granu is more interesting. A Celtic literary revival of sorts was taking place in the late eighteenth century, and United Irish propaganda reveals a familiarity with Old Irish myths and sagas.[51] These sagas had to be sanitized for republican adoption. Queen Grainne, the faithless wife of Finn, becomes Mother Ireland. The sexually aggressive and independent women of myth are transformed into dignified, stainless, but also vulnerable matrons. Recent studies of gender and imperialism suggest that it is common for the colonizer to ascribe negative, feminized qualities to the colonized. This was the case, certainly, in early seventeenth-century English accounts of the Irish.[52] Discursive strategies of colonial resistance tended to absorb and then invert the moral polarities implicit in the gendered imperialist, civilizing project. Thus the identification of Ireland itself as feminine is maintained, but now invested with female virtue rather than vice, while the virtues of English civility are exposed as a mere veil for a vicious, predatory masculinity. Swift's injured lady or the United Irish Erin, like the blameless and virtuous victims of eighteenth-century sentimental novels, engages herself to John Bull in good faith, only to find him an unkind, inconstant, and bigamous lover. It is her female virtue, her passivity, her becoming silence, and her innocence of the corruption of the public sphere that make her vulnerable.[53] Irish subjection is thus the result of an English lack of manly chivalry and morals, not of Irish weakness or corruption. The dignified and virtuous mother abused by a rakish John Bull lifted responsibility for Ireland's conquest from the shoulders of Irish men, easing masculine anxieties about the source of their subjection, permitting them to retain their own gendered virtue.

It is this moralization of politics that runs to the heart of civic republican discourse and also underscores a certain popular image of Anglo-Irish relations. Modern Irish nationalists were inclined to see these relations as a series of polar opposites—the land of saints and scholars versus the workshop of the world, asceticism versus materialism, community versus destabilizing individualism, and virtuous rusticity versus corrupting sophistication. Subjected Ireland, idealized, vulnerable, passive, and feminine, thus assumes the moral high ground, the occupation of which also adds legitimacy and authority to an assault on British rule. Virtuous femininity could ill defend itself alone against unscrupulous and unchivalrous male abuse. Freeing Erin from this loathsome embrace required an assertion of virtuous masculinity, tested in combat, stoic in the face of death. Until then, Ireland would remain, as Drennan lamented, "a nation of abortive men."[54]

NOTES

1. See, e.g., Joan B. Landes, *Women and the Public Sphere in the Age of the French Revolution* (Ithaca and London: Cornell University Press, 1988).
2. For a discussion of this civic humanism and its adoption by the United Irishmen, see Nancy J. Curtin, *The United Irishmen: Popular Politics in Ulster and Dublin, 1791–1798* (Oxford: Clarendon Press, 1994), 13–37.
3. For loyalist adoption of civic humanist ideas, see Jacqueline Hill, "The politics of Dublin Corporation, 1760–1792" in *The United Irishmen: Republicanism, Radicalism, and Rebellion,* ed. David Dickson, Daire Keogh, and Kevin Whelan (Dublin: Lilliput, 1993), 88–101.
4. For this liberal nationalism, see. E. J. Hobsbawm, *Nations and nationalism since 1780* (2nd ed., Cambridge: Cambridge University Press, 1992), 14–45.
5. Theobald Wolfe Tone, *An Argument on Behalf of the Catholics of Ireland . . . by a Northern Whig* (Dublin: P. Byrne 1791).
6. For United Irish social composition, see Curtin, *The United Irishmen,* ch. 5.
7. J. G. A. Pocock, *The Machiavellian Moment: Florentine Political Thought and the Atlantic Republican Tradition* (Princeton: Princeton University Press, 1975), 183–218, 401–22.
8. Lenore Davidoff, *Worlds Between: Historical Perspectives on Class and Gender* (New York: Routledge, 1995), ch. 8.
9. Anna Clark, *The Struggle for the Breeches: Gender and the Making of the British Working Class* (Berkeley: University of California Press, 1995), ch. 8.
10. Linda Colley, *Britons: Forging the Nation, 1707–1837* (New Haven: Yale University Press, 1992), ch. 4, 6; G. J. Barker-Benfield, *The Culture of Sensibility: Sex and Society in Eighteenth-Century Britain* (Chicago: University of Chicago Press, 1992), ch. 7.

11. See Landes, *Women and the Public Sphere.*

12. R. R. Madden, *Literary Remains of the United Irishmen of 1798* (Dublin: James Duffy, 1887), 46.

13. For the real contributions of women to the United Irishmen, see Nancy J. Curtin, "Women and Eighteenth-Century Irish Republicanism," in *Women in Early Modern Ireland,* ed. Margaret MacCurtain and Mary O'Dowd, (Edinburgh: University of Edinburgh Press, 1991), 133–44; Daire Keogh and Nicholas Furlong, eds., *Women of 1798* (Dublin: Four Courts, 1998).

14. R. R. Madden, *The United Irishmen, their lives and times* (1842–5; 12 vols., New York: Catholic Publication Society of America, 1916), 10: ix-x.

15. Madden, *Literary Remains,* 89.

16. Charles Hamilton Teeling, *History of the Irish rebellion of 1798 and sequel to the history of the Irish rebellion of 1798* (1876; Shannon, Ireland: Irish University Press, 1972), 11.

17. Madden, *Literary Remains,* 41–2.

18. Ibid., 86.

19. Ibid., 41

20. Ibid., 34.

21. *Press,* 3 Mar. 1798.

22. National Archives of Ireland, Rebellion papers, 620/53/14.

23. *Press,* 30 Nov. 1797.

24. Jonathan Swift, *The Story of an Injured Lady* in *Swift's Irish Pamphlets: An Introductory Selection,* ed. Joseph McMinn (Savage, Md.: Barnes and Noble, 1991), 22–8.

25. Madden, *Literary Remains,* 133.

26. *Belfast News-Letter,* 22 Sept. 1797.

27. Madden, *Literary Remains,* 150.

28. John Sheares's proclamation of the provisional Irish government, May 1798 (*The Report of the Secret Committee of the House of Commons, with an appendix* [Dublin: n.p., 1798], 208); intercepted United Irish letter, 28 Jan. 1798 (National Archives of Ireland, Rebellion papers, 620/35/71); see also Tone's epitaph on Orr, "Let Orr be the watchword of liberty" (Trinity College Dublin, Madden papers, MS 873/33).

29. *Press,* 31 Oct. 1797

30. Madden, *Literary Remains,* 47.

31. Ibid., 204.

32. Quoted in Robert Kee, *The Green Flag, Vol. I: The Most Distressful Country* (London: Quartet Books, 1976), 168.

33. Ibid., 169.

34. [Herbert Moon Pim], *What Emmet Means in 1915: A Tract for the Times* (Dublin: Irish Volunteer Headquarters, 1915), 12, 14.

35. For Matilda Tone see Nancy J. Curtin, "Matilda Tone and Virtues Republican Femininity," in Keogh and Furlong, *Women of 1798.*

36. William Sampson, *Memoirs of William Sampson, and Irish Exile, Written by Himself* (1807; London: Whittaker, Treacher and Arnot, 1832), appendix, 392–3.

37. For a discussion of the women in the Dail in 1921 responses to their rhetoric, see Jason Knirck, "'Ghosts and Realities': Female TDs and the Treaty Debate," *Eire-Ireland* 32–3 (Winter 1997/Spring-Summer 1998): 170–94.

38. Quoted in Margaret Ward, *Unmanageable Revolutionaries: Women and Irish Nationalism* (London: Pluto, 1983), 167.

39. John O'Leary, *Recollections of Fenians and Fenianism* (London: Downey & Co., 1896) 2: 56.

40. *Irish People,* 19 Dec. 1865.

41. Mary Ann McCracken to Henry Joy McCracken, 16 Mar. 1797 (Public Record Office of Northern Ireland, McCracken papers, T.1210/7).

42. Theobald Wolfe Tone, *Life of Theobald Wolfe Tone,* ed. William Theobald Wolfe Tone (Washington: Gales and Seaton, 1826) 2: 554–5.

43. For a discussion of this film see Luke Gibbon, *Transformations in Irish Culture* (Cork: Cork University Press, 1996), ch. 8.

44. Quoted in Ward, *Unmanageable Revolutionaries,* 178.

45. For the argument that gender matters as an analytic category, see Joan Wallach Scott, *Gender and the Politics of History* (New York: Columbia University Press, 1988).

46. Clark, *Struggle for the Breeches,* 8.

47. Curtin, "Women and eighteenth-century Irish republicanism," 138–43.

48. Lynn Hunt, *Politics, Culture, and Class in the French Revolution* (Berkeley: University of California Press, 1984).

49. For this last, see A. T. Q. Stewart, "'A stable unseen power': Dr William Drennan and the origins of the United Irishmen," in *Essays Presented to Michael Roberts,* ed. John Bossy and Peter Jupp (Belfast: Blackstaff Press, 1976), 80–92.

50. *Press,* 6 Jan. 1798.

51. Mary Helen Thuente, *The Harp Re-strung: The United Irishmen and the Rise of Irish Literary Nationalism* (Syracuse: Syracuse University Press, 1994).

52. See, e.g., Clare Carroll, "Representations of Women in some Early Modern English Tracts on the Colonization of Ireland," *Albion* 25 (Fall 1993): 379–94.

53. For a discussion of the particular vulnerabilities of virtuous women in eighteenth-century literature, see Barker-Benfield, *The Culture of Sensibility.*

54. Madden, *Literary Remains,* p. 46.

Chapter Three

Women Troubles, Queer Troubles: Gender, Sexuality, and the Politics of Selfhood in the Construction of the Northern Irish State

Kathryn Conrad

The concept of human rights is not, at the end of the day, a numbers game.

—David Norris, Senator, Seanad Eireann, and gay rights activist[1]

In the summer of 1998, the "Good Friday Agreement" peace accord was approved by 70 percent of voters, the Northern Ireland Assembly was elected, and we were given the most hope in thirty years for a peaceful resolution to the euphemistically named "Troubles" in Northern Ireland. The depth, breadth, and practical detail of this groundbreaking agreement remains encouraging, as was the fact that the full Assembly, including members of radical unionist and republican parties[2] who never before had to confront each other face to face, met for the first time on 1 July. That optimism was palpable until 5 July 1998, when security forces physically backed the Parades Commission's 29 June announcement that the Portadown Orange Order would not be allowed to march down the nationalist Garvaghy Road. The whole of Northern Ireland was rocked by mainly loyalist riots, arson, shootings, and bombings committed in response to the standoff and to the Good Friday Agreement more generally; the most notable of the attacks resulted in the death of three young boys in Ballymoney, County Antrim. Dissident republican forces expressed their displeasure with the peace process in late August with a car bomb in Omagh that killed more than 25 people and left more than 100 injured.

In the face of these historic moments, perhaps the last thing on the minds of much of the international community is gender and sexuality and their relation to the construction and maintenance of the State. But gender and sexuality are not only useful areas to examine closely when trying to understand the dynamics of power in the North: they are essential. As Lorraine Dowler argues, "in Northern Ireland today the primary role of women remains that of the reproduction of the body politic."[3] Her comment resonates with my own work on women and reproductive debates in the Republic of Ireland;[4] with cultural critic Lauren Berlant's analysis of gender, sexuality, and politics in the United States;[5] and, more generally, with Nira Yuval-Davis's overview of the relationship between gender and nationalism.[6] The future of Northern Ireland rests firmly in the numbers: though Protestants have a 57 percent majority, this is predicted to change to a Catholic majority by 2050.[7] Dissident Irish republican and feminist Bernadette Devlin McAliskey has said, "Unionists must ensure that nationalists don't outnumber them. On the other side what are we confined to—outbreeding them? What are our choices? Either we shoot them or we outbreed them. There's no politics here. It's a numbers game."[8] Women on both sides of the sectarian divide are constructed through the often masculinist discourse of sectarian groups as those who must do the work of outbreeding "them." And, as McAliskey's comment indicates, that work of "outbreeding" is not considered "politics" in the current political discourse of Northern Ireland. This construction of women's place in the political sphere is more often tacit than explicit, coded in idealized images of passive women articulated through patriarchal Church teachings, punishments for women who cross sectarian lines, and taboos about discussing reproductive choices. It might be fair to assert that women have the greatest investment in the peace process—not because, or not only because, it is "their men and children" being killed in the violence, as recent popular films such as *Some Mother's Son* and *The Boxer* would have it, but because the current entrenched sectarian binary requires women to sacrifice political agency for the so-called greater good of the (unionist or nationalist) community. As Rosemary Sales has argued, however, the sectarian nature of the Troubles has often meant that women must put aside questions of "politics"—defined narrowly as sectarian politics—in order to deal with issues common to women, such as childbirth, reproductive freedom, health- and child-care, and gender discrimination. Ultimately, Sales states, "social policy in Northern Ireland has both been shaped by gender and sectarian divisions, and has also been important in shaping and sustaining them. Official policy has accommodated to the sectarian divide, even where it has been officially 'religion blind,' and many of the policies of the Direct Rule period have served to entrench the separation of the two communities further."[9] She asserts that "politics has remained polarized around community loyalties, placing severe limitations on the development of class-based or gender-based loyalties."[10] This has meant that the politics of reproducing for the community has not been discussed at length, because such a discussion would mean opening the wounds of sectarian division—despite the fact that this state of affairs is true for nationalist and unionist women alike.

The issue of reproduction also affects how queers[11] are seen in the political sphere. The causes of homophobia and heterosexism, like misogyny and sexism, can be traced to multiple sources. But resistant nationalisms, such as unionism and Irish republicanism, remain invested in reproducing their body politic, and they thus rely on and work to ensure the inviolability of the heterosexual family unit to ensure that reproduction.[12] Following this logic, queers do not contribute to the reproduction of the nationalist community; indeed, they are seen as a challenge to the heterosexual family unit and are constructed, in the words of theorist Carl Stychin, as the "nation's other."[13] Both in early twentieth-century Irish nationalist discourse and in later Irish discussions about the AIDS crisis, homosexuality is regarded as a kind of foreign pollution, a threat from outside.[14] The most memorable Northern Irish example of this view was the Democratic Unionist Party's 1977 "Save Ulster from Sodomy" campaign, a response to recommendations from the European Court of Human Rights that the 1967 liberalization of British laws on homosexuality be extended to Northern Ireland. Even when political parties have held a more tolerant view of homosexuality, however, politicians have resisted actively pursuing rights for queer people—perhaps out of fear of alienating the more conservative members of their constituencies, but also perhaps because queers are not seen to contribute to the sectarian cause.

The Good Friday Agreement, while ensuring "partnership, equality and mutual respect" and "the right to equal opportunity in all social and economic activity, regardless of class, creed, disability, gender or ethnicity," continues to mean that Northern politics must remain locked in sectarian binary opposition.[15] The requirement that all designated issues requiring cross-community support in the new Assembly be approved by either "parallel consent, i.e., a majority of those members present and voting, including a majority of the unionist and nationalist designations present and voting," or by a "weighted majority (60 percent) of members present and voting, including at least 40 percent of each of the nationalist and unionist designations present and voting," further reinforces the definition of the

North as a sectarian community divided in two.[16] The practical result of this stipulation in the Agreement is that cross-community groups such as the Alliance Party and the Women's Coalition must choose sides—nationalist or unionist—for votes that are seen to have ramifications for "both" communities. The numbers game remains, and the voices that challenge such a construction of the state of affairs are inevitably subsumed into sectarian politics.

Despite the participation of the Women's Coalition in the multi-party talks and in the new Assembly and the Agreement's calls for civil rights, gender and sexuality issues continue to be put on the back burner both by the politicians in the North and by those in the British Parliament. I argue that this absence of discussion of gender and sexuality is not only harmful for women and queers, regardless of political affiliation, but also for the future of the North. That stasis can only be changed by challenging what is meant by "self-determination" in the North: individuals and groups can currently only have access to a politically-recognized "self," I argue, if they define themselves in sectarian terms. By attempting to participate in political discourse anyway, women and queers trouble that static view of selfhood: thus the title of this chapter. To support this claim, I will examine the so-called division between public and private spheres through the politics of information and the politics of space. The tension between public and private can serve as a window through which we analyze the larger politics of the self.

THE PRIVATE PUBLIC SPHERE,
THE PUBLIC PRIVATE SPHERE

In order to illuminate the specific situation in Northern Ireland, I would first like to examine briefly some of the theoretical debates about the public and private spheres and their relationship to gender. The public sphere has often been invoked and celebrated as the place in which political debate and action happens; the private sphere has generally been described as the site of the individual and, oftentimes, the family—as the concept of the "right to privacy" implies—as well as the site of the economy. In the introduction to the collection of essays entitled *The Phantom Public Sphere,* however, Bruce Robbins explores the changing meanings of the terms "private" and "public" in philosophical-political tracts, starting with discussions in the 1920s and continuing to present-day struggles with the term on both ends of the political spectrum. As he notes, "leftists of the 1990s do not know how to argue for the democracy we want without mobilizing an image of the public so hazy, idealized, and distant from the actual people, places, and institutions around us that it can easily serve purposes that are anything but democratic."[17] The situation described above—women's loss of political agency in the name of the greater, "public" good as defined by those on either side of the sectarian divide—certainly supports that point: such a vision of the "public good" excludes women implicitly from the public forum of participatory democracy. Robbins celebrates, instead of a wholesale rejection of the public/private dichotomy, a recognition of and attention to "the actual multiplicity of distinct and overlapping public discourses, public spheres, and scenes of evaluation that already exist, but that the usual idealizations have screened from view,"[18] ultimately hoping to tease out a notion of the public that "would be adequate to the connectedness of power."[19]

An admirable theoretical goal. But can a space in which multiple discourses and bodies have agency, equal respect, and freedom without violence be imagined within the ways "private" and "public" are currently invoked? Robbins states summarily that "the lines between public and private are perpetually shifting, as are the tactical advantages of finding oneself on one side or another."[20] Surveying the tensions between private and public outlined by feminist critics Catherine MacKinnon, Nancy Fraser, Rosalyn Deutsche, and Iris Marion Young—in short, how private and public are both terms invoked strategically to reify patriarchal relations—Robbins asserts that "feminist efforts would seem better aimed at the immediately disputable power to redraw the public/private line rather than the utopian goal of effacing all such lines."[21] Such a claim, however, does not address the recurring points in MacKinnon's, Fraser's, Deutsche's, and Young's arguments and thus the underlying problems with the invocation of the public/private binary. All of these theorists point to the ways in which the public/private dichotomy relies on a fixed set of gendered power relations. For instance, Catharine MacKinnon, in *Toward a Feminist Theory of the State,* warns of the difficulties of using the language of "choice" to combat anti-abortion legislation. While the goal of securing women's agency is admirable, the language of the United States's *Roe v. Wade* decision links personal choice with privacy. MacKinnon argues that "privacy is by no means a gender-neutral concept;" the liberal notion of protection of privacy assumes that, within the private sphere, all individuals are free and equal, which, as many women recognize, is not the case. As she argues, "for women the measure of the intimacy has been the measure of the oppression. This is why feminism has had to explode the private. This is why feminism has seen the personal as the political. . . . Feminism confronts the fact that women have no privacy to guarantee."[22] She suggests that we need to recognize the extent to which abortion issues have never been wholly "private" nor wholly "choices."

Taking the critique further, Nancy Fraser has effectively analyzed the gendered implications of the often-invoked Habermasian model of public/private relations.[23] Jurgen Habermas distinguishes between not only public and private but also "lifeworld" and "system": the nuclear family is a private "lifeworld" institution, and the (official) economy is a private "system;" the public sphere of debate and political participation is a public "lifeworld" institution, and the official administration of the State is a public "system." Habermas criticizes the "colonization" of the private lifeworld by the systems of the official economy and the State, particularly in the late capitalist welfare State. But, as Fraser points out, the private lifeworld—the nuclear family—is by no means originally separate from and unaffected by these systems. Fraser complicates Habermas's model by suggesting the extent to which gender already informs not only the private lifeworld but also the participatory model of democracy celebrated by Habermas. As Fraser suggests, gender structures all of the systems and lifeworld institutions Habermas names. His model occludes our recognition of the ways these systems depend upon the patriarchal model of familial relations that defines the private lifeworld and women's ability to participate in and affect both the public (lifeworld) sphere and public systems. As Sales has argued, for instance, "Northern Ireland's model of social policy has been based on the British model, which is still based on the notion of the male breadwinner;" the result of such a structure means women bear a heavy, unpaid domestic burden.[24] This situation means that women are practically limited in their ability to participate in the public sphere, and that the private sphere is assumed by public policymakers to be patriarchal and heterosexual. The economy (a "private system") as well as the public sphere are thus exposed as already gendered. Habermas might argue that this gendering is a result of the colonization of lifeworld by system (the State in the form of public policy), but such an argument assumes that systems are not informed by lifeworlds. The language of public debate (a lifeworld sphere) is most certainly gendered, as feminist cultural critics have been pointing out for years; this is certainly no less true in Northern Ireland than elsewhere. So-called private sexual relations serve as a foundation upon which the public sphere, both lifeworld and system, is built. Patriarchal heterosexuality—which, as Judith Butler argues, creates the gender system[25]—is in itself a system that cuts across public and private lifeworlds and systems. And it is a system that has helped to ensure that women and queers with political agency are deemed threatening in the public sphere—a notion that must be destabilized to ensure that civil rights for all are not, to paraphrase David Norris, reduced to a numbers game.

To make this point clearer, and to further challenge the concept of the distinctness of the public and private spheres, I would like to turn to the notion of information, a notion that effectively cuts across public/private lines, though it depends upon the distinction between the two to operate as an oppressive system.

THE POLITICS OF INFORMATION

This essay was originally inspired by an article by Sean Cahill written shortly after the 1994 cease-fire first declared by the Irish Republic Army (IRA) and later by loyalist paramilitary groups. In that article, based on his 1994 visit to Northern Ireland, Cahill makes two claims in particular that caught my attention. The first: "closeted gay men cruising along Derry's Foyle River are picked up by police or soldiers and threatened with out-ing to their friends and families if they don't become informants."[26] The second: "as part of their sting [on Sinn Fein members in Derry], RUC [Royal Ulster Constabulary] officers raided the Well Women's Center . . . confiscating its records full of confidential information. Since Catholics don't trust the Northern Irish State in general and the RUC in particular, reports of rape, domestic violence, and other crimes are made in confi-dence to health clinics. Women's activists in Derry were devastated at the potential for blackmail and pain these records could produce in the hands of the RUC hungry for informants."[27]

Dr. Robbie McVeigh's study of harassment in Northern Ireland, pub-lished by the Belfast-based Committee for the Administration of Justice, suggests that harassment by security forces (here defined as the RUC and the several forces of the British Army stationed in Northern Ireland), in-cluding the types mentioned by Cahill, is a widespread problem. McVeigh distinguishes between sexist and homophobic harassment and political ha-rassment. He argues that "the political harassment of Gay people occurs when they are harassed because of assumed knowledge or contacts and their sexuality is perceived to be a 'vulnerability' which will encourage them to 'co-operate' with the police."[28] That perceived vulnerability can be said to apply too to the women clients of the Derry Centre—whether Catholic or Protestant.

These claims expose the State's control of the bodies both of women who attempt to control their reproductive abilities and, in the situations Cahill recounts, of men who have sex with other men. These incidents of harassment are also a useful starting point for a critical analysis of the place of information in the larger context of the construction and maintenance of the State. To inform and to inform against are closely related; whether the agent is the State controlling access to abortion information, or an in-dividual relaying information about another individual's political activi-ties, "informing" helps to define the boundaries of the State, sectarian communities, and the individual subject. "Inform" has a number of meanings that are related to the formation of identity and the control of subjects. Information, or "knowledge communicated concerning some particular fact, subject, or event," as well as informing, or "lay[ing] or exhibit[ing] information, bring[ing] a charge or complaint," both work to in-form, or "to give form to, put into form or shape . . . mould, or train" the subject.[29] The State's manipulation of information has the effect of shaping the boundaries of the subject. For one subject to shape and control another, s/he must control the flow of information about and through that subject. The security of the State depends on the control both of information and informers.

The State can use the threat of "information," or exposure of personal details, to secure its own self-interest. In both cases Cahill mentions and in the general critique leveled by McVeigh, the threat of public exposure of private information is used by the State in order to extort more information necessary to maintain the borders of the State. The tension between private and public allows the State to manipulate the flow of information among subjects, who remain understandably invested in preserving the distinction between public and private that ostensibly serves their own (private) interests—that is, self-preservation. But the private, as in the cases mentioned above, can serve simply as another arm of the State, wielded in order to ensure its perpetuation.

Further research uncovered differing accounts of the aforementioned "information" that productively inflect my reading of informing. According to the coordinator of the Derry Well Women's Centre, officers of the RUC did raid the Centre and confiscate private phone records under the provisions of the Northern Ireland (Security Provisions) Act of 1991, legislation building on and consolidating earlier acts intended to allow the British crown forces to quell suspected terrorist activity.[30] The raid provoked a general outcry amongst the citizens of Derry, particularly from women concerned about the possible use and abuse of private records in the hands of police. Although the Centre has not been raided since, the event awakened concern about the security of confidential medical and counseling records—even though no patient files were taken in the raid (despite news reports to the contrary). This concern is far from paranoid, and not limited to those seeking the services of this particular clinic. As the incident suggests, the Northern Ireland (Security Provisions) Act allowed the police a great amount of leeway in their decisions about what constitutes a demonstrable link between a client of confidential services and terrorist activity. In this case, the records of calls to the clinic were confiscated because the police claimed that one of the clinic's clients was associated with an elected Sinn Fein city councilwoman—an arguably tenuous link to terrorism at best.

Those at the Centre fear that to return public attention to this event will heighten women's fear of using the Centre's confidential services. Cahill's report was based on the mistaken belief that confidential patient records were confiscated. The misinformation circulated in the press only served to heighten women's fear about their private lives being used for the so-called public good (as assumed by the act). Many of the women who use the service are in search of pregnancy counseling. Though abortion and abortion information is legal in the North, they are by no means easily available; the 1967 abortion law that made abortion available in the rest of Great Britain has not been extended to Northern Ireland, despite the work of several pro-choice groups over the years.[31] Women who seek abortions still find themselves subject to prejudice and ostracism, and women's centers and their workers often find themselves subject to violence and threats of violence from sectarian groups.

Women's centers are not the only organizations both subject to and concerned about discussing police harassment. My contacts with lesbian and gay organizations in the North have led to conflicting reports about police abuse.[32] One member of an organization stated summarily that such abuse did not occur and suggested that my investigation into such claims could stir up bad feeling; another suggested that active homophobic abuses on the part of the police were rare and were, at any rate, a thing of the past, though I later discovered that queers in the community had often reported such abuse to him. Other individuals, however, directed me to the McVeigh report and concurred with its findings, noting that the abuse of gay men in particular has been allowed under "public decency" laws: gay men are either accused of sexually propositioning other men in public or of participating in sexual activity in public space. The illegality of these actions creates more vulnerability that can be exploited by the police.

The concerned and sometimes contradictory responses to my inquiry into police abuse suggest tension about the safety of the public sphere for women and queers. Both the Derry Women's Centre and certain members of the queer community were understandably invested in keeping secret the abuse leveled by the State, abuse sanctioned under the Northern Ireland (Security Provisions) Act and ostensibly leveled in the name of the "public good." The State is not the only entity that can abuse the private sphere thus, but it clearly has the edge because it is what Max Weber calls "a human community that (successfully) claims the *monopoly of the legitimate use of physical force* within a given territory" (original emphasis).[33] In practice, then, the good of the State equals the public good. The State can "legitimately" use the threat of violence to achieve its ends, especially given what McVeigh calls the "infrastructure of emergency"[34] and the lack of structures of "liaison and democratic control" with respect to the Royal

Irish Regiment (RIR) and the British Army.[35] The State thus is the most effective and officially legitimized controller of information. One can also say with certainty that the State's control in Northern Ireland has at the very least shaped sectarian battles, if not in fact necessitated them. Such battles have thus spawned control of information (and the often violent control of informers) within republican and unionist communities. The private lifeworld, in short, is up for grabs in the public, sectarian battle over who gets to control the State, and women and queers are caught in the middle—shaped, often violently, by competing political forces.

All sides of this sectarian struggle rely on the sanctity of the private sphere to create anxiety about the public regulation of bodies: entering the public sphere means "publicity," or anxiety, shame, and ultimately retreat, for those who do not fit into socially acceptable norms. The public sphere, both lifeworld and system, thus remains the province of the State and those who can personally, professionally, socially, and/or financially afford public battles with it or for it—groups like the IRA that have funding from outside sources, for instance, or those protected by employment laws focused on preventing discrimination based on "political" affiliation. Those who cannot afford such battles are, of course, those for whom privacy is the most sacred, since privacy is the only protection from public censure—and often, violence. Privacy is thus ironically both the only protection for queers and women who do not toe the family line and the way in which they remain oppressed, for they do not have public recourse.

Public protection for such marginalized groups has historically been minimal. During the '90s peace talks, however, the British government, under pressure from the United States, drafted a document intended to replace the MacBride human rights principles (which were rejected because of the nationalist sympathies of its drafter, Sean MacBride). The resulting guidelines, the Policy Appraisal and Fair Treatment (PAFT) guidelines, came into effect in 1994. The government stated that "the aim of the PAFT initiative is to ensure that issues of equity and equality inform policy making in all spheres and at all levels of Government activity, whether in regulatory and administrative functions or in the delivery of services to the public."[36] The guidelines, a sweeping statement of support for public equality, state that "it shall be unlawful for a public authority to discriminate unfairly, directly or indirectly, against anyone in Northern Ireland on any ground such as race, gender, pregnancy, marital status, political or other opinion, ethnic or social origin, color, sexual orientation, age, disability, religion, conscience, belief, culture, language, birth, nationality, national origin, or other status."[37] In another case of State control of information, however, those guidelines, produced under pressure from outside, were never circulated to those groups in the North whom they would most benefit. Knowledge of PAFT came slowly to groups in the North, circulated primarily by word of mouth. Were these guidelines to be made legally binding, those groups most affected by police abuse of private information and by discrimination would have an unprecedented amount of protection under the law, and the abuse of private information by public officials could be appealed. Currently, however, the guidelines are guidelines and not law. Making PAFT legally binding would be a first step toward destabilizing the abusive power that results from the public/private divide. But as long as public systems and the public lifeworld are dominated by those who can abuse private information, whether they be public (government) officials, politicians, paramilitaries, or others, the result will continue to be violence, both emotional and physical, against those who are limited because of their inability freely to access the public sphere.

Those groups who define themselves in terms outside sectarian language often find respite in "neutral" spaces in Northern Ireland. Women and queers in particular, groups that potentially threaten the secure reproduction of the sectarian politics of the North, have both tried to articulate theoretical space and secure physical space in which they can be "themselves"—acts that are in themselves politically challenging. The concept of space, like the concept of information, is essential to understanding the politics of selfhood in Northern Ireland. Selves or subjects do not only exist as abstract concepts: they require space. The next section will thus engage briefly with "space" and its role in gender, sexuality, and national subjectivity in the North.

THE POLITICS OF SPACE

Space is highly politicized in Northern Ireland—a place where sectarian divides are marked by curbs painted in the flag of the nation to which a given community pledges allegiance, or wall murals that invoke static histories of community triumphs and oppressions; where skirmishes are fought over stretches of road down which one community wishes to march and which another claims as its own; where religious and ethnic differences are still sometimes pseudo-scientifically "measured" by the distance between a person's eyes; and where surveillance cameras and security outposts watch over large segments of the population. Political and (para)military battles are often fought over space—who gets it and who controls it. Space can be seen as another manifestation of the numbers game. If you have the numbers, you have the space, and vice versa. In short, space is territory, and territory in Northern Ireland is a geopolitical concept, marked by actual physical boundaries.

These are the spaces that are discussed in Northern Ireland and that dominate media presentations of the province. But other spaces—sometimes quite tangible, sometimes more abstract—are rarely commented upon publicly. The parceling out of territory along sectarian lines has often meant little space for communities that do not define themselves along those lines. The Downtown Women's Centre in Belfast, for example, is a single building that houses a number of cross-community women's organizations, including Women Into Politics, an initiative that is attempting to get more women participating in the public sphere and public systems; Women's News, a cooperative that prints the feminist monthly of the same name; and the Women's Support Network, which coordinates and serves as a "neutral space" for various community women's centers around Belfast. All of these projects work to provide a space for women to voice their concerns outside of the territorialized communities in which they are often, literally and figuratively, contained. The Downtown Women's Centre is in what is in itself considered to be a geographically neutral space—that is, a space not defined by sectarian loyalties. As a result, women feel freer to voice their concerns about issues that would be more contentious in their own community centers, issues such as abortion, for instance, or cross-community programs. The building in which the Centre is housed, however, is up for sale, and the Centre's lease expired at the end of summer 1998. The business development of the city center has meant that it will be very difficult for the women's groups to find an affordable "neutral space."[38] Most of the inexpensive sites would be located in the more financially depressed sectarian spaces of the city, the very spaces from which women often need respite and in which they often find themselves quite literally under siege.[39] Even if the Centre managed to maintain its lease, its hold over that physical space, in which a more theoretical and potentially borderless "feminist space" can flourish, is clearly unstable.

Another community that often finds itself in need of space is the queer community. As Carola Speth of *Women's News* has put it, Belfast is "a city which doesn't offer much for gay people" in terms of space.[40] This has been partially remedied in 1998 by the formation of Queer Space, a grassroots-funded collective "space maintained by & for the community— OUR COMMUNITY."[41] The community to which the Queer Space Mission Statement refers is the lesbian, gay, bisexual, transgender (LGBT) community, but Queer Space also aims to "make sure it stays open, accessible, and known both to the LGBT community AND the general/mainstream population," and the Queer Space Policy document states that "Queer Space rejects discrimination on the basis of: gender, sexual/political identity, class, race/skin color/ethnicity/nationality, religion, age, physical ability, employment status, HIV status, immigration status or other aspects of identity."[42] The formation of this space and the reclamation of the word "community" from its often-invoked sectarian meanings challenges the notion that territories in the North can only be defined in sectarian ways. Like the Downtown Women's Centre, Queer Space has been located in the so-called neutral downtown area of the city. And like the Centre, it recently faced the problem of finding another adequate safe space troubled neither by sectarianism nor, just as importantly, gay-bashing, both verbal and physical. Though Queer Space did successfully relocate in September 1998, the concerns about maintaining a safe and accessible space remain.

Lorraine Dowler, in the conclusion to "The Mother of All Warriors: Women in West Belfast, Northern Ireland," argues that "true political solidarity does not exist within the borders of Irish Nationalism, rather it exists in the frontiers of Irish feminism. . . . We must perhaps try to escape from a territorialized, hermetically sealed cell-like view of human communities."[43] The politics of selfhood in the North, however, make the realization of such a goal difficult in the current political climate. Subjects need space in which to exist; bodies occupy space. And many such spaces are, as I have discussed above, under siege from forces that threaten the very existence of these bodies. Dowler's statement points to the problem of territorialization in West Belfast in particular. We can extend that argument more generally to the North as a political entity. Where sectarian groups and the State clash over geopolitical territory—that is, the spatial boundaries of Northern Ireland—there is violence. But the violence is not only perpetrated on those who choose to engage with one definition of the national self or another: it is also inflicted on those who have no space in which and no recognized public voice with which to express their own notion of political subjectivity.

When the song that is in me is the song I hear from the world I'll be home.
—Paula Meehan, "Home"[44]

As I have argued above, the recent breakthroughs in the peace process are far from solving the problems facing Northern Ireland, because many in the region do not have free and equal access to the so-called public sphere. Access to the public sphere is shaped by patriarchal and heteronormative assumptions; the individual "self" that engages in the public sphere can only do so if it conforms to those assumptions. The public sphere is also further delimited by sectarian concerns that reinforce patriarchal heteronormativity: women must reproduce for the cause. Allowing people to have agency over their sexuality means destabilizing the secure reproduction of sectarian communities. But as long as the North remains a numbers game, as long as politics remains defined by allegiance or challenge to the existing geopolitical boundaries, women and queers will by default continue to be denied space for alternative definitions of the self. Politics must have a broader definition, and different selves must be recognized, before the North can find a lasting peace.

NOTES

I would like to thank the University of Kansas Center for Research, Inc. for the New Faculty General Research Fund grant that enabled me to complete the research for this article.

1. David Norris, "Human Rights for Homosexuals" (Letters to the Editor), *Irish Times,* 29 June 1998.
2. "Unionist" and "loyalist" are used interchangeably throughout the essay to refer to those who support Northern Ireland's union with Great Britain. "Republican" and "nationalist" are used to refer to those who do not support the union and instead want Northern Ireland to reunite with the Republic of Ireland as a single sovereign nation.
3. Lorraine Dowler, "The Mother of All Warriors: Women in West Belfast, Northern Ireland," in *Gender and Catastrophe,* ed. Ronit Lentin (London and New York: Zed Books, 1998), 78.
4. See "Fetal Ireland," in *Eire-Ireland* (forthcoming).
5. See Lauren Berlant, *The Queen of America Goes to Washington City: Essays on Sex and Citizenship* (Durham: Duke University Press, 1997), especially ch. 3, "America, Fat, the Fetus," 83–144.
6. Nira Yuval-Davis, *Gender & Nation* (London: Sage Publications, 1997).
7. Dowler, "The Mother," 78.
8. Bernadette Devlin McAliskey, quoted in Sean Cahill, "Occupied Ireland: Amid Hope of Peace Repression Continues," *Radical America* 25 (1995): 57.
9. Rosemary Sales, *Women Divided: Gender, Religion, and Politics in Northern Ireland* (New York: Routledge, 1997), 135.
10. Ibid., 202. Begoña Arextaga has also explored the relationship between gender and political activism, primarily in Catholic West Belfast, in *Shattering Silence: Women, Nationalism, and Political Subjectivity in Northern Ireland* (Princeton: Princeton University Press, 1997).
11. I use "queers" to denote lesbians, gay men, bisexuals, transgendered people, and all others who fall outside of definitions of supposedly normative heterosexuality.
12. For an examination of the centrality of "family" to the discourse of the nation, see especially Anne McClintock, "Family Feuds: Gender, Nationalism and the Family," *Feminist Review* 44 (Summer 1993): 61–80.

13. Carl F. Stychin, *A Nation of Rights: National Cultures, Sexual Identity Politics and the Discourse of Rights* (Philadelphia: Temple University Press, 1998), 9.

14. See especially Kieran Rose, *Diverse Communities: The Evolution of Lesbian and Gay Politics in Ireland* (Cork: Cork University Press, 1994); and Kathryn Conrad, "Queering the Nation: Homosexuality in Irish Nationalist Discourse," in *Cultural Studies* (forthcoming).

15. "Northern Ireland Political Agreement," published by British Information Services, http://www.britain-info.org/bis/nireland/keysettl.htm.

16. Ibid.

17. Bruce Robbins, *The Phantom Public Sphere* (Minneapolis: University of Minnesota Press, 1993), xii.

18. Ibid.

19. Ibid., xiii.

20. Ibid., xv.

21. Ibid., xvi.

22. Catherine MacKinnon, *Toward a Feminist Theory of the State* (Cambridge: Harvard University Press, 1989), 191.

23. Nancy Fraser, *Unruly Practices: Power, Discourse and Gender in Contemporary Social Theory* (Minneapolis: University of Minnesota Press, 1989). See especially ch. 6, "What's Critical about Critical Theory? The Case of Habermas and Gender," 113–143. Fraser focuses her critique on Jurgen Habermas, *The Theory of Communicative Action,* vol. 2, *Lifeworld and System: A Critique of Functionalist Reason,* trans. Thomas McCarthy (Boston: Beacon Press, 1987).

24. Sales, *Women Divided,* 135.

25. See Judith Butler, *Gender Trouble: Feminism and the Subversion of Identity* (New York and London: Routledge, 1990), especially ch. 1, "Subjects of Sex/Gender/Desire," 1–34.

26. Cahill, "Occupied Ireland," 53.

27. Ibid., 54.

28. Robbie McVeigh, *"It's part of life here . . .": The Security Forces and Harassment in Northern Ireland* (Belfast: Committee on the Administration of Justice, 1994), 136.

29. *Oxford English Dictionary* (Oxford and New York: Oxford University Press, 1996).

30. Based on a telephone conversation between the author and the coordinator of the Derry Well Women's Centre, December 1997.

31. Those groups most recently include the Alliance for Choice and the Irish Abortion Solidarity Campaign.

32. I have not received permission to quote from these individuals, so I have chosen not to identify them or the groups to which they belong.

33. Max Weber, "Politics as a Vocation," in *From Max Weber,* ed. H. H. Geth and C. W. Mills (London: Routledge and Kegan Paul, 1970), 77 (as cited in McVeigh, "It's Part of Life," 53).

34. McVeigh, "It's Part of Life," 24.

35. Ibid., 37.
36. Cited in Christopher McCrudden, *Benchmarks for Change: Mainstreaming Fairness in the Governance of Northern Ireland—A Proposal* (Belfast: Committee on the Administration of Justice, 1998), 3.
37. Ibid., 23.
38. Based on a conversation between the author and Marie Mulholland of the Downtown Women's Centre, July 1998.
39. It is worthy of note that a not-for-profit public space is under threat from the public forces of sectarian violence on the one hand and the private forces of the market on the other. The effect of the increasing influx of global capital on politics in Northern Ireland is an important area for further investigation.
40. Carola Speth, "Queer Space," *Women's News* (Belfast), Feb. 1998, 13.
41. Ibid., 13.
42. "Queer Space Mission Statement" and "Queer Space Policy," 1998. Available at http://www.geocities.com/WestHollywood/Heights/7124/about.html.
43. Dowler, "The Mother," 88.
44. Paula Meehan, "Home," *f/m* 1 (Summer 1997): 12.

Chapter Four

Familist Ideology and Difficult Identities: "Never-Married" Women in Contemporary Irish Society

Anne Byrne

INTRODUCTION

Ireland has been described as a society moving from private to public patriarchy, from the household as the main site of women's oppression to public sites such as employment and the state.[1] Though the concept of patriarchy has come under critical scrutiny, it does highlight structures and practices that give rise to women's continued disadvantage in gender relations. While some research examines the consequences of patriarchy for women's lives in employment, education, health, welfare, and sexual violence, little attention has been paid to how women cope and lead meaningful lives in the face of powerful, oppressive social structures, institutions and practices. Paying attention to structures, institutions and practices of patriarchy is crucial to explaining patterns, identifying problems, and making the case for change—part of the project of emancipatory, feminist research.

What is obscured in Irish research is how women respond to or resist patriarchal power at the level of the individual. Individual agency and the potential for effecting change is neither observed nor analyzed. Some research attempts to explain the changes in family practices where marriage and reproduction have become uncoupled, leading to a marked increase in single parenthood, a situation unthinkable thirty years ago. Pat O'Connor argues that women themselves have led the changes in re-negotiating marriage and family-making in Ireland.[2] I argue here that a general focus on identity issues demonstrates that transformations at the individual level are also going on, transformations that have collective consequences and significant implications for our understanding of womanhood and especially what it means to be a woman in contemporary Irish society.

The "founding fathers" of Irish national and cultural identity deliberately constructed a national identity based on familism, religiosity, and nationalism in an effort to secure legitimacy for and adherence to the newly emerging state. The connection between the endorsement of familism (and the concomitant construction of femininity and masculinity) and the developing economy of the Irish Free State/Irish Republic cannot be emphasized enough. Low marriage rates, higher age of marriage, higher fertility within marriage together with patterns of postponed marriage, and high rates of singleness (described as "permanent celibacy") in the 1940s and 50s were tied to improving the economic life of the nation.[3] The stem-family system of inheritance, allowing only one son (or daughter in the absence of a son) to inherit property, was devised to consolidate land holding and contribute to greater economic prosperity. The inheriting son could marry, his wife bringing a dowry into the household, thus allowing one daughter to marry. Such a system meant that there was a real constraint on the number of people who could marry and reproduce in the population, thus giving rise to a high rate of singleness, a status which, though economically necessary, was neither socially nor culturally valued, particularly for women.

Considering this context and the resultant effects of social and economic policies that gave preferential treatment to those actively engaged in the civilizing and modernizing of Irish society, it is somewhat surprising that there has been little sociological interest in an analysis of the consequence of approved and dominant social identities for individual lives and personal identity. Tom Inglis is concerned that Irish research on sexuality is sparse, arguing that the Catholic Church's monopoly over sexual discourse has deterred social scientists from reflecting "critically on the creation of our personal and social being."[4] Heterosexuality, marriage, and parenthood were and continue to be regarded as prime practices through which approved gender identities are constructed for women and men, yet their contribution to the process of identity composition and the consequences for individuals "who choose to do otherwise," remain largely unexamined.

The effects of familism continue to deeply resonate throughout many of our political and social institutions, despite changing family practices. A case in point concerns the recommendations of the Constitutional Review group in reference to Article 41 on the family, which offered constitutional protection to the "traditional" (marital) Irish family, composed of breadwinner husband, full-time housewife with "home duties," reflecting their central position in the then developing rural economy and a family form considered key to maintaining social (albeit Catholic) order.[5] In an appendix to the report of the Constitutional Review group, Kathleen Lynch critically observed that an opportunity to re-evaluate the current constitutional definition of family as constituted by marriage was not taken. Whatever the merits of re-affirming and offering constitutional protection to the marital, two-parent, heterosexual family as the preferred family form, this preference continues to locate nonmarital families in outsider positions.

To understand familism it is necessary to recognize that it is an ideology, encompassing in one sweep, the "natural" order, the division of labor, and the promise of love and care. Familism is created and maintained by the privileging of heterosexuality, marriage, and reproduction in the composition of approved gender identities.[6] Familism is premised on a division of labor between those who earn a wage outside the home and those involved in full-time caring work in the domestic space. Familism is an ideology in which the family is treated as a social, political, economic, and affective unit that is antithetical to individualism or the realization of autonomy for its female and child members, aspects that are key to achieving the status of full personhood in contemporary society. What it is to be a woman or man are contained within the ideology of familism, captured in the breadwinner husband and stay-at-home wife model of the family economy.

Tony Fahey has located Irish families as largely in this stage, with some moving on to the dual income, dual earner stage.[7] Though increasing numbers of married women continue to join the labor force, most are engaged in "home-duties" full-time (Census of the Population classification for house-wives, i.e., married women working in the home as unpaid laborers), a pattern that distinguishes Irish women from their European sisters. While family size is generally decreasing, suggesting that women's life-time dedication to home duties is no longer necessary, and though the number of nonmarital families continues to grow, familist ideology continues to inform conceptions of what it is to be a woman. The persistence of a traditional familist ideology, despite changes in family practices, forms, and values, is necessary, I suggest, to bolster the practices and organization of patriarchy.[8]

Traditional familist ideology remains functional in contemporary Irish society, I suggest, in order to bolster the practices and organization of patriarchy. A full-time domestic (house) worker, married (wife), mother, caretaker, economically dependent, a conception idealized in Article 41 on the Family in Bunreacht na hEireann, remains ideologically relevant in Irish culture.[9] To claim womanhood in this order is to demonstrate to others that you can sexually attract a man, form an intimate, enduring, exclusive, marital relationship with him, and reproduce and care for children. Others assume that until this form of "emphasized femininity" is achieved, one cannot be considered a woman, an adult, or a full person.

Kathryn Conrad points to the lack of "space" available to develop alternative definitions of self-identity for those positioned outside heterosexual familism.[10] The evidence from my study shows that single women are developing alternative definitions of self-identity. A focus on identity issues reveals how some women actively negotiate familism, and in so doing challenge the dominance of traditional familism, move beyond it, and create new, alternative ways of being a woman in contemporary Irish society.

SINGLE STIGMA

During the period 1995–1998, I carried out a collaborative study with thirty single (never-married), noncohabiting, childless women, over the age of thirty, in the West of Ireland, about the meaning of singleness and single identity to them. The Single Study was concerned with examining the relationship between self-identity (personal identity) and social identity (collective identity),[11] with the accuracy of relational models of self-identity for woman, asking if nonmarital, nonreproductive pathways to adulthood existed in contemporary, modern Irish society. In the Single Study, self-identity is understood to be composed in relationship with others—the dynamic between self-identity and social identity constituting concepts of personhood. Interview, workshop, and evaluative material generated by single women participants was analyzed using a voice-centered relational method, allowing for a focus on individual narratives set in the context of women's relationships with others.[12] Three categories of women participated in the study, identified by acceptable social identities for single women—career women, women carers, and women actively seeking a partner.

Despite the normative acceptability of the choices single women made in developing successful careers, in carrying out essential family and kinkeeping work, in demonstrating to others that they were interested in heterosexual coupledom and intimacy, all reported and described the existence of single stigma. Being constantly questioned about their singleness and asked for explanations for their failure to marry by family, friends, acquaintances, and strangers was a commonly reported experience. Women's reports of remarks made by others provide evidence that singleness is still perceived as a discreditable social identity. Women are deeply aware that the continual intrusion into their "marital" status is because singleness is still not an acceptable social identity for women. For example, Siobhan said:

> the unspoken expectation in society is that you will marry unless you have stated that you are a homosexual, which I am not. So therefore maybe you are seen as something of an aberration as the older you get . . . people . . . they would say "she is a spinster." They would note that. Whereas the norm is that you would be a married woman. So somewhere along the line you have failed to meet society's expectations of you and there might be "why is this the case." That is meant by asking me questions. I would be aware of that. . . . (Siobhan, Partner-Seeker, age 37)

Most of the persistent questioning of single women is concerned with marriage intentions, bearing children, and sexuality. Single women's assumed lack of commitment to marriage, reproduction, and heterosexuality results in others perceiving them as not quite adult, as not full persons. Bonnie, a thirty-two year old woman, said:

> In the eyes of my mother . . . I am still a girl and that comes across very strongly and I vehemently hate that. And also that it is not enough to be in a relationship, that until you have the baby, you are still a girl and no matter what age you are. . . . (Bonnie, Partner-Seeker, age 32)

A single woman carer said she is treated with derision because she is not married. Margaret is pained by the fact that though single women such as herself have placed the needs of family over her own desires, she is regarded as not having completed the appropriate female rites of passage that would enable her to claim adult status. She feels that the work of single women carers is not valued and that "nobody acknowledges them."

Single sexuality is also regarded by others as a legitimate topic of interest, inquiry, and scrutiny. Being celibate and being sexually active are both bases for criticism and query. Women's lack of sexual activity is regarded as a burden, one that any male can relieve. Women reported the lack of respect and sensitivity shown by family and strangers when talking openly about single women's sexuality. Women reported, for example, that the husbands of married friends spoke to them with sexual innuendo, inquiring about their sexual availability and offering to have sex with them. Though done in a jocose manner, with wives laughing in the background at their husbands' "antics," for single women it was just one more occasion on which they were perceived as sexual "targets" for men. Being perceived as sexually available and being approached for sex is described as a frequent occurrence for women alone or in the company of other single women in pubic settings.

Sexual orientation was also a source of stigma. Women reported being identified as lesbians either because they were over thirty, single, or because they socialized with other single women or were physically affectionate toward other women in public settings. Some women were more uncomfortable than others with being perceived as lesbian. Cara's brother assumed that because she was single, she was lesbian. She is now careful "to show him that I am chatting up a lad or that I would fancy a fellow." Cara has learned that in order to avoid being further discredited, she must display to others that she is an active heterosexual woman, supporting the status quo. The fear of being labeled lesbian illustrates the intensive pressures to conform to which single women are particularly subject. Homophobia and reproductive expectations intersect to stigmatize singleness.

Marriage, reproduction, and demonstrable, active heterosexuality are still regarded as the only legitimate pathways to adulthood for Irish women, one that single women do not take. As a result, the gender and sexual identity of single women is often questioned by others, but also is of concern to single women themselves. Significantly, having to deal constantly with others' inquiries about one's singleness and receiving messages that one is an immature adult can undermine one's self-identity as a mature, adult woman. Some women, for example, reported feeling "like an outsider looking in," as "different to others," and having constantly to examine who they are.

MANAGING SINGLE STIGMA

Evidence from the Single Study showed that singleness was a deviant social identity for women that intruded into single women's relationships and interactions with others. Other consequences were also evident, such as the exclusion of single women from coupled society in family, work, and leisure settings, leading to isolation from others and legitimating a social context that marginalizes singleness as a valued characteristic. Having interviewed seven Irish, child-free, never-married women on their "opinions and experiences" of singleness, Breeda Duggan found no evidence of change in the salience of approved social identities for women based on marriage and motherhood, despite the supposed expansion in women's choices in modern Irish society.[13]

In this study, several stigma management strategies were observed. All of the women had developed a repertoire of stories to explain their singleness to others in order to reduce the effect of the stigma.[14] Women learned to avoid social situations such as weddings and coupled, family occasions that marked them as "outsiders" and as "not belonging." They learned to avoid being further discredited in work and social settings by concealing personal information about themselves. Some deliberately misled others, inventing boyfriends, wearing wedding rings, pretending to be partnered, married, engaged, drawing attention away from their continuing single-ness. But most significantly, the majority of women categorized themselves as "involuntary singles," a strategy used, I suggest, to distance themselves from the perceived and felt social stigma of singleness. Women stressed re-peatedly "I did not choose to be single," citing devoting time to develop-ing career and education, parent or family care responsibilities, the lack of suitable partners, and broken romances as among the constraints that pre-vented them from marrying. In talking about the lack of a partner in her life, Emer explained

> I was never very good at it. Maybe I didn't apply myself to find a man, maybe I haven't been out and about enough and I have spent a fair bit of time studying and working and maybe I am not interested enough either. (Emer, Career Woman, age 33)

Celie, like many others, stressed that women of her acquaintance did not choose to be single.

> It is just that they can't meet Mr. Right or they have not met Mr. Right. Anybody that I know, it is not that they want to be single, they don't mind it, but it would not be their choice. (Celie, Career Woman, age 36)

By claiming to be an involuntary single, these women suggest that they should not be held responsible for the failure to marry. The claim is some-what disingenuous, as I will show below, but is presented in an effort to offset some of the worst effects of the stigmatized social identity.

Drawing on Erving Goffman's early work on stigma, it would seem that women have learned and well understood the process of stigmatization, at-tempting to manage information about themselves so that they "pass" as "normals," and have also learned to ease social interaction by "covering."[15] Goffman noted that all of the adjustment in interaction falls upon the stig-matized, while "normals" remain undisturbed in their identity beliefs. The concept of self-identity that is being utilized here is drawn from the Mea-dian understanding of the self as composed in interaction with others. As-suming that they have learned the process of stigmatization (the identity beliefs of normal society and the consequences for themselves of being stigmatized), it is likely that women's self-identities have been affected in this process and altered in a direction so as to provide support for famil-ism. Stigma effectively works to elicit support for dominant beliefs, prac-tices and values, while controlling those who, for whatever reason, "choose to do otherwise." This argument gives rise to a conception of single women as conformists, agreeing with the normative ideas of what it is to be a woman and thus contributing to the continued marginalization of singleness. However, this is a conception that cannot be validated by the Single Study.

Did either the stigma management strategies or women's social identity location as "career women," "carers," or "partner-seekers" effectively act as a shield against single stigma? Stigma management strategies may seem to be effective on an individual, short-term basis, within a specific context, in that they allow interaction to proceed; however they do not fundamentally challenge the marital, reproductive, and sexual status inequalities that continue to be maintained and served by the stigmatizing of singleness as a social identity for women. Considering the increased participation of married and single women in the labor market and marked occupational advance in career development terms, it could be assumed that choosing to commit oneself to one's working life and demonstrating financial and entrepreneurial success invites approval and validation from others. However, I found no evidence that the social identity of career woman sufficiently overcame single stigma. Career women enjoyed higher levels of income and had a busy social and leisure life, a number owning their own homes; they were ambitious and were achieving satisfaction in their careers. Nevertheless, their singleness remained an issue that they had to confront and deal with in everyday interaction. "Having an extraordinary career" or acting outside the married/reproductive role cannot be considered as a sufficiently robust strategy to neutralize singleness as a stigmatized social identity at this moment in Irish society.

It might also be assumed that carers are less subject to single stigma than other groups of single women. The evidence from this research does not support this view. Though caring is a valuable social identity and provides long-term, essential support to families, single stigma continues to intrude into caring women's relationships with others. It is somewhat surprising to learn that caring as a social identity does not neutralize the stigmatizing consequences of singleness as a social identity. This would suggest that the fact of not marrying is more consequential for a woman in the context of social interaction. This points to one of the aspects of singleness that is problematic for others; if one-to-one, enduring, sexual relationships with men are not evident it is assumed that the single life-style is defined by the lack of relationships. Singleness is equated with separation from others. Other relationships that women may forge are not recognized either in terms of their importance in a woman's life or in terms of conferring a social identity. Despite the contribution of single women carers to families and the immeasurable work of long duration undertaken by those providing constant care, the fact that they are single and not married is more salient and as-cribes to them a social identity that has negative characteristics.

Partner-seekers as a category could be assumed to be demonstrating to others that they are attempting to correct the deviant trait. Compared to career women and carers, the seekers are more aware of the stigmatizing consequences of being single. Seekers are highly situation conscious and are working to change their single status not only for the sake of their in-teractions with others, but importantly also for themselves. They are dedi-cated to looking for a partner, want to be part of a couple, and desire a long-term sexual relationship. Half want to marry. Women in this category have committed themselves to their goal, have invested time, energy, and resources to finding a suitable partner, have exposed themselves to public scrutiny, and have taken risks that other women have been able to avoid. Partner-seekers are not waiting for relationships "to happen naturally." For example, women whom I interviewed engage in voluntary work, sporting, educational, and recreational pursuits, place and answer newspaper adver-tisements in friendship columns, join dating agencies, attend singles func-tions, and go to bars, pubs, clubs, and dances all over Ireland to meet another person with whom they can build a long-term intimate relation-ship. Ironically, they report that they are often perceived as a threat to other women who are partnered, being cast as "loose women" or "seductresses" challenging particular couples.

The effects of stigmatization cannot be undone by individual stigma management strategies or locating oneself within identity sites suppos-edly approved for and available to women who do not marry/are not yet married. In the face of the persistence of the stigma, what do single women do?

VALUING THE SINGLE LIFESTYLE[16]

I observed that single women constantly reflect on who they are and on the quality and extent of their relationships with others. Women talked at great length about the benefits of the single lifestyle and what a single lifestyle means to them. The vehemence with which women stressed the importance of independence, being a self-directed and self-reliant person cannot be adequately expressed in a written text, but was evident in the strong tone of voice used in interviews and recorded on tape. As Susan told me:

> Yes, I am very much aware of being single; . . . being single is being re-sponsible for myself and not necessarily for others. I don't have the com-mitments of a partner; . . . [it] has given me much more freedom, much

more independence, with regards to travel, doing what I want to do and not having to consider other people. (Susan, Career Woman, age 45)

Being alone confers freedom. The absence of others allows individual independence; the potential to realize autonomy as a single person is recognized, is talked about, and is valued.

While self-reliance means an orientation toward oneself, it can also mean that women are less likely to ask for help from others. A woman who is looking for a partner, but who is very aware of her single identity, said that she has become more self-reliant with time.

> I think of myself as being on my own. The person I can feel that I rely most on is me. My friends, yes they are there for me and I value them, but at the end of the day I look at most situations as being my decisions . . . and I find it difficult to look for help. I suppose I have become very independent. (Cliona, Partner-Seeker, age 37)

Although women value their friendships, being single means that one has to take responsibility for oneself; care for and about the self cannot be assumed as forthcoming from another person. Single women know and have learned the importance of being self-reliant—a capacity that once acquired, endures.

The benefits of the lack of ties, of freedom from the constraints that the presence and dependency of intimate others bring, are strongly emphasized. Being single for Cara is "very uncomplicated," a benefit of not being in an intimate relationship.

> Life is very clear and if you can create your own highs, it is great . . . great freedom. (Cara, Career Woman, age 39)

The absence of certain types of relationships, particularly intimate, sexual relationships and familial child-parent relationships, are clearly marked as facilitating single "positive independence" and "genuine freedom." Being free to make decisions on one's own, being self-reliant, and "self-esteem remaining intact" are cited advantages of not being enmeshed in intimate, dependent relationships with others or having responsibilities and obligations to others. Brenda, who has her own business, regards her independence as

> positive . . . you are not responsible for anybody but yourself; . . . if I went bust, I have nobody to think of, only myself. . . . If you have a family, you have huge responsibilities. (Brenda, Career Woman, age 31)

Not having to worry about children or concerned about a husband is also a distinct benefit of being independent and single for Annie, who is, however, actively looking for a partner.

> One of the things that it means to me is that I haven't had children or probably won't have children. . . . That I actually don't have any worries or cares about children or worries about husband. So there are advantages to it. (Annie, Partner-Seeker, age 42)

Women speak about the "regularity" and "predictability" of the single lifestyle, "the evenness" of being single, aspects that they are loath to loose or cede. Emer, a career woman, despite the stigma attached to being single, recognizes her satisfaction with how her life is now.

> Do I accept it (singleness)? I do. I want to accept it very much. I know that I am certainly an awful lot happier now than in a lot of relationships that I have been in. I love the evenness of it. I'd be very slow to give that up. I wish society didn't feel all those things. I wish I didn't pick up the vibes that I pick up out there. I wouldn't trade it. I wouldn't get married to get rid of those vibes. I'll just carry on. (Emer, Career Woman, age 33)

Single women's attachment to independence as a value and to autonomy as a principle for organizing one's life informs and builds their life-style choice. In making a commitment to the single life-style and valuing independence, women attempt to de-couple cherished lifestyle from stigmatized social identity. The single lifestyle is personally meaningful, but for it to be sustained, single self-identity must also be secured. This is achieved in the context of relationships with others, some of which are freely chosen, others of which are deliberately suppressed in order to realize female autonomy. In general, traditional marital relationships and motherhood are rejected by single women on the grounds that they are inimical to those values that support autonomy. Developing adult relationships with parents and siblings, respecting female friendships, and seeking egalitarian intimate relationships were regarded as facilitating the composition of autonomous self-identities. Balancing independence and relationship can be achieved by women.

THE MEANING OF AUTONOMY FOR WOMEN

Classical psychoanalytical feminist positions on the mechanisms of gender identity acquisition argue that the autonomous individual is constructed on the basis of separation from the mother, thereby becoming male. Female individuality is construed as maintaining attachment to the mother figure, learning the importance of relationality to feminine iden-tity.[17] Relationality or autonomy is understood to reside in the self. An implicit assumption is also made concerning the female, maternal, cou-pled, body as constitutive of feminine identity, in that the body is equated with self-identity. This same theme runs through the socially approved preference for marriage and childrearing, particularly for women. Au-tonomy is associated with masculine identity and behavior, which lauds independence, individualism, emotional and physical separation from others, protecting the interests of self and extensions of self (such as fam-ilies) above others, and control of self and one's environment. In this con-ception, the autonomous male self is less tied to the body than the female relational self is to the maternal body. It is what is absent in the male body that most defines autonomy (the mark of childbearing, the sign of having been coupled), while what is present in the female body (the po-tential to bear children, the body as site of erotic attraction) evokes a re-lational identity. Overall, autonomy is denied in the female and relationality is denied in the male. Autonomy is regarded as asocial and largely not embodied.

These views, while convincing in their explanatory power to explore gender differences, are less useful when it comes to devising a framework for exploring the meaning and making of gendered self and social identi-ties. Thinking only of female identity as relational conceals the possibility of relational-autonomy, a disruption of either-or categories. In conceptu-alizing self-identity as social, it follows that autonomy as an aspect of iden-tity cannot be regarded as separate from social relationships. Marilyn Friedman also considers this tension between autonomy and sociality, ar-guing that autonomy is social and that while some relationships are inim-ical to autonomy, there are others that are constitutive of autonomy.[18] Susan Brison argues that the autonomous self and the relational self are in-terdependent and even constitutive of one another.[19] The connection be-tween autonomy and the social is, however, highly complex and remains a matter of some controversy. Friedman calls for an exploration of how so-cial relationships promote and hinder the realization of autonomy, offering an opportunity to re-construct the relational, feminine, social versus the autonomous, masculine, individual dichotomies. I argue that such di-chotomies obscure and mask the realization of female autonomy, which is already partly constitutive of women's lives but not recognized. It is most visible when single women describe their relationship choices and their at-tempts to construct a viable meaningful lifestyle in the context of a stig-matized social identity.

How can autonomy be best understood? Autonomy is regarded as the state of being self-governing, self-determining, of being in charge of one's life.[20] Friedman defines personal autonomy as "individual determination over those aspects of our lives in which we are not bound by moral requirements and may choose among a variety of morally permissible alternatives."[21] Diana Tietjens Meyers advises paying attention to choice and the basis on which decisions are made; for her, autonomy is a competency that is characterized when self-identity and one's life-plans are in harmony. Autonomous people know themselves, know what they really want to do and then act according to the values that inform their idea of themselves. Having the capacity to make autonomous choices is the mark of an autonomous person. An autonomous choice is different from a noncoerced choice, the former being tied to values, beliefs, and commitments that provide personal meaningfulness. To be autonomous one does not necessarily have to swim against the tide, and choices may seem conformist, though critically they are not made as a result of external pressures alone. Choices that fit with one's values and with one's idea of oneself are autonomous choices. For Meyers, autonomy competency "makes it possible for people to develop a sure sense of their own identities and to act accordingly—that is to be self-governing."[22]

An autonomous decision is one made by a person drawn from one's own resources, based ultimately on one's own sets of reasons, values, and beliefs. The skills required to make such decisions are, however, wholly learned, acquired so that individuals can become competent in self-definition, self-direction, and self-awareness (all of which are vulnerable to the effects of socialization). Autonomy competency provides the ability to shape life-plans, to be self-directing, to build a secure and distinct self-identity with which one is content, and to live according to one's values. While Meyers accents the importance of autonomy-enhancing socialization in early childhood, I argue that autonomy competency can also be fostered in later adulthood by virtue of one's social location or status vis-à-vis others, particularly if that status is regarded as somehow deviant from the norm; by one's relationships and interactions with others; and by having a set of values that inform decisions about how one's life should be organized and lived.

REFUSING RELATIONSHIPS FOR AUTONOMY

Of the thirty women interviewed, half said they would like to think marriage might be an option for them in the future, but very few actually expect to marry. Only eight women in total described themselves as "actively seeking a partner." Overall, women were very critical of the institution of marriage, regarding it as "over-rated" and meaningless. The devaluing of marriage may in part be a way of combating the social stigma of being unmarried, but these women were also concerned about the highly unequal structure of marital relationships. Marriage is equated with dependency, the abuse of power, and unequal relationships between men and women. The women in this study emphasized the poor and often violent relationships of parents, siblings, and friends that they have witnessed. Annie, who wants to be in a relationship, thinks that marriage

> is a highly over-rated structure. I mean there is this view that society evolves around the family, and family implies marriage, and I think there is so much hypocrisy around the whole area. The abuse that goes on, the abuse of children, the abuse of wives, the abuse of women as partners in marriage, the violence and all of this and yet society holds on to this. Marriage is the sacred cow and there are so many faults with it. (Annie, Partner-Seeker, age 42)

Women observe and witness marital and intimate relationships and assess what they see as not measuring up to expectations of relationships as mutual, enduring, satisfying, safe, and pleasurable. Women have very clear expectations of intimate relationships in which companionship, support, compatibility, equality, and, significantly, not feeling threatened within the relationship were cited as important factors. Sexual intimacy was regarded as secondary to companionship, demonstrating women's dissatisfaction with intimate relationships that are eroticized and based on relations of dominance and oppression. A number of women commented that despite the pressure to marry, they would never marry "for the sake of it" and would ensure that with or without a marriage, they would remain capable of looking after their own emotional and material needs. Kit (Career Woman, age 39) would not be involved in a relationship that would "compromise" her, and "that is why I would make sure that I would never need to do that—that I have a job that I like and a home that I like and plenty of friends."

While women spoke of their regret in not having children, only five women talked about life plans to have a child in the future. Most of the women have made the "choice" not to have children, but as with choosing to be single, most of the women do not wish to be represented as voluntarily child-free. Women do not wish their social identity choices to be represented as voluntary, as a free choice made in the absence of constraint; this is in recognition of the continuing, powerful dominance of heterosexual, marital, and familistic ideologies in a patriarchal society. Portraying oneself and, crucially, the stigmatized group to which one belongs as "involuntary singles" and as being "involuntarily childless" is a contextual, self-protective response to familism as a normative, cultural, and gendered construct of Irish society. This label purposely masks the other life lived by many; it obscures the everyday practices and values that inform independent, autonomous, single living and conceals the evidence that these are, in fact, women living without men and children. In talking about considering parenthood, women struggle with external constraints, their own needs and desires to have children and children's own needs. Most of the women interviewed said that the main reasons for not having a child alone are parental disapproval, marriage as prerequisite, religious beliefs, having to care for elderly parents, career commitments, not wanting to mother, beliefs that a child needs two parents, questioning their own ability and capacity to care for a child alone, and the difficulties of rearing children in a modern, drug- and problem-oriented environment. Annie explained her position on single parenthood:

> I wouldn't have wanted to have a child by anybody that I was not totally, madly in love with, . . . but I think I would want the father to be around if I had a child. And as well I think the demands of my job are very strong and that probably has an effect too. I certainly cannot see myself doing all the things I am doing now if I was working as a single mother. I couldn't, there is no way I could do it. (Annie, Partner-Seeker, age 42)

A number of women consider the child's welfare rather than their own desire to mother in their decision not to have children. Kelly (Career woman, age 36) regards single parenthood as being unfair to the child; satisfying her own desire would be "selfish." While single women desire and value relationships with others, most of the women interviewed would not consider giving up their single life-style for marriage or motherhood.

CHOOSING RELATIONSHIPS FOR AUTONOMY: PARENTS AND FRIENDS

Most women committed to living the single life-style had developed a variety of relationships with others that supported the life-style or did not threaten it. I report here on parental relationships and friendships. I observed three responses to familial relationships: 1) women continue to nurture and maintain their connection to their parents and siblings using a narrative of love and comfort to talk about these relationships; 2) they maintain contact and provide assistance to those in need in the family, speaking in terms of duty, obligation, and the responsibility of family members to support one another; 3) or women live out their lives separate from their families, having little contact with brothers and sisters or parents, revealing little to them about their personal lives. The first two responses are more typical of caring relationships between daughters and parents, while the latter signify relationships that are not based on having to provide care. The status of familial relationships indicates an affirmation or rejection of women's singlehood.

When speaking about their "good relationships" with parents, it is evident that women receive comfort, support, attention, security, protection, and respect for their life-style choices in these relationships, and in turn they look after and care about their parents. A career woman, Celie, living with her parents, describes their relationship as follows:

> I have lovely parents. It is a home not a house. They are very supportive in whatever I do. . . . They are very important to me. . . . In return I am very good to them. . . . We do share a lot fifty, fifty. (Celie, Career Woman, age 36)

All five women who live in the parental home provide care for their parents. Other women not living with their parents also speak about their strong attachment to their families and the importance of family as a source of emotional support. Sisters and brothers are described as close friends. In this context, when families and parents in particular make demands on a single woman's time, women respond by saying they "don't mind." If families are providing affirmation for the single life-style, it is hardly surprising that women continue to nurture these relationships. I could find no evidence that women who spoke with love and affection about parents and siblings, who continued to live in the parental home, who regarded their siblings as friends or who willingly provided care (not out of a sense of obligation or duty), could be said to be any less autonomous than others. It is true that women speak about these relationships in reciprocal terms, emphasizing the give and take, but women also speak about their closeness to parents and the importance of retaining a loving bond with them. Women describe their mothers in particular as being "very important" to them and the bond between mother and daughter as "very close." Bonnie (Partner-Seeker, age 32) described her mother and sister as "my best friends."

This continued mutual attachment to parents could be interpreted as a very sophisticated resolution of the wish for relationship, which does not compromise, but rather supports single self-identity. Friedman has requested that we give up the "unqualified assumption that social relationships are necessary to the realization of autonomy," arguing that some are supportive and should therefore be nurtured, while others are destructive of autonomy and should therefore be abandoned.[23] Thus, the severing of marital and mother-child relationships by single women in order to maintain their autonomous self-identity makes sense. Likewise, maintaining parental relationships that do not restrict daughters' choices and that create opportunities for independent living represents choosing a social relationship that "promotes the realization of autonomy." In this sense, single women's practices and choices can be understood as autonomous-relational.

The response was different where women caring long-term for their parents spoke about relationships in terms of duty and obligation. For example, Sadhb explained why she gave up her full-time job and income to care for her father and a neighbor in her own home.

> I believe that anybody has a duty to their parents for a start, no matter who they are. . . . If you don't respect your parents, you don't respect anyone. . . . Daddy wasn't able to manage and he couldn't cope here on his own any longer, so I gave up my job to stay home with him. (Sadhb, Carer, age 33)

This "choice" at one level could be regarded as highly inimical to autonomy. This is particularly so when the difficulties and challenges of providing constant care for another are outlined. Sara Ruddick, however, points to the possibilities for female autonomy within traditional caring relationships.[24] Some women may abandon a previous life-style and choose to engage in a long-term caring relationship instead, on the basis that the values underpinning the single life-style are maintained. Placing others' needs before one's own desires may indeed be more indicative of autonomy, and choosing to care should not be judged simply as an outcome of convention or coercion.[25] At least three women clearly represented their choice to care in terms of recognizing and responding to another's need, a choice that at the same time served the single life-style.

The third response concerns women who have abandoned parental and familial relationships, apart from a routine, ritualized contact. Women reveal little of their private lives to families, having suffered from lack of support, protection, attention, care, and respect. For example, Annie talked at length of the insensitivity of her brothers and sisters to her singleness and gave an example of comments made about her sex life. She said her sister treated an old boyfriend as an "object of derision," and comments made were

> always very insensitive; . . . they knew I was going out with somebody, but it was only in terms of "how is your sex life, are you getting much of it." And it was so crude. So that was the way they viewed me. (Annie, Partner-Seeker, age 42)

How families speak about single women's relationships matters very much; this woman observed the lack of respect evident in her siblings' treatment of her and also their lack of concern with her needs for being supported and nurtured. In response, she has decided to remove herself from being overly involved with many of her brothers and sisters and retains only a ritual contact with parents. A significant minority of women felt unsupported by their families in their chosen life-styles. They felt that despite emotional and material support given to their families, their families did not recognize either their own need for care, protection, and love or their relationships with single daughters or sisters as involving reciprocity. Women talked about themselves as "second-class" and "invisible" in these relationships, which were often filled with descriptions of acrimony between siblings, instances of families uttering hurtful and demeaning remarks, family occasions in which the single woman felt excluded or important events in the woman's own life which passed unremarked or not celebrated by those with whom she felt in relationship.

As regards friendships, many single studies have focused on the vital importance of friends and friendship networks in supporting the single lifestyle. Friends meet personal needs and provide one-to-one companionship; friends also bring the single woman into the company of others, socializing, travelling, and moving about in the world. Friends can also provide ideological support for an alternative value system, sustaining the choice to be single in the face of a coupled, heterosexual world. Maggie regards her friends in the lesbian community as an alternative support system to families, and having lots of friends is important to her. She said:

> I didn't have enough realizations what friends could be . . . because I was into the marriage model and the family model. (Maggie, Partner-Seeker, age 41)

Prior to coming out as a lesbian, she said she could not "see" any alternatives to marriage and families. For Kelly (Career Woman, age 36), friends are what make her life "enjoyable, even bearable." Without the support of her "very good friends and family," she would be "definitely married." The maintenance of the single life-style requires the ongoing support of significant others; the support of friends and family helps women to sustain choices to remain single.

The loss or absence of friends is felt deeply by women, particularly when they live in a remote rural area and feel isolated from the local community. Women spoke about the significance of their friendships and were clear about the expectations and obligations of friendship. Concern with reciprocity was a marked feature of friendship relationships. Friendships were deeply meaningful and sustained women on a day-to-day basis. Loyalty, confidentiality, and "being there for me" were among the most commonly mentioned aspects women valued. Women were prepared to invest a lot of time in maintaining their friendships, recognizing that these were valuable relationships that could not be easily replaced. Friends most commonly included other single women, sisters, married women, and occasionally married men. However, friends cannot fulfill all expectations, all needs, all desires; satisfaction with one's life must also come from "within." Compared to the expectations associated with ideal, intimate, sexual relationships, the role of actual friendship relationships was more bounded. Mary explained

> I would only call on my friends if I really needed them, in an emergency. . . . I don't expect somebody to be there. Your friends are your friends, they are not your partner. (Mary, ex-Carer, age 44)

Friends could not and should not be relied upon completely either as a source of support, advice, or companionship. Friends were not unreliable, but women's own self-reliance was in tension with their recognition of the ongoing significance of friendships to them. Women talked about the necessity of not being "too needy" in friendship relationships nor too dependent on them. This may be a peculiarity of Irish friendship patterns in that expectations of friendships are generally low, or it may be that families remain a primary source of support and reference for many. I observed that many single women looked after their friendships, minding them, holding them, but never wanting to over-burden them.

CONCLUDING COMMENTS: ACHIEVING AUTONOMY IN RELATIONSHIPS

What is evident from the Single Study is the primacy of independence and autonomy as values, as a way of being in relation to others and as a characteristic of the single life-style. It is often wrongly assumed that independence precludes sociality, that autonomy does not require intimacy. Women's caring work, their search for intimacy, and relationships with friends and family are evidence of the existence of the autonomous, but other-oriented (relational) woman.

I argue that autonomy for women is possible, discernible, and attainable, despite adverse, normative gender socialization and the ideological dominance of familism in Irish society. Reconsidering the notion of autonomy as a competency, as recognizing and responding to the needs of others, as a disposition to consult the self, as an ability to act upon one's own beliefs and values, and as a goal expressing control over the direction of life plans brings "female" or relational-autonomy into focus. Due to their stigmatized and deviant location and their struggle to attain a secure self-identity in this context, single women are highly motivated to achieve autonomy.

Familism remains a strong ideological force in Irish culture and society, countering a view of women as independent and autonomous. Familism remains necessary for patriarchy; marital status and compulsory heterosexuality continue to define what it is to be a woman. But single women actively move beyond marital status and reproduction in claiming adulthood and womanhood, in their struggle to build meaningful lives despite a stigmatized collective identity. By living the single life, by choosing the single life-style but rejecting the stigmatized social identity, the dominant model of womanhood is challenged and traditional gendered ideologies are significantly weakened. The improving socio-economic context and the liberalizing of social values allow for a greater expansion, not only of women's roles, but also of women's self and social identities. In valuing independence and relationship, in making autonomous choices, single women compose a self-identity that will affect how we think about womanhood in contemporary Ireland. I leave the last word to Cara:

> I suppose, what I would love would be if being single was OK. If society would allow people to be single and I suppose I could argue that must come from in here first and I probably have a conditioning that makes it difficult even for me to allow single to be OK; . . . the next generation hopefully won't think that it is so important to be married. I think this generation wouldn't have the same, I hope, sort of urgency to impose marriage on their children. (Cara, Career Woman, age 39)

NOTES

A special thank-you to Ricca Edmondson and Mary Owens whose useful comments on this chapter are much appreciated.

1. See Evelyn Mahon, "Ireland: A Private Patriarchy?" *Environment and Planning* 26 (1994): 1277–1296.
2. See Pat O'Connor, "Women, Marriage and the Family," *Irish Journal of Sociology* 5 (1995): 135–163.
3. See Robert Kennedy, *The Irish: Emigration, Marriage and Fertility* (Berkeley: University of California Press, 1973). Currently the proportion of women who never marry is increasing; see Anne Byrne, "Single Women in Ireland: A Re-examination of the Sociological Evidence" in *Women and Irish Society: A Sociological Reader,* ed. Anne Byrne and Madeleine Leonard (Belfast: Beyond the Pale, 1997).
4. Tom Inglis, "Irish Sexuality," *Irish Journal of Sociology* 7 (1997): 5–28.
5. See Thomas K Whittaker, *Ireland: Report of the Constitution Review Group* (Dublin: Stationary Office, 1996); also Kathleen Lynch, "Defining the

Family and Protecting the Caring Functions of Both Traditional and Non-Traditional Families," in Whittaker, *Ireland,* 627–9.

6. Familism is "the propagation of politically pro-family ideas"; see Michelle Barrett and Mary McIntosh, *The Anti-Social Family* (London:Verso, 1982), 26.

7. Tony Fahey, "Family and Household in Ireland," *Irish Society: Sociological Perspectives,* ed. Patrick Clancy, Sheila Drudy, Kathleen Lynch, Liam O'Dowd (Dublin: Institute of Public Administration, 1995).

8. See Christopher Whelan and Tony Fahey, "Marriage and the Family," in *Values and Social Change in Ireland,* ed. Christopher Whelan (Dublin: Gill and Macmillan, 1994), on contradictory cultural attitudes toward family issues.

9. Article 41.2 of the Irish Constitution (Bunreacht na hEireann) reads: "1. In particular, the State recognizes that by her life within the home, woman gives to the State a support without which the common good cannot be achieved. 2. The State shall, therefore endeavour to ensure that mothers shall not be obliged by economic necessity to engage in labor to the neglect of their duties in the home."

10. See Kathryn Conrad, "Women Troubles, Queer Troubles: Gender Sexuality and the Politics of Selfhood in the Construction of the Northern Irish State," in this volume.

11. My understanding of self and social identities is derived from social constructionism and feminist philosophical theoretical work, which positions identity as constructed in relationship with others. See George Herbert Mead, *Mind, Self and Society from the Standpoint of a Social Behaviourist* (Chicago: University of Chicago Press, 1934), ed. C. W. Morris; Diana Tietjens Meyers, *Self, Society and Personal Choice* (New York: Columbia University Press, 1989); Marilyn Friedman, "Autonomy and Social Relationships: Rethinking the Feminist Critique," in *Feminists Rethink the Self,* ed. Diana Tietjens Meyers (Boulder: Westview Press, 1997), 40–61.

12. See Natasha Mauthner and Andrea Doucet, "Reflections on a Voice-Centred Relational Method. Analysing Maternal and Domestic Voices," in *Feminist Dilemmas in Qualitative Research. Public Knowledge and Private Lives,* ed. Jane Ribbens and Rosalind Edwards (London: Sage, 1998), 119–146.

13. Breeda Duggan, "Single Women" (M.A. thesis in Women's Studies, University College Cork, Ireland, 1993), 66.

14. Explanations for singleness included: being emotionally independent, prior importance of work; achieving educational ambition; having to care for others; not finding the "right man"; a broken romance; not interested in or incapable of forming intimate attachments; and "something that just happened."

15. Erving Goffman, *Stigma: Notes on the Management of Spoiled Identity* (Harmondsworth, Middlesex: Penguin, 1963).

16. The term "life-style" is used to denote "decisions taken and courses of action followed" even in conditions of constraint. See Anthony Giddens, *Modernity and Self-Identity: Self and Society in the Late Modern Age* (Cambridge: Polity Press, 1991). Choosing and sustaining a preferred life-style, I argue, is based on values that one holds dear.

17. See Nancy Chodorow, *The Reproduction of Mothering: Psychoanalysis and the Sociology of Gender* (Berkeley: University of California Press, 1978).

18. Friedman discusses the severing of relational ties, the challenging of shared values, and the questioning of expectations often required in achieving autonomy.

19. Susan J. Brison, "Outliving Oneself: Trauma, Memory, and Personal Identity," in Meyers, *Feminists Rethink the Self,* 12–39.

20. John Christman, "Feminism and Autonomy," in Dana E. Bushnell, *"Nagging Questions": Feminist Ethics in Everyday Life* (Lanham, MD: Rowman and Littlefield, 1995), 30.

21. Friedman, "Autonomy and Social Relationships," 41.

22. Meyers, *Self, Society and Personal Choice,* 84.

23. Friedman, "Autonomy and Social Relationships," 55.

24. Sara Ruddick," Maternal Thinking," in *Feminist Social Thought: A Reader,* ed. Diana Tietjens Meyers (New York: Routledge, 1997), 583–603.

25. This is a difficult position to maintain in the face of studies that show that the responsibility of providing dependent relative care is shared unevenly in families. Those who are unmarried, without children, with low integration in the labor force are the most likely candidates. See Joyce O'Connor and Helen Ruddle, *A Study of Carers in the Home* (Dublin: National Council for the Aged, 1988). Others are critical of interpreting dependency work as "freely chosen," given the effect of socialization on women to develop character traits and the volitional personality structure required for caring work; see Eva Feder Kittay, "Human Dependency and Rawlsian Equality" in Meyers, *Feminists Rethink the Self,* 219–66. However, if the capacity to recognize and respond to the needs of others is valued by the self and regarded as constitutive of autonomy, then the choice to care can arguably be regarded as an autonomous choice.

Varieties of Masculinity ▣

Chapter Five

The Ideal Man: Irish Masculinity and the Home, 1880–1914

Joanna Bourke

R ecent historiography has placed immense emphasis on the importance of gender in defining identities and structuring relationships
in the past. As long ago as 1975, Gayle Rubin distinguished between "sex" (meaning anatomical differences) and "gender" (referring to the
social construction of these differences).[1] Since then, historical analyses of
the social construction of femininity have proliferated, particularly in
women's history and feminist studies, and the history of masculinity (as opposed to femininity) has slowly begun to be incorporated into the mainstream, thus opening doors for a truly "gendered" history to be written. Yet,
in Ireland, while women's history is currently generating some of the best
work, the history of Irish masculinity has scarcely commenced.[2] However,
the construction of manliness in Ireland is a potentially exciting field, ripe
for overturning a number of dominant myths. This chapter examines one of
these myths—one concerning the ideologies and experiences of domesticity for Irish men of the laboring and small farming class in the period from
1880 to 1914. The alleged alienation of these Irishmen from this sphere is
commonly reported, despite the fact that a wide range of organizations came
to target the domesticity of Irishmen at this time. The Board of Education,
Department of Agriculture and Technical Instruction (D.A.T.I.), Congested
Districts Board (C.D.B.), and the Irish Agriculture Organization Society
(I.A.O.S.) turned their attention to the construction of Irish manliness at
home. From the late nineteenth century Irishmen (*as men*) came increasingly
under the supervisory eye of these institutions. Before this period control

over men in the domestic sphere had been maintained primarily by religious representatives and by formal policing systems. However, in these three decades, a much wider range of Irishmen came to be affected by the intervention of organizations with very clear notions of ideal manliness and with a determination to "reform" real-life Irishmen. Critics of "separate sphere" ideologies have tended to dismantle only one side of the equation: that is, the containment of women in the "private" sphere. It is helpful also to question the imprisonment of men within the "public" sphere. Cultural constructions of masculinity and femininity cannot be viewed in isolation.

While sharing some characteristics with its British counterparts, the manly ideal in Ireland was not identical to the ideal being pursued across the Irish Sea. Clearly, differential settlement patterns meant that Irish norms of manliness were skewed toward the rural rather than the urban environment. Even within rural settings, men in Britain were more influenced by urban culture than the Irish peasant farmer. Demographically there were also major differences between Ireland and Britain. Irish masculinity placed a greater emphasis on celibacy. The "devotional revolution" led by Archbishop Cullen after the Famine increasingly enticed men into chaste service within the Catholic Church. Even excluding this pious cohort, a large proportion of Irishmen never married. In 1911 this included 27 percent of all Irish men, and those who did marry tended to delay the event until the relatively late age of 31. In the words of the historian David Fitzpatrick: "In 1841 English and Irish men were equally likely to be celibate. But sixty years later the English proportion was unchanged whereas Ireland was competing with Iceland for the honor of heading the European celibacy league."[3] Furthermore, the status of the married man in Ireland was enhanced by the increasing age differential between couples. By the turn of the century, husbands tended to be ten years older than their spouses. The never-marrying man exemplified a very different masculinity from the marrying man. Finally, Irishmen had more radical options than Englishmen. In the 60 years following the Famine, approximately 5 million people emigrated from Ireland: approximately half of these people were men, and two-thirds went to America. Such high levels of emigration meant that the dissatisfied Irishman—or the man who did not feel comfortable within categories of Irish masculinity as defined by his particular family, village, or neighborhood—could quite easily escape. The celibate Irishman was one who found single life in Ireland preferable to both married life at home and life abroad.

In the context of the late nineteenth century, with what one historian has called the wholesale attempts to "kill Home Rule with kindness," British reformers approached the Irish economy with very definite ideas about what were appropriate forms of work for men and women.[4] Notions of masculinity in English workshops were applied to the Irish context that had different norms of the appropriateness of "women's" and "men's" jobs. For instance, by one stroke of the pen, the factory acts led to a massive substitution of male labor for female labor in rural industries, leading to an increasingly segregated workforce. In 1891 about one-fifth of all men were working in occupations where not one woman was employed; by 1911 this had risen to over one-third.[5] In part such shifts were due to sectoral shifts in Irish industry, but economic reformers also made a deliberate effort to move men into jobs formerly performed by women. State-led encouragement of technology had a similar impact. From the 1890s subsidies for the purchase of harvesting machinery and the establishment by the I.A.O.S. of large and technically sophisticated creameries resulted in a direct substitution of male for female labor on the grounds that the use of machinery was a "masculine" pursuit unsuited to Irish femininity. Commissioners in the D.A.T.I. demanded that important export-oriented industries (such as the dairy and poultry industries) be withdrawn from women and placed into men's hands. After all, they reasoned, women were "confined to the narrow circle of the home" (which was actually not the case in Ireland at this time) and rural industries needed men's "broader vision."[6] Due to such assumptions, only men were allowed to attend classes concerned with the dissemination of scientific and managerial knowledges. Consequently, institutions like the Albert Agricultural College that had provided special dairying courses for women in the early 1880s restricted their new classes in creamery management to men in 1885 and by the end of the decade had discontinued all classes for women. In the words of R. A. Anderson, secretary to the I.A.O.S.: "In days gone by cows were all milked by women. There was no such thing as a man milking a cow. Men would not consider it their work to milk a cow. Whatever be the cause, women have gone out of the business, and in a great number of cases, therefore, cows have got to be milked by men and boys."[7] Or, from a different perspective, as one elderly Corkman complained in 1938, "in years gone by the women always milked the cows an' fed the pigs an' cattle, an' men about forty years ago wasn't able to milk, nor wasn't asked to milk. . . . Now it's the men must do all, milking an' feeding, an' that spoils a good part of the day."[8] The economic intervention of these reformers was based on assumptions of masculinity (imported from Britain) and led to shifts in gender roles within Ireland.

Even more than in the paid employment market, in the unpaid sphere these reformers enthusiastically intervened in the self-conscious construction (they might have said reconstruction) of Irish manliness. The role and attitudes of both married and unmarried Irishmen in the domestic sphere has been widely scorned. Some of the clichés employed at the time and recycled by historians include maintaining that Irishmen kept at a considerable distance from their womenfolk, that they valued their pig or heifer more than their spouse, and that they made friends with the people with whom they drank (rather than slept).[9] Within this narrative, domestic violence was thought to be ubiquitous. Evidence can be found for all of these generalizations. The Irishman's "proudest boast" was that he could not boil an egg, bitterly noted the infamous Kathleen Behan.[10] Mary Waldron, a tenement dweller in the early decades of this century, accused Irishmen of worse crimes: "He was your husband and when you married him you had to do what he told you. Like it or lump it! Or you'd get a few punches." Or, in the words of Mary Doolan of Dublin: "The men was the men. Men made sure they were kings. Everything had to be done for them. You wouldn't have a word to say—or they'd bang you with the leg of the chair!"[11] Clearly, many men did associate their status as "men" with dominating, ugly, and frightening behavior.

However, the "breadwinner" against whom women struggled cannot be portrayed as unchanging, universally unrepentant, and fundamentally undomesticated. It is important to note that Irishmen were never excluded from the domestic sphere. In a 1958 survey carried out by the Irish Folklore Commission only fifteen percent claimed that men did no housework.[12] In households consisting of unmarried men, men might do all the washing, cooking, and cleaning with or without the help of a domestic servant. As one man put it:

> Men that lived alone had to do all that class of work [housework] themselves. Some of them could bake and cook and wash as good as any woman. Some men could do their own knitting and there were men that could sew as well as any woman. They could patch their clothes, and there were men that could make up butter as good as a woman would do it—they'd make it better than some women. There was many an unfortunate man that his wife died and left him with a family of small children, and that poor fellow had to wash and clean the children and cook and mend for them. . . .You'd see two or three old brothers living together, and no woman in the house, and one of them would have to do the baking and cooking and mending and washing and all the work that a woman would do about a house.[13]

As the proportion of men-only households increased dramatically from the Famine, and as the number of domestic servants plummeted in the late nineteenth century, such forms of male labor would have been increasing.

Domestic labor was not only reserved for unmarried and widowed men: married men were never excluded from the domestic sphere. There were some chores that they avoided. Carrying a child in petticoats, or pushing a pram, might be considered unmanly even for the most devoted father; similarly, it was unusual for men to do the baking or washing.[14] In 1909 the Department of Agriculture and Technical Instruction observed that men would eagerly attend cookery classes to learn how to cook for others, "but for themselves they will not cook. Domestic service in some wealthy person's house is an aspiration, but domestic service in their own home is a useless drudgery."[15] However, during whatever period we care to examine, boys and men played some part in carrying out conventional domestic tasks. Their roles often changed with shifts in the life cycle. Male domestic labor was high in childhood, would decline in adolescence, but increase again once they had children of their own, only to soar after retirement. Young boys might do a considerable amount of housework. Typically, James Cousins (who was born in Belfast in 1872) spoke about his childhood chores of lighting the fire and sweeping the floor.[16] Many people in the early years of this century emphasized the need for boys to learn needlework, especially how to mend their clothes and darn their socks.[17] Male domestic labor was expected while the wife was nursing a newly born infant. While fathers might be relatively unhelpful in caring for young children, they were important in the raising of older children. As an unnamed woman at the 1910 conference of United Irishwomen noted: "Most men do not deserve to be called parents until their children are about 12 years old, when they begin to assume airs of proprietorship, whereas when the child was in petticoats he would be ashamed to be seen in its company."[18] Adult men had certain parts of the house that were their responsibility: the yard, outside walls, and fire, for instance. Certain culinary traditions included men—they were involved in the food process at its earliest stages, such as slaughtering pigs, digging potatoes, or providing grain for bread-making. Male visitors were expected to "give the meat a spin" when meat was cooked on spits, and men took part in preparing meats for "special" occasions, such as cooking the goose at Christmas. Old men were crucial in the care of their grandchildren.[19]

The sexual division of labor within the home was justified according to a number of principles, including the distribution of skills and of strength. Men were supposed to be simply "better at" certain jobs if only on the spurious grounds that they had been taught how to do them by the parents of their own sex. It is important to note that the sexual division of labor within the home was not simply one of men taking care of the "house" (outdoor work, carpentry, whitewashing) while women took care of the "home" (indoor and cleaning). If there was a "spare" man in the household, he would do the churning, since "it was too heavy a work for women." But if there was only one man in the house, "the woman would keep at it." "Heavy" forms of housework were more likely to be seen as male responsibilities, but there were as many definitions of "heaviness" as there were household tasks (the most obvious example being the fact that women did the very laborious labor of washing clothes, while men repaired cupboard handles).

What is interesting, however, is that the propensity of Irishmen to perform certain forms of domestic labor changed between the 1880s and 1914. The primary use of time for Irishmen continued to be in the fields or other place of paid employment, but the Irishman's home increasingly contained a masculine space. From the late nineteenth century changes in the Irish economy and household infrastructure meant that Irishmen came to be performing more housework (of certain kinds). Although it is probably true that as children began spending more time in school, fathers had to take responsibility for the domestic chores previously performed by older children, men did not necessarily do more cooking, cleaning, and child-care from the late nineteenth century. Indeed, married Irishmen were probably doing less cooking, cleaning, and child-care as Irishwomen increasingly moved out of many forms of paid employment and began devoting more of their labor to full-time domesticity. Elsewhere, I argue that this movement of Irish women into full-time domesticity was less of a coerced shift than a response to changing economic conditions, which meant that the decision to work in the domestic sphere seemed to minimize women's risk of poverty and to maximize their power.[20] However, while women were increasingly excluding men from certain forms of domestic labor (or, at the very least, insisting that women should be the primary managers of their menfolk within these traditional areas of domestic labor), there was simultaneously the expansion of other forms of domestic labor for which men (again, under women's supervision) were considered suited. The most important of these forms of domestic labor were those associated with household repairs, decoration, and small-scale food production for immediate household use.

The overall improvement in Irish living standards was crucial for the evolution of masculine housework. Improvements in Irish housing probably had the biggest impact. In 1891 nearly half of all rural dwellings were third- or fourth-class housing—that is, small huts made of mud or cheap materials. By 1911 nearly three-quarters of dwellings were classed as first- or second-class houses—that is, good farmhouses, having more than five rooms and possessing many windows.[21] The reasons for such dramatic changes are complex, but state investment in rural housing must be seen as an important influence. Furthermore, much of this investment was carried out with gender relations explicitly in mind. For social reformers, housing was a moral and social question. Human surroundings either "elevate or degrade"—if Ireland was to contain a "moral, sober, intelligent, healthy and industrious population" they must have improved homes.[22] As middle-class reformers had been saying since the mid-nineteenth century, comfortable housing and improved diet helped entice men to spend time at home. Men also became responsible for maintaining standards of domestic beauty; they enjoyed the touch of wood and plants; their domestic work symbolically reaffirmed their manly role as "providers." Male forms of housework brought a new sense of accomplishment while enhancing men's masculinity. It gave a man "something about his own home which is attractive for him to work at," in the words of the J. P. and leading member of the County Committee of Agriculture and Technical Instruction for Donegal, William James Hanna, in 1907.[23] In conjunction with higher levels of home ownership, men were provided with a rationale for investing more and more time in the domestic sphere. Male domesticity promised to increase the "comfort" of the home. In the words of "A Woman Worker" in the reforming journal *Irish Homestead* in 1899:

> The husband, as well as the wife, can do his share in increasing the home comfort. . . . A window box in which she could grow mignonette, musk, or gay nasturtiums, the whitewashing of the ceiling and coloring of the walls, also the making of cement or concrete floor, . . . are all things that could be done better by a man than a woman, and, last but not least, the comfort of that ardent home ruler, the baby, might be increased by his help.[24]

The development and expansion of masculine forms of housework thus required a little economic surplus. The dramatic improvements in the rural infrastructure and housing meant that more and more Irishmen had a domestic space within which to express this new manliness.

Although economic incentives were clearly paramount, this is not to ignore ideological factors. The most important of these is, of course, the church. Ironically, the increased power of the Catholic Church after the Famine not only cemented the position of women as wives and mothers (exclusively); it also emphasized the responsibilities of men within self-contained, nuclear, and private households. Anti-drinking campaigns and church-run youth organizations also emphasized the ideal man as residing within a devoted, family-centered environment (that is, unless they claimed a "vocation"). Thus, it was not uncommon for priests to exhort men to embrace more family-centered values. Walter MacDonald, for instance, was the Prefect of the Dunboyne Establishment, St. Patrick's College (Maynooth) between 1888 and 1920. In 1911 he delivered a lecture to the Catholic Men's Society on "The Manliness of St. Paul" in which he argued that St. Paul was the "manliest" of men; he was athletic, strong, courageous, independent, bold, and soldierly. But then McDonald went on to declare that St. Paul was the "manliest" of men because he was "womanly." The saint possessed "all the delicacy of feeling, courtesy and tenderness of soul we are want to associate with the noblest woman; womanly tact, too, when needed; [a] heart that yearned for love and loved deeply in return. . . . That and much more was Paul the woman."[25] The ideal Catholic man embraced nurturing, domestic values.

Furthermore, the expansion of masculine housework from the last decades of the nineteenth century was deliberately promoted by the state. Housework is "natural" to neither men nor women, but is part of a complex of cultural interactions. Irish boys learned their role as manly houseworkers from a range of sources. Obviously, their parents played the largest part in their socialization. As with girls, however, the state also intervened in the domestic education of Irish boys. Elsewhere, I have examined the state-sponsored domestic education of Irish girls, but equivalent attempts to intervene in the domestic education of Irish boys were taking place at the same time.[26] In a handful of schools from the early 1880s, and more generally from the 1910s, manual classes were set up for boys. In addition, itinerant classes for boys were established by all the rural reforming organizations, including the D.A.T.I., the C.D.B., and the I.A.O.S. Most of the training consisted of making simple furniture, indoor household repairs, and being taught to look after the outside of the house and yard. The classes that were established from the turn of the century were not intended to train boys in marketable trades—in the words of George Fletcher, Assistant Secretary to the D.A.T.I., the aim was to train "young fellows . . . to do what would ordinarily be left undone; . . . it supplants no workman but it does create a handyman."[27] Or, as the 1912–13 report put it: the manual classes were intended to make boys "useful in their homes for such repairs as require to be done in houses and about farms."[28] They were to "domesticate" boys: to ensure that they did not "run wild."[29] It was "moral training."[30]

Manual training was explicitly introduced to dovetail with girls' domestic education, and they were discussed in the same paragraph (and often in the same sentence) by the promoters. As one report of the manual training provided in Connemara by the C.D.B. in 1914 explained: "girls were taught housewifery and the young men were being taught to make household furniture for their new or improved houses."[31] Or, as William James Hanna of the County Committee of Agriculture and Technical Instruction for Donegal told the commissioners in 1907 when arguing for an extension of manual training: "boys should be instructed in their role in life as well as the girls." He went on to stress that the training was not "with a view of earning, but making them useful in their homes."[32] In 1908 the Very Rev. Patrick Finegan agreed, arguing that manual instruction had been successful in training boys. He said that the training was immediately put to "profitable account" and when asked "such as?" responded: "working in their own homes; making gates, doors, and other things useful for the household."[33] Irish boys and their parents strongly supported the classes—so much so that there were serious problems with over-crowding.[34] Both the girls' domestic education classes and the boys' manual classes were intended to teach gendered roles within the household.

Why was the state so concerned with the domestic skills of Irishmen? There was a range of agendas, many operating simultaneously, but a few strands predominated. In the rural reform movement, both British and Irish spokesmen and women argued that manual training was necessary to bring Irishmen up to the standard of their English brothers. In 1902, one rural reformer identified the "Irish problem" as not being related to poverty or lack of property rights, but as part of a more insidious failure in Irishmen as men. In his *Letters from Ireland,* he wrote:

> It is a sad reflection that if a Dutchman or an Englishman be set down in a hut in the midst of a bog he will in a few years have transformed his dwelling, and made it a bower of greenery, whereas, an Irishman put into a cottage with a trim garden will too often neglect the plants, and let them run to seed and weed.[35]

Irishmen needed to be educated according to Dutch and English standards. The manual classes for boys were part of an agenda to make Irishmen more "thoroughly respected abroad" (as one instructor put it in 1904).[36] Ireland as the inferior and colonized "other" had to be repudiated.

At the same time, it was seen as contributing to the mission of stemming emigration. Male labor around the house would make it a more pleasant environment and this would "keep our people at home."[37] Irishmen needed to be encouraged to remain in Ireland; even seasonal migration was frowned at on the grounds that it "unmanned" Irishmen who returned in winter after their womenfolk had taken care of the plot, and thus were idle (in winter, Irishmen should be working on their own domestic environment instead of idling their time away until the next harvest, the reformers believed).[38] As in England at this time, there was great concern about the degeneration of the Irish physique and mental stability. Dr. Kelly, the Lord Bishop of Ross, went so far as to tell the Interdepartmental Committee on Physical Deterioration in 1904 that if he rigidly adhered to canon law, which forbade him to admit amongst the clergy any person who had insanity in his family, he would "exclude practically all the applicants; . . . there would be practically nobody left [in the priesthood]!"[39] Irishmen were suffering from "cerebral excitement" (as Sir Charles A. Cameron, Dublin's Medical Officer for over thirty years, put it in 1904) due to "questions about land and politics;" they needed their energies to be re-channeled.[40] Finally, the government had a direct fiscal and political interest in the profitability of all economic sectors of the community—household as well as agricultural. Just as land reform was intended to meet certain social and political ends, domestic instruction of both sexes was part of a value-laden policy to shape the two genders in ways that would conform to the needs of the state and increase the wealth and pacification of the people.

This is not to argue that such a policy succeeded in forging "happy families." There is an important factor that has been left out of this discussion so far. In its feminine and masculine forms housework is about power. Who produced what within the household is important. Just as compulsory domestic instruction for girls caused friction between daughters and their mothers (and mothers-in-law) and cemented relationships of subordination and dominance between men and women, so too boys' manual training had important implications in terms of power. On the one hand, it threatened established power relations within the home: young boys were more adept at this work than their fathers and tensions might arise between sons and fathers. On the other hand, such instruction retained conventional power relations between men and women. Despite the increased presence of Irishmen in the home, this made little difference to the respective power positions of men and women within the home. It is true that many women sought to retain control over the feminine aspects of housework. Men had their domestic sphere; they were responsible for its more menial side: scrubbing boots, dirty cleaning, carting water, "wielding his weapons" (that is, carving meat), and work connected with rough woods, cold metals, and dirt. While Irishwomen's domestic work was slowly becoming sanitized and mechanized through the sale of cleaning fluids, a diversification of kitchen and dinnerware, and (in the inter-war years) the spread of electricity, men retained those jobs connected with primitive dirtiness. However, there was little in the growth of male domesticity to promote equality within the home. Irish men had to remain "men." After all, Irish republicans were supremely conscious of the "feminization" of Ireland by its colonizers, and anxieties about the agenda behind some of the state's concern with men within the domestic sphere could not be lightly dismissed. Masculine housework had to remain "manly"—an Irishman might fashion a crib for the baby but never rock it.

Of course, there was much more diversity in the experiences of the rural small-landholder than this chapter has acknowledged. There was neither one "Irishman" to which a uniform "masculine code" was applied, nor was there a single, dominant "British" ideal being applied. The landless man who did not participate in the benefits of economic restructuring, the wealthy landlord who would not stoop to servile domestic chores, and the homosexual who could not participate in the heterosexual or celibate ideals being propagated had very different experiences. Furthermore, men could exhort the ideal at one moment, and then flout it in the next moment. After all, there was a flourishing trade in prostitution to feed the sexual appetites of men who did not act in accordance with their consciences.[41] Irishmen were both more "domestic" in private, and less influenced by external pressures to conform than this chapter may have implied. But, just as historians have been exhorted to publicly reject what Betty Friedan once famously called the "feminine mystique,"[42] it is time that the Irish "male mystique" was spurned, giving way to a more nuanced vision of the ways in which men were molded by official organizations and how they invented themselves as men in the past. Between 1880 and 1914 the subtle interaction between economic re-structuring and growth, ideological shifts toward the church, a new emphasis on domesticity for both married and unmarried people, and pressure from rural reformers, with British norms in mind, all served to create a space within the home for men-as-men. Even the declaration of war in 1914 and the ensuing renewal of violent political protest—both of which separated thousands of men from congenial domestic environments and the nurturing ethos—did not permanently dent the commitment of Irishmen to the creation of homely spaces where they could act as men.

NOTES

1. Gayle Rubin, "The Traffic in Women: Notes on the 'Political Economy' of Sex," in Rayna Reiter, ed., *Toward an Anthropology of Women* (New York: Monthly Review Press, 1975), 157–210.
2. There are some notable exceptions, the best being Patrick F. McDevitt, "Muscular Catholicism: Nationalism, Masculinity and Gaelic Team Sports, 1884–1916," *Gender and History* 9 (August 1997): 262–84.
3. David Fitzpatrick, "Marriage in Post-Famine Ireland," in Art Cosgrove, ed., *Marriage in Ireland* (Dublin: Dublin College, 1985), 117.
4. Andrew Gailey, *Ireland and the Death of Kindness. The Experience of Constructive Unionism 1890–1905* (Cork: Cork University Press, 1987).
5. See my "The Best of all Home Rulers: The Economic Power of Women in Ireland, 1880–1914," *Irish Economic and Social History* 18 (1991): 36.
6. House of Commons (H.C.), "Departmental Committee on the Irish Butter Industry: Minutes of Evidence, Appendix and Index," *Parliamentary Papers,* 1910, *Department of Agriculture and Technical Instruction,* Cmnd. 5093, 1910, vol. 8, p. 464.

7. *Department of Industry and Commerce. Commission of Inquiry into the Resources and Industries of Ireland: Minutes of Evidence, I, City Hall, Dublin* (Dublin: Department of Industry and Commerce, 1919), 9.

8. Irish Folklore Commission (IFC) 58: 411–12.

9. No one exemplifies this more than K. H. Connell, "The Land Legislation and Irish Social Life," *The Economic History Review* 9 (1958): 1–7; and idem., "Peasant Marriage in Ireland: Its Structure and Development Since the Famine," *The Economic History Review* 14 (1961–62): 502–23.

10. Kathleen Behan, *Mother of All the Behans* (London: Arrow Books, 1985), 70.

11. See, e.g., Kevin C. Kearns, *Dublin Tenement Life: An Oral History* (Dublin: Gill and Macmillan, 1994), 50–1.

12. IFC 1024.

13. John Cullen, speaking to P. J. Gaynor, in IFC 1024: 380–81.

14. Richard Denihan, aged 86 years, talking to Colm O Danacain, January 1951, Co. Limerick, IFC 1210.

15. "Home Life in Ireland. A Social Revolution," *Irish Homestead,* 25 May 1909, 406.

16. James H. Cousins and Margaret E. Cousins, *We Two Together* (Madras: Ganesh and Co., 1950), 7.

17. W. D'Esteere Parker, "Correspondence. Commission on Manual and Practical Instruction," *Irish Textile Journal,* 15 Mar. 1897, 34, and "What Boy's Should Learn," *The King's Chronicle,* 27 Mar. 1913.

18. "Notes on the Week. United Irishwomen in Conference," *Irish Homestead,* 8 Oct. 1910, 832.

19. See, e.g., John M. Synge, *The Aran Island* (Leipzig: Bernhard Tauchnitz, 1926), 48.

20. See my *Husbandry to Housewifery: Women, Economic Change and Housework in Ireland, 1880–1914* (Oxford: Oxford University Press, 1993).

21. Censuses of Ireland, 1861–1911.

22. "Working Women's Corner," *Irish Worker,* 19 Aug. 1911; Mary Fogarty, "Influence of Home on Life," *Irish Education Review* 3 (July 1910): 604; Eibhlain MacNeill, "The Place of Women in the Irish Revival," *Irish Peasant,* 6 Jan. 1906, 3; "The Provision of Labourers' Cottages in Ireland," *Irish Builder* 26 (1 June 1884): 155–6.

23. H. C., "Minutes of Evidence Taken Before the Departmental Committee of Inquiry," *Parliamentary Papers,* 1907, *Department of Agriculture and Technical Instruction* (Ireland), Cmnd. 3574, 1907, vol. 18, p. 444, evidence by William James Hanna, J. P., member of the County Committee of Agriculture and Technical Instruction for Donegal.

24. A Woman Worker, "Household Hints. The Husband's Share," *The Irish Homestead,* 29 Apr. 1899, 308.

25. Walter McDonald, "The Manliness of St. Paul," in *The Manliness of St. Paul and Other Essays,* ed. Walter McDonald (Dublin: Clonmore and Reynolds Ltd., 1958): 11, 26, 29, a lecture to the Catholic Men's Society in 1911.

26. See Bourke, *Husbandry to Housewifery.*

27. H. C., "Royal Commission on Congestion in Ireland, Fourth Report of the Commissioners," *Parliamentary Papers,* Cmnd. 3508, 1907, vol. 36, p. 109, evidence by George Fletcher, Assistant Secretary to the D.A.T.I.

28. H. C., "Twentieth Report of the Congested Districts Board for Ireland," *Parliamentary Papers,* 1912–12, *Congested Districts Board,* Cmnd. 6553, 1912–13, vol. 12, p. 30; House of Commons, "Fourth Annual General Report of the Department, 1903–04," *Parliamentary Papers,* 1903–04, *Department of Agriculture and Technical Instruction (Ireland),* Cmnd. 2509, 1905, vol. 11, p. 6.

29. D. A. T. I., "Minutes of Evidence," 565, evidence by John F. O'Hanlon of the Cavan Joint Technical Instruction Committee.

30. "Fourth Report of Commissioners," 112.

31. H. C., "Twenty-Third Report of the Congested Districts Board for Ireland," *Parliamentary Papers,* 1912–19, *Congested Districts Board for Ireland,* Cmnd. 8076, 1912–19, vol. 24, p. 20; "Fourth Report of Commissioners," 109–110; D. A. T. I., "Minutes of Evidence," 445.

32. D. A. T. I., "Minutes of Evidence," 444, evidence by William James Hanna, J.P., member of the County Committee of Agriculture and Technical Instruction for Donegal.

33. H. C., "Royal Commission on Congestion in Ireland, First Appendix to the Seventh Report. Minutes of Evidence (Taken in Ireland, 16 May to 11 June, 1907), and Documents Relating Thereto," *Parliamentary Papers,* Cmnd. 3785, 1908, vol. 49, p.138, evidence by The Very Rev. Patrick Finegan; see also "Fourth Report of Commissioners," 111.

34. For a few examples, see D. A. T. I., "Minutes of Evidence," 309, 327, 373, 444, 495; "Twentieth Report of C. D. B.," 30.

35. H. B., *Letters from Ireland* (Dublin: *New Ireland Review,* 1902), 48.

36. Kathleen Ferguson, "The Peasant's Home. How Pat and Mary Started Housekeeping," *Irish Homestead,* 6 Feb. 1904, 116.

37. D. A. T. I., "Minutes of Evidence," 444, evidence by William James Hanna, J.P., member of the County Committee of Agriculture and Technical Instruction for Donegal.

38. H. C., "Report from the Select Committee of Distress from Want of Employment Together with the Proceedings of the Committee, Minutes of Evidence, Appendix and Index," *Parliamentary Papers,* Cmnd. 321, 1896, vol. 9, p. 78, evidence by John Fitzgibbon, merchant of Castlerea, County Roscommon.

39. H. C., "Interdepartmental Committee on Physical Deterioration. Minutes of Evidence Taken Before the Interdepartmental Committee on Physical Deterioration, vol. ii—List of Witnesses and Minutes of Evidence," *Parliamentary Papers,* Cmnd. 2210, 1904, vol. 32, p. 411, evidence by Dr. Kelly, Lord Bishop of Ross.

40. Ibid., 406–7, evidence by Sir Charles A. Cameron, medical officer for Dublin for over 30 years.

41. See the discussion by Dympna McLoughlin, "Women and Sexuality in Nineteenth Century Ireland," *The Irish Journal of Psychology* 15 (1994): 266–75.

42. See, e.g., Mary Cullen, "History Women and History Men: The Politics of Women's History," *History Ireland* (Summer 1994): 31.

Chapter Six

Losing It All:
The Unmanned Irish Landlord

Vera Kreilkamp

> Their country seats are surrounded by enormous, amazingly beautiful parks,
> but all around is wasteland, and where the money is to come it is impossi-
> ble to see. These fellows are droll enough to make your sides burst with
> laughing. Of mixed blood, mostly tall, strong, handsome chaps, they all wear
> enormous mustaches under colossal Roman noses, give themselves the false
> military air of retired colonels, travel round the country after all sorts of
> pleasures, and if one makes an inquiry, they haven't a penny, are laden with
> debts, and live in dread of the encumbered estates court.
>
> —Frederick Engels, May 23, 1856

Frederick Engels' impression of the Anglo-Irish landlord highlights
not substance but surface: the impressive physique, prominent aristocratic nose, and hedonistic military air mask a persistent anxiety.
Within that handsome body, presumably without a penny in its pocket, re-
sides the soul of an insecure man; he is, in fact, much less of a man than he
seems.

Criticism of the Irish landlord appeared persistently in the nineteenth
century, from tenants, foreign visitors like Engels, and English journalists.
In March 1847, at the height of the Famine, the *Northern Whig* protested
that the unmanly Irish landlord expected to be rescued by England:

> It is but proper the English people should be told that the sons of a broken
> down gentry—a gentry full of beggarly pride, but utterly destitute of the

spirit of manly independence—are deriving the chief advantage from the present enormous expenditure of money.[1]

On occasion, such criticism was echoed from within Big House society itself, by landowners concerned with their declining authority. Addressing his fellow landlords in 1886, in a period of "fierce agrarian agitation," Standish O'Grady denounced the failures of his own class—the rightful "masters" of Ireland—to overcome that "fatal crutch," their crippling dependence on England.

> I believe there never will be, as I know there never has been within the cycle of recorded things, an aristocracy so rotten in its seeming strength, so recreant, resourceless and stupid in the day of trial, so degenerate, outworn, and effete. You have outlived your day.[2]

For O'Grady, the landlord's faults arise not from the gender-determined weakness of defenseless women or children "whom ruffians may mistreat," but from the shame of "brave men," who have collectively—"as an aristocracy"—turned soft and lazy. Although he uses terms like "effete" and "degenerate" that to the modern reader might mistakenly signal an assault on the very gender identity of the landlord—or, in the terminology I will use in this chapter, on his very masculinity—O'Grady's attack is directed elsewhere. His jeremiad is instead loosened against an aristocracy being destroyed by its pursuit of "personal gratification,"[3] not by a waning sexual energy or, in the terms of a more modern preoccupation, by a growing effeminacy.

O'Grady's rhetoric emerges from a tradition that Linda Dowling analyzes in *Hellenism and Homosexuality*, where she observes that terms like "corruption" and "luxury" invoke a classical public discourse of civic alarm about a nation's historical decline. The term "effeminacy" in such discourse has "nothing to do with maleness and femaleness, in the modern sense," but rather refers back to ancient civic standards involving the public valor of citizen-soldiers.[4] O'Grady addresses Irish landlords in 1886, less than a decade before the vilification of a fellow Irishman for a polluting male love, and a year after the passage of the notorious Labouchere Amendment to the Criminal Law Amendment Act, under which Oscar Wilde was successfully prosecuted for gross indecency. But O'Grady's rhetoric echoes an older language of endangered civic virtue; he indicts the landlord's failure to subordinate private interests to the public good, his failure to conduct himself according to that "classical republican probity,"[5] which underscores an ideology of martial civic virtue claimed by both conservative and republican traditions. At stake is the landlord's failure of manly courage and resolve, not his sexual identity.[6] He is vilified for his failure to be a "true shepherd" to his flock, for the loss of an ancestral "heroic ardour," for his philistinism and corrupting sloth. Against the contemporary landlord's piti-ful and unmanly dependency on England, O'Grady juxtaposes an ahistor-ical golden era of martial stewardship: "With your household troops and war-tenants you once ruled and regulated and gathered in your rents, spending them again in a manner mainly human and rational."[7]

The ongoing public discourse surrounding the nineteenth-century landlord accompanied a growing assault in Irish fiction, where represen-tations of that figure dominate a narrative of Big House decline.[8] Since Maria Edgeworth's *Castle Rackrent,* writers emerging from a Protestant Anglo-Irish culture churned out novel after novel about the deeply flawed proprietor, depicted as risking and often losing his land, his money, and his social position as he refused to adapt to changing eco-nomic and political conditions. In theory if not in reality, the landlord was the patriarch of a neo-feudal rural community, charged with fulfill-ing the roles of magistrate, relief officer, and agricultural advisor. In Irish fiction, however, he was viewed as a failed patriarch; rather than the dis-interested proprietor overseeing his holdings, he was an improvident ab-sentee, gauging rent from helpless tenants and refusing to exercise stewardship. If in an older classical discourse described by Dowling, the manor house was "the irreplaceable nursery of civic virtue,"[9] the Anglo-Irish Big House was the site of disorder and corruption. The sheer weight of such negative literary representations in both elite fiction and the folk record provides useful evidence about perceptions—although not necessarily the reality—of the Big House from within and from out-side its demesne walls.[10] But in this cultural record the proprietor's iden-tity is defiantly male, and the teasing sexual implications of Engels' handsome hunk with his empty pocket, all mask and no substance, are undeveloped; whatever the state of his pocket, the landlord's masculine prowess—if not his civic virtue and manhood—remains intact.

Early nineteenth-century novelists like Edgeworth and Lever, writing from within Ascendancy Ireland, created narratives about the landlord's failures of stewardship; he is not generally represented as a sexual predator. But references to his licentiousness—envisioned as a lawless rather than dysfunctional male sexuality—have long existed in a concurrent folk tra-dition. Séamus MacPhilib's compilation of material from folklore records describes, among other transgressions, the landlord's first night rights over village brides (*ius primae noctis*), his brutal attacks on young servant girls, and his fathering of illegitimate offspring among the peasantry.[11] MacPhilib cites dozens of examples of sexually predatory proprietors, but only one of a landlord whose masculinity was impaired. This wealthy

County Tipperary landowner remained childless despite offering marriage to any woman who would conceive a child by him—and was humiliatingly memorialized in the folk record: "What good is / Damer with all his riches, / When he has got nothing in his breeches!"[12] But such ridicule of the unfortunate Damer's sexual inadequacy is the striking exception in a widely disseminated folk tradition of aggressively male landlords.

That tradition became absorbed into Irish fiction when, for example, William Carleton, a writer emerging from the tenant cabin, described a sexually marauding gentry family in the *Squanders of Castle Squander.*

> Alas! it is grievous to reflect upon the number of similar cases that have occurred in Ireland, where the otherwise virtuous girl, surrounded by destitution and despair, has been tempted to forfeit virtue and character under the base promise of her landlord's son—that the next gale of rent would be remitted, or that the rent itself would be reduced to such a reasonable standard as might enable her father and his struggling family to live in comfort. No wonder, indeed, that the curse and judgment of God has come down upon so many of the Irish landlords and their families.[13]

And by the twentieth century, even novelists from within gentry society associated Big House decline with sexual license. Somerville and Ross's 1925 *The Big House of Inver* was inspired by Violet Martin's letter describing the fall of an actual family in Galway after generations of misalliance with the local peasantry.[14] In *Woodbrook,* David Thomson's 1974 memoir, the narrator weaves local memories of brutal Big House assaults against peasant women into his account of a fading ascendancy culture in the early decades of the twentieth century.[15]

The characterization of the colonial landlord as aggressively masculine in much nineteenth- and early twentieth-century cultural discourse reflects ruling-class assumptions about gender in a colonial society. The intersection of gender and imperialism is by now a familiar theoretical crux for postcolonial critics, who emphasize the masculinity of the colonist's self-definition and the state's concomitant constructions of a feminized subject people.[16] Mimicking the universalizing impulses of the imperial state, an emerging nationalist movement constructed new binaries—usually as constricting as those they replaced. David Lloyd posits an essential congruence between the agendas of both imperialism and nationalism, arguing that both traditions attempted to unify diverse groups through their cultural programs. The emergence of a literature engaged in national self-identification created an identity limited by constraints imposed by an older imperial hegemony. From such pressures, Lloyd argues, emerged the repetition of old binaries.

While nationalism is a progressive and even necessary political movement at one stage in its history, it tends at a later stage to become entirely reactionary, both by virtue of its obsession with a deliberately exclusive concept of racial identity, and more importantly, by virtue of its *formal* identity with imperial ideology. Ultimately, both imperialism and nationalism seek to occlude troublesome and inassimilable manifestations of difference.[17]

This chapter will map out such a reactive binary in several texts of a post-Independence fiction that sought to replace the imperial construction of gender identity with an alternative one—specifically that of the hypermasculine Irishman and the sexually dysfunctional Anglo-Irish or English landlord. If imperialism bestowed a feminine identity on native Irishman, one strand of a newly ascendant nationalist culture sought to undo the former overlord's masculinity, to reinvent him as an impaired survivor of a defeated world, as a sexual as well as an economic and political loser.[18]

Representations of the landlord, a pivotal figure in Irish cultural discourse, reveal changing constructions of gender that accompany a triumphant nationalism. The new attack on the landlord's intimate sexual identity—not simply his social and political behavior—appears after Independence and after what commentators have termed the "male drama" of World War I.[19] In these texts, issues of politics and gender identity have become virtually inseparable, even interchangeable. By the mid-twenties Irish men had indeed asserted their claim to a martial manhood in the traditional terminology of civic virtue: they had liberated a feminized nation from centuries of dishonor and successfully borne arms against a mighty imperialist oppressor. Tellingly, the three post-Independence authors I discuss all saw some active service in the republican cause.[20] Padraic Colum (*Castle Conquest,* 1923), Sean O'Faolain ("Midsummer Night's Madness," 1932), and Liam O'Flaherty (*Famine,* 1937 and *Land,* 1948)[21] created young Irish revolutionaries whose sexual challenges to the Big House undermined any remaining aura of power surrounding the landlord and constructed a post-Independence vision of republican masculinity. Their attack on the sexual potency of the landlord, occurring after a revolution had been won, represents a long delayed psychological confrontation with the colonial power structure—the false, usurping stepfather. This psychological assault against the English or Anglo-Irish colonial stepfather (who has brutally ravaged the family home) occurs as a continuation of the more frequently analyzed rebellion of Irish sons against their real fathers who had submitted to such usurpation. The impulses I describe impelling the rebellion are more triumphal and reactive than Joyce, Synge, and O'Casey's anxiously nuanced confrontations with parental inadequacy, which Declan Kiberd maps out in his chapter "Fathers and Sons," in *Inventing Ireland.*[22]

And this post-Independence assault against the landlord advanced a sternly puritanical masculinity for the new state, thus helping defeat the liberating goals of Joyce and some revivalists. The androgynous formulations of gender being developed by both Joyce[23] and Yeats,[24] for example, have no role in the reactive binaries established in the texts I consider below.

Although undoubtedly emerging from age-old patterns of youthful revolt against patriarchy, this new preoccupation with declining male authority and potency in the Big House occurred concurrently with an international modernist sexual anxiety about changing gender relations—in what Sandra Gilbert and Susan Gubar term a "no man's land of mad women and unmanned or maddened men."[25] But whereas the emasculated men that populate modernist texts—Ernest Hemingway's Jake Barnes, D. H. Lawrence's Clifford Chatterley, T. S. Eliot's Prufrock, for example—arguably emerged from an anxiety about rising female aspirations and the appearance of the new woman, the unmanned Irish landlord can be viewed in more local and transparently political terms. In these texts, the assault by the colonized sons against their newly defeated political stepfathers (landlords and government officials) represents the working out of the sexual dimension of revolution in a postcolonial state—not simply the expression of a free-floating modernist gender neurosis.

Often the landlord is simply too old, too much the product of worn-out and in-bred stock to perform; the persistent trope of his decaying house becomes a metaphor for his sexually inadequate body. Several works portray the rage of an old man living with memories of a past ascendancy, but reduced now to the role of ineffectual cuckold, his physical impotence serving as emblem of his social and political losses. In the decade following Independence, Padraic Colum and Sean O'Faolain invoked both the new nation's resentment of the defeated imperial fathers and its ambivalent efforts to assert superiority over the discredited past. In Colum's *Castle Conquest* the sexually inadequate master of an ancient Big House—an old man married to a young girl—fearfully rages against the men he sees in teasing encounters with his nubile wife. The roofless castle, a barrack-like eighteenth-century Big House, and a hostile landlord arouse an "obscure jealousy" stemming from a "racial enmity" in the young republican hero. In his voice we hear the litany of past dispossessions and attempted repossessions that lie behind the mythology of modern republicanism—with the Big House and its lands assuming the emblematic role of the forfeited Irish nation. Fittingly, he first pledges an oath of loyalty to the IRA in the tower of Castle Conquest; in the epilogue of the novel, the Castle has been transformed into an IRA camp, and the son of the largest landlord represents the British forces in negotiating the final transfer of power to the new Irish state. The novel thus enacts a new nation's sexual and political ascendance over its past.

The humiliating decline of a formerly ascendant class is explored with far more subtlety in Sean O'Faolain's short story "Midsummer Night's Madness," in which a young IRA soldier-narrator is billeted in a Big House and encounters the aging ascendancy landlord Alec Henn. A demonic figure in community mythology, remembered as running naked through the fields terrorizing neighborhood girls, Henn is now a victim of a new dispensation during the War of Independence, as young republicans ignite neighboring ascendancy houses. The narrator's ambivalent tone toward Henn shifts between awe and contempt, fascination and disgust. The old man is presented as a grotesque—a rheumy-eyed, half-blind lecher, ludicrous and pitiful in his sexual posturing, but capable, nevertheless, of challenging the republican certainties of the narrator and of displaying a rage that evokes memories of a lost ascendancy:

> Henn's hand shook, and all his legs as he pulled himself up on his stick, taller when he stood than any of us, his bent back straightened, made gigantic by the great shadow that climbed the wall behind him. I could see what a man he was in his heyday, what a figure on a horse, wielding the rod from the top of a rock, a wiry, bony giant. There was almost majesty in him as he pointed his trembling stick to the door.[26]

The young soldier reacts to the old libertine's invocation of his phallic power (the stick, the gigantic shadow, the rod) with a predictable assertion of political animus, but swiftly moves beyond politics to express the sexual triumph of youth over age.

> You may pity him as I tell you of him, but I, riding along the darkling lanes that night, had nothing in my heart for him but hate. He was one of the class that had battened for too long on our poor people, and I was quite pleased to think that if he lived he lived only in name; that if he had any charm at all left he would need it all now to attract even the coarsest woman. For no London light-o'-love would be attracted to his ruin of a house now for other reasons.[27]

Surrounded by a great five-mile estate wall, Henn's aptly named Red House is as encrusted with age as its master. Its threadbare carpets and dusty lace curtains mock the old libertine's sensuous desires for an Ireland producing lovely silks or flowers, rather than the narrow provincial poverty he deplores. The narrator, never entirely free of his awe before a distant Ascendancy world, is shocked: "I could not believe that even such a house would fall so low."[28] Unable to suppress his disgust as he watches Henn's withered old hands caressing a pregnant tinker girl, he witnesses his sergeant (who has himself impregnated the girl) force the old lecher into marriage with her—the final sexual and social shame inflicted on a once proud Ascendancy landlord.[29]

But in Liam O'Flaherty's fiction sexual dysfunction in the Big House has far more sensational sources than mere age and decrepitude. In *Famine,* the absentee's agent (or surrogate landlord) has been literally unmanned—presumably castrated—by a more distant subject people during imperial service in India, a narrative detail that neatly displaces a savage act of reprisal (the empire strikes back) to a more distant and "heathen" group. Chadwick's sexual harassment of peasant women is strikingly aberrant; after ruining the reputation of his female servant, he promises to save her sister from starvation only if she will permit him to lash her for each gold coin he offers. His dependence on these women to satisfy transgressive sexual needs imposes a heavy aura of decadence around the collapsing Big House he occupies. This drunken, broken, impotent Marquis de Sade and his sadistic passions, particularly when viewed in the context of O'Flaherty's republican ideology, embodies some significant social encoding: if the conquering English race has historically been the masculine force in a feminized Celtic colony, what better revisionary characterization of an English oppressor than that of an aging lecher unable to perform? Through the words of his loyal groom, the emasculated Chadwick becomes an explicit symbol indeed of the colonizer—now gelded by his former subjects in India; "not having it in him to be natural," he expresses his impotence through sexual sadism.

> . . . the stories he used to tell about foreign parts and about his old father and how the sun got at him in India. The heathens got at him, too, sir, and he caught in an ambush, where they cut off half his shame, saving your presence, he let it out one night when he was drunk. . . . Lord have mercy on him, for any queerness. He had no right to take the people's stock, with the hard times, but he was driven to it, one way and another. . . . The devil came in with her, and he not having it in him to be natural, same as a man would be, so he could get her out of her mind.[30]

O'Flaherty's fascination with decadence in the Big House generates its own antithesis. Although his melodramatic *Land* is populated by several sexually compromised males, in Michael O'Dwyer the novel constructs a stern model of nationalist masculinity, a potent hero destined for death as a Fenian martyr. In this novel, republicanism is not only the most moral of callings; it is also the most masculine. Although preoccupied by forebodings of his death—the "self-immolation on the altar of the nation" that Curtin identifies as a defining characteristic of Irish republicanism[31]—O'Dwyer is a remarkably vital character: six feet tall, with a rugged and bronzed face, jet-black hair and intense blue eyes. Even when he first appears, dazed by the wounds he has incurred in an attack on the landlord, his muscular body conveys "extraordinary power." Springing up from his apparent coffin in a resurrection into masculine sexual vitality, he looks at and captivates his future bride, a beautiful and well-born Anglo-Norman girl educated in Paris.

O'Dwyer's particular brand of masculinity unlocks his mate's womanliness; after her first sight of him she is preoccupied with an emotion specifically described—in some very unfortunate prose—as an "awareness of beauty still in the womb, at whose door life is waiting with a key for the moment of birth."[32] This "key" of love—and eventual source of a child in her womb—unlocks her with significant energy, for O'Dwyer is no gentle lover. Although too intelligent to be the simple "primitive" that the bride's father first deems him, he is uncouth—interrupting conversations suddenly, staring at the ceiling, burdened by social convention. When he sits in the parlor, the sudden brusque movements of his muscular body disarray his clothing, "as if a savage impulse in him sought to tear off their constraint."[33] Although O'Dwyer is a figure of ruthless vitality, his identity is animated far less by his sexuality than by a devotion to politics and by his gloomy sense of his own inexorable doom. The pleasures of an ordinary sensuality seem quite alien to him; thus the heights of intimacy achieved on his honeymoon occur when the young husband initiates his bride into the orgasmic fulfillment of terror and teaches her to see beauty only in life-threatening danger. In describing how Michael lashed her to the stern of a boat and willfully sailed with her through the eye of a North Atlantic hurricane, the bride invokes not what the modern reader might easily read as some new and exotic sexual adventure, but rather a puritanical hostility to the sensual that controls the novel. After Michael sacrifices his life to the republican cause, his virtuous and pregnant widow will presumably raise a future Fenian leader; the fulfillment of the O'Dwyer marriage is the male child who signals continuing insurgency—never mere sexual or domestic pleasure.

O'Dywer's fathering of a rebel son suggests a republican ideological insistence on the generative role of sexuality. Fiction about the Big House, on the other hand, is filled with instances—from Edgeworth's *Castle Rackrent* on—of the failure of dissolute or improvident landlords to perpetuate their family lines. In Molly Keane's novels the landlord's children—spinsters, frigid wives, or homosexual sons—typically produce no heirs. And in Tomas Bairéad's 1936 Irish language short story, "Mná Chaointe na Linnseach," the only heir of a decaying and corrupt Big House is a pampered lap dog.[34] O'Dwyer's procreative sexuality thus operates as a critique of ruling class decadence, illustrating George Mosse's thesis that modern nationalism is concerned with sexual control and restraint, with providing the means by which sexuality can be "absorbed and tamed into respectability." O'Flaherty's handsome Fenian and his beautiful wife validate Mosse's observation that nationalism de-eroticizes beauty—that the "beautiful body as the personification of the beautiful nation was . . . to transcend its own sexuality."[35]

In contrast to O'Dwyer's chaste, stern, and potently martial masculinity, O'Flaherty depicts a pervasive sexual decadence among English and Anglo-Irish men. Careful distinctions are made. A dispossessed Anglo-Norman landlord—a barrister-at-law who has returned from political exile in France and dresses like a fop—is rescued from his decadence by becoming a celebrated strategist for the Fenian movement, who invents the concept of boycotting and welcomes O'Dwyer as his son-in-law. The novel's mapping out of masculinity is otherwise fairly straightforward.

As wielders of military might in Ireland, English men, in particular, are overtly manly, but that identity is only skin deep. For example, Fenton, the District Inspector of the Royal Irish Constabulary charged with capturing O'Dwyer, is handsome and fair, with well-shaped and firm features but with a troubled sensibility lurking behind his imperial arrogance. Like Engels' Irish landlord with no money in his pocket, Fenton exists at odds with his role—as a man living behind a mask. And without his "mask," we are told, "it was the face of a rather common man in pain."[36] His distaste for the policing and brutal evictions he must supervise and his shamed responses to the political contempt he meets among the rural Irish drive him into moral collapse. His breakdown is most tellingly signaled by heavy drinking, gratuitous cruelty, and by an uncontrollable lust for his superior's wife. In O'Flaherty's construction of a post-Independence masculinity, real men are never slaves to their passions. Fenton's thralldom to his illicit longings for the landlord's sadistic wife—who comes to seduce him dressed in the boots and tight trousers of a cavalry officer—is in striking contrast to O'Dwyer's response to temptation. The heroic Fenian rejects the lascivious allure of a village beauty who throws herself at him and sternly distances himself even from his young bride when he must reassume his insurgent role. The English officer, however, is humiliated, driven to drunken violence, and finally to professional and personal ruin when he runs off with Barbara Butcher and the money she has stolen from her husband. His undisciplined submission to a corrupt woman—particularly one who favors "warlike male dress" and has a history of cross-dressing—unmans him.[37]

The real villain of the piece is, of course, the English landlord, appropriately named Butcher, who has bought up the estate of the decaying old Norman family and combats growing Fenian challenges to his plans to depopulate his land for cattle grazing. But this landlord is not simply the high-booted oppressor, still in his prime, evicting helpless families, hounding and entrapping Fenians—and regretting that England's Liberal politicians prevent him from suppressing his Irish enemies with the same rigor that his sons turn on the Zulus and Afghans on more distant frontiers of Empire.[38] In the course of the novel, Butcher's masculine identity collapses into political and sexual humiliation. Once shot in the buttocks by a Fenian whose son will finally kill him, he is forced to wear metal protective gear and to surround himself with bodyguards and a bloodhound. Cuckolded by his cross-dressing wife first with his groom (who sings love songs to the wife in Gaelic) and then with the English officer assigned to protect him, he is isolated, terrorized, stripped of his cattle, and finally shot by the Fenians.

Although Butcher's preoccupation with assaults on his body (in one strange scene he insists on showing "a deep hole" in his buttock to Fenton[39]) suggests some degree of homoerotic anxiety in this nineteenth-century man whose wife wears trousers, the homosexual landlord makes a late appearance in Irish fiction. In a country that decriminalized homosexual acts between consenting adults only in 1993, and in which, as Kieran Rose points out, it was difficult prior to that time to find evidence of gay and lesbian life except in legislation intended to control that behavior,[40] Ireland's belated literary attention to such motifs is hardly unexpected. Although Forrest Reid's 1931 *Uncle Stephen*,[41] written from a northern Protestant perspective, obliquely idealizes a homoerotic landlord of a manor house in Northern Ireland, the portrayal is so heavily encoded that its implications have been, until recently, ignored or criticized for their indirectness.[42]

But in a cameo scene toward the end of Julia O'Faolain's 1985 novel, *No Country for Young Men*,[43] we learn about a dying proprietor, Demi Devereux, who seems to emerge from the post-Independence tradition of sexually dysfunctional landlords. Demi is looked after by his old servant Timmy and Timmy's sons and their families, all of whom eventually came to live on the estate to service him. Homosexual Demi epitomizes the regendering of the once ascendant landowner. Having satisfied his sexual needs first with Timmy, the peasant boy educated with him at home, and then with Timmy's sons and grandsons, Demi reflects a familiar novelistic preoccupation with Big House decadence and exploitation—but expressed now in homosexual rather than heterosexual transgressive sexual behavior. This post-Independence landlord is indeed unmanned in the terms of a nationalist gender ideology.

Demi Devereux's French name suggests Anglo-Norman antecedents and a European decadence, as well as his position as only half ("demi") a man. That punning given name is a useful reminder of the intersection of gender and politics in twentieth-century Irish fiction. The landlord's predatory character, now brilliantly adopted and used against him by his former servants, recalls and parodies earlier versions of Big House sexual license in fiction written both from within and outside the demesne. But appearing in a feminist novel that mounts a fierce attack against a post-Independence republican patriarchy—against a shopworn version of Michael O'Dwyer's brand of heroic masculinity—Demi's homosexual exploitation of Timmy and his boys and their subsequent victimization of him represent something quite new in Irish fiction.

No Country for Young Men dissects a society controlled by virile homosocial republican men who conceal the truth in order to preserve nationalist mythologies that destroy women; in such a context, Demi's sexual inclinations appear no more predatory than those of the hyper-masculine men who have replaced him and created a new ruling class. And Timmy and his boys are no mere victims. While their wives give the dying landlord food guaranteed to increase his dyspepsia, they blackmail him and force him to sign his patrimony over to them. The gradual takeover of Devereux's estate by Timmy's clan is characterized as "a bit of do-it-yourself land reform, a take-over of the sort not foreseen by politicians."[44] The revenge of the dispossessed—now willingly ingratiating themselves into the private and public spaces of the landlord (his bed and his house and demesne)—undoes easy moral judgments. If Demi is unquestionably a loser, so too are the new generations of Irishmen who have inherited his lost ascendancy.

Julia O'Faolain's homosexual landlord—when juxtaposed with the aging IRA men who have inherited political power—problematizes the triumphant nationalist construction of masculinity in post-Independence Ireland. (A subsequent and related undermining of gender certainties occurs in the 1992 film *The Crying Game,* where both the shock value of Neil Jordan's depiction of Fergus, a sexually ambiguous IRA terrorist played by Stephen Rea, and the unwillingness of many reviewers to acknowledge Fergus's homoerotic desires[45] suggest the enduring power of a narrow republican construction of masculinity.) I have argued that such a construction rested, to some significant extent, on a projection of sexual differences, ambiguities, or dysfunctions on to a newly defeated ruling class—now stripped of its former political, economic, and sexual ascendancy. Former landlords had to become sexual losers, so the republicans who had defeated them could become winners. And by embracing such a reactive binary, Irish nationalism constricted its own range of available masculinities.

NOTES

1. Quoted in Kevin Whelan, "Immoral Economy: Interpreting Erskine Nicol's *The Tenant," America's Eye: Irish Paintings from the Collection of Brian*

P. Burns, ed. Adele Dalsimer and Vera Kreilkamp (Boston: Boston College Museum of Art, 1996), 62.

2. Standish O'Grady, *Toryism and the Tory Government* (London: Chapman and Hall, 1886), 213.

3. Ibid., 215, 216, 247.

4. Linda Dowling, *Hellenism and Homosexuality in Victorian Oxford* (Ithaca: Cornell University Press, 1994), 5–6. Dowling's analysis suggests the problems modern gender critics meet when they attempt to impose, for example, current interpretations of homosexuality on classical uses of "effeminacy" as civic enfeeblement and self-absorption (10).

5. See Nancy J. Curtin's "'A Nation of Abortive Men'" in this volume, 34.

6. The horror at what was perceived as Oscar Wilde's breakdown of gender identity—a perversion or male "effeminacy" now perceived in explicitly physiological terms—can be read in Arthur Symonds homophobic tirade in the Tory press many years after the 1885 trial. Symonds refers to the "swollen, puffed out, bloated, and sinister" Wilde as particularly hideous because of his hermaphroditic appearance. Not only was he morally polluting, but he also seemed to be literally turning into a woman—losing his essential and visible masculinity. See Joseph Bristow, *Effeminate England: Homoerotic Writing after 1885* (New York: Columbia University Press, 1995), 17.

7. O'Grady, *Toryism,* 234, 242, 229.

8. See Vera Kreilkamp, *The Anglo-Irish Novel and the Big House* (Syracuse: Syracuse University Press, 1998), 1–25.

9. Dowling, *Hellenism and Homosexuality,* 19.

10. See, e.g., Ruth-Ann Harris' "Negotiating Patriarchy" in this volume for a far less malevolent portrayal of the landlord than that provided by the literary record I explore.

11. Séamus MacPhilib, "*Ius Primae Noctis* and the Sexual Image of Irish Landlords in Folk Tradition and in Contemporary Accounts," *Béaloideas* 56 (1988), 97–140.

12. Ibid., 132.

13. William Carleton, *The Squanders of Castle Squander* (London: Illustrated London Library, 1852), 1:109.

14. E. O. E. Somerville and Martin Ross, *The Big House of Inver* (1925; London: Quartet, 1978), 313.

15. David Thomson, *Woodbrook* (Harmondsworth, Middlesex: Penguin, 1976), 18.

16. Both Ashis Nandy, *The Intimate Enemy: Loss and Recovery of Self Under Colonialism* (Delhi: Oxford University Press, 1983) and Edward Said, *Orientalism* (New York: Random House, 1979) describe how nineteenth-century British imperialists in India characterized their subject people as emotional, passionate, and thus implicitly feminine, in contrast to the inherently rational and more masculine colonizers. See also Mrinalini Sinha's *Colonial Masculinity: The 'Manly Englishman' and the 'Effeminate Bengali' in the Late*

Nineteenth Century (Manchester: Manchester University Press, 1995). Recent cultural analyses of Irish colonialism similarly explore how nineteenth-century British imperial discourse in Ireland was influenced by Matthew Arnold's enumeration of the "feminine" virtues of the Celtic race: emotion, imagination, love of beauty, charm, spirituality, and sensuality. See, e.g., David Cairns and Shaun Richard, *Writing Ireland: Colonialism, Nationalism, and Culture* (Manchester: Manchester University Press, 1988), 42–57.

17. David Lloyd, *Nationalism and Minor Literature* (Berkeley: University of California Press. 1987), x.

18. The response of Dublin audiences to Synge's 1903 *The Shadow of the Glen* as an attack on Irish manhood suggests how a developing hyper-masculinity intruded itself upon Irish culture years before Independence. David Cairns and Shaun Richards, "Women in the Discourse of Celticism: a Reading of 'The Shadow of the Glen,'" *Canadian Journal of Irish Studies* 13 (1987): 43–60, contextualizes the riots greeting the play in an emerging nationalist opposition to the traditional imperial feminizing of the Irish character. The foundation of the Gaelic Athletic Association in 1884, the worship of a cleansing violence in subsequent nationalist discourse, and a growing puritanical attitude toward sexuality all played their role in this developing cultural construction of a nationalist masculinity.

19. See Joanna Bourke, "'Irish Tommies': The Construction of a Martial Manhood 1914–1918," *Bullán* 3 (1997): 13–25. Bourke argues that despite the much analyzed disillusionment with the war experience, many of the more than 200,000 Irish men participating in World War I experienced pleasure in "outpourings of aggression" (13).

20. Although Colum left Ireland for residence in America in 1914, prior to his departure, he joined the Irish Volunteers and participated in gun running at Howth. O'Faolain served with the IRA both in the War of Independence and the Civil War. O'Flaherty fought both in World War I and with the republicans in the Civil War.

21. Padraic Colum, *Castle Conquest* (New York: Macmillan, 1923); Sean O'Faolain, "Midsummer Night's Madness," in *The Collected Stories of Sean O'Faolain* (Boston: Little Brown, 1983), 9–43; Liam O'Flaherty, *Famine* (Dublin: Wolfhound, 1984) and *Land* (New York: Random House, 1946).

22. Declan Kiberd, *Inventing Ireland: The Literature of the Modern Nation* (London: Cape, 1995), 381–94.

23. *Ulysses'* celebration of Leopold Bloom, the cross-dressing womanly man, and the novel's parody of the nationalist construction of a martial xenophobic manhood in the Citizen suggest Joyce's transcendence of any such simple gender binaries.

24. Elizabeth Cullingford's *Gender and History in Yeats's Love Poetry* (Syracuse: Syracuce University Press, 1996) explores the "fissured" contradictions of Yeats's "discourse with patriarchy" (6). Cullingford argues that although "[a]s a nationalist poet [Yeats] was expected to produce 'manly' verse in order to counteract the colonial stereotype of the Irish as effeminate and

childish . . . [He] conceived of his poetic vocation as demanding a 'feminine' receptivity and passivity" (11). Her analysis of the poet's inability to identify with late nineteenth-century "norms of masculinity" and of his recurring identification of poetry with femininity—in the context of his growing hostility to post-Independence Irish social policy and personal sympathy with unconventional sexualities—compellingly demonstrates how Yeats's career deconstructed those very patriarchal binary oppositions that were being embraced by Irish republicans.

25. Sandra M. Gilbert and Susan Gubar, *Sex Changes,* vol. 2 of *No Man's Land: The Place of the Woman Writer in the Twentieth Century,* (New Haven: Yale University Press, 1989), 40.

26. Sean O'Faolain, *Famine,* 26.

27. Ibid., 12.

28. Ibid., 13.

29. This undermining of the landlord's sexual prowess also appears in an Irish language novel written in the 1920s. Philip O'Leary has alerted me to Mícheál O Gríobhtha, *Buaidh na Treise* (Baile Átha Cliath: Muinntir C. S. Ó Fallamhain, Teo. i gcomhar le bOifig an tSolásthair, 1928), a novel in which a son's unhealthy relationship with his mother, the bigoted English widow of a just landlord, causes the son to bully his tenants. The tenant protagonist of the novel triumphs over such behavior by learning the art of boxing, thrashing the new landlord in a fist fight, and winning the hand of a woman also being courted by him. And more than a half-century after O'Faolain's "Midsummer Night's Madness," Molly Keane, writing from within the demesne, offers yet another version of the fall of a Big House womanizer in *Good Behavior* (London: Abacus, 1982). Paralyzed by a stroke, Keane's helpless landlord receives pleasure—liquor and masturbatory sexual relief—from the hands of a newly ascendant Irish housemaid.

30. O'Flaherty, *Famine,* 291.

31. Curtin, "'A Nation of Abortive Men'," 36.

32. O'Flaherty, *Land,* 79.

33. Ibid., 80.

34. "Mná Chaointe na Linnseach," *Cumhacht na Cinneamhna* (Baile Átha Cliath: Oifig Díolta Foillseacháin Rialtais, 1936), 93–100.

35. George Mosse, "Nationalism and Respectability: Normal and Abnormal Sexuality in the Nineteenth Century," *Journal of Contemporary History* 17 (April 1982): 222, 223.

36. O'Flaherty, *Land,* 99.

37. Barbara Butcher's behavior—certainly aberrant in nineteenth-century rural Ireland—suggests that O'Flaherty, like Joyce, was acquainted with late nineteenth- and early twentieth-century traditions of androgyne cross-dressing—often with roots in sadistic Victorian pornography. But as Gilbert and Gubar suggest, such pornography is "perversely reversing, exaggerating, and thereby parodying the male dominance-female submission that the authors of these works believe to be quite properly associated with

male female relationship" (*Sex Changes,* 333–34). In later Irish fiction about the Big House written from within the demesne walls, Molly Keane and Jennifer Johnston also demonize the landlord's wife, but for arrogance or cruelty to children and servants—never for such sensational sexual transgression.

38. O'Flaherty, *Land,* 52.
39. Ibid., 51.
40. Kieran Rose, *Diverse Communities: The Evolution of Lesbian and Gay Politics in Ireland* (Cork: Cork University Press, 1993), 9.
41. Forrest Reid's *Uncle Stephen, The Retreat,* and *Young Tom* were published together as *Tom Barber* (New York: Pantheon, 1955).
42. Reid's version of the homoerotic landlord in *Uncle Stephen,* the last volume of the Tom Barber trilogy, suggests the constraints and literary costs of official state homophobia on its literature. The novel describes a romanticized implicitly erotic affection between a sensitive young boy escaping from the philistinism of professional and commercial Ulster society into the secret world of his mysterious uncle's country mansion. Uncle Stephen's cultivated hellenism—the garden of an abandoned lodge on his demesne is adorned with the naked statue of a pagan boy—signals an idealized homoerotic alternative to the muscular masculinity of his nephew's background. See Colin Cruse, "Error and Eros: The Fiction of Forrest Reid," *Sex, Nation, and Dissent in Irish Writing,* ed. Éibhear Walshe, (New York: St Martin's, 1997), 60–86, for a discussion of how Reid both defended and obscured homosexuality through the language of a nineteenth-century patrician discourse of classicism.
43. Julia O'Faolain, *No Country for Young Men* (Harmondsworth, Middlesex: Penguin, 1980).
44. Ibid., 337.
45. See Lance Pettit's "Pigs and Provos, Prostitutes and Prejudice: Gay Representation in Irish Film, 1984–1995," in Walshe, *Sex, Nation, and Dissent,* 270–2.

Chapter Seven

Putting Masculinity to Work on A Northern Ireland Shopfloor 🔲

William F. Kelleher

This ethnographic chapter makes use of poststructuralist feminist theory and a narrative theory of identity to make visible the gendering of class relations in a glassmaking factory, the Drumcoo Glassworks, in Ballybogoin, Northern Ireland.[1] Poststructuralist feminist scholars have cleared a path toward more fully relational studies of gender and its articulations to class, race, and ethnicity through their critiques of theories that propose an ontological specificity to women as childbearers, as social mothers, or as fundamentally relational.[2] They criticize such essentializing theories for relying on identity categories that not only describe but also normalize and, therefore, exclude. Feminist developments of poststructuralist thought believe "women" cannot be totalized and ought to signify "an undesignatable field of differences."[3] The refusal to categorize men in essentializing identity terms follows from this argument. The terms masculine/feminine designate symbolic references, not the physical bodies of male/female. This theoretical position, then, moves away from the Enlightenment tradition that defines masculine/feminine in terms of the opposition of abstract qualities: masculine as strong, rational, and public and feminine as weak, irrational, and private.[4]

Joan Scott has connected this critique of identity categories to the category of class. Working from approaches that understand class and class consciousness as the same thing, she theorizes that gender, understood as social understandings of sexual difference, constitutes class relations. Gender marks class relations and class struggle because it provides a convenient and available resource to register difference. It refers to nature, to physical bodies, so gender appears natural and immutable, even though it varies across space and time. Gender is apprehended here not as a thing added to social relations, but as social knowledge that may exert force in those relations, may transform them, and gets made and remade in various locations. "As a social process, we need to think of *gender* not only as a noun but also as a verb," Ava Baron writes, and the study of gendering, in this sense, "is concerned with how understandings of sexual difference shape institutions, practices and relationships."[5]

This essay examines such a gendering process at the Drumcoo glassworks. Gender entered the history of the firm, was attached to its geographical location, and was expressed in the struggles that occurred there at the end of 1984 and the strike that ensued in the spring of 1985. It profoundly shaped the institutions, the relationships, and the practices at the glassworks. Gender figured into the workplace struggles that led to the strike, the strike itself, and its aftermath. This essay will track this identification process at the glassworks and will attempt to understand the gendering of social relations and social action at the glassworks. It draws on the identity theory of action developed by Margaret R. Somers, who combines the insights of feminist theory with recent research on narrative. Somers has developed a set of concepts for understanding social action that takes into account structure and social order along with ontology, social being, and identity.[6] From this position, no ontological specificity is accorded to any category, whether it be men, women, or workers. Instead, narratives are understood to provide the means through which social actors come to know their world. Actors organize the self through narratives and become who they are by locating themselves in stories that are negotiated in time and space.

Somers has proposed four dimensions of narrativity—ontological, public, conceptual, and meta-narrativity. Ontological narratives are the stories actors deploy to make sense of their worlds and act in them. These are discourses about the self and define who a person is. A person, then, is a narration made intelligible through ongoing relationships in time and space. Actors understand themselves and others by placing their actions in the context of preceding and subsequent events, and the ontological narratives they construct are integrally related to public narratives. Public narratives are the products of the interpersonal webs of relationality that transform narratives over time. They include narratives of family, nation, church, and workplace among many others, and individuals configure their ontological accounts and changing relationships in close relation to these public narratives.

Narratives give events historicity and relationality. Actors relate events to other events through the mediation of a plot, and "the narrative identity approach embeds the actor within relationships and stories that shift over time and space and thus precludes categorical stability in action."[7]

These emplotments not only give significance to events, but they also work to make social orders. People in all societies are called to account for their actions and do so through narratives that draw on and reproduce social orders. Such accounts are not only retrospective, they are anticipatory. When actors give accounts or tell stories, they affirm or challenge the ordering criteria by which their actions and those of others will be evaluated in the future.

People size up situations within narratives. In emplotting events, social actors measure some types as being of worth and not others. In doing so, they endorse some narratives and disclaim others.[8] When social actors do this evaluative work they mobilize some social ties and networks, while they disentangle themselves from others. As David Stark writes: "Accounts mobilize ties: they link social beings in orders of worthiness with measuring instruments that inscribe value" and social ties "mobilize accounts: they transport accounts across settings through networks of affiliation."[9] This intersection of ties and accounts makes a social order, and all modern societies have more than one.

Social actors make their social orders, and, in turn, are made in relationship with them. Conceptual narratives, Somers' third dimension of narrativity, address this process. Ontological narratives and public narratives alone do not produce social action. Wider social forces such as market patterns, institutional practices, and organizational constraints exert powerful effects. Conceptual narratives analyze these social forces, and their challenge is "to devise a conceptual vocabulary that we can use to reconstruct and plot over time and space the ontological narratives and relationships of historical actors, the public and cultural narratives that inform their lives, and the crucial intersection of these narratives with the other social forces."[10] The ethnography that follows is a conceptual narrative of the glassworks and the struggles that occurred there. It foregrounds the discursive practices and the narratives through which actors evaluated and acted before, during, and after this strike.

MEN AND MASCULINITY AT THE DRUMCOO GLASSWORKS

"He's a bull of a worker," Dolan, the managing director of the Drumcoo Glassworks, told me as we watched Liam, a skilled glasscutter approach his cutting wheel. Liam, who overheard, gave Dolan a broad smile and pulled four crates of heavy glassware to his cutting machine from the marking area, where Margaret McCann, the one woman who worked in the main factory shopfloor, marked the designs to be cut. Most other workers pulled one crate at a time or possibly two.

Liam was one of the most skilled glasscutters. With the highest production and the best weekly pay, management considered him their model
worker. They pointed to him and his work habits when other workers
complained of poor pay. They used him to advance public relations. When
tourists and government officials visited the factory, Dolan explained the
glasscutting process by highlighting Liam. Dolan told Liam that I was an
anthropologist who had come from the United States to study the factory,
and joked with him, saying, "usually we visit the Yanks to learn about business not the other way around." After a short conversation, Dolan led me
out from the shopfloor and said, "we are doing great things around here."

This utterance indexed Dolan's identification with Liam. This process
of identification, the "we" that Dolan invoked, was a complex one as the
events of the next ten months would show, but, at that time and place,
Liam identified with the subject position in which Dolan's discourse
placed him. Dolan's speech action was determinate; it was taken up by
Liam because it followed the story line of Liam's ontological narrative, his
worker autobiography, one closely articulated to the public narrative of the
firm.[11] At that time Liam was considered management's man by his fellow
workers. In his mid-thirties, he was one of the three remaining employees
from the glassworks' original blue-collar workforce, and this job had enabled him to fulfill his responsibilities and desires. With pride he showed
me a house he was having built for his family, his wife, and two sons. Satisfied with his situation and his choices in 1984, Liam identified with the
subject position that Dolan located him in.

Dolan connected to Liam through a masculine idiom. Dolan's utterance
positioned Liam as masculine, "a bull," and the first person pronoun, "we,"
enabled him to take responsibility for the "great things" the firm was doing
while he assigned joint responsibility for that success to Liam and his bullish practices. Liam accepted that partnership in productive prowess, so
Dolan's utterance became a speech act; it was adopted by Liam. And the
pronoun "we," as used in that situation, is best understood for its indexical
functioning. An indexical carries information about the speaker's identity
and is creative when it sets up new relations or makes them explicit.[12] The
"we" here indexed Dolan and Liam as occupying the same spatial location
and the same moral position in Ballybogin's moral order.[13] This was a positively valued position. It depended on the speaker's moral standing in relation to the counter-speakers and others in the moral community, and, at
the time Dolan produced this speech act, he was a respected figure in
Ballybogin. He had rescued the glassworks, a community enterprise
whose goal was to produce jobs for local people in a region that had the
highest unemployment rate in the United Kingdom of Great Britain and
Northern Ireland in 1984. Dolan had put the glassworks, in his words, "on

a solid footing," and he had won the respect of both Protestant and Catholic members of this bitterly divided "community."

The ontological and public narratives that contextualized this speech act enable understanding of why this masculine type was valued by Liam and Dolan. Liam's ontological narrative makes that interpretive process possible. Liam had left school in his mid-teens and had been working as a laborer for two years in the mid-1960s when Father Finbarr, the Roman Catholic priest, raised enough money to establish the glassworks and start training male workers. Apprenticing at the glassworks paid very little and offered little status, but Liam joined the twelve young men that constituted the original group of trainees, several of whom had given up better paying jobs for the chance to become a skilled worker. They collected jam jars from parishioners of the local Roman Catholic parish, cut them and sold them cheaply at local demonstrations. They named themselves "the twelve apostles." Liam told me he joined the glassworks because he wanted to settle in the area and have a family. The cutting job offered the possibility of stability.

At that time, Father Finbarr instituted a foundational narrative for the firm, a public narrative he used to raise money from his parishioners, other townspeople, and the state development authority. Through this narrative Father Finbarr founded a group dedicated to local economic development and redressing what he and local Catholics perceived to be the discriminatory actions of the state and unionist, Protestant businesses. Grounded in the philosophies of Catholic Action, a conservative organization he adapted to construct local institutions of self-help, Father Finbarr surveyed demographic trends among young Roman Catholics in the early to mid-1960s and believed these statistics proved discrimination against local Catholics that threatened the Irish nationalist community's viability.

Father Finbarr chose to address this crisis of social reproduction by attending to the family. He founded a development association that raised money to address family needs. His first project was a cooperative housing development for families who were living doubled or tripled up in the homes of parents or siblings. Then he focused on employment discrimination against Catholic men by organizing plans for the glassworks. At that time, he proposed that investment be made into the organization of home-based production sites for women, the knitting of Irish woolens for the tourist trade, the painting of ceramics, and the packaging of the products of the small industries he hoped would develop, but these jobs for women never materialized. The money that was raised went toward creating jobs for local men.

The major aims of the local development association, Father Finbarr wrote, were "to provide opportunities for employment by the setting up of small local industries in which the emphasis would be on the personal skill of the worker and secondly by attracting outside industrialists to set up production in the area." "Drastic action" was necessary, he contended, because of "the economic facts of life, in this area, which are directly attributable to the policies of the unionist government at central, and more particularly, at local government levels." The "facts" were that the emigration rate of those leaving Catholic schools in nationalist areas of the region "ranged from 35 to 43% in the age group of 15–25 years," that "the average unemployment in the six counties of Northern Ireland is 7%," and that "the average male Catholic unemployment rate in the Nationalist (sic) areas . . . ranges from 20% to 26%, and this in spite of the huge emigration rate."[14]

Through such appeals to the community and the state, Father Finbarr marked young working-class Catholic men as capable individuals who could provide for families, and he raised the capital for the Drumcoo Glassworks, his favorite project. Capital did not get raised for the proposed women's jobs. Father Finbarr's narrative produced an ideology for the firm, one that reproduced the local nationalist theme of anti-Catholic discrimination and the consideration of women as domestic workers only. Father Finbarr transformed this narrative by adding the idea that, if given a chance, Catholic males would become skilled industrial workers. This narrative attracted young Irish nationalist men like Liam, who left jobs they believed had no future for them. Father Finbarr constructed for them the belief that, as Liam told me, "we had something better in us," that they could support a family in Ballybogoin and did not have to emigrate. Father Finbarr enabled choice. He provided an agentive discourse. His narrative was taken up by "the twelve apostles," and they emplotted their futures through it.[15]

Father Finbarr imagined the glassworks as a firm that required skilled craftspeople who, once trained, would not be "made redundant." His story contested the dominant discourse about culture and economy in the area, which held that Catholics operated from personal and cultural deficits that rendered them unreliable industrial employees. One economist who became a key adviser to Northern Ireland's unionist governments in the 1960s wrote the following about Northern Ireland's Catholics in 1955:

> For generations they were the underdogs, the despised "croppies," the adherents of a persecuted religion, who were kept out of public affairs by their Protestant conquerors. They were made to feel inferior, and to make matters worse they often were inferior, if only in those personal qualities that make for success in competitive economic life.[16]

Several workers and many Ballybogoin Irish nationalist townspeople remembered feeling inferior during the time that Father Finbarr was building his local development association. They recalled that Father Finbarr countered that feeling, one produced by discourses that marked Catholics as other in Northern Ireland's industrial world. Liam remembered those days and identified with the struggles of many people he knew who did not have proper houses when he made the decision to become a glasscutter.

Asking, as Joan Scott recommends, "how implicit understandings of gender are being invoked and reinscribed" in general social processes enables these narratives of the 1960s to be connected to the events of 1984 and 1985.[17] Liam related his work autobiography to the desire to support a family, to work hard and be a man, an opportunity that, the public narrative of the firm proposed, was denied to him by the local labor market. He realized masculine values at the glassworks. The glassworks, in this reading, afforded his self-realization as a local masculine subject while meeting the instrumental values attached to providing for his family. Both ideal and instrumental values constituted the glassworks.

Dolan narrated stories that reproduced these masculine values when I asked him about his history at the firm. He performed that masculinity in his everyday managerial practices, such as his daily visits to the two shops, the glassblowing shop and the glasscutting shop, which were housed in two buildings over one mile apart. At both of these sites Dolan produced speech acts like that introducing the ethnographic section of this essay, and those acts articulated to a variety of stories analogous to but different from Liam's. Dolan, a Roman Catholic whose religious identity was revealed by both his Christian name and his surname in the Northern Ireland process of "telling" that establishes one's communal/religious identity on the basis of bodily or verbal signs, was born and raised in an eastern region of Northern Ireland, with a Protestant majority. This marked him as different for Ballybogoin's Catholics. They believed he did not interact artfully the way Ballybogoin people did. Many local Catholics considered him bullish and brutish. For his part, Dolan desired recognition of his difference from the Ballybogoin nationalist community. During my first interview with him, he told me how he transformed sales by going personally to clubs and ladies' societies, the vast majority of which were politically unionist and religiously Protestant. He hated the way he was immediately interpreted as Catholic in those spaces, and he tried to make clear what his political position was. He did not want to be identified with Sinn Féin, the political party allied to the Irish Republican Army (IRA), an identity that many unionists assigned to Catholics from this western region of Northern Ireland.

Dolan was known around Ballybogoin as "a dealing man," one who "could buy and sell you." Irish nationalists used metaphors like "bull" to describe him, figures they also used to name their Protestant fellow townsmen in their politically divided town. He was "a dealing man" because he would become "bullish" and "ignorant" if his desires were not met. Although he was both respected and reviled for this trait, being like a bull was one he identified with, as shown in his comments about Liam.

Dolan identified with Liam's bodily acts, his strenuous physical exertion, and his speed at work. These bodily practices signified value iconically. They exhibited value in themselves, and, as signs, they were part of a more comprehensive whole.[18] For Dolan and Liam such signs and their associated values constituted an intersubjective spacetime, "a spacetime of self-other relationships formed in and through acts and practices," that makes male groups in Ballybogoin.[19] Dolan attempted to institute those practices and values that constituted this form of intersubjective spacetime at the glassworks through his favoritism of Liam. He desired to create networks that fostered the masculine values for which Liam's work practices, his bodily acts and the organization of his time, served as signs.

The stories Dolan recounted about his strategies in reorganizing the glassworks when he took over in 1981, around the time of the Irish Republican Army (IRA) hunger strikes, served to justify the reorganization he imposed on the workforce and his departure from the firm's foundational narrative. Dolan assumed control of the glassworks when it was failing and about to be put out of business by the Northern Ireland Development Association (NIDA), which had taken it over when the local development association could not turn a profit. Dolan offered a different account of the workplace than did the workers and local people. In interviews, Dolan referred to Liam as "a man with work in him," and he opposed Liam, a man from the rural area outside the town, to men from the working-class housing estates of the town, who, Dolan said, "had no work in them." Dolan identified himself as "a man from the country" as well, but he differentiated himself politically from "the men from the country" around Ballybogoin. He told me "men from the country around here are daft" as he recounted to me the fact that the majority of Irish nationalists from those areas voted for Bobby Sands, the chief of staff of the IRA and the leader of the 1981 IRA hunger strike, as their Member of Parliament at Westminster. Dolan believed that the men from the town with "no work in them" were solid supporters of Bobby Sands and the IRA. He fired most of those workers when he became managing director of the glassworks in 1981, reducing the blue-collar employees from 135 to 65. Most men from the country kept their jobs even though many of them, Dolan believed, had questionable political ideas, but they were quiet about it. Liam, a man from the country, was a quiet supporter of Sinn Fein, so for Dolan even he was marked with ambivalence despite his self-discipline and productivity.

Still, Dolan regarded Liam's acts as valued ones because they had the capacity to produce value in both its economic/objective and sociological/subjective senses. They produced more glassware and, therefore, profit for the firm. They fit the accountants' story line that Dolan highly valued. Liam's work habits extended the social relationship between Dolan and Liam, manager and worker. Linguistic practices, like the masculine banter that took place when Dolan visited the shopfloor everyday, constituted this connection. When I asked Dolan how he viewed the firm's foundational narrative, the public narrative of the firm that Father Finbarr promulgated, he scoffed. He said he admired and respected Father Finbarr, but believed his idealism was wrongheaded. The business was about sales, Dolan insisted, not about community. Dolan understood Liam's acts as profitable and manly and valuable because they opposed the discourse that Catholics had no work in them, but he did not see the glassworks as an employment scheme for Catholics. He told me that the workers he kept on were interested in building houses for their wives and children, as Liam and several other of the better paid workers had started to do. Dolan saw Liam's upward mobility and family responsibilities as insurance for his firm. During that first interview he told me he could keep the trade union at a distance if the workers were building houses and had mortgages like Liam had. Such practices served as a hedge against the firm's uncertain future, and he invested much in that narrative of masculinity and family responsibility that articulated to the firm's public narrative, one that emphasized the importance of men getting jobs to provide for women and children.

IDENTITIES: NARRATING
STRUGGLE/EMPLOTTING MASCULINITY

The differing articulations of Liam and Dolan's ontological narratives to the two operating public narratives, the firm's and the local nationalist one, indicated the instability of their identities and registered the evanescence of the unity that Dolan's speech act achieved. The relationship between Dolan and Liam was an unstable ordering of multiple possibilities, as was that between management and workers, and even among the workers themselves. The social order at the factories constituted incompletely managed factors of difference from 1981, when Dolan took over, until late September 1984. During that period, there were no strikes and no extended conflicts, although Dolan fired more than one third of the total workforce. That uneasy stability began to transform in September 1984, when labor unrest at the glassblowing factory began.

The glassblowers carried out a one-day strike that management resolved by calling in the Northern Ireland Labor Relations Agency (the

LRA), which proposed a fact-finding study of the entire glassmaking process. That study produced eleven recommendations. These included the assignment of an additional shop steward for the glasscutters who had no skilled worker to represent them and the re-timing of jobs in the company by outside time-study experts who would reassign value to the items workers produced. The glasscutters elected Liam as their shop steward and anticipated the 1985 re-timings with trepidation. They feared time studies, because when they underwent them in 1977, they transformed them into masculine contests, racing each other to see which man was the strongest and fastest among them. These races, they later realized, led to lost time and money. They had no desire to repeat that history, so they exchanged stories that hypothesized possible strategies of resistance. They worried about Liam, whom they admired as a worker but mistrusted as a shop steward. They identified him as "a company man," and believed management got the shop steward they desired when the workers elected him. In early 1985, when the production manager, Sean Murphy, lowered the payments the edge cutters would get on 1984 glassware items, this reading of Liam appeared accurate.

The edge cutters struggled to make the wages they were accustomed to after Murphy's price change. At the end of March they protested, met with management and agreed to prepare lists of unsatisfactory edge cutting piece rates. Two days later the edge cutters banned overtime pending a determination of those piece rates they found unsatisfactory. Liam, a flat cutter who was not directly affected by the new prices, prepared the edge cutter list in consultation with those workers and discussed the issues several times with management. Management adhered to the lower prices, and the edge cutters walked out of the factory after a May 6 meeting. That evening Liam told me "the strike is the fault of one man, Sean Murphy." Murphy had arbitrarily assigned new prices to old items, and the workers believed someone from outside the factory should have re-timed those contested items. Liam thought the edge cutters should try the new price scheme for two months and then discuss the wages by looking at the average earnings over the period. "Some of the edge cutters are being stubborn," he said, and he added "the LRA report was a useless whitewash and I don't know why they bothered." The next morning the flat cutters and the ancillary workers in the cutting factory voted to join the edge cutters on strike. Six days after the edge cutters walked out, both the skilled glassblowers and the blowing factory's ancillary workers voted to strike in support of their cutting factory colleagues.

The picket line was manned 24 hours a day, but it was not well organized. Ten to fifteen men participated regularly while the rest showed up sporadically. All of the nationalist, Catholic women workers but one and half of the unionist, Protestant women workers came to the factory gates the first two days of picketing, but they did not walk the picket line. They stayed in their cars and watched the men and explained that they felt excluded and believed the men would "slag" them if they exited their cars. After the first week, none of the female workers came, and they did not participate in the three major trade union meetings that were held at the Roman Catholic parish hall. On the picket line several males reproduced the masculine banter that characterized Dolan's dealings with the secretarial staff, commenting on the clothes and bodies of their female colleagues and female passers-by. These speech acts excluded women workers and, since women worked in the glass cleaning and packaging rooms physically separated from the men and operated under different work rules, they did not identify strongly with the men's cause.

Liam, who was becoming the leader of the strikers, did not participate in this masculinist talk, but he engaged the picketers in conversation. They sat or stood in circles more often than they marched in line. They exchanged stories of the problems they encountered. The overarching theme in the glassworkers' conversations was relationships—how to make and unmake them. Their interactions with Dolan preoccupied them. They recalled that his daily visits to them on the shopfloor gradually declined after the September one-day walkout until they had almost no interaction with him. In the process of remembering the speech acts that placed them and Dolan at the same moral location, the workers realized that the distance between them and Dolan had increased. Some workers still believed Dolan could be persuaded to agree with their position in the first two weeks of the strike. Many workers believed, as Liam did, that Murphy was the cause of the strike. One glassblower said that he talked to Dolan once about the timings, and Dolan confessed that he did not understand the piece rate and bonus systems. "Murphy has baffled him with science," this man said. Several remembered that they worked hard for Dolan when he saved the firm from NIDA, which they believed desired to shut it down, and one glasscutter noted that "everyone worked hard for him because we thought he was more or less like us." "Now," this skilled edge cutter said: "He gets all the credit. We never get any, and we created the profit." Murphy, they said, never talked to them and Dolan was getting like him. One of the younger, unskilled workers interjected with an observation about social distance. He said: "We give a good, natural hard time to Peter, Francie and Adrian (the younger, white-collar male staff), as they drive through the gate, but we are quiet for Dolan, Murphy and Mullally (the senior management team) because they have power over us and could get us back when we go back to work." He added: "It's like striking against God. They could make life tough for you."

Dolan had demonstrated his distance and his power that very morning, the end of the strike's third week. Workers with families and mortgages expressed anxiety over the strike's duration, and Liam had become frustrated with management's intransigence. During the strike the union's area representative, a woman, Kathleen McGinn, who was the shop steward at a nearby poultry plant, stopped at the picket line on her way to and home from work. She taught Liam about workers' rights, possible strategies for action, union members' responsibilities, and shop steward leadership. Meanwhile, Dolan offended Liam because he talked at Liam not with him in their negotiating sessions. Their "we" was unraveling, and that morning it snapped.

Dolan and a salesman, O'Leary, a local man who was a white-collar union member, loaded up the trunk of O'Leary's car with glassware. Liam walked through the gate to warn O'Leary that he would report him to his union for crossing a picket line, a principle of trade union solidarity that he learned from Kathleen McGinn. Dolan made a remark that no one could decipher, but it was read as provocative by the workers who watched. It angered Liam, who walked back to the gate. As O'Leary drove out, Liam kicked the wheel of his car, punched the hood and started pounding the roof. Dolan went to his office and summoned the police, the Royal Ulster Constabulary (RUC), who arrived minutes later and began to apprehend Liam, who had returned to "the picket line." The police stopped their action when a passerby told them that they had no warrant, that Liam was not causing a disturbance, and therefore they could not arrest him. The police let Liam go.

The passerby warned the picketing men to watch out for the police and informed them of their rights. Deeply skeptical of RUC action like most nationalists, this man had performed a fairly routine act in this particular nationalist community, where many Catholics believed the RUC was an illegitimate, sectarian force. Most of the workers believed that, and since Dolan was now identified with the police, they understood him as even more removed from them and the narrative of the firm. Their conversations moved from questioning his distance to interpreting it, and his acts began to be emplotted in local narratives of the British State. Stories circulated that Dolan took down the photograph of Father Finbarr that overlooked the lobby when Protestant unionists visited the factory. The strikers remembered how many times they had seen newspaper photos of Dolan giving crystal glassware as prizes at unionist events. They emplotted Dolan as a character that participated in the state's exclusion of them. They made sense of this event in terms of the local Irish nationalist narrative.

The shop steward for the ancillary workers began a conversation involving the themes of that narrative the next morning. The steward, Kevin, had received permission from the union to cross the picket line to keep the furnaces burning in case the strike was settled, because the furnaces took weeks to re-ignite and get back to working temperature. At the picket line, he offered his interpretation of the encounter between Liam, Dolan, and the RUC. He said that England needed a revolution, and one of his interlocutors uttered "yeah, the problems would be solved if we burned all the Protestants." Immediately, another man exclaimed "What?" and the speaker changed his statement to "burn all the governments" while Kevin continued saying "the government in Russia is no worse than the government here." This engendered an immediate reply from the firm's youngest worker who said "No, that's not so!" Kevin asked him "how is it different?" The sixteen-year old replied "we can move around here more," and one of the skilled workers in the circle shot back: "How many days can you leave your house and go up the town without being stopped?" The young fellow winced, shook his head in agreement and sunk it in his shirt collar.

It was a point taken up by the workers, and it signified not only the surveillance rampant in the town during those years but also the gendering of public space. Ballybogoin, located in the western, majority Catholic half of Northern Ireland, underwent much violence in the 1970s and 1980s. Ballybogoin itself had been one of the most bombed towns in Northern Ireland throughout the 1970s, and it was a prime site of assassination in the 1980s. The roads leading to and from Catholic working-class housing estates were often blocked off by RUC or British army patrols. The nationalist rural areas had Special Air Service (SAS) units camping out in fields and sometimes commanding country roads at night. The workers often spoke of their inability to move and talked about how free they felt when they crossed the nearby border to the Republic of Ireland, a place through which they could move relatively unhampered. Sometimes workers arrived late to work because they had been interrogated at roadblocks. This restriction of their mobility feminized them. They feared certain neighborhoods in Ballybogoin and believed the police would not protect them if they entered those spaces. The young man who believed striking against Dolan was "like striking against God" told a story about an encounter with the RUC he had had a few nights before. He had one pint of beer with several other workers before going home and was stopped by the RUC on the country road he took home. They told him he had the smell of rum on his breath and took him to the inspection area near his border village, tore through his car, yelled at him for being an "Irish drunk," and, while waiting for a breathalyzer test, kept screaming at him, interrogating him as to the place he drank and whether it was a place they would be welcome. He felt they were naming pubs where militant nationalists gathered, and told the police he did not drink there. He was one of the least political men in the factory and not sympathetic to the IRA. He finally got his breathalyzer test, and there was so little sign of alcohol it was laughable. The police let him go. Restriction of movement, being confined to domestic spaces, feeling unsafe under the eyes of patriarchal authority were aspects of all nationalist Catholic workers' lives in this area, but as the story of the workers' treatment of their female colleagues from the picket line shows, nationalist Catholic women were the objects of those practices within their own "community" as well.

CONCLUSIONS

Ballybogoin started off in 1984 with a male unemployment rate slightly over 40 percent, and it remained over 30 percent for most of the next two years. Catholics were 2.5 times as likely to be unemployed as Protestants for the remainder of the decade.[20] The glassworkers feared job loss, and they had little hope of transferring their skills to another place of employment. During the fourth week of the strike, management composed a letter that they sent to all workers' homes. The letter stated: "The industrial action, which has continued since 6 May 1985, has now caused a situation where the Company can no longer continue the recurring expense of firing the furnaces. . . . Accordingly, these furnaces will be 'turned off' on Monday 3 June 1985." It concluded: "It is with deep regret that we take this course, since the Drumcoo Glassworks furnaces have never been turned off before."

Letters in hand, most of the male workers showed up at the picket line the next morning. Again, the women did not participate. All but one of the Protestant blue-collar women had found other jobs, but none of the Catholic woman had. Margaret, the one woman who worked on the main cutting factory space, decided to quit because she planned to get married the following month. After receiving the letter, workers argued over possible strategies of action. The following conversation at the factory gates, starting with a short discourse about Dolan, depicts the story lines that informed their deliberations:

> Worker 1: That's his last card he can play. What else can he do, sure? Let him, I know, but he could've played that last, that was his last card. And everybody knew it that was his last card from day one that we came out on strike. Now he has played. It's up to the lads to stand their ground.

After twenty minutes of argument, the conversation turned to the topic of returning to work but continuing to resist.

Worker 1: That's right. If you get the lads in there, you'll not get them back. You're finished. If the majority says to go back in I'll keep my 75p. (This meant that he would not remain a member of the union whose dues were 75p per week). Everybody's saying about Peter, Peter Hughes. Peter Hughes needs a fuckin' medal cause the last negotiations fuckin' broke down this road over a pay rise. Peter left the union. Yes, he was fuckin' right.

Worker 3: I'm gonna leave the union myself, Patrick.

Worker 1: Ah, fuckin', if it's gonna be a union, stand together. Aye.

Worker 4: Well, that's what he's gonna get if you don't go in and stand together.

Worker 3: They can break the union if they want. Back on Monday he's gonna close it down and not take anybody back.

Worker 5: Not if we all stand together.

Worker 4: How can we all stand together if we're all on the dole signing on? Worker 1: If we stand together, then we don't go back.

Worker 4: How do you stand together when you? I have a wife and child up there, a fucking big mortgage. How do I stand together with that there? I go for money, that's what I'm fucking here for.

Worker 1: There. We should've, we shouldn't've held the strike on. We never should've asked for the strike. Yous should've said: "All right, forget about it. I can't afford to go on strike."

Worker 4: Before we were out on strike I was worried about taking an hour off to go to take the fuckin' car off for an MOT (motor vehicle inspection). That's about all I was fuckin' worried about. We've been on strike now for four fuckin' weeks.

Worker 1: That's why we got to hold out now.

The narrative of family, the masculine provisioning of it, the story of the firm that Dolan had invested in, dominated the discussions for the rest of that day and during the final union meeting when the workers decided to end their strike. Mortgages and children got the blame from the men, who realized that accepting management's terms meant losing the strike. They represented that position by invoking "the wife." Many men uttered: "The wife won't let me stay out" during that day and during the final trade union meeting. This meeting occurred after the shop stewards, Kathleen McGinn from the poultry plant, the regional trade union representative and even the Northern Ireland leader of the union negotiated the terms of the workers' return. The only concession they got from management was a promise not to victimize any strikers. Otherwise, the workers had to go back under the terms that led them to strike.

When the ATGWU (Amalgamated Transport and General Workers' Union) representative told the workers the news about no victimization, they all cheered. Everyone knew that meant Liam would keep his job. The promise not to victimize depended on Liam's removal from his union post.

A new election would have to take place. After this announcement one of the ancillary workers stood up and said, "There's no better man than Liam McBride, and they made him lose the head off him. That's what happens when he gets no thanks for all that he's done." The workers cheered and took up a collection for Liam for all he had done for them. Dolan had castrated the bull, and the workers wanted to compensate him.

Two days later the workers went back to work. That night I went to a local pub with several of them. As we sat drinking, a pint was delivered to me by the barman. He pointed to a stool at the bar where O'Leary, the salesman whose car had been kicked and pummeled by Liam, sat. After a few minutes, I went to sit with him since the pint was a message to do just that. O'Leary, who obviously did not want to engage the workers, told me all that he knew. He informed me who the four workers were who voted against management's "agreement." He explained Liam's transformation during the strike: "That woman from the poultry plant, Kathleen McGinn, she led Liam astray." He cast me a knowing look and presented his evidence. Liam, he heard, had gotten into a car with Kathleen one night as the picket line was under way, and the windows had steamed up. I pointed out to him that such an occurrence was not unusual on damp Irish nights when people talked in their cars, and that Kathleen had been advising Liam on the workers' rights and trade union tactics during the first eleven days of the strike when the workers could not get a response from union headquarters. He did not recognize my emplotment of these events, and his version circulated among his middle-class networks in Ballybogoin.

For many of the middle-class people in the Ballybogoin Irish nationalist "community," Liam's reputation as family man was thrown into question. The "we" that this model worker had established with management's narrative network had dissolved. The workers' story line, that "no finer man" than Liam existed and that "he lost the head" because management did not recognize either Liam or them, did not move beyond working-class networks. The third-person references to Dolan that marked the first exchanges in the workers' conversations above located him as socially distant, not sharing the same moral order. Patrick said that Dolan "played his last card," and he had no doubt that Dolan intended to win. It was a zero sum game, and Dolan's "last card" had more power than any move the workers could muster. The narratives through which both management and workers emplotted the strike had profound effects. The narrative of masculine family provisioning, in which Dolan had invested so much, returned and provided the rationale for most workers' acceptance of management's harsh terms. The hegemonic social order had been gendered—naturalized and made immutable. Many workers represented themselves through a non-agentive discourse: "the wives" would not let them stay out, so women were assigned responsibility for the break-up of male, trade union solidarity. At the same time, management's gendered emplotment of the strike positioned a woman as the source of disorder.

At the final union meeting, another narrative emerged. The workers complained to the trade union officials that the media misrepresented them as violent and disorderly. Liam's outburst, always featured in local media accounts, became a metonym for the strike as a whole. The workers told of townspeople telling them: "The community owns that factory, and you have no business shutting it down. Get back to work." They attributed this interpretation to management's having "the media locked up." The media story line was management's, and the narratives that circulated informally through the middle-class networks around the town after the strike imagined a woman as the cause of that perceived disorderliness. They emplotted the transformation of Liam from model worker to disorderly strike leader as feminine, and they disconnected Liam from the narrative of male support for family reproduction that the firm so highly valued. Liam lost his location at the center of the factory and became a marginal figure because he took advice from a woman, Kathleen. She had the workers at her own factory take up a collection to buy chicken that they roasted after work hours and brought to the strikers on the picket line. Kathleen's gesture fostered solidarity between the members of her own union and the glassworkers, who gave support when the trade union officials at headquarters did not respond to Liam's urgent requests for help. She won the respect of the striking glassworkers although she never established a connection with the glassworks women.

Kathleen and Liam, as shop stewards, had tried to instigate a different social ordering, a new intersection of ties and accounts, a working-class one, but more powerful narrative networks halted those practices. They fought masculine discourses along with class ones, and the trade union lost. With the "agreement," workers became alienated from the union. No skilled worker would take up Liam's shop steward position after he was forced to resign. The glassblowers' shop steward voluntarily resigned, and no skilled worker would take up his position either. Ancillary workers assumed those positions, but workers did not make use of the union after that. The union had been implicated in the workers' loss and humiliation and did not factor into their workplace strategies after the return to the shopfloor. Gendered categories figured the transformed relationships and identities produced by the strike. The workers' loss appeared natural and immutable. Some workers made peace with management by accepting arrangements on piece rates through an internal labor market that individuated skilled craftsmen. Maybe that young worker was right—striking against Dolan was "like striking against God," God in all his maleness.

NOTES

The research reported here was carried out with the support of a dissertation research grant from the Social Science Research Council's Fellowship Program for Western Europe. Sponsored jointly by the American Council of Learned Societies, funds for the program were provided by the Ford Foundation, the William and Flora Hewlett Foundation, and the National Endowment of the Humanities. I thank all these institutions for their generous support. Jo Thomas applied her keen editorial insight and offered criticisms that increased the clarity of this chapter. Charles R.Varela offered suggestions for reading that helped me to work through problem areas. Marilyn Cohen and Nancy Curtin helped me to better relate the feminine and the masculine. My thanks to all of them.

1. Following common anthropological practice, the names of the firm, of the town, and of individuals are fictitious. The individuals are not presented as composite characters. In doing this ethnographic work I told those who spoke to me that I would not reveal their identities. Obviously, those who know the area could identify these persons and this firm if they desired. I hope the honesty and integrity of all those involved in these events will be honored.

2. On poststructuralist feminist theory see Joan Scott, *Gender and the Politics of History* (New York: Columbia University Press, 1988). For the sociolinguistic perspective adopted here see Peter Mühlhäusler and Rom Harré, *Pronouns and People: The Linguistic Construction of Social and Personal Identity* (Oxford: Basil Blackwell, 1990). On the narrative theory of identity see Margaret R. Somers and Gloria D. Gibson, "Reclaiming the Epistemological 'Other': Narrative and the Social Constitution of Identity," in *Social Theory and the Politics of Identity,* ed. Craig Calhoun (Oxford: Basil Blackwell, 1994), 37–99. For Somers' position on class formation debates see Margaret R. Somers, "Deconstructing and Reconstructing Class Formation Theory: Narrativity, Relational Analysis and Social Theory," in *Reworking Class,* ed. John R. Hall (Ithaca: Cornell University Press, 1997), 73–105.

3. Judith Butler, "Contingent Foundations: Feminism and the Question of 'Postmodernism'," in *Feminists Theorize the Political,* ed. Judith Butler and Joan W. Scott (New York: Routledge, 1992), 16.

4. Joan Scott, "On Language, Gender and Working Class History," in *Gender and the Politics of History,* 63.

5. Ava Baron, "Gender and Labor History: Learning from the Past, Looking to the Future," in *Work Engendered: Toward a New History of American Labor,* ed. Ava Baron (Ithaca: Cornell University Press, 1991), 36.

6. Somers and Gibson, "Reclaiming the Epistemological 'Other'," 40.

7. Ibid., 65.

8. David Stark, "Recombinant Property in East European Capitalism," *Cornell Working Papers on Transitions from State Socialism* 94.5 (Ithaca: Marion Einaudi Center for International Studies, 1994), 31.

9. Ibid., 31.
10. Somers and Gibson, "Reclaiming the Epistemological 'Other'," 62.
11. Bronwyn Davies and Rom Harré, "Positioning: The Discursive Production of Selves," *Journal for the Theory of Social Behaviour* 20 (1990): 43–63.
12. On indexicality see Michael Silverstein, "Shifters, Linguistic Categories and Cultural Description," in *Meaning in Anthropology,* ed. Keith Basso and Henry Selby (Albuquerque: University of New Mexico Press, 1976), 11–55. For an interesting discussion of indexicality and class, racial, and ethnic divisions, see Bonnie Urciuoli, *Exposing Prejudice: Puerto Rican Experiences of Language, Race and Class* (Boulder: Westview Press, 1996).
13. Rom Harré, "Agentive Discourse," in *Discourse Psychology in Practice,* ed. Rom Harré and Peter Stearns (London: Sage, 1995), 121–136.
14. These sentences appeared in first-page stories in local Ballybogoin newspapers. I cite them using Father Finbarr's papers.
15. Rom Harré, "Agentive Discourse," 123.
16. Thomas Wilson, ed. *Ulster under Home Rule* (Oxford: Oxford University Press, 1955), 208–209.
17. Joan Scott, "Gender: A Useful Category of Historical Analysis," in *Gender and the Politics of History,* p. 49.
18. Nancy D. Munn, *The Fame of Gawa: A Symbolic Study of Value Transformation in a Massim (Papua New Guinea) Society* (Durham: Duke University Press, 1986), 16.
19. Ibid., 9.
20. Department of Economic Development Statistics, 1984; 1991 Northern Ireland Census of Population; Liam O'Dowd, "Development or Dependency? State, Economy and Society in Northern Ireland," in *Irish Society: Sociological Perspectives* (Dublin: Institute of Public Administration, 1995), 132–177.

Domesticating Political Economy

Chapter Eight

Asenath Nicholson's New Domestic Economy

Gordon Bigelow

In the spring of 1844, Asenath Nicholson traveled from New York to Dublin and toured Ireland "for the purpose," as she put it in the subtitle of one of her books, "of personally investigating the poor." She stayed for four and a half years and wrote two books about her visit. The first, *Ireland's Welcome to the Stranger,* published in 1847, describes travels around Ireland in 1844. *Lights and Shades of Ireland,* published in 1850, offers an account of the relief work she took up in the gathering crisis of 1845–47 and documents conditions among the poor in these years.[1] Born Asenath Hatch in rural Vermont, to a family of strict Congregationalists, Nicholson passed her early life as a schoolteacher before moving to New York sometime around 1830. There she married a business man, William Nicholson, and with him ran a number of temperance boarding houses in the city, which themselves became meeting places for a variety of abolitionists and political reformers.[2] "It was in the garrets and cellars of New York," she writes in her first volume, "that I first became acquainted with the Irish peasantry, and it was there I saw they were a suffering people."[3] Nicholson committed herself to the redress of the massive social inequalities she saw in New York's immigrant slums, and after the death of her husband in 1843 she decided to travel, alone, to Ireland. She writes:

> I came to gather no legends of fairies or banshees, to pull down no monarchies, or set up any democracies; but I came to glean after the reapers, to gather up the fragments, to see the poor peasant by wayside and in bog, in the field and by his peat fire, and to read to him the story of Calvary.[4]

She aims in part to bring the Bible to Catholic Ireland, to "read . . . the story of Calvary" to anyone prepared to listen. But what becomes more evident in her writing is her determination "to see the poor peasant," to see the "fragments" of Irish life more or less obscured by previous tourists, Celticists, and surveyors. Her books develop a keenly observed critique of Irish social and economic conditions, one that resonates in profound ways with a larger critique of British political economy that was gaining currency in the 1840s.

I have used the phrase "new domestic economy" in my title as a gesture toward economist Pedro Schwartz's book, *The New Political Economy of John Stuart Mill*. In this work Schwartz positions Mill within the history of economic thought in the nineteenth century, describing him as an influential critic of the cold rationality associated with the names Smith, Malthus, and Ricardo. Mill referred to this body of theory as "the old political economy," and he argued for a more humane science of wealth and progress.[5] Mill's major works on economics are exactly contemporary with Nicholson's two volumes, spanning the middle years of the 1840s, and if we attend to the economic perspective Nicholson develops in her portraits of the Irish poor, we find that the two writers have a great deal in common. Nicholson's critique of "the old political economy," however, invokes the domestic household as a model of economic efficiency tempered and motivated by sentimental feeling. She proposes a "new political economy" through the vision of a transformative "new domestic economy."

Nicholson deploys the values associated with domestic femininity in this period to develop a radical and scathing critique both of British government policy during the Famine and of laissez-faire political economy in general. Under the force of this and similar critiques waged by Nicholson's generation, "the old political economy" was discredited, but it was superseded in the last decades of the nineteenth century by the so-called Marginal Revolution in economics, a movement that lay the foundation for the neoclassical school that still dominates economics in the academy and in public policy today. This was the most important shift in economic thought of the nineteenth century, for it succeeded eventually in cleansing political economy of the bad reputation it carried in the wake of the Irish Famine, and it laid groundwork for the reemergence of laissez-faire theories of poverty and progress in the twentieth century. The beginnings of this shift, I argue, are visible in Nicholson's texts, as they are visible in the work of Mill and of many Irish political and economic thinkers who lived through the years of the Famine. The critique of political economy in Nicholson works through her idea of domestic femininity; an early element of neoclassical thought is present, I will argue, in her idea of romantic nationalism.

Nicholson arrives in Ireland in the early summer of 1844, and it is clear from the start of her first book, *Ireland's Welcome to the Stranger,* that she has in mind a study of Irish economic conditions, not a simple travel log. Having described the landing at Kingstown, the first thing she mentions is the loss of all her money: "Putting my hand into my pocket to get a shilling for my ticket, I missed my pocketbook; this pocketbook contained all valuables of purse and scrip, and not a farthing had I out of it."[6] After a moment of panic, the wallet is returned by an honest passerby, but as she proceeds to the train, she continues: "I found I had lost my ticket; ran into the office, paid for another, and lost my keys."[7] Immediately Nicholson focuses us on the distribution of objects and articles of value, their circulation, appearance, and disappearance, presenting a model of economy like that of the sucking stones in Beckett's *Molloy*.[8] Nicholson highlights this metaphor linking the arrangement of personal possessions and the total management of resources in a society (what we think of now as "the economy") at the close of this passage. She relocates all her goods "after considerable bustle, and then commence[s] regulating government affairs a little."[9]

That Nicholson is undertaking an economic analysis and not compiling a collection of sights and impressions is made clear again almost immediately. Given a letter of introduction to a wealthy family in the Dublin suburbs, she is attracted on her way to the first small cottages she sees: "I had never before seen a thatched roof," she writes, "an earthen floor, or the manner of cabin housekeeping."[10] She interviews the family here about their rent, their diet, and their expenses and concludes, "This being my first arithmetical calculation on Irish labour and economy, I was at a loss to understand how the thing could be possible."[11]

As she grows familiar with the hungry street people of Dublin and the attitudes of the elite Protestant classes, she first proposes the solution to poverty in Ireland that will carry through all her work, describing travels over the whole of Ireland from 1844 to 1848. She writes:

> Suppose fifty ladies in the city, who have leisure, should go out at ten in the morning, and mingle promiscuously with the poor upon the street, ascertaining who is worthy, and who unworthy . . . who are idle from necessity, and who from choice. . . . By four o'clock in the afternoon each could ascertain the true condition of twenty persons at least, making in all a thousand, who might be truly deserving, and who, with a little assistance of work and necessaries, would soon be placed beyond want.[12]

Middle-class women here spread to the poor the principles of thrift and economy. They discern the diligent from the lax and assist the former in setting up independent households, where they can support themselves by the careful rational management of market rate wages. These middle-class women "mingle promiscuously with the poor," like both the government inspectors and reporters on poverty in this era, and the prostitutes who were frequently objects of their official interest. Here and throughout her work Nicholson frankly asserts the responsibility of women to go out alone, risking as they did the scandal of being seen as a streetwalker, to spread the cure of economic efficiency.

In her second book she praises the mostly Protestant women of the Belfast Ladies' Association on this account. This group has set up a series of "Industrial Schools" for poor children. Nicholson argues that the schools have succeeded because they are organized and supported not by paid public administrators, presumably male, but by volunteers, that is by women. Professional relief workers, she argues, sequester themselves in offices and when touring among the poor "take the highest seat in a public conveyance . . . the most comfortable inns [and] . . . the best dinner and wines."[13] Volunteers, however, work out of a "kindly spirit" and are "found mingling with the poorest, often taking the lowest seat, curtailing all unnecessary expense."[14] They "loo[k] into the causes of distress, that [they] might better know how to remove them."[15] In other words, volunteers apply the principles of domestic economy to the task of helping the poor, mingling the techniques of efficient administration with feelings of affection and care.

Through the public work of these women, Nicholson writes, "the highways and hedges were faithfully visited, the poor sought out, their condition cared for, and the children of the most degraded class were taken and placed in a school, which continues to flourish on an extensive scale."[16] Like Charles Trevelyan in his notorious report on treasury expenditures, Nicholson here sees poor relief as a means to bring a "hidden," premodern Ireland into the light of industrial modernity.[17] In the description that follows this passage, the "industry" taught in the industrial schools becomes a consuming metaphor for self-improvement, in language reminiscent of Charles Babbage or Andrew Ure, proponents of the supposedly healthful qualities of repetitive machinery labor:

> The happy effects of industry on the minds of the children were striking. That passive indifference to all but how a morsel of bread should be obtained, was exchanged for a becoming manner and animated countenance, lighted up by the happy consciousness, that industry was a steppingstone which would justly and honourably give them a place among the comfortable and respectable of the earth. . . . While these benevolent women were teaching the practice of industry to the poor, they found the benefit react upon themselves, for they too must be industrious.[18]

However, for Trevelyan, Babbage, and Ure, machines and money reshape private desires and domestic habits. For Nicholson the process is exactly the reverse: In her hands "industry" is first of all a quality of human behavior, a value best taught at home, which will itself radiate through the public arena of the market and transform it.

The power of domestic economy is most fiercely defended in Nicholson's description of the first moments of crisis, in the winter of 1845–46, when starving people began to multiply on the streets of Dublin, and when the first shipments of American cornmeal were released by the English government into Irish wholesale markets. She opens this chapter not by describing the conditions of suffering among the poor, though she does go on to specify these in compelling detail, but by excoriating the domestic habits of rich women. While the Irish poor had been widely accused of laziness, she argues that it is "the rich" who "are idle from a silly pride and long habits of indulgence. . . . Their late hours of rising and of meals necessarily unhinge all that is good in housekeeping, and where all is left to servants, economy *must* come in by the by."[19] Here, where money and class status afford leisure, the effects of "industry" are strikingly absent. No productive work is accomplished; no moral improvement enabled. In Nicholson's view, good economic habits among middle-class women will circulate wealth and productivity throughout the society, in a model of self-sustaining exchange. The rich household, however, is a model of economic and moral stagnation, producing nothing, circulating only poverty and crime:

> Here is one of the sources of the evil: the "ways of the household," which are specially allotted to the "prudent wife" are made over to the uninterested servant; because this poor servant was "glad" to work for a little more than nothing. The keys of the house are peculiarly the care of the mistress, and with these well-pocketed she prevents all inroads into her larder.[20]

This practice of keeping everything locked up, we are told, is meant "to keep servants from theft—the surest method of making them thieves."[21] The problem here is a failed transmission of the codes of femininity, as Nicholson understands them. Rather than training poor servants in skills of domestic management, nurturing the nurturing instinct, as it were, rich women neglect their staff and thereby encourage suspicion and inefficiency. This same failure of gender codes prevents young women among the gentry and aristocracy from cultivating personal "industry." The typical daughter of this class, Nicholson complains, "is sent to school, and goes the routine of a genteel education. She can work Berlin wool, perhaps read French, and possibly German, play the piano, and write a commonplace letter, in angular writing, made on purpose for the ladies; but with all this her mind is not cultivated, her heart is not disciplined."[22]

This indiscipline at the heart and hearth of what should be, in Nicholson's view, Ireland's leadership class, results in disaster at the time of national crisis:

> When the Famine had actually come, and all the country was aghast, when supplies from all parts were poured in, what was done with these supplies: Why the best that these inefficient housekeepers could do. The rice and Indian meal, both of which are excellent articles of food, were cooked in such a manner that, in most cases, they were actually unhealthy, and in all cases unpalatable.[23]

After describing the widespread rejection by the poor of "Peel's Brimstone," she concludes, "Had the women of the higher classes known how to prepare these articles in a proper manner, much money might have been saved, and many lives rescued, which are now lost."[24] Again, the extremes of suffering and the most intense aspects of economic crisis result, in this analysis, from a misunderstanding of what it means to be a good woman. The crisis of the Famine is a crisis of motherhood.

In one way it might seem that Nicholson's emphasis on good housekeeping here is simply an extension of the principles of market efficiency and self-sustaining growth that were proposed by the classical political economists. But these principles, which we now associate with the work of Adam Smith, were not part of what the phrase "political economy" generally meant in the 1840s. The most common understanding of the precepts of Smith, Malthus, and Ricardo, from the 1820's through the time of the Famine, was a simplistic advocacy of free trade and an opposition to the poor laws. In this era, which Boyd Hilton has called "the age of atonement," the idea of divine retribution for earthly improvidence, which ran through Malthus's population theory, was reinforced by both Anglican and dissenting churches. The resulting popular conception of political economy was one that stressed personal responsibility for poverty and hard work as atonement for sin.[25] In this view, to interfere in labor or trade contracts was a follied attempt to perfect an irrevocably sinful life on earth. This was the loose set of theories Mill referred to as "the old political economy" and set out to overturn. Nicholson was certainly a free-trader of a sort. Her discussion of Irish history focuses on the English inhibition of Irish trade as a perennial cause of poverty.[26] Certainly also, she prefers private voluntary relief, organized by efficient concerned women, over government efforts by male professionals. But she is starkly set off from the popular "atonement" school of political economy, most clearly in her view of the Famine. "The old political economy" insisted that starvation was a divine judgment against Irish imprudence, overpopulation, and laziness. Nicholson overturns all these presumptions, arguing that only the rich are lazy, and that their inaction has led to starvation, rather than any intervention by the hand of God.[27] Moreover, she espouses a kind of Smithian optimism about the improvements that domestic economy will bring. Popular political economy saw prudence as a spiritual duty, not necessarily a social benefit: a good investment was evidence of rectitude, not a means of increasing the aggregate wealth of the nation. But for Adam Smith economic efficiency, in the form of the division of labor, yields public good, just as for Nicholson domestic efficiency, organized by what she calls "the rational mother,"[28] spreads productivity through an entire society.

Nicholson's economics are, in addition, concerned with sentimental as well as market values. Her understanding of economic efficiency is characterized not merely by the harsh disciplining lessons of poverty, but by, in the phrase I quoted above, a "disciplined heart." This concept of a rationally ordered love, a typical Romantic linking of what were considered masculine and feminine principles, appears also in Nicholson's metaphor of domestic efficiency as a kind of industrial machine. In her discussion of the Belfast Ladies' Association, she comments on the "mutual confidence" these women feel in each other. She argues that to "those moving in the machinery," that is the metaphorical machinery of the industrial school system, this mutual confidence was "like a heavenly influence distilling unperceived into the hearts of all."[29] The sentimental heart of the industrial machine here is like the loving domestic home, the center of an industrial economy whose free movement and efficiency is only heightened by its love.

Nicholson's particular politics of domesticity draws from a number of popular movements in this period. It exemplifies a growing American emphasis on domestic femininity, as proposed for example in Catherine Beecher's 1841 *Treatise on Domestic Economy,* a volume reprinted many times through the 1840s and '50s.[30] Students of the English novel will also recognize what Catherine Gallagher has called the metonymic discourse of domesticity, where the maternal power of the household is shown to benefit every person who comes in contact with it, transforming national morality and economy as its example slowly spreads.[31] The politics of domesticity in these movements formed one important cultural wing of the critique of "the old political economy." Against the cold logic of the market, they pose the warm affections of the heart. Nicholson's insistence on the political and broadly social power of domestic feeling echoes also with the widespread critique of industrialization in the 1840s. Her metaphor of the machine with the feeling heart anticipates the cruder pronouncements of Dickens's *Hard Times* in 1852.

But another intellectual touchstone for Nicholson's texts is a new evolving understanding of the concept of nationality and its true meanings. Nicholson's first book presents documentary evidence of Irish poverty on the eve of the Famine. The second presents stronger demands for action to stem the mortality of the Famine and prevent its recurrence. Perhaps to further her claim to the authority of these arguments, Nicholson opens the second volume with a two-hundred-page summary of Irish history. Throughout this section of the book, she favors the view held out to her by the Irish poor: that Ireland was a great nation in ancient times, a land of saints, whose history had been rewritten by its conquerors into a string of defeats. She notes, "when searching for truth concerning a nation 'scattered and peeled,' as the Irish have been, the true ore can better be found in the unpolished rubbish, in the traditions of a rude nation, retained from age to age, than among the polished gems of polite literature, written to please rather than instruct, and pull down rather than to build up."[32] In describing her travels, she stresses the truth-value of the spontaneous speech of unlettered peasants and the potentially corrupting influence of education. She celebrates one Connemara girl she encounters who speaks only Irish, and whose "broadly spread feet ... had never been cramped by cloth or leather. . . . She had another qualification," Nicholson continues, "viz. that of singing: this was always performed in Irish and with tones and gestures which made every auditor feel to the bottom of his soul."[33] Among Irish speakers from remote regions, this power of the voice exists alongside what Nicholson calls the "ruling passions" of hospitality and politeness.[34] Even when near death, she writes, "that *heartfelt* greeting which they give the stranger, had not in the least died within them."[35] In the towns, however, where they are presumably exposed to the "polished gems of polite literature," the poor lose this instinctive politeness: "The Irish, whether unlike all others I do not pretend in this particular . . . do not become less savage and impetuous by a superficial, and what may be termed common, education. The labouring classes in towns and villages are less courteous, less humane, and more impetuous, than in remote mountains."[36]

In this way Nicholson elaborates a Rousseauean, Romantic vision of the Irish, one that relies on a theory of the origin of language in the prehistory of the human species, and on a particular historiography of civilization. While the remote Irish speakers are "savage," they possess an innate "humanity." Their original (Irish) instinct toward courtesy is only defaced by the conventions of an (English) education. While they believe in a variety of superstitions, which Nicholson occasionally enumerates, these "are more poetical than frightful, and they generally turn all supernatural appearances to a favourable account."[37] The vision of the Irish here conforms to the prescriptions of romantic language theory. The Irish, for Nicholson,

speak in the way Shelley describes the first humans: a race of poets. She
sees their conception of the world as Rousseau characterizes primitive language: an encoding of literal perceptions in metaphorical or "poetic"
signs.[38] Nicholson takes a "phonological" position here, stressing the au-
thenticity of spoken language over the artificiality of writing, attributing
spontaneity and sincerity to oral performance, corruption and duplicity to
literate culture. The seeming praise of oral culture rests on the theory that
orality is more primitive than literacy. Through her travels among the Irish
poor, Nicholson becomes convinced "that man, fresh from the hand of the
maker, needs no missionary societies to teach him benevolence, nor
schools of the polished to teach him gentility; and it is because these have
been so defaced by man's education that they must be rubbed up and put
on by artificial training."[39] The race character of the Irish here corresponds
to the position of the child in romantic poetry, where the child enters the
corrupt world in a position of original innocence, "trailing clouds of
glory" from his or her divine beginnings.[40] "It is greatly to be regretted,"
Nicholson writes at one point, "that civilized life, as it is too falsely called,
should suppress [the] fine feelings of the heart."[41]

Beginning as she does with these assumptions, Nicholson suggests that
only by understanding the spontaneous poetry and generosity of the Irish
can one shatter the stereotypes of Irish laziness and provide the correct sort
of education to develop good industry, public and private. This belief in the
importance of understanding core, essential, national characteristics is one
Nicholson is far from alone in holding in the 1840s. Her characterization
of the Irish as coming "fresh from the hand of the maker" in fact fits neatly
with Thomas Davis's idea of a "Young Ireland,"[42] which despite its potentially militant character embraced the idea, as David Lloyd has argued, that
Ireland was one of the "minor" or relatively primitive members of the family of nations.[43] Davis's economics followed from this view; he argued the
case for peasant proprietorship in Ireland rather than the wage-labor system urged by free traders in England.[44]

This was also the position of John Stuart Mill, and for similar reasons.
Mill's major work on economics, his 1848 *Principles of Political Economy,*
arose out of his interest in the positivism of French philosopher Auguste
Comte. Comte borrowed from the revolution of empirical and positive
methods in the physical sciences and argued for their application to the
analysis of social processes. "The human mind," he wrote in 1830, "has created celestial and terrestrial physics, mechanics and chemistry, vegetable
and animal physics, we might say, but we have still to complete the system
of the observational sciences with social physics."[45]

Mill makes the case for Comte's positive method in his only full-length
philosophical work, the *Logic* of 1842. He argues here that the scientific

study of human behaviors and social processes will lead ultimately to a positivist "ethology," a study of peoples.[46] He proposes that political economy should be replaced by "a science of national character," a compromise Mill called "political ethology."[47] His conviction that only through a specific knowledge of national, or what we would now call racial, character could one form economic policy caused him to refrain from drafting his thousand-page treatise on political economy during the Famine to submit a series of letters to the *Morning Chronicle* arguing for peasant proprietorship in Ireland.[48]

In arguing for a specifically Irish political economy, Mill allied himself with a critique of British economic policy that gained momentum from the time of the Famine, a critique which Thomas Boylan and Timothy Foley have documented in their *Political Economy in Colonial Ireland*.[49] The laissez-faire, anti-poor law policies that comprised the system of early Victorian political economy were attacked by John Mitchell, Isaac Butt, and others in the worst years of the Famine. The universalizing and coldly rational "old political economy" was run down, and a specifically Irish political economy, formed on the basis of national characteristics, was proposed to take its place. The value of what Mill called "ethology" had become widely recognized by 1881, when Gladstone spoke out in the House of Commons against those who would apply the "principles of abstract political economy to the people and circumstances of Ireland" as if "proposing to legislate for the inhabitants of Saturn and Jupiter."[50] This concern with the concrete specificities of character and custom crept into British policy across the empire. As S. B. Cook argues in his *Imperial Affinities*, legal and economic policy in both India and Ireland after 1850 was set to conform with what were thought to be authentic local customs. The Hindu legal system and the 1870 and 1881 land reform acts in Ireland were both justified in these terms.[51] It is in this context we should place Nicholson's economic thought, though of course she works the flip side of the model drawn up by her male counterparts. For her, trade or land legislation, even when devised in line with local custom, could never have the transformative power of the maternal household.

The crisis in economic analysis, which the critique around the time of the Famine inaugurated, was resolved in two different directions. One was the so-called Historical School, which advocated an analysis purely dictated by empirical observation, not based on any prior axiom or theory. The Irish economist Cliffe Leslie's 1876 essay "On the Philosophical Method of Political Economy," for example, argued for a wholly inductive method, refusing any universal or metaphysical starting point, but rather building conclusions from the statistical evidence of a particular market. This movement was to have some impact on policy in a number of Euro-

pean governments, but by far the more influential response to the critique
of political economy that Nicholson's generation mounted was the so-
called Marginal Revolution of the 1870s. This new wave of theorizing, associated in England with the work of William Stanley Jevons, focused on
the consumer's subjective perception of commodities and their "marginal
utility." But while it is easy to see how a historical theory of economics
might evolve out of a critique of the universalist and judgmental prescriptions that had been justified in the name of Ricardo, it is more difficult to
see how Nicholson's generation might have produced the Marginalists.
This task would be an important one, however, for marginal utility, as consolidated at the end of the nineteenth century in the work of Marshall,
would establish the founding principles of neoclassical economics as practiced up to the present.

I argued that Nicholson's perception of economic solutions to poverty
in Ireland is directly parallel to Mill's, that both suggest a knowledge of national character is necessary before any formulation of social and economic
policy can proceed effectively. This position leads Mill, in the *Principles of
Political Economy,* to a theory of race-based variation in the desire for
wealth, what he called "the effective desire of accumulation."[52] In nations
where this "desire" was weak, as Mill considered it to be among the indigenous North Americans, for example, nothing is saved for the future, no
effort is spent on the long-term accumulation of wealth. The "effective desire of accumulation" Mill considers to be an inherent "moral attribute" of
a nation, one of the natural conditions, like climate or the number of nav-
igable rivers, that will limit any particular market.[53]

William Stanley Jevons, England's first Marginalist thinker, argued in
1870 that political economy should not involve itself with moral or social
questions, that it should confine itself to a mathematical analysis of the real
actions of individuals and groups in the marketplace, and that, to signal its
narrowed emphasis on the calculation of relative value, the discipline ought
to shift its name from "political economy" to "economics" plain and simple.[54] The name change stuck, along with the general housekeeping oper-
ation Jevons imagined. "Economics" became increasingly distant from
"politics" and cultivated a patina of scientific objectivity based in numerical analysis. It eschewed judgments about why certain people or nations
were rich and others poor, focusing only on concrete actions of economic
actors. Economics as a discipline shifted from being a normative science,
one concerned with defining "normal" standards of human work, comfort,
and survival, to a positive one, a purely descriptive modeling of market relations as they already exist. So while the popular versions of political
economy in the early nineteenth century could generate explanatory
judgments (for example, the judgment that the Irish starved because they

were lazy, or because they were deficient in the "effective desire of accumulation") twentieth-century economics generally refuses to offer moral or social reasons for poverty, believing, as Jevons put it, that "every mind is inscrutable to every other mind."[55]

However, while Jevons argued that the question of why people behave as they do in the market should be outside the scope of economics, a racial foundation of economic behavior is still visible in Jevons's epoch-making *Theory of Political Economy,* where he argues that "in minds of much intelligence and foresight, the greatest force of feeling and motive arises from the anticipation of a long-continued future."[56] In this regard Jevons follows Mill in arguing that wealth is an implicit measure of racial intelligence and an inborn level of economic prudence. "That class or race of men who have the most foresight," he argues, "will work most for the future. The untutored savage, like the child, is wholly occupied with the pleasures and the troubles of the moment; the morrow is dimly felt; the limit of his horizon is but a few days off."[57] Economic productivity is ranged along a scale of world historical development, from the "childish" to the "mature."

Thus we could say that, through the transitional figure of Jevons, economics took Asenath Nicholson's advice, along with John Mitchell's, Thomas Davis's, and J. S. Mill's. Of course Nicholson's ideas about the active principle of "feminine" efficiency fell on deaf ears among male economists. But with Jevons economics dropped its overtly punitive attitude toward poverty and accepted a seemingly more benevolent theory of the progress of the races, of savagery and civilization, of industry and idleness.

A history of gendered and racialized concepts in economic thought has yet to be written, though a number of scholars have taken up work in this direction. Cultural critic Regenia Gagnier's comparative study of economics and aesthetics in nineteenth-century culture has made visible some of the slips and exclusions built into early neoclassical theory.[58] The International Association for Feminist Economics (IAFFE), formed in 1994, has sought to encourage an ongoing critique of contemporary economic policy and theory. The IAFFE journal, *Feminist Economics,* offers a forum for researchers "challenging the merits of narrowly situated economic theories and research agendas."[59] Introducing the journal's debut issue, editor Diana Strassman argues:

> Whether engaged in discussing welfare reform, childcare, family planning, economic development, structural adjustment, domestic abuse, sexual harassment, discrimination, affirmative action, pay equity, family leave, or the feminization of poverty, feminists have initiated a sweeping debate on economic policy issues vital to the economic wellbeing of the majority of humans.[60]

Meanwhile, though a feminist and anti-racist revision of economic theory gains some attention in academic circles, the neoclassicists continue to
dominate the field. While the neoclassical defense of the free market tried
at the close of the nineteenth century to purge itself officially of moral
judgments about poverty and wealth, it becomes increasingly clear in the
1990s that such judgments still surround us. Debates in U.S. politics routinely rest on assumptions about moral character (witness, to be very brief,
the contempt for "welfare mothers," a code for the supposed economic irrationality of poor African-American women, and the reflex against funding for third-world aid agencies, while huge profits flow to the United
States from low-wage labor markets in third-world countries). It is because
of such racialized judgments, which continue to function in the metaphysical backgrounds of economic analysis, that I argue that perhaps the
most important consequence of an anniversary reevaluation of the Irish
Famine has to do with the economics of the event: that is, both the policies that caused it, and the theoretical positions it both demolished and enabled. Tracing gendered and racialized categories through the history of
economic thought is a crucial opportunity presented by Asenath Nicholson's work, and by the current renewal of scholarly interest in the Famine.

NOTES

1. More detailed publication history of Nicholson's works is provided in the
   excellent reissue of Nicholson's *Annals of the Famine,* a revised 1851 edition of *Lights and Shades of Ireland,* ed. by Maureen Murphy (Dublin: Lilliput, 1998); see Murphy's introductory essays, 5–19.
2. Ibid., 10.
3. A[senath Hatch] Nicholson, *Ireland's Welcome to the Stranger, or An Excursion
   Through Ireland in 1844 & 1845 for the Purpose of Personally Investigating the
   Condition of the Poor* (New York: Baker and Scribner, 1847), iii.
4. Ibid., iv.
5. Pedro Schwartz, *The New Political Economy of J. S. Mill* (London: London
   School of Economics, 1968).The quotation is from a letter to Harriet Taylor in 1854, which Schwartz takes as his epigraph for ch. 1.
6. Nicholson, *Ireland's Welcome,* 24.
7. Ibid., 25.
8. Samuel Beckett, *Three Novels by Samuel Beckett* (New York: Grove Press,
   1965), 69–74.
9. Nicholson, *Ireland's Welcome,* 25.
10. Ibid., 27.
11. Ibid., 28.
12. Ibid., 39.
13. Asenath Nicholson, *Lights and Shades of Ireland* (London: Houlston and
    Stoneman, 1850), 253.

14. Ibid., 254. A discussion of Nicholson's practices of visiting can be found in Margaret Kelleher's "The Female Gaze: Asenath Nicholson's Famine Narrative," in *Fearful Realities: New Perspectives on the Famine,* ed. Chris Morash and Richard Hayes (Dublin: Irish Academic Press, 1996), 119–130.

15. Nicholson, *Lights and Shades,* 254.

16. Ibid., 250.

17. Charles Trevelyan, "The Irish Crisis," *The Edinburgh Review* 87 (January 1848): 229- 320. Note, for example, the controlling metaphors of enlightenment and legibility in Trevelyan's pronouncement that "Irish affairs are no longer a craft and mystery. The abyss has been fathomed. The Famine has . . . exposed to view the real state of the country, so that he who runs may read" (214).

18. Nicholson, *Lights and Shades,* 251–252.

19. Ibid., 217 (emphasis in original).

20. Ibid.

21. Ibid.

22. Ibid., 218.

23. Ibid., 218–219.

24. Ibid., 220.

25. Boyd Hilton, *The Age of Atonement: The Influence of Evangelicalism on Social and Economic Thought, 1795–1865* (Oxford: Clarendon, 1988).

26. Like John Mitchel, whose 1847 volume *Irish Political Economy* reprinted Swift's pleas for the development of Irish manufactures, Nicholson also makes a historical case against the English restriction of Irish economic growth, and she mounts similar praise of Swift. See especially her discussion of Swift and eighteenth-century economic history in *Lights and Shades,* 99–104.

27. Ibid., 239.

28. Ibid., 244.

29. Ibid., 253.

30. Catherine Beecher, *A Treatise on Domestic Economy* (1841; New York: Schocken, 1977). On the publication history of Beecher's work, see Kathryn Kish Sklar's introduction to this edition, vi.

31. Catherine Gallagher, *The Industrial Reformation of English Fiction: Social Discourse and Narrative Form, 1832–1867* (Chicago: University of Chicago Press, 1985). The concept of metonymy is developed in Part Two of this volume, "The Family versus Society," especially in Gallagher's discussion of Dickens's *Hard Times.*

32. Nicholson, *Lights and Shades,* 7.

33. Nicholson, *Ireland's Welcome,* 187.

34. Nicholson, *Lights and Shades,* 272.

35. Ibid. (emphasis in original).

36. Ibid., 428.

37. Ibid., 427.

38. Jean-Jacques Rousseau, "Essay on the Origin of Languages," in *On the Origin of Language,* trans. John H. Moran and Alexander Gode (New York:

Ungar, 1966), 57. See especially ch. 3, "That the First Language had to be Figurative." I have drawn here on Jacques Derrida's reading of Rousseau's "Essay" in *Of Grammatology,* trans. Gayatri Chakravorty Spivak (Baltimore: Johns Hopkins University Press, 1974): Part 3.2. Shelley's ideas on the original poetry of human speech are in his "Defense of Poetry" in *Shelley's Poetry and Prose,* ed. Donald H. Reiman and Sharon B. Powers (New York: Norton, 1977), 478–510. For a history of European philosophies of language in the eighteenth and nineteenth centuries, see the work of Hans Aarselff, From *Locke to Saussure: Essays on the Study of Language and Intellectual History* (Minneapolis: University of Minnesota Press, 1982) and *The Study of Language in England, 1780–1860* (Princeton: Princeton University Press, 1967).

39. Nicholson, *Lights and Shades,* 206.
40. The phrase is Wordsworth's, from "Ode: Intimations of Immortality from Recollections of Early Childhood," line 64.
41. Nicholson, *Lights and Shades,* 206.
42. Davis's pivotal articulation of a cultural nationalism is first laid out in his "Young Irishman of the Middle Classes," a talk delivered to the undergraduate Historical Society at Trinity College, 1840, in *Essays of Thomas Davis,* ed. D. J. O'Donoghue. (New York: Lemma, 1974), 151.
43. David Lloyd, *Nationalism and Minor Literature: James Clarence Mangan and the Emergence of Irish Cultural Nationalism* (Berkeley: University of California Press, 1987), 76.
44. For this program, see Davis's "Udalism and Feudalism," in *Essays of Thomas Davis,* 528–529.
45. Auguste Comte, *The Essential Comte,* ed. Stanislav Andreski (London: Croom Helm, 1974), 27. Discussion of Comte's impact on Mill can be found in W. J. Ashley's Introduction to Mill's *Principles of Political Economy with their Applications to Social Philosophy,* ed. W. J. Ashley (London: Longman, 1915) xii; and in Schwartz, *New Political Economy,* 634.
46. John Stuart Mill, *A System of Logic,* in *Collected Works of John Stuart Mill,* ed. F. E. L. Priestly (Toronto: University of Toronto Press, 1967), 8:864.
47. Ibid., 904.
48. See Richard Ned Lebow, "J. S. Mill and the Irish Land Question," in *John Stuart Mill on Ireland* (Philadelphia: Institute for the Study of Human Issues, 1979), 322.
49. Thomas A. Boylan and Timothy P. Foley, *Political Economy in Colonial Ireland: The Propagation and Ideology of Economic Discourse in the Nineteenth Century* (London: Routledge, 1992).
50. Quoted in Boylan and Foley, 138.
51. S. B. Cook, *Imperial Affinities: Nineteenth Century Analogies and Exchanges between India and Ireland* (New Dehli: Sage, 1993).
52. Mill, *Principles of Political Economy,* 170.
53. Ibid., 165. In the earlier *Logic* Mill had referred to his projected discipline of political ethology as "a theory of the *causes* which determine the type

of character belonging to a people or to an age" (905, my emphasis). Thus he seemed to advocate a study of what today one might call subject formation: that is, how certain material and ideological conditions produce and replicate cultural characteristics on an individual and social level. However, his application of this method in the *Political Economy* is much more ambiguous. Here Mill's discussion of the "desire to accumulate" comes within Book One, on the *a priori* "laws" of production, laws that "partake of the character of physical truths" (199). While he had suggested earlier that social institutions like government and education produce the economic "character" of a nation, he indicates in the *Political Economy* that character itself causes disparities of wealth, functioning as part of the "physics" of production that precedes human intervention:

> there is, in different portions of the human race, a greater diversity than is usually adverted to, in the strength of the effective desire of accumulation. A backward state of general civilization is often more the *effect* of deficiency in this particular, than in many others that attract more attention. (167, my emphasis)

54. William Stanley Jevons, *The Theory of Political Economy,* 5th ed. (New York: Kelley and Millman, 1957), v–vi, xv–xvi.
55. Ibid., 14.
56. Ibid., 34.
57. Ibid., 35.
58. Regenia Gagnier, "On the Insatiability of Human Wants: Economic and Aesthetic Man." *Victorian Studies* 36 (1993): 125–153. I also work toward a critical genealogy of neoclassical economic thought in my "Technologies of Debt: Bank Finance and the Subject of Economic Thought." *New Orleans Review* 24 (Summer 1998): 14–22.
59. Diana Strassman, "Creating a Forum for Feminist Economic Inquiry?" *Feminist Economics* 1 (Spring 1995): 4.
60. Ibid. An excellent introduction to the aims of a feminist economics can be found also in the anthology edited by Marianne A. Ferber and Julie A. Nelson: *Beyond Economic Man: Feminist Theory and Economics* (Chicago: Chicago University Press, 1993).

Chapter Nine

Spinners and Spinning in the Political Economy of Pre-Famine Ireland: Evidence from County Cavan

Jane Gray

The question of de-industrialization after the Act of Union continues to be a central theme in contemporary scholarship on the economy of pre-Famine Ireland. While there is sharp disagreement on its causes, extent and character, scholars agree that the loss of income from spinning linen yarn by hand was a significant dimension of the process. As prices for their yarn declined, handspinners increased the intensity and duration of their labor, snatching more time for the wheel from the interstices of their daily routines, and working into the night. But de-industrialization was neither sudden nor unilinear. In a recent article Frank Geary calculated that "the process of replacement of handspun by mill-spun yarn to 1850 was less than half complete by 1839." In other words, the spinning mills could not have supplied sufficient yarn to produce the volume of cloth exported from Ireland. Who were the women who made up the difference, and why were they willing to work so hard at producing yarn that sold for little more than the price of raw flax? In this chapter I present evidence from a sample of the surviving 1821 census manuscripts for County Cavan in an effort to locate spinners and spinning in the political economy of the pre-Famine era. I suggest that despite the shortcomings of these documents in relation to the reporting of female occupations, it is possible to make reasonable inferences about the variable significance of spinning in different household types and in different localities. I argue that the embeddedness of spinning in the self-provisioning activities of rural households is a central feature of proto-industrialization in Ireland, and thus has key implications for understanding the protracted and uneven nature of de-industrialization in the countryside. The chapter begins with a brief, critical discussion of the scholarship on proto-industrialization in order to lay the theoretical background for the empirical discussion and analysis that follow.[1]

GENDER AND PROTO-INDUSTRIAL DIVERSITY

The theoretical perspective adopted in this chapter is based on a critical assessment of the "demo-economic" model of proto-industrialization developed by Peter Kriedte, Hans Medick, and Jürgen Schlumbohm. They argued that increased demand for labor in cottage industry lifted the restrictions on marriage and household-formation that were an integral part of the European peasant system. The dynamic of proto-industrial growth inhered in the "peculiarly stable and at the same time flexible" relationship between the profit-oriented merchant and consumption-oriented household. Merchants reaped a "differential profit," because household producers who retained access to small plots of land provided part of the cost of their own subsistence and reproduction. Moreover, their willingness to engage in "self-exploitation,"—that is, to increase the amount of labor allocated to manufacturing when prices declined—enabled merchants to meet the rapidly growing demand for low-cost goods, especially textiles. On the other hand, the related tendency of household producers to withdraw their labor, when higher prices enabled them to meet their consumption targets with less effort, operated as a constraint on proto-industrial growth that was eventually transcended by the introduction of centralized, mechanized forms of production. Industrialization thus led to de-industrialization in many formerly proto-industrial regions. Household producers who could not revert to agricultural production attempted to survive by ever increasing self-exploitation, sometimes leading to great misery. Empirical research over two decades has uncovered a great deal of diversity in the paths followed by rural industrial regions. Neither the tendency toward population growth nor the tendency toward immiseration has been found to be universal. Current scholarship aims to identify principles of differentiation in the proto-industrialization process. Here I focus on arguments that have highlighted the significance of gender.[2]

From the beginning the labor of women and children has been recognized as central to the dynamic of proto-industrial growth. According to Hans Medick it provided the crucial marginal work effort that made possible the super-exploitation of proto-industrial households. In the "ideal-type" household it was the capacity of women and children to expand and contract their labor input to the manufacturing process that facilitated the flexible relationship between merchants and producers. Ulrich Pfister has recently observed that theories of proto-industrialization assume the existence of a dualism between a market and a subsistence sector, which implies the possibility of "under-utilized factors." At the level of the individual household, it is primarily women's labor that is subject to under-employment. It must be recognized, however, that under-employment is socially defined. I have argued elsewhere that because women's work was ideologically associated with the daily reproduction of the household, it was more expandable than men's: women were expected to make time for spinning in the interstices of their household activities. Men's underemployment, on the other hand, was generally defined in seasonal terms—weaving was often carried on during slack periods in the agricultural year.[3]

Case studies of European proto-industrial regions have shown that proto-industrial households were not always integrated production units. In cases where only some members of the household were engaged in manufacturing activities, or where different household members were engaged in unrelated manufacturing activities, the gender composition of the labor force could have significant consequences for household dynamics and the pattern of proto-industrial growth. Based on her research in northern France, Gay Gullickson argued that where work in commercial agriculture was available for men, and proto-industrial activities were confined mainly to women, the predicted fall in marriage age and population increase did not occur. Addressing the problem from a different perspective, Pfister has suggested that the gender composition of the proto-industrial labor force depended on the productivity of labor in manufacturing relative to that in agriculture. Where it was low, proto-industrial growth occurred through geographical expansion, and manufacturing tended to be confined to women and children. Under these circumstances "Household dynamics remain largely unchanged and consequently, increases in overall output are not accompanied by population growth." Where it was high, on the other hand, proto-industrial growth could occur through the allocation of greater amounts of household labor to manufacturing activities, and consequently "gender- and age-specific work roles follow a greater variety of patterns." Under these circumstances proto-industrialization was sometimes accompanied by population growth in the manner predicted by the theory.[4]

Pfister noted that mature proto-industrial systems were often characterized by the first variant at their peripheries, and the second at their cores. He attributed this to transaction costs, but in an important article on the Irish case, Brenda Collins pointed out that the gender division of labor could itself lead to regional differentiation in proto-industrial systems. Individual household production units were often subject to labor imbalances because spinning was so much more labor-intensive than weaving. Using evidence from some 1821 census manuscripts for Cavan, Collins argued that households attempted to make up for a shortfall of female labor by employing kin and "itinerant" spinners. Ultimately, however, the weaving districts became partly dependent on the "yarn counties" of northwest Ireland to meet their needs. Pfister treats gender as exogenous to his model of proto-industrial growth—the allocation of women to low-productivity tasks is not problematized. But spinning and weaving are not simply different tasks; they are stages in a subdivided labor process. Elsewhere I have argued that the gendered allocation of these tasks within linen-manufacturing households had direct consequences for the overall development of the industry, including the emergence of cores and peripheries. The yarn trade within Ireland was a form of "unequal exchange," because households in the weaving districts were able to draw on the cheap and expandable labor of women and children in the yarn districts, the cost of which was supplemented by their own and their men's labor in subsistence production.[5]

LOCATING SPINNING IN THE
PRE-FAMINE ECONOMY: LOCAL CONTEXTS

According to Kevin Whelan four regional archetypes may be distinguished in eighteenth-century Ireland: the pastoral, the tillage, the small farm and the proto-industrial. Cavan was an integral part of Ireland's proto-industrial zone centered on the linen market of Armagh to the north, but encompassing most of Ulster and parts of north-Connacht and north-Leinster. This zone was characterized by relatively poor land occupied by small-farm households that combined agricultural production with spinning and weaving linen yarn and cloth. Within the proto-industrial zone it is possible to distinguish three main sectors: a core weaving district centered on the "linen triangle" delimited by the towns of Dungannon, Belfast, and Newry; an outer weaving district stretching to the west and south of the triangle, and including much of County Cavan; and a surrounding peripheral sector integrated to the proto-industrial zone primarily through spinning.[6]

In the early part of the eighteenth century, demand for produce and domestic cows from the linen triangle led to a surge of agricultural improvement throughout south Ulster. At this time the linen industry in Cavan seems to have been concentrated along the banks of the River Erne in the north-central part of the county. Belturbet was described as

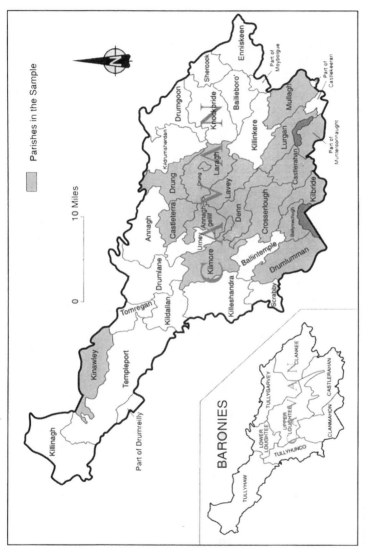

Map 9.1

the most important linen market in Cavan in 1739, but by the second half of the century it had clearly been displaced by Cootehill to the east, although Cavan town remained the principal yarn market in the county. When Arthur Young visited this area in 1776, he found that the linen manufacture "consists principally in spinning, which is universal all over the county for girls and women." In 1783 some linens were still sold at fairs in Cavan, Ballyconnell, and Ballyhaise, but Cootehill accounted for 76 percent of the value of all linens sold in the county. There was a secondary linen market at Killashandra, in the southwest of the county. According to William Crawford widespread crop failure and cattle losses at the middle of the century had contributed to the spread of linen weaving beyond its Protestant base throughout the religious and social hierarchy.[7]

In 1796 the Trustees of the Linen Board in Ireland instituted an extra-ordinary, once-off scheme to promote the cultivation of flax: for each rood of flaxseed sown, they distributed a spinning wheel. The published "List of Persons to whom Premiums . . . have been adjudged" gives an indication of the spatial distribution of flax cultivation and spinning in County Cavan at the end of the eighteenth century (see Table 9.1 and Map 9.1). As elsewhere in Ireland, the great majority of claims (almost 90 percent) were for just one wheel. Smyth has pointed out that a rood of flax would have provided approximately enough raw material to absorb the spinning capacity of an individual household.

In County Cavan, two parishes adjacent to the major linen markets made the greatest number of claims. Focusing on those parishes where more than a hundred wheels were awarded, two zones of flax-cultivation and spinning may be identified. The first, stretching from Annagh to Drumgoon, corresponds to the northern proto-industrial zone described above. The second zone comprises a southwestern arc, stretching from Killashandra to Munterconnaught. It is noticeable that in the latter set of parishes, the proportion of claims for two or more wheels tended to be slightly higher than in the former. For example, the ratio of claimants to wheels in Kildrumsherdan was 1:1.06, whereas in Kilbride, at the other extreme, it was 1:1.46. Those parishes claiming smaller numbers of wheels comprised a third zone, stretching across the center of the county from Kilmore to Enniskeen (the exception is Bailieborough). There appear to have been no claims from the northwestern barony of Tullyhaw, which may therefore be described as a fourth zone. The four zones correspond remarkably well to the nineteenth-century landscapes that P. J. Duffy has traced to the seventeenth-century Ulster plantation and Cromwellian land grants.[8]

At the end of the eighteenth century, the value of sales at Cavan's linen markets grew dramatically from £68,000 in 1783 to over £180,000 in

Table 9.1 Spinning Wheels Awarded under the Flax Premium Scheme in County Cavan in 1796, by Parish (Ranked by Number of Persons Awarded)

Parish[1]	Number of Awards for:				Total Persons	Total Wheels
	Four Wheels	Three Wheels	Two Wheels	One Wheel		
Kildrumsherdan	0	2	16	296	314	334
Killashandra	2	2	14	177	195	219
Kilbride	4	12	40	110	166	242
Crosserlough	0	2	17	146	165	186
Annagh	1	1	9	147	158	172
Drung	2	2	6	135	145	161
Drumgoon	2	3	9	107	121	142
Ballintemple	0	1	15	102	118	135
Munterconnaught	3	4	25	73	105	147
Drumlumman	0	3	8	78	89	103
Bailieborough	1	4	13	58	76	100
Kilmore	1	2	2	66	71	80
Enniskeen	2	1	10	56	69	87
Castlerahan	0	4	17	41	62	87
Denn	2	0	4	54	60	70
Ballymachugh	1	0	2	56	59	64
Larah	0	2	3	54	59	66
Castletarra	0	0	4	53	57	61
Drumlane	1	1	4	51	57	66
Knockbride	0	0	1	47	48	49
Lavey	0	0	1	47	48	49
Killinkere	3	0	9	33	45	63
Annagelliff	0	0	3	35	38	41
Killan (Shercock)	0	0	3	34	37	40
Kildallan	0	0	3	29	32	35
Mallycoram[2]	0	0	8	23	31	39
Urney	0	0	1	26	27	28
Collumkill[3]	0	0	2	15	17	19
Lurgan	0	0	1	6	7	8
Total	25	46	250	2155	2476	2893

Source: County of Cavan. A List of Persons to whom Premiums for sowing Flaxseed in the year 1796 have been adjudged by the Trustees of the Linen Manufacture (Dublin, 1796).

Notes: 1. For convenience, I have altered the eighteenth-century spelling of parish names to conform to the standard spelling adopted in mid–ninteenth century, except where it was not possible to identify the parish in question.

2. I have not been able to identify this parish.

3. The civil parish of Collumkill is in County Longford. It is possible that in this context it refers to the adjacent parish of Scrabby, in County Cavan.

1803, when they accounted for eight percent of the total value of sales at open markets in Ulster. During this period there seems to have been an increase in the distribution of weaving in the southwest of the county, with the emergence of Arvagh and Ballynagh as significant markets. The output of yarn probably increased even more rapidly. In 1816 James Corry described Cavan as "a very great yarn county." Sales at the linen markets had begun to decline, however, as the industry entered a period of recession, and by 1820 they had fallen back to about £100,000 per annum. From the end of the eighteenth century, Cavan experienced a new wave of agricultural commercialization in response to sustained increases in corn prices during the Napoleonic period, followed by a period of crisis from 1816 to 1826, as prices dropped precipitously.[9]

The National Archives in Dublin hold manuscript copies of the 1821 Census Enumerators' Schedules for fifteen parishes in County Cavan. I drew two samples from the returns. The first consists of the population of households where at least one weaver was resident. The second is a systematic random sample of every fifth household where no weaver was resident. The combined data file (hereafter the 1821 Cavan sample) amounts to a stratified random sample of the population of enumerated households in the returns. For each household I recorded the number of acres reported, the total number of inhabitants, number of inhabitants less than twelve years of age, and number of inhabitants aged twelve years or more. For each inhabitant aged twelve or more years I recorded their relationship to the head of household, sex, age, and occupation.[10]

There is significant variation across parishes in the proportion of individuals for whom occupations were recorded by the enumerators. Three patterns can be identified. In one cluster of parishes (Castlerahan, Crosserlough, Kinawley, Munterconnaught, Lurgan, and Mullagh), more than 95 percent of all individuals aged fifteen years and older had an occupation recorded. At the other extreme, in a second cluster of parishes (Annagelliff, Ballymachugh, Castletarra, Drumlumman, and Kilbride), more than 50 percent had *no* occupation recorded. In an intermediary cluster (Denn, Drung and Larah, Kilmore, and Lavey), approximately one third had no occupation recorded. Across all three clusters almost all household heads and nonfamily household residents had occupations recorded.[11]

Women were far more likely than men not to have an occupation recorded; just 16 percent of men in the Cavan sample were without an occupational title, compared to 41.8 percent of women. Table 9.2 compares the distribution of occupations for men and women in the Cavan sample as a whole with that of the sub-sample of parishes where almost all individuals had an occupation recorded. It can be seen that just two occupa-

Table 9.2   Occupational Distribution of Men and Women Aged 15 Years or Older in 1821 (Cavan Sample and Sub-Sample of Parishes)

(i) Men

	Cavan Sample		Cavan Sub-Sample	
Occupation	Weighted N	Percent	Weighted N	Percent
Farmer	1432	30.6	474	28.4
Laborer	1421	30.4	746	44.7
Weaver	300	6.4	107	6.4
Spinner	0	0.0	0	0.0
Other Artisan	252	5.4	107	6.4
Servant	399	8.5	152	9.1
Other	124	2.8	53	3.7
No Occupation	751	16.0	28	1.7
Total	4679	100.1	1668	100.4

(ii) Women

	Cavan Sample		Cavan Sub-Sample	
Occupation	Weighted N	Percent	Weighted N	Percent
Farmer	133	2.9	55	3.3
Laborer	12	0.3	7	0.4
Weaver	2	0.0	0	0.0
Spinner	2023	42.6	1323	78.7
Other Artisan	48	1.0	30	1.8
Servant	515	10.9	205	12.2
Other	31	0.5	13	0.8
No Occupation	1985	41.8	47	2.8
Total	4749	99.9	1682	100.0

Source: Cavan sample.

tions accounted for most of the variation—that of laborer for men, and spinner for women. This yields an important insight about the nature of spinning as an occupation within the peasant family economy. Spinning was embedded within the everyday reproductive activities of the household. Proto-industrialization occurred when traders began to draw on existing consumption-oriented production in order to supply regional and overseas markets. In this respect spinning differed from weaving as a proto-industrial activity. Weaving was a *trade,* and thus for the 1821 census enumerators a clearly defined male occupation, in contrast to laboring, which

was a general title for sons and other male relatives assisting in the reproduction of the household—as spinning was for female relatives.

This distinction between spinning and weaving is further demonstrated
in Table 9.3, which shows that a substantial proportion of weavers—over
15 percent—could not clearly be identified as relatives of the head of
household. Over 6 percent were identifiably *unrelated* to the household
head.[12] By contrast, only 7 percent of spinners could not clearly be identified as relatives. On the other hand 9 percent of all spinners were relatives
who were not members of the nuclear family, as opposed to just over 3
percent of weavers. This may indicate that households tended to draw on
family and kinship networks for additional labor in spinning, whereas
weaving households were more likely to employ unrelated tradesmen.

Those enumerators who dutifully recorded an occupational title for all
adults, therefore, did not necessarily perform a service for historical soci-
ologists. All women span as part of their household duties, and spinners
were almost all family members before they were employees. In order to
determine whether or not a given parish was incorporated into the proto-
industrial zone through spinning, we would need to know either what
proportion of women's time was given over to spinning, or how important
the cash income from spinning was to household budgets in that parish.
Below, I attempt to develop a proxy measure for this. Before proceeding to
do so, it will be useful to summarize local and class differences amongst
weaving households, in order to provide a baseline image for comparison.
The summary below draws on a more detailed and extensive analysis of
weaving households that I have presented elsewhere.[13]

Table 9.3   Spinners and Weavers by Relationship to Head of Household

Relationship to Household Head	Spinners		Weavers	
	Weighted N	*Percent*	*Weighted N*	*Percent*
Head	112	5.5	709	52.4
Spouse	882	43.6	0	0.0
Son/Daughter	702	34.7	501	33.5
Brother/Sister	97	4.8	36	2.4
Other Relative	88	4.4	15	1.0
Other	80	3.9	93	6.2
Missing	63	3.1	143	9.6
Total	2023	100.0	1497	100.0

Source: Cavan sample.

Three main categories of households engaged in weaving may be distinguished in the Cavan sample. The largest category (33.9 percent) consisted of farmers with weavers resident in their households, most of whom were sons. These farmers tended to report larger acreages (median=9) than farmers without resident weavers (median=7). Amongst households headed by weavers, the census enumerators distinguished between farmer-weavers and weavers. Farmer-weavers comprised 30.9 percent of all weaving households. They tended to have smaller landholdings (median=6) than either category of farmers. Weavers comprised 28.4 percent of all weaving households. Almost 90 percent of them reported either no land or gardens of less than one acre. There were interesting differences in family and household composition amongst the three categories of weaving household. Farmers employing weavers tended to have larger households, to be more likely to employ servants or to have non-relatives resident, and (partly by definition), to have reached a later stage of the family life-cycle when all of their children were older than twelve years. Both farmer-weavers and weavers were more likely than any of the other main social categories (including farmers and laborers), to be in an early stage of the life-cycle, when all of their children were younger than twelve years. On average, farmer-weavers had higher mean numbers of children under twelve years than any other main social category.[14]

Weaving households (that is, households with at least one weaver resident) comprised 8.6 percent of all households in the area covered by the Cavan sample. Higher than average proportions of weaving households were found in the parishes located along an axis linking Cootehill to Killashandra (neither of which, unfortunately, is in the surviving records for 1821). Crosserlough, in the south-central part of Cavan, had the highest proportion of weaving households at 17.2 percent. The lowest proportions of weaving households (less than five percent) were found in the southeastern parishes of Kilbride, Lurgan, Mullagh, and Munterconnaught. The three types of weaving household were not distributed evenly across the parishes. Farmer-weavers predominated—that is, comprised more than a third of all weaving households—in the north-central parishes of Annagelliff and Castletarra, and in the northwestern parish of Kinawley. A combination of farmers employing weavers and farmer-weavers predominated in the east-central parishes of Drung and Laragh, and Lavey. Farmers employing weavers predominated in the south-central parishes of Dennand Crosserlough, and in Drumlumman in the southwest. It was not possible to identify a predominant type for Kilmore, but in other respects this parish was similar to Drumlumman. Landless weavers predominated in the southern parishes of Ballymachugh and Castlerahan.

Examination of the landholding structure revealed further, overlapping differences amongst the parishes in the sample. The north- and south-central parishes were characterized by relatively high degrees of land poverty, defined in terms of the proportion of households holding less than the sample median of seven acres. On the other hand, they had relatively low proportions of households headed by landless laborers. In the south-central zone, where the quality of land was poorer, there were proportionally more households at an earlier stage of the family life-cycle. The southwestern and southern parishes stretching from Kilmore to Mullagh were characterized by relatively high proportions of households headed by landless laborers. Within this zone, a number of further distinctions can be made. The western parishes Ballymachugh, Drumlumman, and Kilmore were characterized by higher than average proportions of weaving households. The southeastern parishes of Lurgan, Mullagh, and Munterconnaught were characterized by much poorer quality land. The northwestern parish of Kinawley may be considered part of a fifth zone. Here, while the average size of landholdings was quite large, the quality of land was extremely poor, and the proportion of households headed by landless laborers was relatively small.

Table 9.4 summarizes the spatial distinctions described above. Two observations may be made. First, the distinctions amongst parishes in the 1821 Cavan sample add complexity to the four zones observed in relation to the flax-seed premiums. Notably, in the parishes stretching to the south of Killashandra, proto-industrialization seems to have been grafted onto a local economy characterized by somewhat larger (and unevenly distributed) landholdings, and relatively high proportions of landless households. This is in contrast to the north-central parishes nearest to the market of Cootehill in the sample, where the landholding structure conforms more closely to the pattern predicted by the theory of proto-industrialization. The second observation is that spinning was far more widespread than weaving, both in spatial terms and in terms of its distribution throughout the population. The flax-premium data suggest that spinning may have been important in some parishes—notably Kilbride and Munterconnaught—where the proportion of weaving households in 1821 was very low. Moreover, if the degree of land poverty in the north-central parishes in the sample was caused by proto-industrialization, then spinning must have been the main factor in this process; while the proportion of weaving households in these parishes was higher than in the sample as a whole, they still represented a minority of all households (less than 10 percent).

Having identified the major patterns associated with weaving in the Cavan sample, we must turn our attention to the more difficult problem of identifying patterns of spinning. Table 9.5 gives three estimates of the

Table 9.4 Regional Variation in the Cavan Sample by Valuation and Household Economic Characteristics

Zone	Parish	Land Valuation (Pence per Acre) 1841	Weighted N	Household Characteristics (1821)			
				Weaving (%)	Main Weaving Type	Headed by Laborers (%)	Land Poor (%)
North–Central	Annagelliff	60	116	8.8	FW	14.6	31.7
	Castletarra	60	198	6.2	FW	13.8	34.2
	Drung & Larah	56	411	9.9	F/FW	9.2	34.0
	Lavey	50	163	8.7	F/FW	16.7	30.3
South–Central	Crosserlough	54	285	17.3	F	17.8	30.1
	Denn	52	164	14.1	F	6.9	30.7
South–Western	Ballymachugh	73	103	10.9	W	23.4	30.6
	Kilbride	73	136	1.5	—	33.2	19.4
	Kilmore	70	237	8.9	EQ	22.5	25.6
	Drumlumman	60	246	10.0	F	27.4	23.1
	Castlerahan	57	190	7.0	W	22.6	24.6
South–Eastern	Muntercon.	52	84	1.4	—	35.6	13.1
	Mullagh	48	158	2.7	—	22.8	17.4
	Lurgan	47	209	3.6	—	26.1	21.5
North–Western	Kinawley	17	97	6.8	FW	13.5	19.5

Source: Cavan sample; *General Valuation of Ireland, County of Cavan* (Newry: James Henderson, 1841).
Key: FW = Farmer–Weaver; F = Farmer; F/FW = Farmer and Farmer–Weaver; W = Weaver; EQ = Equal Distribution.

significance of spinning in each parish in the Cavan sample: the percentage of women reporting the occupation "spinner" in 1821; the percentage of young women in service in 1821; and the percentage of women reporting an occupation "ministering to clothing" in the published 1841 census returns.

The first estimate is obviously subject to the problem of differences in the rate of occupational reporting discussed above. Clearly, these figures must be treated with a good deal of skepticism, but it is nonetheless notable that there appears to be a correspondence between very high proportions (more than 70 percent) of women reporting the occupation "spinner" and low land valuation, where the proportion of households engaged in weaving was lower than average (the exceptions are Castlerahan and Crosserlough). This raises the possibility that the enumerators were more likely to record the occupation "spinner" in 1821 where it represented a significant source of household income, *relative* to that earned by men. By this estimate the most important spinning districts in Cavan were on the poorest lands, at a distance from the major linen markets, in the southeast and northwest of the county.

The second estimate represents an attempt to gauge the importance of spinning in the local economy by examining the proportion of young women in service. In pre-Famine Cavan, just as elsewhere in pre-industrial Europe, service was a regular feature of the individual life-cycle, especially for women. In the 1821 Cavan sample, about one in five women between the ages of 15 and 24 were servants—that is, in the years before they married and set up households of their own. According to proto-industrialization theory, in areas where income was available from manufacturing activity, small-holders were less likely to send their daughters into service and more likely to maximize the labor capacity of their households. In parishes where spinning was vital to the family economy, then, we would expect to find lower proportions of young women in service. However, this is not a perfect proxy for spinning, as rates of service were also affected by household life cycle. Households where the wife was young, and in all probability pregnant, or caring for young children, were more likely to employ servants than households where the wife was older, and where at least some of the children were old enough to assist in household duties. Thus a low proportion of households in an early stage of the life-cycle might independently lead to lower proportions of young women in service.

A glance at Table 9.5 suggests that, in 1821, the proportion of young women in service tended to be lower in the core weaving parishes, especially in those parishes closest to Cootehill, where the farmer-weaver type prevailed. This is what the proto-industrialization thesis would lead us to expect. Conversely, the proportion of young women in service tended to

Table 9.5 Estimates of the Distribution of Spinning in the Cavan Sample Area, 1821–1841

Zone	Parish	Land Valuation (Pence per Acre) 1841	Individuals Reporting Occupation "Spinner" 1821 (%)	Women Aged 15–24 in Service 1821 (%)	Women "Ministering to Clothing" 1841 (%)
North-Central	Annagelliff	60	4.9	18.7	55.0
	Castletarra	60	4.9	17.5	42.8
	Drung & Larah	56	14.8	22.1	58.9
	Lavey	50	22.1	15.6	50.3
South-Central	Crosserlough	54	40.4	28.2	38.9
	Denn★	52	19.1	Missing	40.9
South-Western	Ballymachugh	73	1.0	29.1	29.7
	Kilbride	73	0.2	22.9	23.8
	Kilmore	70	26.8	18.4	23.0
	Drumlumman	60	0.0	22.7	43.9
	Castlerahan	57	39.0	23.9	34.6
South-Eastern	Munterconn.	52	35.8	26.2	40.3
	Mullagh★★	48	41.0	17.0	18.1
	Lurgan	47	40.4	26.2	31.5
North-Western	Kinawley	17	37.3	23.7	56.4

Source: Cavan sample; House of Commons, "Census of Ireland, 1841," *Parliamentary Papers,* 1843, vol. 24, pp. 411–416.

Notes: ★The enumerator for the parish of Denn failed to distinguish between servants and other unrelated household residents.

★★The percentage of women for whom an occupation was recorded in Mullagh (28%) was particularly low in 1841, suggesting a greater degree of error in this case.

be higher in those parishes where the proportion of weaving households was low, or where weaving occurred in the context of relatively high proportions of landless laborers. However, there are many anomalies and the pattern is far from straightforward. The first problem is that the enumerator for Denn failed to distinguish servants from other household residents, for whom a relationship to the head of household was unstated, so that this case has to be considered missing. The second problem is that Kilmore and Mullagh are anomalous cases: both have much lower proportions of young women in service than the parishes to which they are otherwise similar. Finally, Crosserlough represents a contradictory case, insofar as the proportion of young women in service in this parish was higher than in any of the parishes where the proportion of weaving households was low, despite the fact that Crosserlough is otherwise similar to the core weaving parishes (and indeed had the highest proportion of weaving households in the sample). This measure, like the first one, seems to be a less than satisfactory indicator of the significance of spinning in the local economy. Nonetheless it may highlight aspects of the importance of women's labor to the household economy that were not reflected in the recording of occupational titles. This impression receives some support when both indicators from 1821 are compared with data from the 1841 census.

Many commentators have argued that outlying weaving counties like Cavan were already in the midst of de-industrialization by 1825. Thus according to Liam Kennedy, "It is likely that a substantial decline in the numbers of weaving households occurred within the period 1815–40 in many parts of Cavan and Monaghan." The Ordnance Survey Memoirs for Drumgoon and Kildrumsherdan, dating from 1835, indicate that weaving was much reduced in extent and profitability, while in Drung and Larah it was said to be "almost extinct." However, Collins has pointed to reports of increasing sales at Cavan's linen markets in the late 1830s and 1840s. As I indicate below, this is consistent with evidence of a strong recovery in Irish linen exports during this period.[15]

The published returns from the 1841 census provide a detailed breakdown of occupations by county, but unfortunately give only an aggregate breakdown by broad category at the parish level. However, in the detailed data for County Cavan, more than 90 percent of all women reporting an occupation under the category heading of "ministering to clothing" were spinners, so it seems likely that this category represents a reasonable proxy for spinning. Like the census of 1821, the 1841 census consistently underreported occupations for women. However, the rate of reporting varied much less from one parish to another in 1841, suggesting that the figures may be more reliable.[16] Table 9.5 shows that in two kinds of parishes in the sample area more than 50 percent of all women reported an occupation "ministering to clothing" in 1841: first, the core proto-industrial parishes (with the exception of Castletarra), where low proportions of young women were in service in 1821, and low proportions of households were headed by laborers; second, the northwestern parish of Kinawley, which was characterized by very low land valuation, and by very high proportions of women reporting the occupation "spinner" in 1821, together with a low proportion of households headed by laborers.

SPINNING AND DE-INDUSTRIALIZATION IN LOCAL AND WORLD CONTEXTS

Comparative analysis of parish data from County Cavan in the pre-Famine period has revealed a substantial degree of complexity in the social and spatial distribution of proto-industrial households, and in the significance of spinning in the local economy. This complexity can be explained by the uneven proto-industrialization of different parts of the county in the context of regional incorporation to the Atlantic sector of the world economy during the eighteenth and early nineteenth centuries. Uneven proto-industrialization led in turn to correspondingly different paths of de-industrialization.

In 1796, when the Trustees of the Linen Board distributed almost 3,000 spinning wheels in the county, the Irish linen industry had reached the culmination of a period of extraordinary dynamism. Linen cloth exports, at almost 47 million yards, had more than doubled since 1780, growing at an average rate of 8 percent per annum. This period was marked by an increase in the proportion of Irish linens destined for colonial markets.[17] Sales at Cavan's brown linen markets grew comparably between 1783 and 1803, and this period may have seen the emergence of new markets in the southwest of the county. The allocation of wheels by parish in 1796 suggests that spinning was concentrated in two zones centered on the main linen markets: along the northern border with County Monaghan, and along the southern borders with Counties Longford and Meath. Fewer wheels were claimed in the poorer parishes in the center and east of the county, and there appear to have been no claims from the remote, northwestern barony of Tullyhaw.

In the early decades of the nineteenth century exports of Irish linen cloth stagnated, and outlying markets like Cootehill and Killashandra in County Cavan entered a period of steady decline. The value of sales halved at each of the main linen markets in Cavan between 1803 and 1820. The 1821 census manuscripts reveal differences in the consequences of proto-industrialization in the two main zones, and the spread of spinning to new areas of poor quality land in the southeast and northwest of the county. In the sample parishes nearest to Cootehill, proto-industrialization appears to have followed a "classic" trajectory, leading to land fragmentation and the predominance of the farmer-weaver type of weaving households, but to lower proportions of landless households than elsewhere. Here, relatively low proportions of young women in service suggest the importance of women's labor in spinning to the family economy of farmer-weavers and small farmers.

By contrast, in the sample parishes nearer to Killashandra and its satellites to the south and east, weaving seems to have coexisted with larger landholdings and a more numerous population of landless laborers. Here the relatively high proportions of young women in service suggest that spinning was of less significance in the family economy of farmers, some of whom employed their sons as weavers. Finally, the 1821 census manuscripts suggest that spinning had emerged as an important source of income in two zones of poor quality land that were relatively remote from the linen markets, namely the southeast and northwest of the county. We cannot be certain that these areas were newly incorporated to the proto-industrial zone after 1796, but if this was in fact the case, it begs the question of why new spinning districts were emerging during a period of relative stagnation in the industry. Perhaps either high population densities or estate rationalization in lowland areas had caused displacement onto poorer lands where families attempted to survive through a combination of spinning and subsistence agriculture.

According to calculations published by Solar, Irish linen exports went through a prolonged depression in the late 1820s and early 1830s, followed by a recovery in the second half of the 1830s. Solar suggests that a jump in exports occurred in 1836 due to an increase in the price of raw cotton, which "gave the linen industry a chance to claw back sales from its arch rival" at a time when the American and British economies were booming. While the peak year of 1836 was followed by a sharp decline in 1837, exports recovered and remained strong at about 55 million yards per annum in the late 1830s and early 1840s. Cavan's linen markets may have experienced a temporary recovery due to this increase in demand. The period from 1821 to 1841 was marked by significant changes in the structure of the industry, however. The port of Belfast achieved near-monopoly in the export of Irish linens, and Liverpool, rather than London, became their principal destination. The proportion of linens sold at open markets declined as increasing numbers of weavers worked for large-scale manufacturers. During the 1830s mill-spun yarn began to displace the hand-spun product, leading to the slow concentration of the industry in the vicinity of the mills around Belfast.[18]

Despite the introduction of mill-spun yarn, women in many parts of Ireland persisted in their attempt to glean a "scanty profit" through "almost incessant application to the wheel" and, as we have seen, substantial numbers of them reported the occupation "spinner" to the 1841 census (almost 40 percent of all women in Cavan as a whole). The evidence presented in this chapter suggests that spinning remained an important source of income in two kinds of proto-industrial district during the process of de-industrialization: core districts where the farmer-weaver pattern had prevailed, and where the extent of land subdivision made a return to full-time farming unviable, and peripheral districts of poor-quality land that appear to have been incorporated quite late to the proto-industrial zone, and that were characterized by low proportions of households headed by laborers. By contrast the evidence suggests that spinning was never as important in districts of better-quality land where the proportions of households headed by laborers was relatively high, and that it may have declined in importance in those districts with high proportions of laborers on poor-quality land. O'Neill has argued that by the 1830s laborers were experiencing extreme poverty because of population growth and declining demand for their labor. He also found that in Killashandra in 1841, laborers' daughters were much less likely than farmers' daughters to operate unprofitable wheels. Increasing "application to the wheel" in the context of declining prices occurred primarily in small-farm households. These were concentrated in mature proto-industrial districts and in newly incorporated "yarn districts" on marginal lands.[19]

Commentators often suggest that women continued to spin because of the absence of any other source of employment. Thus according to Collins, "Although spinning was regarded merely as an alternative to idleness its production continued because the family labor which produced it was an invariable overhead cost." Similarly, Geary observed that "Hand spinners . . . did not receive a contractual wage; their earnings were realized when the household web was sold or when they sold their yarn. In this latter circumstance, constrained by a lack of alternative employment opportunities, they appear to have acted as price takers." No doubt if other sources of money income were available for women, spinning would have been more widely abandoned (or indeed might have been less widely taken up). But women were not "content to sit up in the evening without a light and charge little or nothing for it" because they literally had nothing to do. As laborers explained to the Poor Law commissioners, it was difficult for their wives to combine long hours of spinning with domestic responsibilities, and there is no reason to believe they differed from small farmers' wives in that respect. Women found themselves in the position Geary describes because the household division of labor consigned them to a low-productivity phase of the production process, and because in the prevailing ideology spinning was not distinguished from women's other household tasks, even when it was integrated into regional and international markets.[20]

The following passage from the Ordnance Survey Memoir for Aghalurcher, in County Fermanagh, is a particularly good illustration of the gendered construction of work and leisure in proto-industrial households in the context of de-industrialization:

> In the leisure time intervening sowing and harvest time the more industrious among the young men apply themselves to weaving coarse linens. Weaving, however, is not carried on to any great extent in this parish.
>
> The female part of the community invariably spin and earn but a very scanty profit for their almost incessant application to the wheel. The women, however, are not excused from the labors of husbandry, and during the more busy periods of the year may be seen with their husbands or brothers assisting in the business of farming. It is to be lamented that there does not exist other employment to occupy the spare time of the agriculturalist, which sad to say is too often spent in idleness and drinking. These remarks apply chiefly to the very small farmers, for to apply it generally would be doing injustice to a great proportion of steady, well-doing farmers.[21]

That women's "spare time" was invariably occupied by spinning, whereas weaving had been generally abandoned and most men had leisure for drinking, can only be understood in terms of the unequal gender relations that were an underlying feature of the proto-industrial family economy. Women continued to spin because their application to this labor-intensive task was the decisive factor both in the overall growth of the linen industry under proto-industrialization, and in the labor-consumer balance of individual proto-industrial households. The defining features of such households were first, that their economic activities were oriented toward "customary family subsistence and economic self-sufficiency," and second, that they retained access to small plots of land that went part of the way toward meeting those needs. Under de-industrialization, it made sense to suspend or abandon the more capital-intensive process of weaving, where in relative terms the loss of income was greater, in order to devote more labor to agriculture. The gender division of labor ensured that women (rather than men) compensated by increasing their "self-exploitation" in the labor-intensive process of spinning. By contrast, households in farming communities that were already more fully incorporated to the money economy might diversify into spinning and weaving under favorable market conditions, but because the underlying logic of household production was different, de-industrialization there had different consequences. Labor-

ing women whose households felt the brunt of "overpopulation" and declining demand for agricultural labor ceased to spin, not so much because
the cost of the equipment made spinning irrational (as O'Neill suggested),
but because their lack of access to land made it so.[22]

I have argued in this chapter that the extent to which spinning was embedded in the family economy of rural households determined both the
course of proto-industrialization and the experience of de-industrialization in the pre-Famine period. Using evidence from County Cavan, I have
shown that local differences in the significance of spinning depended
partly on the timing and mode of incorporation into the world economy,
and partly on distinct local features such as the quality of land. Underlying
these processes was a gender division of labor that created the possibility
of proto-industrialization, shaped its local and regional development, and
prolonged the process of de-industrialization in some localities. Finally, the
analysis adds complexity to our understanding of regional differentiation
in the development of the linen industry. Future research should explore
not just the emergence of core/periphery relations between spinning and
weaving districts but also the impact of the timing of incorporation into
the world economy through proto-industrialization, and the possibility of
differences amongst spinning districts.

NOTES

Some of the material in this chapter was presented at the European Social
Science History Conference, Amsterdam, 5–7 March, 1998. Research on
which the analysis is based was funded by the Woodrow Wilson Foundation Women's Studies Program, the Economic and Social Research Institute of Ireland and an Indiana University South Bend Summer Faculty
Fellowship. I would like to thank James Keenan for producing the map,
which was funded by a Publication Grant from the National University of
Ireland, Maynooth. I would also like to thank Marilyn Cohen and Nancy
Curtin for their comments. Any errors are my responsibility alone.

1. Frank Geary, "De-industrialization in Ireland to 1851: Some Evidence
   from the Census," *Economic History Review* 51 (1998): 512–541, 523. The
   de-industrialization debate centers on the question of whether or not the
   Act of Union, by introducing free trade between Ireland and Britain, made
   it impossible for Irish industry to compete. For discussions see Geary cited
   above and below, and Joel Mokyr, *Why Ireland Starved: A Quantitative and
   Analytical History of the Irish Economy, 1800–1850* (London: George Allen
   and Unwin, 1983), 278–294; Cormac O'Grada, *Ireland Before and After the
   Famine: Explorations in Economic History, 1800–1925* (Manchester: Manchester University Press, 1988), 25–36; idem., "Industry and Communica-
   tions, 1801–1845," in *A New History of Ireland, Volume 5, Ireland under the
   Union I, 1801–70*, ed. W. E. Vaughan (Oxford: Clarendon Press, 1989),

137–157. Geary has argued that loss of manufacturing employment in Ireland was "limited to the effects of technical change on flax spinning" up to 1851; see Frank Geary, "The Act of Union, British-Irish Trade, and Pre-Famine De-industrialization," *Economic History Review* 48 (1995): 68–88, 87; idem., "Regional Industrial Structure and Labor Force Decline in Ireland Between 1841 and 1851," *Irish Historical Studies* 30 (November 1996): 167–194.

2. Peter Kriedte, Hans Medick, and Jürgen Schlumbohm, *Industrialization before Industrialization: Rural Industry in the Genesis of Capitalism,* trans. Beate Schemp. (Cambridge: Cambridge University Press, 1981). For an overview of perspectives on proto-industrialization, and recent scholarship, see Sheilagh C. Ogilvie and Markus Cerman, eds., *European Protoindustrialization* (Cambridge: Cambridge University Press, 1996); Peter Kriedte, Hans Medick, and Jurgen Schlumbohm, "Proto-industrialization Revisited: Demography, Social Structure and Domestic Industry," *Continuity and Change* 8 (August 1993): 217–252.

3. Hans Medick, "The Proto-Industrial Family Economy," in Kriedte et al., *Industrialization before Industrialization,* 62; Ulrich Pfister, "A General Model of Proto-Industrial Growth," in *Proto-industrialization: Recent Research and New Perspectives in Memory of Franklin Mendels,* ed. Rene Leboutte (Geneve: Librairie Droz, 1996), 73–92, 75; Jane Gray, "Rural Industry and Uneven Development: The Significance of Gender in the Irish Linen Industry," *Journal of Peasant Studies* 20 (July 1993): 590–611.

4. Gay L. Gullickson, *Spinners and Weavers of Auffay* (Cambridge: Cambridge University Press, 1986); Pfister, "A General Model," 79–81.

5. Ibid.; Brenda Collins, "Proto-industrialization and Pre-Famine Emigration," *Social History* 7 (May 1982): 127–146; Gray, "Rural Industry and Uneven Development."

6. Kevin Whelan, "The Modern Landscape: From Plantation to Present," in *Atlas of the Irish Rural Landscape,* ed. F. H. A. Aalen, Kevin Whelan and Matthew Stout (Cork: Cork University Press, 1997), 67–103. For an authoritative discussion of regional differentiation within the proto-industrial zone, see William H. Crawford, "The Evolution of the Linen Trade in Ulster before Industrialization," *Irish Economic and Social History* 25 (1988): 32–53; see also Collins, "Proto-industrialization and pre-Famine Emigration."

7. Arthur Young, *Arthur Young's Tour in Ireland (1776–1779), Volume 1,* ed. Arthur W. Hutton (London: George Bell and Sons, 1892), 211. This account of the development of the linen industry in Cavan owes much to William H. Crawford, "Economy and Society in South Ulster in the Eighteenth Century," *Clogher Record* 8 (1975): 241–258. For the value of sales at Cavan markets, see William H. Crawford, *The Handloom Weavers and the Ulster Linen Industry* (Belfast: Ulster Historical Foundation, 1994), 78.

8. *County of Cavan. A List of Persons to whom Premiums for sowing Flax-seed in the year 1796 have been adjudged by the Trustees of the Linen Manufacture*

(Dublin: n.p., 1796); William J. Smyth, "Flax Cultivation in Ireland: The Development and Demise of a Regional Staple," in *Common Ground: Essays on the Historical Geography of Ireland,* ed. William J. Smyth and Kevin Whelan (Cork: Cork University Press, 1988), 234–252, 238; Patrick J. Duffy, "The Making of the Cavan Landscape," in *Cavan: Essays on the History of an Irish County,* ed. Raymond Gillespie (Dublin: Irish Academic Press, 1995), 14–36, 25.

9. *Minutes of the Trustees of the Linen and Hempen Manufactures of Ireland, containing the Reports of their Secretary on a Tour of Inspection through the Province of Ulster,* (Dublin: W. Folds and Sons, 1817), 62; Kevin O'Neill, *Family and Farm in Pre-Famine Ireland: The Parish of Killashandra* (Madison: University of Wisconsin Press, 1984), 72–85.

10. National Archives of Ireland, CEN 1821/1–15, Shelf Numbers 2/436/4–7.

11. I have calculated proportions of those aged 15 years or older in order to facilitate comparison with published data from the 1841 census. From this point onwards, "men" refers to males aged 15 years or older, and "women" refers to females aged 15 years or older.

12. That is, they were identified as journeymen, apprentices, or lodgers.

13. Jane Gray, "Incessant Application to the Wheel: Spinning and Weaving in Two Irish Counties, 1800–1840." Unpublished paper presented to the European Social Science History Conference, Amsterdam, 5–7 March 1998.

14. The acreages reported by the enumerators were probably not statute acres, but rather "Cunningham" or "Plantation" acres, equivalent to 1.29 or 1.62 statute acres. See O'Neill, *Family and Farm,* 42 and Terence C. Cunningham, "Notes on the 1821 Census of Lavey Parish," *Breifne* 1 (1960): 192–208. Since the reliability of farm size data in the 1821 Census manuscripts is uncertain, they should be treated as crude indicators of differences amongst social groups, rather than as accurate measures of the structure of landholding. The "main social categories" in the Cavan Sample were households headed by farmers without weavers resident (52.1 percent), farmers with weavers resident (2.9 percent), laborers (20.2 percent), artisans other than weavers (5.8 percent), farmer-weavers (2.7 percent), weavers (2.4 percent), spinners (4.0 percent), others (3.7 percent), and occupation unspecified (6.1 percent).

15. Liam Kennedy, "The Rural Economy, 1820–1914," in *An Economic History of Ulster, 1820–1939,* ed. Liam Kennedy and Philip Ollerenshaw (Manchester: Manchester University Press, 1985), 1–61; Collins, "Proto-industrialization and pre-Famine Emigration," 142.

16. There were two outliers in the 1841 data—Mullagh, where only 28 percent of women had an occupation recorded, and Lurgan, where 83 percent of women had an occupation recorded. Otherwise, the rate of reporting of women's occupations varied from 39 percent to 67 percent in the Cavan sample. By contrast, in 1821 the rate of reporting varied from 14 percent to 99 percent.

17. R. C. Nash, "Irish Atlantic Trade in the Seventeenth and Eighteenth Centuries," *William and Mary Quarterly* 42 (July 1985): 329–356, 349. Annual data on the volume of linen exports are published in Conrad Gill, *The Rise of the Irish Linen Industry* (Oxford: Clarendon Press, 1925), 341–343.

18. Peter M. Solar, "The Irish Linen Trade, 1820–1852," *Textile History* 21 (1990): 57–85.

19. O'Neill, *Family and Farm,* 148–149.

20. Collins, "Proto-industrialization," 142; Geary, "De-industrialization in Ireland to 1851," 535–536. See the testimony of Adam Finlay and John McCrome, laborers from the barony of Upper Iveagh in County Down, and "universal opinion" in the barony of Lecale, County Down. House of Commons, "Reports From Commissioners, Poor Laws (Ireland), Appendix D," *Parliamentary Papers,* 1836, vol. 31, pp. 93, 115.

21. Angelique Day and Patrick McWilliams, eds. *Ordnance Survey Memoirs of Ireland, Volume Four, County Fermanagh I, 1834–5: Enniskillen and Upper Lough Erne,* (Belfast: Institute of Irish Studies, 1990), 12.

22. Medick, "The Proto-Industrial Family Economy: The Structural Functions of Household and Family During the Transition from Peasant Society to Industrial Capitalism," *Social History* 3 (1976): 291–315, 299; O'Neill, *Family and Farm,* 149.

Chapter Ten

"A Girdle around the Globe": Spinning Transnational Bonds between Gilford, Ireland, and Greenwich, New York, 1880–1920 ◼

Marilyn Cohen

> The weekly spinning of the Greenwich company would put a girdle around
> the globe, while the quantities spun daily at the Gilford house would encir-
> cle it several times.[1]

INTRODUCTION

Although migration is integral to Ireland's cultural ethos, the dominant
contextual setting for most nineteenth-century research remains the post-
Famine rural west. Rural migrants formed part of a larger urbanization
process in which they left their native country to live in cities and towns
on both sides of the Atlantic.[2] Young single women comprised a large proportion of these rural Irish migrants in the late nineteenth and twentieth
centuries, and their numerical superiority has ensured them a visibility
apart from the reductionist familistic framework.[3]

The Irish female migrant remains, however, a "novel field of study."[4] The
depiction of the typical Irish female migrant as rural and often western reinforces a stereotypical dichotomous image of women's migration as a transition from traditional to modern life.[5] Such ideological and ethnocentric

assumptions dominated cross-cultural analysis of female migration until the early 1980s.[6] The extension of this model to late nineteenth-century Ireland appears logical, since women from the patriarchal rural west have been depicted as economically redundant, as repressed and oppressed, with little prospect for either marriage or employment. For these rural women, apparently left behind by the modernization process, migration has been interpreted as a pathway to modernity.[7] I will argue here that the modernization model lacks historicity, denies women's agency, and has little relevance in the industrialized northeast, where "modernized" women comprised the backbone of the industrial labor force in the linen industry from 1825.

Post-Famine migration patterns from northeast Ulster have been neglected by scholars, since employment opportunities for women and men in the linen industry often provided an alternative to emigration. Although scholars have recognized a link between economic cycles in the linen industry and older pre-Famine migration patterns between 1815–1830, there are no studies linking the fluctuating fortunes of the industry after 1880 with migration patterns.[8] Further, there are few studies of Irish migration that apply the transnational conceptual framework developing within anthropology: "Immigrants are understood to be transmigrants when they develop and maintain multiple relations—familial, economic, social, organizational, religious and political—that span borders."[9] This approach highlights links between transnational migration patterns and changes in the global capitalist system and facilitates the systemic comparison of continuities and changes in cultural values, strategies, ties between migrants and their native community, and the integration of macro- and micro-level factors influencing individual migration decisions.[10]

The transnational framework can be methodologically applied to the past by linking migrants from particular communities and households in the sending country to communities in the receiving country.[11] This chapter attempts such a study by linking 34 migrant households in two factory towns dominated by the spinning of linen yarn and thread: Gilford, County Down and Greenwich, New York between 1880 and 1920. It offers an interdisciplinary approach to migration combining record linkage with anthropology's emphasis on the experiences and social fields of real people, the significance of place, and human agency.[12] By locating migrants within fields of family, community, and work relations, the continuity and changes in social relationships during the migration process are explored.

The chapter's core questions emerge from the relationships among sex/gender systems, the economic development of a region, its connection to world capitalism, and migration patterns.[13] The Irish linen industry was from its inception an example of export manufacture, often characterized by a predominantly de-skilled, low paid, female work force.[14] How were transnational patterns of migration from Gilford to Greenwich linked to market changes in the export-oriented linen yarn and thread sector? What were the links between migration and the formation of male- and female-headed households in Gilford and Greenwich? What continuities and changes occurred in household strategies regarding residence, employment, and schooling? What were the significant indicators of social mobility, and to what extent did gender influence their definition and attainment?

THE IRISH CONTEXT:
GENDER, MIGRATION, AND THE LINEN INDUSTRY

Emigration rates from Ulster during the eighteenth and nineteenth centuries were intimately tied to economic fluctuations in the linen industry. After 1825, many young male handloom weavers migrated to North America when the productivity of wet spinning frames depreciated the value of handspun yarn produced by their womenfolk.[15] However, emigration from the parish of Tullylish in northwest County Down to America was reported in 1836 to be "very trifling in comparison with others."[16] Here alternative employment for displaced handspinners as handloom weavers, winders of yarn for manufacturers, and as operatives in the new yarn-spinning mill of Dunbar McMaster & Company existed. This new mill, which opened in 1841, was one of Ireland's largest, with a workforce of over two thousand by 1846.[17]

Despite Victorian familist cultural conceptions of respectable masculinity—defined in terms of breadwinning—and femininity—defined in terms of domesticity—the labor force of the linen industry was overwhelmingly female, and the family wage economy was a necessity. Although the typical female mill worker in Gilford was young, single, and living with her parents, low wages ensured that a significant proportion of households could not make ends meet without the earnings of wives and mothers. Further, as many young single women came to Gilford in search of work between 1841 and 1871, some lived on their own as boarders and others in female-headed households.[18]

Since women earned about half the wages of unskilled men, households headed by women faced formidable economic challenges. It was essential for all members to contribute to the household budget, especially since female-headed households were smaller than those headed by men. The vast majority of widows lived in nuclear family units augmented at times with descendent kin or boarders. Single women who headed households usually reconstituted families by living with sisters, brothers, cousins, or nieces.

Few widows and single women lived alone, since poverty was inevitable and state assistance for the poor was both minimal and stigmatized.[19]

THE AMERICAN CONTEXT:
THE LINEN INDUSTRY IN WASHINGTON COUNTY

Although linen did not dominate the economy of the American northeast as it did the Irish northeast, the influence of the northern Irish on the American industry in its early years was considerable. In the early eighteenth century, linen manufacture in the American northeast was improved "by a number of Protestant people from the North of Ireland who introduced better knowledge of the cultivation and manufacture of flax and the linen or foot wheel for spinning flax."[20] By 1842 increased demand and improved implements "gave an impulse to the business and the flax wheel thence forth-ward became an appendage to almost every farm house and cottage in the country."[21]

Southern Washington and Rensselaer Counties in New York State were the seat of flax production in America.[22] The village of Greenwich in Washington County was as typical of rural industrial settlements in the American northeast as was Gilford in the Irish northeast. Job Whipple of Rhode Island, who gave the town its first name, Whipple City, was one of several early Victorian entrepreneurs who sought suitable sites for textile manufacture in rural industrial locations in New York state dependent on water power.[23] His son-in-law William Mowry established the first cotton manufactory in the state at Greenwich.[24] By 1868, William Weaver and several members of the Cottrell family purchased property on both sides of the Battenkill River and organized the Greenwich Linen Company to manufacture "crash" and other linens. Heavy debt forced foreclosure of the Greenwich Linen Company in 1871, and in 1879, Hugh Dunbar McMaster of Gilford purchased the property and established the Dunbarton Flax Spinning Company valued in 1885 at £31,647.[25]

After the "linen boom" years of the 1860s and 70s in Ireland, the outputs of both linen yarn and cloth fell, resulting in increasing unemployment.[26] The opening of Dunbarton Mill coincided with this recession, and beginning in 1879, a steady stream of machinery and labor flowed over the next 40 years. The population of Gilford fell from 1,324 in 1881 to 1,199 in 1901, while the population of Greenwich rose from 1,231 in 1880 to 1,663 in 1890. Until May 1880, Hugh Dunbar McMaster was present to oversee the new mill. He was replaced by his younger brother John, age 30, who remained as general manager until 1888. John McMaster returned to Gilford, died three years after, and was replaced as manager by James Wallace. All of the machinery and most of the initial labor force were from

Gilford, and by September 1880 there were 125 employees manufacturing linen threads and light twines.[27] As with Dunbar McMaster & Company in Gilford, the specialties of the Dunbarton Mill were internationally recognized high-quality Irish flax threads.[28] The linen yarn, thread, and twine produced by the Dunbarton Mill were sent to all parts of the country from the shoe factories of Boston to the salmon fisheries of Oregon.

GENDERED STREAMS OF LABOR: THE CASE OF BOARDERS

Recent theoretical models relating to transnational migration lack an explicit gender dimension that would highlight differences in the social networks of immigrant men and women and their distinctive contributions to socio-cultural reproduction.[29] Evidence from the 1900 U.S. Census suggests that the typical migrant to Greenwich was in his or her twenties and single—men or women who migrated before marrying and lived as boarders or servants.[30] Although Irish servants have received considerable scholarly attention, there is little analysis of boarders and how they affected household formation and strategies on both sides of the Atlantic.[31]

In 1900, 8.7 percent of the total households in Greenwich were augmented with boarders. There were significant differences in the way gender mediated the connections among this residential strategy, local employment opportunities, and prospects for future independence. There were 118 male boarders in Greenwich, 11.9 percent of whom were from Ireland. Only five had linen mill occupations. Instead, we find these single males employed in a variety of occupations including agricultural laborers, skilled workers, salesmen, and professionals, suggesting cultural links between masculinity and choice of employment, geographic mobility, and independence.[32]

For example, in 1900, Samuel Brown and his sister Annie boarded in the household of Robert Emerson. At age 30, Samuel was a single theology student, while his sister, at age 36, worked in the Dunbarton Mill. Samuel initially worked in the mill and was the first employee to graduate from high school. He later married and became a Presbyterian pastor and a missionary in India.[33]

A larger proportion (27.8 percent) of the 67 female boarders were Irish, and many more of them were operatives in the local linen (17.1 percent) and knitting mills. There are multiple reasons why female migrants chose to board. First, women's wages in the United States between 1880 and 1890 were about 70 percent of those paid to adult men.[34] Male workers in cotton mills in 1890 earned a median wage of $1.33 a day, while females earned .91 cents a day, or 68 percent of the male wage.[35] Thus it would have taken longer for a single female migrant to afford her own accommodations.

Turning to socio-cultural reasons, at the turn of the century, Ireland was a patriarchal society, with adult single men and women characteristically remaining home until marriage. Data relating to occupations suggest that single women tended to remain in a given area. Such norms may have influenced a young female migrant to prefer residence with another household for the protection, security, and companionship offered by kin and former neighbors. Although the overlap between boarders and extended kin is impossible to determine, it is certain that some boarders were relatives, given the strength of sibling and cousin migration patterns among women. Many expected to live with and contribute to the households of kin until they could afford to make a residential change. However, even when Irish boarders were unrelated, they overwhelmingly chose to reside in Irish households. Many chose to live with former Gilford residents, sustaining ties with Irish networks while developing new ones in Greenwich.[36]

Lizzie Shillcock migrated from Gilford in 1892 at age 32 to work in the Dunbarton Mill. She initially boarded with former Gilford resident Joseph Chambers and still lived with him in 1900 at age 40. Although she remained a single winder in 1910, she rented a house and supported herself independently. When she died, she left her personal estate of $578 to her nephew.

Sarah and Robert Meek were siblings who formerly lived on High Street in Dunbarton with their widowed mother and siblings. In 1901 the household in Dunbarton was female-headed, consisting of two sisters, an illiterate unemployed brother, and a female boarder. Although Sarah at age 34 was present during the 1901 enumeration of Gilford, she had migrated to Greenwich with or soon after her brother Robert in 1880, numbering among the mill's first labor force. In 1892 Sarah lived as a boarder with Robert Emerson and worked as a twister. In 1900 she still lived with Emerson but was no longer living there in 1910. Sarah Meek died in 1914 leaving her $1600 estate to her brother Robert.

Sarah Meek's case reflects the persistence of kin ties between migrants in Greenwich and Gilford and how these ties were shaped by gender. The daughter of a widow since 1870, Sarah expected to have enduring obligations to her family. As a child she left day school as soon as legally possible, after Class 4, to begin working full-time. Although she left Gilford as a young adult, by remaining single and a boarder she was unencumbered by children, better able to afford travel between Greenwich and Gilford, and accumulated a personal estate nearly equal to her brother's.

Boarders enhance our understanding of female transnational migration patterns and strategies. Like servants, boarders were unmarried and relatively young, usually in their twenties and thirties, suggesting that individuals chose this option at a stage in their life cycle between young adulthood and marriage. Both servants and female boarders were members of surrogate families who provided a degree of sheltering, preserving their feminine respectability. Both were self-supporting and able to save money despite their small earnings. Both diversified household composition and contributed to the household's economic survival. Some boarders ultimately married or formed independent female-headed households.

GENDERED MIGRATION PATTERNS: MALE AND FEMALE-HEADED HOUSEHOLDS

By 1900 there were 1,071 total households in Greenwich with 16.9 percent of these headed by women.[37] Twenty-four percent of all female-headed households were of Irish descent. Several processes were at work in the creation of these female-headed households. First, migration often takes place in stages with one member initiating the migration chain. When married men migrate first, their households of origin enter a transnational stage that may endure for years. These households were female-headed, dependent upon wages earned by remaining members and remittances sent by those living elsewhere.[38] Ruth-Ann Harris's studies of Famine migrants confirm that husbands were more likely to precede their wives than vice versa.[39] In Greenwich 2.7 percent of households were headed by males who had migrated before their wives.

Although the data relating to average age at first marriage among Irish migrants in Greenwich (21.3 for women and 22.7 for men) supports the position that Irish women in the United States married more often and at younger ages than did those in rural Ireland, high rates of female celibacy persisted.[40] In Gilford and other linen dominated communities of east Ulster, higher rates of female celibacy are partly explained by employment opportunities that attracted a surplus of females. Continuity in labor market opportunities for women in Greenwich, partly reproduced this demographic pattern. Thirty-four percent of the total households included single employed women over the age of 30, and many households contained more than one single woman. Most unmarried women were sisters and daughters of the household head. Some eventually married, others remained in their father's or sibling's household, while others lived in separate female-headed households with kin or non-kin reproducing a wide-spread residential strategy known as "spinster, sister or sibling clusters."[41]

John, Mary, Bella, and Jane Giffen were the children of linen weaver Robert Giffen and Jane Jones of Drumaran, a townland surrounding Gilford. John was the first link in the chain leaving in 1882, followed by his three sisters from the port of Larne in 1888. In 1900 these single siblings lived clustered together in a rented house and worked in the Dunbarton

Mill. Typical of men, John was naturalized in 1894 before his single sister Jennie. Belle, typical of single women, remained an alien. Between 1900–1910 John married, his wife died, and he, along with sister Mary, returned to Ireland for a year. After returning to Greenwich in 1904, Mary married William McCune, age 30, and all three siblings again lived clustered together in a rented house headed by McCune. Jennie and Belle Giffen remained single, working in the Dunbarton Mill as a winder and preparer while John, who never remarried, worked as a hackler. In 1920 Belle, Jennie, and John were still living with William and Mary McCune. When Jennie died in 1941, she had accumulated an estate of $5,000.

In 1900, 24 percent of female-headed households in Greenwich were of Irish descent. The migration strategies of women who were members of female-headed households in Gilford were distinct in several ways. First, widows did not initiate migration chains as did male heads of household. Many were elderly with lives shaped by dependence upon a male breadwinner, domestic responsibilities and, after the death of their husbands, poverty. Instead, we find their children migrating to Greenwich on their own or with siblings, leaving their widowed mothers behind, dependent upon remittances and, at times, parish support.[42] Although many widows' sons eventually formed their own nuclear family households in Greenwich, their daughters were less likely to marry.

In 1901 Owen Murphy, the son of a widow, lived on Tandragee Road in Gilford and worked as a general laborer at Dunbar McMaster & Company. In that year, at age 24, he migrated from the port at Londonderry, leaving behind his widowed, unemployed mother Mary and two sisters. Owen's passage was paid by his maternal uncle, John McCann, and with four dollars he made his way to Greenwich. In 1910 Owen was a 29 year-old dye-house laborer who rented his home. He was married to Alice, a former Gilford woman, for seven years and they had one son, Owen Jr. Owen Sr. remained continuously employed at the Dunbarton Mill for 41 years.

Women migrating from female-headed households, particularly from widow-headed households, frequently did not marry, re-establishing instead female-headed households in Greenwich. For these women, "reformation of the sibling unit, or a portion of it, was . . . the way to reimagine the family unit in America. . . ."[43] Mary Mullan was a 60-year-old widow who lived on Castle Hill Street in Gilford and worked as a bobbin carter at Dunbar McMaster & Company. Widowed since the 1870s, she relied on the wages earned by her daughters Anne, Mary, and Eliza Jane. These girls had left the Gilford Mill Female Day school to begin earning wages before Class 4 and none remained in the Gilford Mill Evening School beyond Class 3. In 1883 daughter Anne migrated to Greenwich to work in the Dunbarton mill, and in 1900 she was 38, single, and a twister. Anne shared her rented house with a 28-year-old boarder Katherine Livery, a former Castle Hill neighbor who migrated in 1884 and also worked as a twister. Back in Gilford, Mary continued to live with her daughter Eliza Jane, while her two other single daughters—Jane, a spinner, and Agnes, a machinist—shared their own house on Sandy Row. Although Mary had maintained her household independent of parish support for over 30 years, by 1903–04 at age 65 she was typical of the aged poor receiving outdoor relief from the local Board of Guardians.

In male-headed households typically the male head or a son initiated the transnational migration process either alone, with his wife, child(ren), or sibling(s). Since men "naturally" were to assume the role of breadwinner, it was culturally appropriate for them to migrate seasonally or permanently in search of work. Male linen industry workers in Gilford also earned at least twice the wages of women. They were, therefore, in a better position to initiate the chain and later send for other members of the family. Further, elderly widowers were less likely to be left behind in Gilford. Although young single men often lived as boarders or with their siblings for a time, they were better able to lay the foundations for heading an independent nuclear, extended, or complex household as the following example illustrates. In 1901 William McCann was a widower and shoemaker living on Tandragee Road in Gilford with his four daughters and a son. His eldest daughter Jane worked in Dunbar McMaster & Company while daughter Bridget kept house. William's brother John (uncle of Owen Murphy) was the first link in the chain, emigrating in 1874. By 1910 John was married with five children and worked as a foreman in the Dunbarton Mill.

In 1896 William's son Arthur had migrated to Greenwich from Liverpool. In 1900 26 year-old Arthur had married millworker Mary Clark and was paying off a mortgage for a house valued in 1915 at $500. Prior to migrating in 1898, Mary had resided in Dunbarton on Hill Street with her widowed mother Elizabeth and two sisters, one of whom was deaf. At this time Arthur's 16 year-old brother Thomas also lived with him and worked in the mill. Between 1900–1920 Arthur held a number of occupations—a bleacher in a dyeworks, a foreman in an underwear mill, and a dyer in the Dunbarton Mill. He also supported six children, his 40 year-old deaf sister-in-law Elizabeth Clark, a single spreader in the mill, and helped finance and support the migration of his own siblings. In 1900 he paid the passage for his brother Patrick, age 14, who arrived with fourteen dollars, and sister Rose, age 19, with $7.50. In 1901 Arthur, Patrick, and Rose sent for their sisters Mary, age 9, and Sarah, age 7. Sister Bridget, his brother William, and father William Sr. also arrived in 1901. Only his sister Jane remained in Gilford.

By 1910 William McCann Sr. had reconstituted a household headed by him and kept by his daughter Bridget as in Gilford. While his sons Patrick and William married and moved into their own separate households by 1920, daughter Bridget, age 35, headed her own female-headed household after her father's death with her two single sisters Mary, 29, and Sarah, 28. Bridget and Sarah worked as shirt makers in the shirt factory and Mary remained a spinner and twister in the Dunbarton Mill for 31 years. Bridget, atypically for women, obtained a mortgage for a home. Sarah died in 1923 and left her personal estate of $500 to her sister Mary.

EMPLOYMENT PATTERNS: MALE- AND FEMALE-HEADED HOUSEHOLDS

Low wages ensured the persistence of the family wage economy with most working-class children leaving school at the earliest legal age to begin waged work.[44] Due to asymmetrical wages, and a higher proportion of co-residing women, economic interdependence was heightened in female-headed households with all members continuously employed.[45] An example is the household of Margaret, George, and Elizabeth Reid. In 1901 William J. Reid lived on High Street in Dunbarton. At this time, Margaret, William, and Eliza resided with him and worked in Dunbar McMaster & Company. Margaret was listed as the occupier of the house through 1908, although she and Elizabeth migrated to Greenwich together in 1907, followed by George in 1908. In 1910 the siblings lived clustered together in a female-headed household headed by Margaret with boarder Eva Mahon. All were employed. Margaret and Eva were spinners, Elizabeth a doffer, and George a laborer. George Reid and Eva Mahon soon married and had two children. Eva died after the birth of her second child and George returned to Ireland where he was decorated for gallantry during World War I.[46]

Employment patterns in male-headed households fluctuated with the wages and occupation of the male head. When the male head earned relatively good wages, as did machinist Joseph Henderson, wives and teenaged daughters could remain out of the workforce. Henderson, a machinist for Dunbar McMaster & Company for twelve years, was the first person to migrate from Gilford to Greenwich in 1879. Henderson married in 1882, was naturalized by 1885, and was one of the first migrants to purchase property and build his own house. He remained a machinist in the Dunbarton Mill for 54 years enabling him to accumulate a sizeable estate by his death in 1928.[47]

Men with secure lower paying jobs, such as flaxdresser Samuel McDowell, were more reliant on the wages of their children. In 1900 Samuel lived with his wife who did not work for wages, his two daughters, who were winders in the mill, and his son, who worked in the machine shop. Laborers were the least secure male occupation at the bottom of the wage scale. John Redpath, a laborer, migrated in 1888 with his wife Eliza and their four daughters. Although his wife was not employed, his four daughters worked in the mill with his eldest daughter Lizzie leaving waged work to keep house only after Eliza's death.

GENDERED INDICATORS OF SOCIAL MOBILITY

Analysis of vertical mobility among the working class should include in addition to occupations small yet meaningful indicators of security.[48] One indicator, as suggested above, is the employment of wives. In 1901, 20.7 percent of wives in Gilford were employed while census data from Greenwich suggests that the vast majority of wives were homemakers. Of the 34 households, only five had working wives, and of these, only one had co-residing children strongly suggesting that most women left waged work at marriage and nearly all left after bearing children. However, because the census does not include data concerning supplemental wage earning activities by wives, it under represents their income-earning contributions.[49] The presence of boarders is a clear case in point.

Robert Emerson migrated in 1880 and was a laborer in 1892. Although his wife was unemployed, all of his four children worked in the Dunbarton Mill, and a boarder, Sarah Meek, lived with them. By 1900 Sarah was joined by two other boarders, Annie and Samuel Brown and Robert's niece, Maggie Allen. Both female boarders worked in the mill. In 1910 Robert was a widower, living with his single son, his daughter, and no boarders. Clearly, caring for boarders was the responsibility of Robert's wife Martha, and after she died, the practice ceased.

Joanna Bourke argues that despite the labor-intensive nature of housework in the late nineteenth century, women in post-Famine Ireland consciously chose unpaid housework over paid employment. One reason is that control over the domestic domain, particularly the household budget, enhanced the power of wives vis-à-vis their husbands.[50] In Gilford both documentary and oral evidence suggests that a working mother was an indicator of poverty and an object of pity. Because women were wholly responsible for domestic work, a working wife had to accomplish her domestic duties after working hours and on weekends, eliminating leisure time.[51] The fact that so few wives with resident husbands in Greenwich were employed is culturally significant, particularly given the favorable labor market for women.

There are several explanations for the low proportion of working wives in Greenwich. In some cases the wages earned by husbands and children were sufficient to allow wives to remain at home. Another explanation is that the ideology of a better life in America was partly interpreted in terms of attaining gendered middle-class standards of respectability where husbands supported their wives and children. A third is that married women with children who desired employment were prevented from working due to a lack of suitable childcare. In 1919 the owners of the Dunbarton Mill attempted to attract more married women into its workforce by building a nursery to care for their children. Eight mothers took advantage of this service on the nursery's opening day. Located in a house close to the mill, the first and second floors had a parlor, a large activity room, a kitchen, bath, and a large porch on the front. The finished basement had five bathrooms with tubs, a shower, and laundry. Women were charged a nominal fee, too small to cover the expenses associated with food, a nurse, and an assistant. Oral evidence suggests that more married women entered the workforce henceforth, but data from the 1920 census is too early to prove a cause and effect relationship.[52]

In Ireland at the turn of the century, a combination of factory and education acts ensured that children remained in school until the Fourth Class or until age 12, when they could begin full-time work. Younger children could work part-time at age 11 as halftimers. In the United States, prior to 1889, children under the age of 13 were not permitted to be employed in a factory. By 1889 the age limit was raised to 14.[53]

Evidence from the 1900 U.S. census suggests that most Greenwich children did not begin earning wages until age 14. Only two 13-year-old children were listed as having linen mill occupations. Still, households relied heavily upon the wage contributions of children since all but one of the 14-year-old children were employed. By 1910 and 1920, however, the evidence suggests that Greenwich parents were keeping their children in school longer. All 14-year-old children are listed as in school with an increasing number of girls between 15 and 19 listed as in school with no occupations. Given the strength of the family wage economy and the opportunities for female employment in the spinning mill, this is a notable change. Although birth order probably was a significant factor in schooling patterns, the ability to support teenage children while in high school may represent a new strategy—providing selected male children with the opportunity for social mobility through education and enhancing the respectability of daughters.[54]

In capitalist societies an individual achieves shelter through the following means: production or self-building; the market, meaning renting or ownership; and inheritance or transfer entitlements. There is a growing literature demonstrating that home ownership confers a greater sense of personal identity, control, autonomy, and security than renting.[55] Scholars have also demonstrated the high rates of home ownership among the Irish in comparison with other ethnic groups.[56] In Gilford none of the working class could own their homes or property. Rents paid either to Dunbar McMaster & Company or to other principal landlords were relatively low, but all household budgets included rent payments. In contrast, sixteen of the linked male-headed households in Greenwich owned their homes entirely or were in the process of paying off a mortgage. The possibility of property ownership by members of the Irish working class in Greenwich was attractive because it represented a tangible increase in their standard of living and security.

"Personal circumstances" such as security of employment, wages, and assets are central to understanding a person's ability to command housing resources.[57] Such personal circumstances are, of course, never gender neutral. Scholars are beginning to address the relationship between lower incomes, housing costs, and access to housing among widowed, divorced, and single women.[58] Although these studies have concentrated on access to housing by female heads of household in contemporary urban regions, their explanations are applicable to the past.

In Greenwich the two principal means of housing entitlement among the working class—the market and inheritance—varied significantly by gender. Since the wages paid to women were substantially less then those paid to men, women were rarely able to obtain mortgages. Only two households headed by single women in Greenwich were able to obtain a mortgage for a home. The few single women listed as owning their homes usually obtained these through inheritance.

Finally, comparative and longitudinal evidence for the linked households between 1892–1920 suggests that in most cases the occupations of migrants were of a similar skill level as family members in Gilford.[59] In five cases, men who initially held working-class occupations in Greenwich, rose to low level managerial positions or skilled artisan occupations. In ten of the 34 linked households, first-generation male occupations indicate upward social mobility either into management positions, skilled artisan occupations, or shopkeeping positions. By contrast, in 1910 only two first-generation daughters had jobs (bookkeeper and teacher) requiring more skill or associated with a higher class or status than their parents. For some women upward mobility was achieved through marriage or inheritance. Since it was less culturally appropriate for single women to hold occupations involving travel, most female occupations closely mirrored local employment opportunities in the textile mills.

In 1888 Joseph Wilson, age 57, his wife Eliza (Sturgeon), and their children migrated to Greenwich. In 1892 Joseph was a laborer, an occupation that he retained, and all of his children worked in the mill. When he died in 1906, Joseph left personal property worth $1000 to his wife and six children. In 1892 Joseph's son Thomas and Thomas's wife and child lived with him. By 1900 Thomas, a flaxdresser, purchased and moved into his own house. This represented considerable security for a man who began working at age 9 as a half-timer in Dunbar McMaster & Company. By 1915 Thomas owned two houses and lots valued at $700 and $2500 and was a village trustee. In 1920 Thomas's 28-year-old son James was married and a foreman in the Dunbarton Mill. When Thomas died in 1943, he had worked in the Dunbarton Mill for 50 years and left his real estate valued at $5000 and personal property worth $10,000 to his wife. His son James remained a foreman for 33 years.[60]

After Joseph Wilson's death his single son William John headed the household. In 1910, at age 57, William John was a retail merchant specializing in groceries and had purchased his father's house. His single brother James, age 43, lived with him and worked as a clerk in the grocery store. William's two single sisters Minnie and Eliza also lived with him, but they worked in the Dunbarton Mill as a reeler and a winder. Their upward mobility was achieved through inheritance in 1915 of their brother's property: the house worth $1000 and the store valued at $1200. Until their death they lived together in a house on John Street close to their married sister, Sarah Reid (Wilson).[61]

CONCLUSION

The Irish who migrated from Gilford to Greenwich were no strangers to "modern" capitalist industry. Although industrialization in the Irish northeast provided alternatives to transnational migration for many, factory towns like Gilford, wholly dependent on the linen industry, were particularly vulnerable to market changes. In the 1880s, when the linen industry faced recession, long-distance migration from Gilford to Greenwich became a more rational choice than local migration within Ulster's linen conurbation.

The hope of a better life is usually a key motivation for migration, and the United States was a more open society in class and religious terms than Ireland between 1880 and 1910. However, comparisons between Greenwich and other nearby textile centers (Troy or Cohoes) with large Irish populations suggest that gender figured prominently in the attainment of a better life.[62] Although there were numerous small quality-of-life indicators of an improved standard of living and examples of upward mobility, low wages and limited opportunities for secondary education ensured the continuity of the family wage economy that tracked many working-class children into working-class jobs. For women in female-headed households—a prominent residential strategy among Irish migrants—there is little evidence of an improved life, since asymmetrical wage scales heightened economic interdependence and usually denied them such tangible rewards as home ownership. Rather, evidence points to significant continuities in material constraints, employment patterns, and residential strategies among female-headed households in Gilford and Greenwich. Although many single women were able to accumulate savings, the extent to which their money improved their own standard of living is unclear. Often it was passed on at death to others who benefited from the commitment of unmarried sisters to their families.[63]

Rethinking transmigrational patterns from a gendered perspective requires that we investigate women's and men's distinct roles in the global economy, both in their countries of origin and in the receiving country, and how their gender-specific roles in sustaining and transmitting transnationalized social commitments and networks differ.[64] Since the double class and gender oppression faced by women linen industry workers remained largely unchanged in Greenwich, models that explain Irish female migration in dichotomous teleological terms have limited explanatory value. Irish labor generally, and Irish female labor specifically, shared many characteristics and problems of cheap migrant labor elsewhere in the peripheries and semi-peripheries of the world economy.[65] The Irish linen industry's dependence on cheap, de-skilled female labor and export manufacture persisted throughout its history, as did mid-Victorian patriarchal familist constructions of gender.[66] Directions of cultural change and adaptation during the migration process should be posed as problematic rather than assumed, requiring historically specific analysis of locales and their connection to world capitalist development on both sides of the Atlantic.

NOTES

1. *Directory of Greenwich for the year 1894–5* (Albany: R. S. Dillon, 1895), 39.
2. John Modell and Lynn Lees, "The Irish Countryman Urbanized: A Comparative Perspective on the Famine Migration," in *Philadelphia,* ed. Theodore Hershberg (Oxford: Oxford University Press, 1981), 358.
3. Brenda Collins, "Families in Edwardian Belfast," unpublished paper presented to the Urban History Group of the Economic History Society annual meeting, University of Aberdeen, 1982; idem., "Irish Emigration to Dundee and Paisley during the First Half of the Nineteenth Century," in *Irish Population, Economy and Society,* ed. J. M. Goldstrom and L. A. Clarkson (Oxford: Oxford University Press, 1981), 195–211; Hasia R. Diner, *Erin's Daughters in America* (Baltimore: John's Hopkins University Press, 1983); Thomas Dublin, *Women at Work* (New York: Columbia University Press, 1979); Daniel J. Walkowitz, "Working-Class Women in the Gilded

Age: Factory, Community and Family Life Among Cohoes, New York Cotton Workers," *Journal of Social History* 5 (1972): 464–90; Daniel J. Walkowitz, *Worker City, Company Town* (Urbana: University of Illinois Press, 1978); Carole Turbin, "Beyond Dichotomies: Interdependence in Mid-Nineteenth Century Working-Class Families in the United States," *Gender and History* 1 (1989): 293–308; Carol Groneman, "Working-Class Immigrant Women in Mid-Nineteenth Century New York: The Irish Woman's Experience," *Journal of Urban History* 4 (May 1978): 255–273; Lynn Hollen Lees, *Exiles of Erin* (Ithaca: Cornell University Press, 1979); Maureen Murphy, "The Fionnuala Factor: Irish Sibling Emigration at the Turn of the Century," in *Gender and Sexuality in Modern Ireland*, ed. Anthony Bradley and Maryann Gialanella Valiulis (Amherst: University of Massachusetts Press, 1998).

4. Kirby A. Miller, David N. Doyle and Patricia Kelleher, "For Love and for Liberty: Irishwomen, Emigration, and Domesticity in Ireland and America, 1815–1920." Paper presented to the American Conference for Irish Studies (ACIS), Villanova University, April 1993.

5. David Fitzpatrick, "The Modernization of the Irish Female," in *Rural Ireland: 1600–1900: Modernization and Change*, ed. Patrick O'Flanagan, Paul Ferguson, and Kevin Whelan (Cork: Cork University Press, 1987), 162–180.

6. Mirjana Morokvasic, "Women in Migration: Beyond the Reductionist Outlook," in *One Way Ticket: Migration and Female Labour*, ed. Annie Phizacklea (London: Routledge and Kegan Paul, 1983), 13–14. For a critique of the modernization paradigm see James Jackson Jr. and Leslie Page Moch, "Migration and the Social History of Modern Europe," in *European Migrants: Global and Local Perspectives*, ed. Dirk Hoerder and Leslie Page Moch (Boston: Northeastern University Press, 1996).

7. Diner, *Erin's Daughters;* Fitzpatrick, "Modernization;" Miller, et al., "For Love and For Liberty;" Murphy, "The Fionnuala Factor," 92; Groneman, "Working-Class Immigrant Women;" Robert E. Kennedy, *The Irish: Emigration, Marriage and Fertility* (Los Angeles, 1973), 7, 84; David Fitzpatrick, "'A Share of the Honey comb': Education, Emigration and Irish Women," in *The Origin of Popular Literacy in Ireland*, ed. Mary Daly and David Dickson (Dublin: University College Dublin Press, 1990), 167–87; Pauline Jackson, "Women in Nineteenth Century Irish Migration, *International Migration Review* 18 (1984): 1004–1019; Janet A. Nolan, *Ourselves Alone: Women's Emigration from Ireland 1885–1920* (Lexington: University of Kentucky Press, 1989).

8. Collins, "Irish Emigration to Dundee and Paisley," 202; William Forbes Adams, *Ireland and the Irish Emigration to the New World from 1815 to the Famine* (New York: Russell & Russell, 1967), 51; Alan G. Brunger, "Geographical Propinquity among Pre-Famine Catholic Irish Settlers in Upper Canada," *Journal of Historical Geography* 8 (1982): 272; Patrick J. Blessing, "Irish Emigration to the United States, 1800–1920: An Overview," in *The Irish in America: Emigration, Assimilation and Impact*, ed. P. J. Drudy (Cam-

bridge: Cambridge University Press, 1985), 13; Dierdre M. Mageean, "Nineteenth Century Irish Emigration: A Case Study Using Passenger Lists," in ibid., 39–61; idem., "Ulster Emigration to Philadelphia, 1847–1865: A Preliminary Analysis Using Passenger Lists," in *Migration Across Time and Nations,* ed. Ira Glazier and Luigi de Rosa (New York: Holmes & Meier, 1986), 276–335; Cormac O'Grada, "Across the Briny Ocean: Some Thoughts on Irish Emigration to America, 1800–1850," in ibid., 79–93.

9. Nina Glick Schiller, Linda Basch and Cristina Blanc-Szanton, eds., *Towards a Transnational Perspective on Migration: Race, Class, Ethnicity and Nationalism Reconsidered* (New York: The New York Academy of Sciences, 1992), ix-x.

10. The exceptions are A. C. Hepburn and Brenda Collins, "Industrial Society: The Structure of Belfast, 1901," in *Plantation to Partition: Essays in Honour of J. L. McCracken,* ed. Peter Roebuck (Belfast: Blackstaff Press, 1981), 210–228; and Collins, "Families."

11. Cormac O'Grada, "Determinants of Irish Emigration: A Note," *International Migration Review* 20 (1986): 650–655; Timothy Guinnane, "Migration, Marriage and Household Formation: The Irish at the Turn of the Century," (Ph.D. diss., Stanford University, 1984); Timothy W. Guinnane, "Age at Leaving Home in Rural Ireland, 1901–1911," *The Journal of Economic History* 52 (September 1992): 651–674; Timothy J. Hatton and Jerry G. Williamson, "After the Famine Emigration From Ireland 1850–1913," *Journal of Economic History* 53 (September 1993): 575–600; Collins, "Irish Emigration to Dundee and Paisley"; Brenda Collins, "The Impact of Out-Migration and Emigration on Sending Communities: Examples From Ireland," in *From Family History to Community History,* ed. W. T. R. Pryce (Cambridge University Press), 169–180.

12. Walter D. Kamphoefner, "Problems and Possibilities of Individual-Level Tracing in German-American Migration Research," in *Generations and Change: Genealogical Perspectives in Social History,* ed. Robert M. Taylor Jr. and Ralph J. Crandall (Macon, Georgia: Mercer University Press, 1986), 311–321.

13. Carole Turbin, "Beyond Conventional Wisdom: Women's Wage Work, Household Economic Contribution, and Labor Activism in a Mid-Nineteenth Century Working Class Community," in *To Toil the Livelong Day,* ed. Carol Groneman and Mary Beth Norton (Ithaca: Cornell University Press, 1987), 47–67; idem., "Beyond Dichotomies."

14. Saskia Sassen-Koob, "From Household to Workplace: Theories and Survey Research on Migrant Women in the Labor Market," *International Migration Review* 18 (Winter 1984): 11–46.

15. Ruth-Ann Harris, "Characteristics of the Famine Emigrants as Derived from the Boston Pilot Newspaper's 'Missing Friends' Column," Paper presented to the ACIS Conference, Villanova College, April, 1993; William H. Crawford, *Domestic Industry in Ireland: The Experience of the Linen Industry* (Dublin: Gill & Macmillan, 1972).

16. House of Commons (H. C.), "Reports From Commissioners, Poor Laws (Ireland), Appendix F," *Parliamentary Papers*, 1838, vol. 33, pp. 335–336.

17. H. C., "Reports by Inspectors of Factories," *Parliamentary Papers*, IUP ser., *Industrial Revolution: Factories*, 1842, vol. 7; report by James Stewart; Public Record Office of Northern Ireland (PRONI), Census of Ireland, 1841–51.

18. H. C., "Board of Trade Report by Miss Collet on Changes in the Employment of Women and Girls in Industrial Centers, Part I: Flax and Jute Centers," *Parliamentary Papers*, 1898, vol. 88; ibid., "Report of an Enquiry of Trade into the Earnings and Hours of Labour of the U.K. Part I: Textile Trades in 1906," *Parliamentary Papers*, 1909, vol. 80; Hepburn and Collins, "Industrial Society," 216–217; Collins, "Families," 4; and Mary Daly, *Dublin: The Deposed Capital* (Cork: Cork University Press, 1984), 307.

19. Marilyn Cohen, "Survival Strategies in Female-headed House holds: Linen Industry Workers in Tullylish, County Down, 1901," *Journal of Family History* 17 (July-August 1992): 303–18; Hepburn and Collins, "Industrial Society," 216–17; Collins, "Families," 4.

20. J. Leander Bishop, *A History of American Manufacture* (New York: Augustus M. Kelley, 1966), 1: 330–333.

21. Ibid.

22. William T. Ruddock, *Linen Threads and Broom Twines: An Irish and American Album and Directory of the People of the Dunbarton Mill, Greenwich, New York, 1879–1952* (Bowie, MD: Heritage Books, 1997), 24.

23. *History of Washington County, New York* (1911; Interlaken, NY: Heart of the Lakes Publishing, 1991), 340.

24. Ibid.

25. Dunbar McMaster & Co. L'Estrange & Brett Papers, PRONI, D.1769/8/1A; E. R. R. Green, "Thomas Barbour and the American Linen Thread Industry," in Goldstrom and Clarkson, *Irish Population*, 217.

26. Emily Boyle, "The Economic Development of the Irish Linen Industry, 1825–1914," (Ph.D. diss., The Queen's University of Belfast, 1977), ch. 5.

27. Irish Census of Population, 1880–1900, PRONI; U.S. Federal Census 1880–1890.

28. Ruddock, *Linen Threads*, 7; *The Directory of Greenwich*, 39.

29. Constance R. Sutton, "Some thoughts on Gendering and Internationalizing Our Thinking about Transnational Migrations," in Schiller, et.al., *Towards a Transnational Perspective on Migration*, 246.

30. Kirby Miller, *Emigrants and Exiles: Ireland and the Irish exodus to North America* (New York: Oxford University Press 1985), 352, 581–2; Lees, *Exiles*, 48.

31. Miller, et al., "For Love," 10; Marilyn Cohen, "The Migration Experience of Female-headed Households: Gilford, Co. Down to Greenwich, New York, 1880–1910," in *Irish Women and the Irish Migration, vol. 4, The Irish World Wide*, ed. Patrick O'Sullivan, (Leicester: Leicester University Press, 1995), 136–137. See also Caroline Brettell, "Women are Migrants Too: A Portuguese Perspective," in *Urban Life*, ed. George Gmelch and Walter Zenner (3rd ed.; Prospect Heights, IL: Waveland Press, 1996), 250.

32. Miller et al., "For Love," 17; Cohen, "Female-headed Households," 136.
33. Ruddock, *Linen Threads,* 28–29.
34. Clarence D. Long, *Wages and Earnings in the United States, 1860–1890* (New York: Arno Press, 1975), 106.
35. Ibid., 95, 105–106.
36. Cohen, "Female-headed Households," 137.
37. Ibid., 135. Lees found a nearly equal proportion (17 percent) of female-headed households in her 1851 London sample (Lees, *Exiles,* 130).
38. Cohen, "Female-headed Households," 136.
39. Harris, "Characteristics," 48.
40. Diner, *Erin's Daughters;* Nolan, *Ourselves Alone.*
41. Olwen Hufton, "Women Without Men: Widows and Spinsters in Britain and France in the Eighteenth Century," *Journal of Family History* (Winter 1984): 361; Nici Nelson, "Surviving in the City: Coping Strategies of Female Migrants in Nairobi, Kenya," in Gmelch and Zenner, *Urban Life,* 265; Dirk Hoerder, "From Migrants to Ethnics: Acculturation in a Societal Framework," in Hoerder and Moch, *European Migrants,* 239.
42. Cohen, "Female-headed Households," 138.
43. Murphy, "The Fionnuala Factor," 99.
44. Lees found that because female wages were below those of male laborers, most would have lived below Seebohm Rowntree's poverty line. This resulted in 75 percent of Irish female heads working as compared with 22 percent of wives with resident husbands (Lees, *Exiles,* 102, 106, 113).
45. Cohen, "Female-headed Households."
46. Ruddock, *Linen Threads,* 36.
47. Ruddock, *Linen Threads,* 14–15.
48. Lees, *Exiles,* 118.
49. Cohen, "Female-headed Households," 140.
50. Joanna Bourke, "The Best of all Home Rulers: the Economic Power of Women in Ireland, 1880–1914," *Irish Economic and Social History* 18 (1991): 24–37; Miller, et al., "For Love, 10–16.
51. Cohen, "Female-headed Households;" idem., "The Migration Experience;" and idem., *Linen, Family and Community in Tullylish, County Down, 1690–1914* (Dublin: Four Courts, 1997).
52. Ruddock, *Linen Threads,* 126–127; Isaac Jackson, oral evidence.
53. Cohen, "Female-headed Households," 140–142; L.1889,c. 560. White v. Wittemann Lithographic Co., 1892, 131 N.Y. 631, 30 N.E. 236.
54. Cohen, "Female-headed Households," 141.
55. Ruth Madigan, Moira Munro, and Susan J. Smith, "Gender and the Meaning of the Home," *International Journal of Urban and Regional Research* 14 (December 1990): 625–647; Cohen, "Female-Headed Households," 140–141.
56. Miller, et al., "For Love," 17; Ruddock, *Linen Threads,* 124.
57. Philip Amis, "Migration, Urban Poverty, and the Housing Market: the Nairobi Case," in *Migrants, Workers, and the Social Order,* ed. Jeremy Eades (London: Tavistock Publications, 1987), 256–257.

58. Susan J. Smith, "Income, Housing, Wealth, and Gender Inequality," *Urban Studies* 27 (February 1990), 67–88; Madigan, Munro, and Smith, "Gender," 633.

59. Cohen, "Female-headed Households," 142.

60. Ruddock, *Linen Threads,* 96–97.

61. Timothy Guinnane's research suggested that the wealthier farm families were less likely to marry than the poorer families. See Guinnane, "Migration, Marriage and Household Formation;" see abstract in *Journal of Economic History* 49 (June 1984): 452–454.

62. Dublin, *Women,* 170–173; Turbin, "Beyond Dichotomies," 300–301.

63. For a discussion of the sense of obligation felt by older sisters and female relatives toward their migrating kin, see Murphy, "The Fionnuala Factor," 96–99.

64. Sutton, "Gendering and Internationalizing," 247.

65. Annie Phizacklea, "Introduction," in Phizacklea, *One Way Ticket,* 5–7.

66. Jane Gray, "Gender Politics and Ireland," *Journal of Women's History* 6 (Winter/Spring 1995): 238–249.

Gender, Class, and
the Transgressive Subject ▓

Chapter Eleven

Negotiating Patriarchy: Irish Women and the Landlord

Ruth-Ann M. Harris

> The possession of land is of immense importance, without it he [the peas-
> ant] must lead the life of a mendicant. The only way in which a woman can
> get an interest in land is by marrying, and the only chance of protection
> from beggary when she loses her husband, or when his powers fail, is to have
> children. The poorest Irish peasant is therefore always married.
>
> —John Revans, 1836[1]

Although scholars have demonstrated the differentiation of the Irish
tenantry, particularly at the bottom of the class ladder, how differentiation was mediated by gender remains both undertheorized
and underanalyzed. Women in Irish tenant households were subject to
double jeopardy from two interconnected and sometimes competing patriarchal systems: first, from a patriarchal landlord class that assumed stewardship over their tenantry, exerting significant control over their material
conditions of life; and second, from their subordinate status and dependence on males within the patriarchal tenant family unit. I will argue,
however, that women's power and agency was more complex than one
might suspect. These dueling systems of patriarchy created opportunities
for women to seize the initiative and employ strategies to protect their
own resources and interests.

Evidence for these arguments comes from a sample of 490 written petitions from tenants and sub-tenants, addressed to the landlord or his agent
on the Shirley estate in southeast County Monaghan, between 1840 and

1855.[2] The issues addressed in the petitions include charity and maintenance, debt and rent, requests for justice, inheritance-related disputes, domestic abuse and violence, dowry (portion was the more usual term) issues,
and requests for assisted emigration. Some petitions reflect directly the impact of the Famine on the tenantry and illustrate vividly the role of assisted
emigration in alleviating distress and resolving problems. The importance of
the extended family networks, including emigrants and other geographically mobile members, is graphically evident. The positive role of emigration within family strategies, and the ways that migration was financed,
provides valuable insight into the family's means of coping with difficult
circumstances. The evidence here does not support the stereotypical view
of emigration as a last resort for the indigent, frequently imposed by cold-
hearted landlords trying to rid their estate of unwanted and uneconomic
tenants. Rather, assisted emigration was bargained for and negotiated by
tenants and sub-tenants who knew they had considerable leverage.

The 182 petitions authored by women confirm that Irish was the principal language of the region, suggesting that traditional social structures,
wherein women played an active role, remained strong.[3] In addition to petitions in which women sought the landlord's intervention, wills and marriage settlements shed light on the distribution of family resources toward
daughters. Women appealed to the landlord to enforce what they regarded
as their rights and entitlements.

In conjunction with census reports, Griffith's Valuation[4], estate records
(including rent rolls), Poor Law commissioners' reports, and emigration
lists, the petitions provide a window through which one can observe the
social and economic conditions of tenants and sub-tenants before, during,
and after the critical Famine decade in Ireland's history. Our usual historical sources on this period impose particular class-specific filters on the reality of the past. The documents used here preserve the voices of ordinary
people, shedding new light on the nature of family relations and the strategies employed for ensuring the survival of the family and accumulating
and controlling wealth.

The Shirley estate was the largest landed property in County Monaghan in the nineteenth century, amounting to some 26,000 acres. Together with the Bath estate it formed the barony of Farney in southeast
Monaghan, of which Carrickmacross was the chief administrative center
and market town. The barony of Farney was Gaelic until granted to the
earl of Essex in 1575. A century later the property was divided between
two branches of the family by marriage, becoming the Shirley and Bath
estates.

The Shirleys were mostly absentee landlords throughout the eighteenth
century.[5] Since they were only resident for about three months a year in

the nineteenth century, they employed estate agents. One result of not administering the estate directly was the middlemen system, meaning most of the estate was leased out to head tenants who in turn broke their leaseholds into smaller units, letting to tenants at considerably higher rents per acre than they themselves were paying. These latter tenants, in turn, sublet ultimately to cottiers who usually occupied little more than a house and garden in exchange for labor. The result of excessive subletting was a sharp rise in the population of the estate.

Patrick Duffy states that the south Monaghan region exhibited the Irish "ecological paradox," with the greatest density of population on the poorest land. In this region, where the rural domestic linen industry was a source of extra income, domestic industry contributed to universally high population densities, one hypothesis of the proto-industrial model.[6] By the early decades of the nineteenth century, Farney had some of the highest rural population densities in all of Ireland, with one reference to 44,107 persons. On the combined estates the rent roll had grown commensurately: from revenue of £8,000 in 1769 to £40,000 by 1843, from which the Shirley estate drew roughly five-eighths.[7]

THE PATRIARCHAL LANDLORD SYSTEM

The Shirley family was not the careless, spendthrift landlord, described by observers such as Arthur Young. As early as the 1780s, they actively encouraged the production of linen, and after his marriage in 1820, Evelyn John Shirley attempted to modernize the estates. The family adhered to the values of paternalism, in which the ownership of property conferred obligations as well as privileges. The landlord was a father writ large, powerful because of his superior status and ability to control his tenants, benevolent in encouraging a responsible tenantry. And in the language of paternalism, a responsible tenant was a male breadwinner, a father writ small, whose authority was legitimated by his ability to secure the well-being of his dependents.[8] In this context it is hardly surprising that landlords heeded women's accusations against the profligacy of their husbands, brothers, and fathers. There was also a practical and immediate reason for the Shirley family and their agents to endorse women's pleas for justice. If not provided for within the family, women could easily become public charges, placing an increased burden on the recently instituted poor rates.

Literary accounts have notoriously stripped the veneer of paternalism from the Irish landlord, exposing him as feckless, greedy, and predatory.[9] This chapter, however, reveals a functioning proprietary paternalism, whereby the landlord's patriarchal authority is both maintained and enhanced by the strategic employment of benevolence.[10] By sanctioning the women petitioners' claims to justice, landlord agency empowered women at the expense of patriarchal authority within the Irish family.

By the late eighteenth century agents on the estate were warning the Shirley family of the growing population of impoverished tenants, advising against renewing leases to marginal tenants and pointing out the enormous profits accrued by middlemen leaseholders. By the late 1830s active measures were underway to reduce the number of persons on the estate; estate papers show agents closely scrutinizing the granting of sub-leases, and by the 1850s middlemen had been eliminated from the estate.[11] In addition, the impending Poor Law held landlords financially responsible for indigent tenants, giving an extra incentive to rationalize production and reduce the number of poor tenants.

By 1843, when William Steuart Trench came to manage the Shirley estate, the problem of rent arrears was reaching crisis proportions, and efforts to collect from defaulting tenants led to dangerous disturbances.[12] Trench recommended a radical restructuring of the estate. Many of his suggestions were ignored—leading to his resignation after about two years as agent—but his most important recommendation, to fund extensive emigration, was accepted.[13] Trench encouraged tenants to submit written petitions as part of his rationalization of estate management. He is undoubtedly responsible for the large number of extant petitions; there were 125 in his first four months as agent in 1844, 40 percent of which were from women.

Under the system of tenant right, long-term leases were transferable. Leases were valuable assets for tenants in a position either to farm the land themselves, to sublease at higher rates, or to sell the lease. While landlord permission for transferring a lease was required, such transfers were usually approved. Landlords' willingness to tolerate transfer of leases, when presumably they could have cancelled them and charged a higher rent, reflected the limitations of landlord power, some of whom feared reprisal such as the successful rent strike by the tenants of Ballykilcline, county Roscommon.

Although the power of landlords vis-à-vis their tenants was extensive, the interdependence inherent in the relationship created a space for tenants to formulate ways to strengthen their security and position. The acquisition of tenancies was thus a means of asset accumulation by peasants, and the inheritance of tenancies played a central part in the distribution of family wealth.[14] On the Shirley estate, as elsewhere in Ireland, there was substantial differentiation among tenants, even within the general categories—farmers with no capital who worked as laborers, and cottiers with sufficient capital to give their daughters substantial dowries. Tenants on the estate were disproportionately Catholic, but religion was not a differentiating feature in the attitudes of the agents toward tenants, and there were Catholics and Protestants at every level.[15]

THE IRISH TENANT FAMILY

The assets controlled by the Irish tenant family were: 1) access to land; 2) the labor power of family members; and 3) reproducible capital in the form of livestock, implements, seeds, dwellings, and household furniture. In addition, there was considerable reliance on earnings from wage labor, particularly from seasonal migration[16] and remittances from longer-term emigrant members of the family unit.[17] The reproduction of these units came through marriage and inheritance.

Marriage could only be considered if males and females each brought resources to the union sufficient to establish a viable unit. Males generally brought land, while females brought dowry, used in part to capitalize the new unit and in part to enable the groom's family to provide dowries for other daughters. Sons without land and daughters without dowry either worked as unpaid labor on the family farm or sold their labor in the cash economy. The distribution of land and dowry was the prerogative of the senior males of the family, and this kept unmarried children subject to patriarchal control. Nevertheless, possession of a dowry gave women power within the household, because women maintained individual claims on their dowries.

Women's economic contribution to the family unit had been significant over time, with the dowry system playing an important role.[18] Women contributed to the domestic cash economy in eighteenth-century Farney primarily through spinning and the production of eggs and butter. By the nineteenth century, however, the importance of spinning woolen yarn was diminishing. Jane Gray asserts that gender inequalities within rural industrial households contributed to uneven capitalist development in the Irish linen industry and partially explains patterns of de-industrialization. Linen yarn districts such as Farney, which lay just beyond the "linen triangle,"[19] were vulnerable to de-industrialization by the 1830s.[20]

It is evident from the petitions that families sought to provide for daughters as well as sons, and it was not uncommon for widows and unmarried women to control assets independently. Inheritance provisions reveal that tenancies were passed on to sons (and occasionally daughters) and to widows with the stipulation that they provide for non-inheriting brothers and sisters. Rapid population growth put increasing pressure on resources. Tenants responded by reducing the average size of holdings and intensifying competition for land that not only pitted family against family in pursuing accumulation strategies, but also sisters against brothers, and mothers against sons. Remarriages were a particular source of tension. Marrying a man with children from a previous marriage set up competition between the new wife and her children. Similarly a widow with children faced competition from the family of her deceased husband, who generally opposed her remarrying. From the perspective of the widow, re-marrying generally gave her power because of the resources she brought to the new union. In this increasingly competitive environment women were actively involved in protecting their interests, seeking the landlord's authority to enforce their claims and the claims of their families.

THE MEE FAMILY

The experiences of the Mee family of Beagh Magheross highlight a range of familial issues and strategies. On 28 November 1843 the widow Alice Mee sought the agent's intervention in a family dispute, stating she was "worn down by grief, age and infirmities and I can do nothing but weep at the thoughts of leaving the world and my Daughter unsettled."[21] There were five sons and one daughter, and the terms of her deceased husband's will called for the family property of fifteen acres in Beagh townland to be divided among the three oldest sons. The land-inheriting sons were to pro-vide the two younger boys with an education and a trade, and each of the three was to give their sister £10 for her dowry. The widow's provision was a lifetime tenant's right to three acres, one from each inheriting son.

A dispute arose when her daughter received an offer of marriage and the two elder sons, Philip and Thomas—required by the terms of their fa-ther's will to pay the share of a deceased brother, James—refused.[22] As a result of the dispute, the widow had conferred with Patrick, one of the two younger sons who received ten pounds in lieu of land. He was will-ing to pay the remaining ten pounds of his sister's dowry in exchange for the right to have his name on the lease of his mother's land. Opportunity for Patrick was created by the death of James, and the widow asked the landlord to overturn her husband's will by transferring her lifetime use of the lease to Patrick. Thus, a written petition from Widow Mee to agent Trench was issued requesting approval of the transaction and enforcement of conditions.

Widow Mee's story illustrates some of the tensions within tenant fam-ilies and the role of the landlord as a semi-judicial authority. The honor-ing of wills and contractual obligations, claims on assets—particularly the sale and transfer of tenancies—frequently strained relationships. This was especially true during the countdown years to the Famine, when family resources were shrinking. Widows and unmarried daughters were partic-ularly vulnerable, and some form of extra-familial authority was needed to enforce justice and protect an individual's rights. While there was re-course to the civil courts for some of these issues, the landlord's author-ity was often sought instead. Civil courts referred plaintiffs to their landlord under the presumption that certain matters were better handled locally. The cultural explanation for landlords' judicial authority stems from their patriarchal role as "father" protecting their "children"—in this case "daughters"—on the estate. In addition to petitions, sources such as Griffith's Valuation are instructive, because the names of leaseholders that survived the Famine are reported by townland. Patrick Mee, the name of the son who was willing to pay his sister's portion in exchange for obtaining his mother's lease, appears in 1860 as having a property of thirty acres in the townland (15 acres more than his father bequeathed to the family) while the two brothers who inherited the family property were no longer present.[23]

A second petition a year later (3 May 1844) continues the family saga. A younger son, Charles Mee, who had been apprenticed to a tailor in lieu of inheriting land, sought assisted passage to America.[24] He wrote (petitions were almost always written in third-person, semi-legal language): "In consequence of the difficulties he has met with in seeking employment and the obduracy of his brothers, please enter his name for America. He has formed a most sanguine wish for emigration where his exertions and good conduct will ensure a means of subsistence which he cannot procure here." Charles Mee also informed the agent that his brothers failed to fulfill their responsibility provided for in their father's will; their mother paid the four and a half pounds for his apprenticeship training.

A third petition adds yet another dimension. Anne M'Cabe of the adjoining townland of Greaghlatacapple submitted a petition of distress on 3 February 1844. While working for Thomas, one of the senior Mee brothers, he had "got her with child" after promising marriage but had now "turned her adrift on the world."[25] Moreover, Anne learned she was not the first girl he had placed in such a predicament. Expressing the anguish of an abandoned unwed mother, she wrote, "wretched infamy awaits her if your Honor deigns not to interpose your Authority, and compel this man to do justice to a poor deluded Orphan, who would be happy in poverty, but never can, in Shame. She therefore most humbly supplicates your Honor to send for him and compel him to do justice, which he will not do for the advice of any other person living." The resolution of her predicament became apparent when her name appeared on a list of emigrants assisted to leave in 1844; she was granted £2 3s. Thomas Mee was compelled to help finance her emigration since the estate's contribution was insufficient for passage. It is clear from these petitions that women had the right to expect support for illegitimate offspring, as was the case with the Reyburn family. If the biological father failed to assume responsibility, it made cultural sense to appeal to the next higher level of fatherhood—the landlord.

EMIGRATION

Emigration was transforming the social landscape of parts of rural Ireland long before the Famine. Landlords were not alone in seeking to prevent families from dividing land between their sons. Families often sought to consolidate their economic position and preserve family farms by encouraging non-inheriting sons to emigrate.[26] Tenants negotiated emigration assistance, frequently using the threat of division of land as leverage. In her petition seeking emigration for a son, Widow Margaret Cassidy stated to George Morant, who replaced Trench as agent in 1845, that she had already sent two daughters and three sons to America "by hard industry" where they now "enjoy a degree of Competency."[27] She now sought assisted passage in lieu of dividing her small farm of five acres between her remaining two sons. She described her son as "a Stout athletic young son who is bent on going to America if he had the means." She was granted £2 10s. "to pay passage of son and to keep the farm for the eldest son."[28]

Emigration was viewed mostly as a positive option, but for some families the departure of family members created problems, such as destitution and desertion, for those who remained. Mary Reilly financed the emigration of her son, Tom, by selling "her spot of land," but was now destitute. "She is very ill for want of a Blanket and the cold coming on."[29] When husbands emigrated families could fall into destitution. Mary Floody was left with eight children when her husband "was compelled to exile himself by seeking employment in a far and foreign climate." In her vivid words, "The cryes of eight craving children daily rings through the cold and destitute cabin that surrounds them."[30] Mary was granted £13 10s. to take seven of the children to America in 1844.

Desertion and the threat of desertion through emigration were reasons for invoking landlord intervention. Alice Keenan Morgan of Raferagh sought protection for herself and four young children against an abusive husband who had threatened to sell his five acres of land and go to America with his two children by a former marriage.[31] Mary Murphy Gartlan's[32] second husband "done well, till the sickness and Death of Cattle, succeeded by the failure of the Potatoe crops, cramped his means, and caused him to fall into one year's arrears [of rent] and in order to better his means, he opened a Public House in Town, which did not answer his expectations and therefore on the 12th of March last [1848], he privately deserted your Petitioner and family, and sailed for America."[33] Mary sought an abatement of rent, saying that she had given up property in the townland of Coolfore and was now reduced to 26 acres. When estate authorities tried to seize her crops she held them off with weapons and threats.

DOWRY

Dowry was the central issue in 12 percent of women's petitions, and it was mentioned in many others.[34] Women's dowries ranged from two pounds to a hundred or more pounds, with the most frequently quoted figure being around fifty pounds sterling. A dowry could also be in land, and in a land-stressed economy, there was potential for strife. Dowry was usually referred to by petitioners as a "portion" or a "fortune." A petition would sometimes read "my portion or dowry" or "my fortune or dowry" suggesting that dowry was an imported term, gradually replacing the vernacular or customary terms.[35] The term portion implies entitlement, and the possession of a portion was critical to a woman's status, giving her a degree of autonomy within the marriage. She faced opprobrium from her husband's family if for some reason her portion was not fully paid, as in the case of Mary O'Here McNally of Lisnaguiveragh, who described ill treatment from her husband's family after his death. Her father-in-law, Bryan McNally, protested that he was promised a dowry of £30 of which only £22 was paid, presumably justification for the abuse.[36]

While under nineteenth-century law the portion may have legally belonged to the husband, by an older system of rights these women regarded the portion as their own, to be used judiciously by husbands and husbands' families. Widow Anne Murray Daly of Clonturk wrote to protest the claims by her husband's family on what remained of her portion.[37] She brought a portion of £50 when she "was married on" John Daly, Jr., who had nine and half acres. The money was used to portion her husband's sister. The new brother-in-law insisted on Anne's husband joining him in a loan of £50 that was used to pay his debts. After her husband's death she had been left with five orphans and feared that the debts imperiled her eldest son Michael's patrimony and access to land. It appears that her petition was successful, because Griffith's shows a Michael Daly with 33 acres in 1860.[38]

A term for portion in Irish is *cleamhnas,* meaning a match, and implying an economic alliance of equals.[39] When the portion was not fully paid, as in a previous case, the wife was in a vulnerable position. Widow Mary M'Enally was persuaded to marry a man "only a little advanced in years." She described her late husband, Owen, as a "good, kind and affectionate husband" whose "comfortable settlement had its own influence in persuading [her] to the union." Her fortune was £30, while Owen's father promised eight acres and a farm on the adjoining Bath estate. Owen's father, however, gave him only six acres and her father only £22 of her fortune. Misfortune followed their marriage; their only child died and then her husband. After her husband's death she was left in a difficult situation when her husband's family sold her only cow. Anticipating a future where she would only be a servant in their household, Mary petitioned the landlord to be provided with shelter.[40]

It is also clear that some women earned their portions and negotiated marriage terms with a prospective husband independent of their families. The petition of Anne Keenan McCabe of Aghacloghan states that she "gathered her hard-earned money" when her prospective husband offered marriage and two acres of his father's land.[41] Anne's money freed her father-in-law, Hugh McCabe, from three years in debtor's prison. Her father-in-law expelled her from the family house while her husband was away working in England, but kept her child, and she sought restoration of her rights through the landlord's intervention.

WOMEN ALONE

Anne Malone was an orphan whose parents left her a heifer in their will. She had saved 25s. from employment "in service." When she sold the heifer to Pat McNally for £7 he refused to pay in cash, offering only potato ground, valued, she claimed, at less than £2. She sought arbitration in the dispute with McNally, who may also have been a prospective suitor; there is the suggestion in the petition that she had expected an offer of marriage from him.[42]

In Bridget and Allice Duffy's case against their brother, Patrick, we can see how one case involving single women was settled. The specific charges against Patrick are not clear, but the phrase "deprived his sisters" suggests that he was not fulfilling his fraternal responsibilities to them. Bridget and Allice were awarded £70, to be divided between them and paid in four equal installments over four years by their brother. They were to get "chattels, meal, frieze, farming implements and the crop of corn, potatoes and flax now growing." In turn the sisters were to pay one year's rent of the farm to Patrick. If they married their portions were to be paid in two installments—one half at marriage and the rest twelve months later. If Patrick continued to mistreat them, he was to pay the total amount of £70 on demand, and if he went so far as to turn them out of his house, he must pay them support of a shilling a day.[43]

WIDOWS

The high incidence of petitions from widows was the consequence of a pattern of late marriage whereby men were marrying women many years their junior. A husband's death frequently left a relatively young widow to struggle, not only with the responsibility of providing for a family, but also with holding off the competing claims of his family. The age difference, estimated from immigrant lists in the estate papers, was 4.5 years between husbands and wives. The median age of marriage for men was 30 while for women it was 25, but there was a large emigrant group in which the age differential was more substantial—from 9 to 25 years.[44] It is quite likely that there were a number of relatively young widows who had to compete for resources with surviving children from previous marriages.

Widows were vulnerable, first because they were dependent on the good will of sons (with whom they were often in dispute), brothers, fathers, and the landlord. Second, their husband's family frequently viewed them as a threat to the security of the family land, particularly if they were to remarry; and thirdly, their natal families usually regarded them as a burden or a pawn. But a widow also enjoyed a protected status and a kind of immunity from the usual norms.

The cases of Thomas Connolly's widow and widow Elizabeth Mee illustrate the vulnerability of widows as well as how they used their status to advantage. The (unnamed) widow of Thomas Connolly of Latinalbany was the subject of a petition by the executors of her husband's estate, seeking to preserve the property valued at £60 for his surviving children.[45] The executors say they "gave his widow every possible assistance in labouring the farm, yet soon after her husband's death, all notions of industry in the widow, seemed to be replaced by a propensity to courtship and idleness, untill various Arts and falsehoods to persuade the late agent Mr. Trench, to allow her to sell the farm and Emigrate with the Children to America, but upon discovery of her real intention, that Gentleman would not allow it, but recommended her friends to assist her, and secure the place for her eldest son, who is now a promising boy of 13." Subsequently, the widow married James Smith, "not worth a shilling whom (after paying for her marriage, and a wedding) she clad with money she got out of the Bank on pretense of Getting a cow for the Children." There is no reported adjudication of the case, but by 1860 there was no James Smith or Connolly.[46]

Widow Elizabeth Mee refused to accept blight-diseased potatoes from her son, Peter. According to his petition, submitted in November 1846, he gave his mother 4 cwt. oatmeal, 12 pecks of eating potatoes (at 32 stone each), the feeding of a cow, and one-third of his crop of dried turf, "according to contract."[47] Refusing the potatoes, she asked for their value in meal. When he refused, she took him to court in Carrickmacross for £11 4s. (the price of the potatoes at 7p. per stone). Apparently the court sent the case back to the estate agent. While Peter was willing to take in his mother and "give (her) every privilege due her age and station;" the destruction of the potato crop had so reduced his resources that he was unable to continue to maintain her in a separate residence.

The reality of being a second wife could be hazardous, and a second wife who became a widow was particularly vulnerable. Jane Gulshinan of Corrybracken, now a widow, had been the second wife of Michael Gulshinan, whose will favored the daughter of his first wife, leaving Jane "bare and naked in the place" with nine orphaned children. After she had paid her stepdaughter nine of the £30 willed to her, "the place is bare."[48] There is no reported adjudication of this difficulty, but five years later Jane was assisted to emigrate. She was 40 when granted £2 10s. to assist her to leave with her daughters Mary, 20, and Rose, 18; and son Edward, 16.[49]

Some widows could not handle their problems alone. Her husband's death left Ellen Connor of Tirnadrola with two young children and ownership of a mill and a kiln. The terms of the will left the running of the mill in the hands of her late husband's brother and another executor who informed her that she was not to see the will until the children were of age. The widow accepted this dictum until she began to suspect that her brother-in-law was running the business for his own profit, thereby endangering her children's future. Moses Connor, the brother-in-law, presented a petition in January 1848, warning that there was a rumor that the widow was "about to solicit leave to marry," requesting that she be prevented from doing this.[50] Two months later Ellen Connor requested advice on remarriage: "I find it impossible to manage or keep my children's property together without some protection from you."[51] Her friends, she said, "advise me to marry an honest industrious young man."[52] By November she had remarried—a James Mee, who wrote to the agent, detailing how he planned to care for the estate and provide for the children. He posted a bond for £100 to become the portion of the second son (the first would inherit the mill property).

The next two cases of widows are notable because they concern women negotiating the public domain. With no families present, the two widows acted independently—one in an independent economic enterprise and the other in the political sphere. Widow Catherine Duffy of Cootelane was accused by four citizens of Carrickmacross of permitting "girls of infamous morals and character" to inhabit a small cabin on the land to the rear of her house.[53] According to the petitioners Widow Duffy refused to dispossess them. Whether or not this was a house of prostitution or simply four men outraged that women would dare to live unsupervised by males cannot be determined. Widow Mary Burns of Corrinenty harbored protestors disguised as women, according to Bernard Hanlon's accusation. Hanlon sought firearms to protect himself from their vengeance. Mary's husband had been "transposed"[transported] for robbery (and presumably died abroad). Hanlon said, "as I was proceeding home I espied at Mary Burns' house . . . some women looking earnestly at me one of them started up the road before me. I suspected her & I staid, when she came some distance, I saw a number of women standing along with her, but they were men in womens clothes. Were it not how I proceeded in haste through the country I really believe I would have been murdered; for the Bundoran girls[54] (a name given to those who disguise themselves) were marching through Cornenty the same day . . . they told me they would give me my doom."[55] Bernard Hanlon, a despised bog ranger,[56] was, according to Griffith's, no longer present in 1860.[57] What is significant is that these protesters—sworn enemies of the landlord—found shelter with the Widow Burns.[58]

ABUSE

Appeals for protection from violence were not uncommon, and abuse between family members was a frequent theme in the petitions. On 4 June 1845 Catherine McKittrick of Alts requested protection from her brother, Martin.[59] Her petition, which is part of a larger family disagreement over their parents' estate, states that Martin became an idler after abandoning an apprenticeship. Next, their father got him into the police force in Armagh (he left after only seven weeks). Catherine claimed that because Martin joined a group of agitators on the estate, their father intended to give him no land. Since their mother's death, Martin had appropriated the management of the family property and was refusing to pay Catherine her portion of £80. Thereafter, matters got worse:

> Early on last Sunday morning, your Petitioner having polished his shoes and procured him every necessary to go to divine Worship—he as if possessed with a Demon turned about, and knocked her senseless on the floor, swearing he would have her life. Upon his return from prayers, he also beat, battered and abused her, and turned her out of the house, which he soon after left also with the key of the Street Door, and returned at 12 O'clock that night, Beastly drunk, and shouted to your Pet[itione]r to open her room door, or he would instantly break it. She being advised and encouraged by the presence of her Brother John, did open the Door, whereupon he seized on her, and nearly beat her to Death, cast her forth out of Doors, and took possession of her bedding, bed and Room, which were expressly willed to her by her mother, and disputed by none but him. Your Petitioner cannot calculate on any secuirty [sic] of her life, from this unnatural Brother's conduct, and therefore submits her case (which can be amply corroborated) to your kind consideration humbly begging your protection and advice.

Martin submitted his own petition on the same day, contradicting Catherine's story.[60] Trouble arose in the family, he said, when he opposed his younger brother's marriage. The agent refused to let them divide the land among the four children, and Martin claimed that the siblings blamed him for this. Arbitrators were chosen to settle the dispute.

Alice Meegan of Tullynaskeagh sought protection against her abusive brother-in-law, Francis Slevin.[61] At her mother's death Alice was left a small cabin, twenty-eight perches of ground,[62] and responsibility for the portions of four sisters—the fifth sister "professed extraordinary Religious Devotion, and was never to marry." Despite this the sister changed her mind and "intruded" Francis Slevin on the household. Alice informed Trench that Slevin was involved in political disturbances which Mitchel, the previous agent, had managed to keep in check. Following the death of her mother from Slevin's abuse (according to Alice), he turned on her: "[Twelve] days ago [Slevin] broke her chest, and 2 chairs, and Threw out her bed and bedding which was torn and destroyed by Pigs, whilst he held a spade threatning to kill her if she came near them, at the same [time] defying your Honor, and your conservators with the most indecent epithets, so that on earth there is not a worse character." In 1860 Francis Slevin was in Tullynaskeagh East with four acres of land.[63]

Husbands occasionally brought petitions against their abusive wives. In September 1845 John Traynor of Drumgurra sought protection from his wife and son, "who constantly provoke me."[64] Trench ordered him room and maintenance in town, but four months later (3 January 1846), following the departure of Trench, John's wife wrote to the agent that she was now totally responsible for "a weak and large family paying a large rent" while her husband was wasting the family's resources "going among idle men in Carrickmacross making sport and diversion." Although the adjudication of this case is not known, a John Traynor held 29 acres of land in 1860, suggesting that the family property survived.[65]

CONCLUSION

Patriarchy as a model for harmonious class relationships is based upon clear cultural constructions of gender and deference that inform the expectations and roles of those at the top and bottom of the social hierarchy.[66] The lives of the inhabitants of Farney, however, were hard between 1840 and 1855 and becoming more difficult by the season, straining the extant fault lines in the overlapping patriarchal systems and creating spaces for agency. Tenants organized resistance to their landlords, and within the tenant family, women challenged the authority of their menfolk. It may have been in the landlord's interest to undermine the patriarchal authority of the male head of household by supporting the claims of women—a classic example of divide and rule. Of the 25 cases presented here, women authored 20 petitions, the vast majority of which were successful, suggesting the limitations of patriarchal authority at both levels. Landlords faced actual and potential rent boycotts, had great difficulties in collecting full rents, and were frequently "forced" to allow the transfer of valuable tenancies when they could presumably have profited by canceling those contracts. Within the Irish family the authority of the patriarch was challenged by conflicting claims by wives, children, unmarried siblings, parents, and affines (in-laws) as dwindling resources in the pre-famine and famine periods put additional pressures on the family.

Women in general had less control over their lives than men did and in many petitions they were not referred to by name, only as wife, sister, or daughter. Nevertheless, women adopted strategies to further their own interests, protect their own claims, and provide for themselves, their daughters, and their sons as far as possible. While poverty, culture, and social structure all limited the degree to which women could act autonomously, these petitions provide an insight into such strategies, including emigration, and provide some measure of their limited successes. Hierarchical systems require some degree of collaboration by the dominated group, and the very existence of these petitions reveals the petitioners' acceptance of the patriarchal authority of the landlord. At the same time, they expose the patriarchal neglect of their menfolk. In this sense the women successfully negotiate with patriarchy in patriarchal, but more importantly, reciprocal terms.

NOTES

I wish to thank the following persons who provided comments while this paper was in preparation: Madeleine Blais, Marilyn Cohen, Brian Conchubhair, Gearoid O Crualaoich, Nancy J. Curtin, Patrick J. Duffy, Marianne Elliott, John R. Harris, Bruce Logan, Joan and Bill Maguire, Christine McIvor, Anne McKernan, Kevin O'Neill, Eileen Moore Quinn, Joan Vincent, Megan Sullivan, and Kevin Whelan.

1. John Revans, the Poor Law commissioner, "Poor Laws in Ireland," *London and Westminster Review* 25 (July 1836): 185–6.
2. Shirley Papers (Public Record Office of Northern Ireland [PRONI], D.3531). I am indebted to the Deputy Keeper of the Records and to the depositor Major J. E. Shirley, for permission to quote from them.
3. W. Steuart Trench, *Realities of Irish Life* (London: Longmans Green & Co., 1868), 70.
4. *General Valuation of Rateable Property in Ireland, Union of Carrickmacross, County of Monaghan, 1860,* hereafter cited as Griffith's (Dublin: Alex. Thom and Sons, 1861).
5. The principal family estates were in Warwickshire.

6. Patrick J. Duffy, *Landscapes of South Ulster, A Parish Atlas of the Diocese of Clogher* (Belfast: The Institute of Irish Studies of the Queen's University of Belfast, 1993), 13–15. Scholars applying the proto-industrial model to Ireland include Jane Gray, "Rural Industry and Uneven Development: The Significance of Gender in the Irish Linen Industry," *Journal of Peasant Studies* 20 (July 1993): 591–609; Eric L. Almquist, "Pre-Famine Ireland and the Theory of European Proto-Industrialisation: Evidence from the 1841 Census," *Journal of Economic History* 39 (1979): 699–718; and Marilyn Cohen, "Peasant Differentiation and Proto-Industrialisation in the Ulster Countryside: Tullylish, 1690–1825," *Journal of Peasant Studies* 17 (April 1990): 413–432.

7. Trench, *Realities,* 70.

8. Leonore Davidoff and Catherine Hall, *Family Fortunes: Men and Women of the English Middle Class, 1780–1850* (Chicago: University of Chicago Press, 1987), 17; Patrick Joyce, *Visions of the People: Industrial England and the Question of Class, 1848–1914* (Cambridge: Cambridge University Press, 1991); David Roberts, *Paternalism in Early Victorian England* (New Brunswick, NJ: Rutgers University Press, 1979); Howard Newby, *The Deferential Worker: a Study of Farm Workers in East Anglia* (London: Allen Lane, 1977).

9. See, e.g, Vera Kreilkamp, "Losing It All: The Unmanned Irish Landlord," Chapter 6 in this volume.

10. For a classic statement of the deference/paternalist nexus limiting landed authority, see E. P. Thompson, "Patrician Society, Plebian Culture," *Journal of Social History* 7 (Summer 1974): 382–405.

11. I am indebted to Kevin Whelan for pointing out to me that evidence in Griffith's shows that middlemen were gone from Farney by 1860.

12. For an evaluation of Trench's tenure as manager of the Shirley Estate, see Patrick J. Duffy, "Management Problems on a Large Estate in Mid-nineteenth Century Ireland: William Steuart Trench's Report on the Shirley Estate in 1843," *Clogher Record* 20 (Spring 1998): 101–122. For studies of estate management, see W. E. Vaughan, *Landlords and Tenants in Mid-Victorian Ireland* (Oxford: Oxford University Press, 1994); James S. Donnelly, *Landlord and Tenant in Nineteenth-Century Cork: The Rural Economy and the Land Question* (London: Routledge and Kegan Paul, 1975); and W. A. Maguire, *The Downshire Estates in Ireland, 1801–1845: The Management of Irish Landed Estates in the Early Nineteenth Century* (Oxford: Clarendon Press, 1972).

13. Trench's book subsequently had a very controversial history in Ireland and in America; see Wayne J. Broehl, *The Molly Maguires* (Cambridge: Harvard University Press, 1964), ch. 3, "Tenant Troubles," 41–70.

14. For a discussion of the role of tenant right in capital accumulation, see Kevin O'Neill, *Famine and Farm in Pre-Famine Ireland, the Parish of Killashandra,* (Madison: University of Wisconsin Press, 1984), 67–69.

15. Richard White, *Remembering Ahanagran: Storytelling in a Family's Past* (New York: Hill and Wang, 1998), 22–76, describes differentiation within a rural

Kerry parish with an excellent description of lower tenants withholding rent and enforcing boycotting.

16. For the importance of seasonal migration in the Irish economy, see Ruth-Ann M. Harris, *The Nearest Place That Wasn't Ireland: Early Nineteenth-Century Irish Labor Migration* (Ames, IA: Iowa State University Press, 1994).
17. In bargaining for the emigration of their children, mothers in particular often cited the contributions of the children they had sent to America.
18. K. W. Nichols, "Irishwomen and Property in the Sixteenth Century," in *Women in Early Modern Ireland,* ed. Margaret MacCurtain and Mary O'-Dowd (Dublin: Wolfhound Press, 1991), 25.
19. The "linen triangle" was comprehended within its vertices of the towns of Belfast, Dungannon, and Newry.
20. See Jane Gray, "Rural Industry," 606.
21. Alice Mee to W. S. Trench, 28 March 1843 (PRONI, Shirley papers, D.3531/P/2).
22. James Mee died in 1826/7 according to the petition submitted by his children, Patrick and Catherine Mee, 30 December 1843 (ibid.).
23. Griffith's, Greaghnaroog, 64.
24. Charles Mee to Trench, 3 May 1844 (PRONI, Shirley papers, D.3531/P/2).
25. Anne M'Cabe to Trench, 3 February 1844 (ibid.).
26. See John Mannion, "The Maritime Trade of Waterford in the Eighteenth Century," in *Common Ground: Essays on the Historical Geography of Ireland,* ed. William J. Smyth and Kevin Whelan (Cork: Cork University Press, 1988), 208–234.
27. Widow Margaret Cassidy to George Morant, 28 March 1846 (PRONI, Shirley papers, D.3531/P/3). Margaret Cassidy held nineteen acres in 1860 (Griffith's, 62).
28. Note appended to petition of 4 June 1846 (PRONI, Shirley papers, D.3531/P/1).
29. Mary Reilly to Morant, 6 August 1845 (ibid., D.3531/P/2).
30. Mary Floody to Trench, 14 March 1844 (ibid.).
31. Alice Keenan Morgan to Trench, c.1844 (ibid.); Griffith's, Lisnaguiveragh, 74.
32. Her first husband was a Carrickmacross shopkeeper and the second was from adjoining county Louth.
33. Mary Gartlan to Evelyn John Shirley, 29 October 1849, 15 November 1849 (PRONI, Shirley papers, D.3531/P/2); Griffith's, Lisnaguiveragh, 74.
34. Analysis of themes in the petitions is derived from a computerized database that permits information to be cross-referenced and analyzed systematically.
35. I am indebted to Brian O Conchubhair for informing me that dowry or portion would be implied in the Irish word *cuid,* which can mean share, quota, portion, meal, livelihood, or property belongings.
36. Bryan McNally to agent Mitchel, 10 July 1833 (PRONI, Shirley papers, D.3531/P/3).

37. Widow Anne Murray Daly to Trench, 13 February 1844 (ibid., D.3531/P/2).

38. Griffith's, Clonturk, 51.

39. I am indebted to Mary Kelly for advising me that the Irish word for dowry—*cleamhnas*—means a match.

40. Mary M'Enally to agent Mitchel, [prior to 1843] (PRONI, Shirley papers, D.3531/P/3).

41. Anne Keenan McCabe to Morant, December 1845 (ibid.).

42. Anne Malone to Morant, n. d. (ibid.).

43. Henry Martin and Patrick Duffy, Sr., arbitrators, 8 January 1846 (ibid., D.3431/P/2).

44. Kevin O'Neill's analysis of the 1841 census data in the Cavan parish of Killashandra determined that on average strong farmers' wives married at the age of 23.07 and laborers' wives at 22.26; farmers married at 28.42 and laborers at 24.5; see O'Neill, *Family and Farm,* 176–80.

45. Bernard Finn and Patrick Ward to Morant, 6 June 1845 (PRONI, Shirley papers, D.3531/P/2).

46. Griffith's, Latinalbany, 76.

47. Peter Mee to Morant, 7 November 1846 (PRONI, Shirley papers, D.3531/P/3).

48. Jane Gulshinan to Trench, March 1845 (ibid.).

49. Griffith's, Clogher, 53.

50. Moses Connor to Morant, January 1848 (PRONI, Shirley papers, D.3531/P/2).

51. Widow Ellen Connor to Morant, 2 March 1848 (ibid.).

52. See Martin McKittrick, 21 January 1848 (ibid.).

53. Anthony Coote, Thomas Armstrong, Peter Hooey and John Dawson to Morant, 2 May 1846 (ibid.).

54. Bundoran, Co. Donegal was the established seaside resort for southwest Ulster. The fashionably dressed young women (or men?) to be found there were objects of ridicule to the local peasantry. I am indebted to W. A. Maguire for suggesting this explanation for why the term was applied to the Farney cross-dressers.

55. B[ernard] Hanlon to Trench, [c.1844] (PRONI, Shirley papers, D.3531/P/3). An alternative system for the protection of the rights of tenants came from secret societies, like the Molly Maguires. Trench described the Molly Maguires as active in Farney. (*Realities,* ch.5). See also Kevin Kenny, *Making Sense of the Molly Maguires* (New York: Oxford University Press, 1998).

56. The Shirley Estate was unusual in leasing bog land separate from the rest. Trench advised Mr. Shirley against the practice, insisting it was an undue burden upon already struggling tenants.

57. Griffith's, Corbane, 56.

58. I am indebted to Kevin O'Neill for his comment that the enforcers calling themselves the Bundoran Girls were probably protecting the widow's right of Mary Burns to take turf from the bog.

59. Catherine McKittrick to Morant, 4 June 1845 (PRONI, Shirley papers, D.3531/P/2).
60. Martin McKittrick to Evelyn J. Shirley, 4 June 1845 (ibid.).
61. Alice Meegan to Trench, 25 May 1844 (ibid., D.3531/P/3).
62. One perch was 30-square yards.
63. There were no Meegans in either of the townlands (Tullynaskeagh East and West), Griffith's, Tullynaskeagh, 53–54.
64. John Traynor to Trench, September 1845 (PRONI, Shirley papers, D.3531/P/2).
65. Griffith's, Drumgurra, 59.
66. Trench, *Realities,* 149.

Chapter Twelve

The Land War in the Irish Northwest: Agitation and Its Unintended Consequences ▨

Joan Vincent

He got them united. And they agitated. They fought for the three F's and
they won. They won the greatest victory Ireland got for years and years.[1]

T he crucial problem to be addressed in this essay is the resistance of
tenant farmers (some) to paying rent to landlords (some) in
County Fermanagh between 1879 and 1882. It focuses in particular on the popular face of Agitation, placing emphasis on families and
crowds, not on the individuals listed in Land League membership records,
criminal registers, and Home Office papers. It is concerned with the actions of followers rather than simply members.

The activities of the Irish National Land League were narrated in three
Fermanagh newspapers: *The Impartial Reporter and Farmers' Weekly* (founded
in 1825, and, by 1879, under the editorship of William Copeland Trimble);
The Lisbellaw Gazette and County Fermanagh Advertiser (established by J. G.V.
Porter of Belleisle in 1879 largely as an expression of his own brand of liberal politics); and *The Fermanagh Times and Northern Counties Gazette*
(founded in 1881 to oppose the Land League and rally tenants around Fermanagh's Orange landlords). I draw on these both for a chronology of
events and for the multivalent rhetoric to be heard at 19 Land Meetings
held between December 1879 and October 1881. The significance of
newspapers in the mobilization process was remarked upon at the time: the
Land League, it was said, "has made the farmers a reading people."[2]

A primary objective of this essay is to place alongside newspaper- and popular culture-speak of Protestants and Catholics the marginalized lexicons of gender and class. It contests any claim that "the Land War was a Catholic movement,"[3] arguing that the real nature of the Irish Land War cannot be fully understood in the sectarian terms employed by its contemporaries. The struggle in Fermanagh, as elsewhere in Ireland, is between the owners of property in the form of land and those who rent land from them. Its underlying dynamic was the combination of large and small tenant farmers, Catholic clergy, and country shopkeepers to resist the rent demands of a small landlord class.[4]

The course of events in Fermanagh was distinctive in two respects: first, the strength of the combination of property owners, Anglican clerics, and the Orange Order—the Ascendancy class—and their virtual control of a landless laboring class,[5] and second, the relatively large number of tenant farmers holding over thirty acres of land. These, in the south of Ireland, were to become "the critical nation-forming class."[6] In Fermanagh constitutionalism was the order of the day between 1879 and 1882. The days of physical force nationalisms lay ahead.

Fermanagh, west and east of Lough Erne, might serve as a microcosm of Ireland west and east. The autochthonous National Land League of Mayo flourished between January and October 1879, supported almost entirely by small farmers and their families.[7] Only later after the National Irish Land League centralized in Dublin had mobilized larger tenant farmers in the east of the country were tenurial concessions won from Gladstone's liberal government.

Postcolonial studies draw attention to the cultural politics of class, gender, and race as *interlocking* "structures of oppression."[8] In Ireland, unlike most capitalist colonies, colonizers and colonized were distinguished by religion instead of race, the post-Plantation tenurial system and penal laws of the sixteenth and seventeenth centuries having fundamentally privileged members of the Protestant faith. The uneven development that ensued through conquest and agrarian capitalist development contributed to the ideological work of gender as it worked itself out through distinctions of class and religion.[9] Cultural mores engendering gender relations are institutionalized in the most fundamental institutions of social being—the taken-for-granted everyday life of domestic groups (households), neighborhoods, work groups, communal gatherings, and the like. They are further writ large in family relations involving roles and responsibilities. Families engaged in Land League agitation because family interests were at stake. Neighborhood and community—networks of familial ties (kin and affines) and friendships—provided the arenas in which Land League branches were formed, evictions protested, and boycotting applied.

Localizing the "Land War" in this way permits an appreciation of paths not taken and goals not achieved. Within certain localities countervailing force was mounted by the Loyal Orange Order and, less directly, by benevolent capitalist landowners. Regardless of social divisions and cultural fault lines, such contradictory political tensions moved Fermanagh society, slowly at times, rapidly at others, wholly in certain locations, partially in others, toward Agitation, and always against the domination, hegemony, and resistance of those in the British parliament whose political and economic policies ultimately controlled everyday lives. Collectively, these tensions help explain why Agitation went only so far and no farther.

"TRIBULATION AND SUFFERING"

Distress in the northwest of Ireland preceded the formation in Dublin of the Irish National Land League, empowering those who became its leaders to raise more funds in the United States than might otherwise have been the case, and requiring that a distinction be made publicly between physical force and constitutional objectives. In Fermanagh this divided the league's local branches. Tribulation in the form of oppression by landlords was not as severe in Fermanagh as in many parts of Ireland. Of the county's 408,942 acres, 37 percent was owned by five individuals with estates of over 27,000 acres—small by Irish and English standards. All five belonged to families that had held the land at least since the seventeenth century and all were resident. Indeed, of Fermanagh's 695 landowners, all but twelve lived in the county or just across its borders. As in much of Ireland, a shift from tillage to pasture had left barely 25 percent of the population engaged in agriculture. Some 8 percent of the tenant farming families held over 100 acres of land, while 59.26 percent held under 30 acres (see Table 12.1). In sum, 8,501 small-farmer families were vulnerable to the near-famine conditions of 1879.

Living conditions in the Irish northwest had been deteriorating since 1877, when unremitting rain in August destroyed the oats and rotted the potatoes in the ground. A poor harvest in 1878 was followed by the wettest and coldest winter on record. The unrelenting savagery of the weather exposed the well-housed tenant farmer to the knife-edge condition of a neighboring small farmer and the misery of the laboring poor. In public memory Agitation was, above all else, a response to the "near-famine" of 1879.[10] Thus was James Maguire long remembered as James the League for his work during the Agitation, as was the equally renowned Thomas Owens, the League's branch secretary at Arney, near Sessiagh, where a massive Land League meeting was held in August 1880.[11] Resistance to "landlordism" and despair over the necessity for emigration suggests that gut issues of habitation and livelihood underlay the farmers' response to distress.

Table 12.1 Landowners and Tenents, 1881 (Co. Fermanagh)

	Landowners	
Acreage	Number	Percentage of Fermanagh's 408,942 Acres
over 27,000	5	37.00
10,000–26,999	3	9.13
5,000–9,999	7	11.98
1,000–4,999	35	19.00
under 1–999	645	22.80
Total	695	98.91

	Tenant Farmers		
Acreage	Population	Number of Families	Percentage of Families
below 10	10,253	2,342	
11–20	17,307	3,589	
21–30	3,406	2,570	
Total	40,966	8,501	59.26
31–50	14,032	2,593	
51–100	10,312	1,928	
101–200	4,380	837	
201–500	1,761	322	
above 500	817	162	
Total	31,302	5,842	40.70

Source: House of Commons, "Landed Proprietors," *Parliamentary Papers,* 1872, vol. 47, pp. 249–253, 785; House of Commons, "The Census of Ireland for 1881, Part 2, General Report," *Parliamentary Papers,* 1882, vol. 76, p. 204.

Distress did not simply precede Agitation in Fermanagh, it accompanied it. Between a first Land Meeting held at Belcoo on 26 December 1879 and a second at Sessiagh in August 1880 nature intervened. Fermanagh suffered a particularly bad harvest. The supply of turf was unusually small, and in many places the potato crop was blighted. Seasonal migrants found no work in England and Scotland. Small farmers owed up to ten times the amount of their annual rent. Farms under £8 valuation, it was estimated, "will utterly fail unless aided."[12]

News of Fermanagh's distress reached New York when letters sent to the *Reporter* were reprinted in the *New York Sunday Democrat* in January

1880.[13] Fermanagh-born merchants established a Fermanagh Relief Association in Manhattan to assist small-farmer emigration. Anna Parnell of the Irish Famine Relief Fund immediately attacked it as sectarian, a charge its officers denied in the *New York Herald*. The association raised around $4,500 but collapsed when its largest contributors asked to extend its scope to the north of Ireland.[14]

That same month Charles Stewart Parnell toured New York State raising a quarter of a million dollars in four days. Obliged to agree that some of the funds raised should be used for relief, his nationalist objectives were curbed by Irish distress. Parnell also cut away ground from under the Irish Republican Brotherhood, which also sought funds to buy arms and mount an agrarian revolution.[15] The amalgamation of 28 existing Irish-American organizations to form an American Land League was the compromise solution.[16]

Parnell's relief aid was lauded at a mass meeting in Fermanagh, the *Reporter*'s eye-catching capitalization technique highlighting the drama as leaguer Thomas Little, a Protestant farmer from Clabby, declared: "While the landlords gave us nothing, WE ATE PARNELL'S BREAD."[17] The *Reporter*'s editor, William Trimble, concurred with Parnell that emigration was not what Ireland wanted and proposed that American funds be sent to Poor Law unions, recognizing the regional dimension of Fermanagh's distress. He singled out as most needy the Fermanagh-Leitrim borderland around Kiltyclogher, "the poor in the mountains" between Roslea and Lisnaskea, and a northern district extending from Lack to the Donegal border. Here "strong men and women are emaciated, and exhausted through tribulation and suffering, and the seeds of disease and death are sown."[18]

A delegation from Ederney, a small town near Lack, instigated the first land meeting in Fermanagh on 26 December 1879, barely two months after the Irish National Land League had been formed in Dublin. Held at Belcoo on the Leitrim-Fermanagh border, it intimated the convergence of forces that would shape Agitation in Fermanagh over the next three years: receptivity to moderate tenants' rights leaders and liberal landowners; the presence on platforms of Catholic and Methodist, but never Episcopalian clerics; and the intimidation of those who attended land meetings. At Belcoo this took the form of threats to wreck the train carrying the crowd home afterward. As the movement grew moderation and constitutionalism persisted, as did opposition, but the complexion of platform speakers changed quite markedly.

Nothing approached in magnitude and intensity the rural agitation that galvanized the county between 1879 and 1882. Historical precepts were contested, ideologies unseated, and radical new alliances formed. "Orange Fermanagh" was shaken to the core, and efforts to restore domination through intimidation and misuse of state power served only to engender defiance on a larger scale. In the space of a few months the movement came to embrace small farmers and their families (men, women, and children), laborers, publicans, a few landowners, and even the journalists who covered its meetings.

Twenty League branches were formed and 19 mass meetings held between December 1879 and October 1881 (see Map 12.1.) Few accepted the league's program in its entirety, the most contentious issue being "constitutionalism" versus "physical force," the latter a legacy from the Fenian and the former from the Home Rule movement. Both were bequeathed directly to Fermanagh by Parnell, John Dillon, and Michael O'Sullivan when they addressed land meetings at Belleek, Enniskillen, and Sessiagh.[19] Reverend Boylan, the county's leading Catholic leaguer, forced O'Sullivan off the platform at Sessiagh for urging adoption of the league's most extreme "no rent" policy.[20]

Of course resistance to exorbitant rent demands was hardly alien to Fermanagh tenant farmers. "Rent at the point of a bayonet" was an established tactic for resisting tithes, withholding Poor Law rates and demanding lower rents. To refuse rent altogether, even when coerced by agent, magistrate, constabulary, and military, was the ultimate protest. It occurred only once, in October 1881 when, on hearing of the arrest of Parnell, Boho members refused to pay all rent. Immediately troops were sent and the proscription of the whole barony threatened. The lord lieutenant requested that more police be stationed in the county permanently. Given the readiness of Fermanagh's power-holders to adopt coercive measures, it is, perhaps, not surprising that Agitation more routinely took the form of recruitment, raising funds, and paying the legal costs of tenants fighting "unjust rents." On the whole, however, rhetoric, rather than militant action, was the order of the day. "Captain Moonlight" was little in evidence in Fermanagh, although "he" claimed credit for damaging the tented camp of evangelical revivalists at Lisnaskea.[21]

Local branches were also divided over whether their ultimate objective should be "peasant proprietary." Most of their leaders, but especially Jeremiah Jordan, a Methodist shopkeeper and the son of a Brookeborough farmer, favored moderation.[22] Led by the middle class—strong farmers, urban shopkeepers (Catholic and Protestant), Catholic priests and Methodists—their struggle was directed towards local ends, restraining local landlords and contesting their hold over local government, rather than challenging the distant national regime. Contesting local elections for guardians in the Enniskillen Poor Law union in April 1881, league candidates won five seats and only narrowly lost in three others.[23]

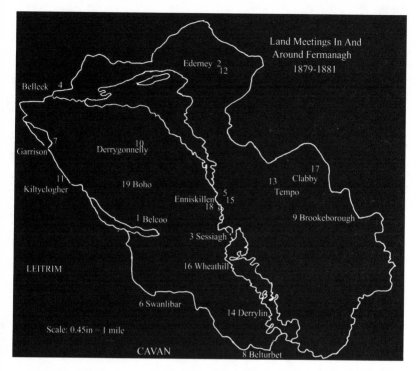

Land Meetings In And
Around Fermanagh
1879-1881

Ederney 2
12

Belleek 4

Garrison 7

Derrygonnelly 10

17
Clabby
13
Tempo

Kiltyclogher 11

19 Boho

Enniskillen 5
18 15

9 Brookeborough

1 Belcoo

3 Sessiagh

LEITRIM

16 Wheathill

6 Swanlibar

14 Derrylin

Scale: 0.45in = 1 mile

CAVAN

8 Belturbet

Map 12.1

The embourgeoisement of Irish rural society led by affluent or aspiring farmers and village traders provided a launch pad for agitation by both men and women, both jointly and categorically. Expectations of mobility for both men and women had been raised by modernization in the Catholic Church[24] and increased professionalization in general. The empowerment of rural women as wives and mothers, controllers of the family purse, gave greater status and authority to women than any form of paid labor, as census data suggest.[25] Methodist and Evangelical revivals had been bringing women into public life for many years in Fermanagh,[26] and by the 1880s an Irish "women's rights" movement had established itself on the Irish scene.[27]

In spite of local branch success in rallying over 2,000 people a time to several land meetings in Fermanagh, in November 1880 the Dublin executive announced that it would be *launching* an "invasion" of the North through Belleek, a small factory town midway between Enniskillen and Ballyshannon. Jordan shared the platform with Parnell, Dillon, and J. J.

O'Kelly, MP.[28] Their speeches did not set Fermanagh alight, but Parnell's traverse of the country from Belleek to Irvinestown, and then across to Ulster east of the River Bann, drew enthusiastic crowds at every train station through which he passed.

The Orange Order immediately countered with a manifesto proclaiming that the Land League was a conspiracy to subvert property rights, Protestantism, and the British constitution.[29] Since virtually all Fermanagh's 695 landowners were Protestant and the 5 largest and most powerful were all Orangemen, their tenants in particular might require a great deal more than rhetoric and symbolism if they were to join the league. A testing moment had come and gone in September 1880 when tenants on the Mayo estate of the earl of Erne (Fermanagh's second largest landowner) rose in protest at the extortionate demands of his land agent, Captain Charles Boycott. The Catholic priest who acted as intermediary between the tenants and the Land League executive in Dublin proposed a march on Castle Crom, the earl's residence in Fermanagh. He was sure that Fermanagh's tenant farmers, Protestant as well as Catholic, would support their brethren. We shall never know; the national executive vetoed the march lest it result in the Mayo tenants offering to pay a portion of their rents to keep their homes. Many Fermanagh landlords had already seized the high ground in 1879 with rent rebates and relief aid and, at that time, it was by no means certain that tenants would unite, as Father John O'Malley predicted, to support their Mayo brethren.

One of the main functions, I suggest, of the 19 land meetings held in and around Fermanagh in the space of 22 months, attracting crowds of between 1,000 and 5,000 and contingents from over 20 miles away, was educating the public about tenurial conditions throughout the county. Landlord response to distress and rent relief varied from estate to estate. For agitation to become class action, tenant farmers under "good" landlords had to be persuaded to join the league for the sake of others. As it turned out the establishment's coercive response to the Brookeborough land meeting was critical in winning their support.

The Brookborough land meeting was organized by the master of one Orange Lodge, the Brookborough district treasurer, and supported by 41 members of another. The day before it was due to be held a placard was circulating calling for loyal Orangemen to assemble at Brookeborough to stop the proceedings by giving "Parnell and his associates a warm welcome."[30] The *Reporter*'s dramatic headlines provide a synopsis:

MAGISTRATES AND THE SPEAKERS
The Authorities Oppose the Meeting
THE RIOT ACT READ

CAVALRY DRAWING SWORDS
EXASPERATING THE PEOPLE
Arrested for Cheering the Queen
THE MEETING HELD!

Its long editorial, preceding full-page eyewitness coverage of the events that occurred, condemned the authorities for the manner in which they interfered with the right of public assembly and concluded "the people had the victory. They held their meeting."[31] National papers concurred, including the *Illustrated London News,* which had an artist on the spot. In the grand scheme of things, a parliamentary inquiry was held to investigate the actions of the magistrates, constabulary, and militia at Brookeborough. In Fermanagh "Brookeborough" fuelled a rapid-fire series of largely Protestant meetings (albeit always with Catholic leaguers and even Catholic priests on the platform) throughout the countryside.

After Brookeborough reports came in that Protestants outnumbered Catholics in the league two to one.[32] For the first time Orange flags and banners were flown at land meetings. Prior to this it had been agreed that banners should not be carried lest they provoke armed opposition. After Brookborough, bands marched and for the first time meetings were held in localities notorious in the past for extreme sectarian violence: Derrygonnelly, Tempo, and Derrylin. A landscape inscribed by conquest and colonial domination was being reinscribed by Land League unity. At this point, culture-speak suggested that Protestants "made their own of the League,"[33] masking the less provincial reality that more large farmers from the densely populated lowlands were throwing in their lot with the league. Along with expansion came an unexpected consequence—an explicit trend toward more gendered rhetoric.

LAND MEETINGS AND THE INSCRIPTION OF GENDER[34]

Cultural geography and gender politics contributed significantly to the league's growth in Fermanagh, where a gendered construction of place had long conditioned public identity. Any privileging of experience historically inaccessible to women and the lower classes diminished along a continuum from private chambers to public rooms to open spaces. In Enniskillen the courthouse was an exclusive site for county and state formal representation, and as in the House of Commons, women were "caged" high up in the visitors' gallery.[35] The town hall was the site of public meetings and balls. It was a signal coup when Enniskillen leaguers held their inaugural meeting there. Admission was by ticket only, in contrast to the demonstration addressed by Parnell, Dillon, and O'Kelly held on the fair green at the east end of town.[36]

Where possible land meetings were held within walking distance from a railway station. Train excursions, famously family affairs, brought supporters from as far afield as Manorhamilton in Leitrim and Ballyshannon in Donegal. The meetings were held in privately owned fields, a hillside creating an auditorium. A litany of sites and the response to its recital inspired and consolidated the growth of the movement, providing a ritualized history of resistance. West of Lough Erne the meetings progressed from marginal border areas (Belcoo and Belleek) to central lowlands (Sessiagh, where a somewhat distanced challenge was offered to the earl of Enniskillen, Grand Master of the Orange Order, and Wheathill on the doorstep of his mansion at Florencecourt) to Enniskillen.

East of Lough Erne, the progress was in time rather than space: from Tempo (6 January 1881) through Enniskillen (3 February 1881) to Clabby (10 March 1881). This second phase in the memorializing of place revealed how much more difficult was the terrain to be mastered. First, more landlords had offered rent rebates early in the distressful period and many had already met tenants' demands for fair rents and fixity of tenure, holding out only against free sale. Second, this was the heartland of Fermanagh Orangedom, and it was not easy for Orangemen—often-favored tenants—to put long-term class action before short-term personal advantage, as league membership required.

Gender politics was much more explicit than that of class interest. Few league orators alluded to women at meetings to the west of Lough Erne, whereas east of the lough many did so. In the west speakers described women as victims—clearly a trope to demonize the landlord and agitate the crowd. East of the Lough Orangemen seemed particularly prone to speak of the agency of their womenfolk in explaining why they became leaguers.

The different gender dialects may have reflected the fact that experiential knowledge of Agitation entered western Fermanagh from Mayo and Leitrim. Speakers at the first wave of land meetings were Catholic small farmers, priests, and the fiery Michael O'Sullivan. When second-wave Agitation took hold in the east, where more of the tenants were Protestant strong farmers, fewer "strangers" were invited and more local branch members spoke. At Belcoo, for example, six strangers and the local priest spoke from the platform and solely to resolutions; at Tempo three strangers and six locals spoke, including one drawn from the crowd and invited onto the platform. Whereas the "strangers" spoke vehemently about "landlordism" or "the land system," locals drew on their own experiences at the hands of an unjust agent or landlord, recounting family histories of harassment.

Two extracts from speeches at the Tempo land meeting on 6 January 1881 serve to illustrate this rhetorical shift.[37] In the first Francis Little, a leading Orangeman from Clabby, chaired the meeting, calling for Fermanagh's unanimous voices to be heard in "the great parliament house in England" as they seized

> liberties in hand to take the opportunity to help themselves. (Cheers). We will muster together, independent of party or creed, and come together unanimously. (Cheers). *Not only the men of Fermanagh but the good ladies of Fermanagh must be with us, and I will tell you today that if I had about 100 of the fair sex of Fermanagh with a few old kale stalks that grew in their gardens I would not be afraid to meet all the landlords in Ireland.* (Great cheering).

Little had been expelled from the Grand Orange Lodge of Fermanagh for organizing the Brookeborough land meeting. At Tempo he was proclaimed "Grand Master for Ireland of the ORANGE LAND LEAGUERS (Great cheering)."[38]

The *Reporter* again had recourse to its capped headline technique to introduce the "family troubles" of one farmer: "MY WIFE TOLD ME." Thomas Carter, an Orangeman, recounted how his wife had warned him that he would lose his "situation" (tenancy) if he spoke out at the meeting, but he told her he had nothing to fear because he would be speaking the truth.

> (I)n coming to speak of our grievances, when our wives are crying (here the speaker visibly gave way to strong emotion)—not feeding pigs and calves, and have nothing at the end of the year but lamentation and woe, I would not be a manly man if I did not come forward for your protection. (Cheers.) . . . If I lose my situation because I came among you, I will have to travel far away and thank God there is a wide world. Many a tear has gone to God from the eyes of tenants who had injustice done to them. There was weeping when people had to go to America to find a home there. . . . (Loud and prolonged cheering)."[39]

An emotional climax reached, Chairman Little had the last word, declaring that "they would not rest till *every man, woman and child* in the county were Land Leaguers (Cheers)."[40]

The nonsectarian membership of all league branches and the practice of at least one loyal Orange Lodge in converting, lock, stock, and barrel, to league status was a phenomenal demonstration of the extent to which Agitation had loosened the hold of Fermanagh's power-holders. But the case must not be overstated. Several individuals were expelled for joining the Land League, and the warrants for two lodges were cancelled because of their members' league activities. Although exceptional in one respect for having fraternized with Catholics, Tempo's Orange leaguers were neither anomalous nor exceptional in their overt acknowledgement of women's role in social life. Women's public role in lodge activities was publicly acknowledged, and their fellowship at Orange soirees and in community service was explicit recognition in local newspapers.

But the bare fact remains that men spoke of women, whether as victim or partner, as social dependents for whom they felt responsible. Appeals to men *through representations of their womenfolk* were not simply the cultivation of masculinity or an essentialist appeal for common *brotherhood* as leaguers regardless of class or denomination but an historically constructed political response to the situation. Michael Davitt later used the same device when he declared that Agitation had been "to save the homes of Ireland—the sacred, domestic domain of women's moral supremacy in civilized society."[41]

Ironically, only three weeks after the Tempo meeting at which gender had played its volatile part in bonding men, the Ladies' Land League (founded in New York in October 1880 to raise funds for Ireland) was asked to take control of the movement in light of the Dublin executive's imminent incarceration. This "remarkable event"[42] tends to obscure the fact that women qualified in their own right for membership in local branches of the Land League.[43] They were mostly widows or, more occasionally, single women, recognized as heads of households. They participated in all forms of land agitation, harassing process servers, boycotting and reinstating evicted tenants. Women faced imprisonment just as men did.[44] Not until the Dublin executive introduced "separate spheres" gender politics into agrarian protest were men and women's activities differentiated and at times, perhaps, separate and antagonistic.[45] At an early meeting of the Ladies Land League in Dublin, Katherine Tynan had asked, "Why ladies, not women?" "Because that would be 'too democratic'," she was told.[46]

Three weeks after the Ladies' Irish National Land League was formally instituted in Dublin in January 1881, women at Kiltyclogher responded to its call: "You cannot prevent evictions, but you can and must prevent them from becoming massacres."[47] Three resolutions were passed: a vote of thanks to Miss Anna Parnell and the ladies of the central branch for "their meritorious exertions on behalf of our suffering people"; a vote of thanks to Mrs. A. M. Sullivan "for her womanlike and tender action in visiting the living tomb where honest and brave Michael Davitt is confined"; and a protest against the government's "so-called" Protection of Life and Property bill, popularly known as "Coercion."[48] The militancy of these women contrasts with the bureaucratic, relief-oriented restraint required of them in collating information on evictions, giving advice and encouragement to victims, and collecting and dispersing funds for emergencies. Gender conspired against class as the ladies' league capitalized—and tended to perpetuate—the service roles expected of women: from keeping household records to teaching school. Yet with foresight they established a Children's Land League principally to teach the injustice of Ascendancy and British domination.[49]

Fermanagh's newspapers were silent on the subject of women's engagement with Agitation with one notable exception. The mode of its telling bears comment. At Belcoo on 18 August 1881, eight tenants were evicted from Slievahon and Kilcoo townlands on the estate of one of Fermanagh's few absentee landowners. A crowd of some 50 persons gathered at house after house as each was "tossed" and the family evicted. James Robinson and his wife were sitting outside by an open fire as the police posse approached his house while John M'Hugh, secretary of the local branch, stood by witnessing his eviction. Widow Catherine Burns was next, followed by her son Thomas, supporting his frail wife as he was driven from his house with his family. M'Hugh tried to intervene but was ordered back by the attending magistrate. Burns's brother, his subtenant and a cobbler, was next, the tossing of his tools of trade delaying the party somewhat.

After evictions at Kilcoo, the party returned to Slievahon to evict Widow Gallagher and her seven small children, Widow Pat O'Brien and Widow Philip O'Brien—all wretchedly poor. Three representatives from the Kilcoo branch of the Ladies' Land League witnessed these events. Melodramatically, patronizingly, the *Reporter*'s man-on-the-spot describes their stance, "kept back by the sabre. They were not daunted." Miss Boyle, Miss Regan, and Miss M'Gourty "filled Land League eviction forms before the agent's eyes: they did their work admirably."[50] Afterward the officers of both Kilcoo League branches met in John Kelly's rooming house to discuss what might be done. We are not told of the outcome.

By and large, the Ladies' Land League did not get good press: "Sensible people in the North of Ireland dislike to see woman out of the place she is gifted to occupy, and at no time is woman further from her natural position than when she appears upon a political platform."[51] Nor, in Fermanagh, did any women who "stirred things up" receive favorable coverage. The empowering of women all around him appeared to agitate Trimble as he learned of Mrs. Amanda Smith's visit to Enniskillen, "an illiterate coloured woman" coming to conduct revival services. "A THOUGHT.—Women are great on this revival business and the men folk are getting smaller just now. When Mrs. Amanda Smith comes we will have four in town."[52]

COUNTER-MOVEMENTS

Land League Agitation cannot be understood unless movements to counter it are also examined. The estate of John Gray Vesey Porter, continuously identified as a "good landlord" since the 1840s, provides a case in point.[53] Space permits only a capsule account of those elements of modernity on Porter's estate that contributed to the retaining power of benevolent capitalists such as he. Porter prided himself that there was no league branch in Lisbellaw, where over nearly half a century he had fashioned a small world of "improvement."[54] He had opened a woolen factory (employing men, women, and youths); seen to it that railway trains stopped at Lisbellaw; and worked for flood control on Upper Lough Erne. Maverick in his politics, he condemned Parnell as a revolutionary as strongly as he excoriated the Orange Order as "the most useless, idle and ignorant Protestants in low hatred of Roman Catholics."[55] A supporter of tenant rights and Isaac Butt's Home Rule principles, Porter had been among the first landlords to give his tenants rent rebates in the near-famine of 1879.

Minutiae in women's public life speak to the gendered middle-class political action that benevolent capitalism begat. As O'Sullivan has so brilliantly demonstrated, many political leaders at the national level were unwilling to accept women and "a range of conflicting images [located] debates concerning gender and citizenship on either side of the domestic door-step."[56] I have suggested that in Fermanagh the politics of gender became broader as the League spread. At a soiree held in Lisbellaw's Orange Hall (described by Porter only nine months before as "now a volcano without fire, but which can still be shown to Tourists and Travellers as a sample of Old Ireland")[57], 16 women joined in the construction of a gendered *communitas* around the fiery local clergymen intent on instilling counter-Agitation sentiments.[58] The soiree was held on Wednesday, 17 November 1880, six days after Parnell and Dillon launched the Land League's "invasion of the North" and a bare three and half weeks before Orangemen were mobilized to attack the league at Brookeborough. The soiree served not only to bond the Loyal Orange lodges by class and sect but also to inculcate that ideological work of gender that the Land League itself was slow to learn.

A few yards away, a flower show had been held in Lisbellaw courthouse, as it had been every summer since 1874, the year in which John Gray Vesey Porter stood as Tenant Right candidate for Fermanagh in the national election. Dissatisfaction with the way the show was run, initially over the same persons (men) receiving the prizes year after year, led a group of women to protest. A new "Flower Show Committee of Management" was fashioned in which women had near equality with men, 13 women serving alongside 15 men.[59]

Porter's relationship with the Land League mirrored that middle constitutional ground on which many Fermanagh tenant farmers stood. He
had been invited to address the first land meeting at Belcoo in 1879 but,
given short notice, sent a letter instead. As the league became more militant, Porter became pointedly more critical, even travelling to Belleek to
protest "quietly and firmly and steadily" the Dublin executive's "invasion
of the North." Advised that his presence might spark a conflagration, he
spent the day out of public sight waiting for the meeting to end.[60]

Porter's long-standing efforts to "modernize" his Lisbellaw tenantry
across lines of class and religion through his patronage (and often instiga-
tion) of a myriad of alternative rural associations (ploughing matches,
farmers' clubs, a Young Men's Improvement Society,[61] an Old Men's Improvement Society, a Mechanics' Reading Room, a farmers' committee
among others) were challenged but not breached by the news and rhetoric
that passed from one land meeting to another. Thus when he offered those
of his tenants who had carried out improvements a second massive rent
abatement, some refused to accept it "on bad advice," presumably that of
the League. A "Lisbellaw delegation" attended (post-Brookborough) the
Wheathill land meeting in late August 1880.

In Fermanagh (with the notable exception of Boho) the Land War
ended with a whimper as large farmers, agitators and nonagitators alike,
flocked to land courts established under the Land Law (Ireland) Act of August 1881 to extract "just rents" from their landlords. Small farmers owing
rent were not eligible for reductions, and to maintain strength the Land
League began to recruit anew, becoming in September 1881 the Irish National Land League and Labourers and Industrial Union. Attention turned
from "the Land Question" to "Home Rule." His own man to the last,
Porter stood for election as the Home Rule party's candidate in South Fermanagh, thus belying the commonplace that "it is easier for a camel to pass
through the eye of a needle than for an Irish landlord to enter the kingdom of Home Rule."[62]

CONCLUSION

Six unintended consequences for better or worse may be garnered from
the subtexts of this essay: (1) the revitalization of the Orange Order
through its counter-Agitation measures; (2) the exposure of new class divisions in the rural districts; (3) the plethora of voluntary associations
that moved people from Manichean formulations of identity couched in
terms of tenant/landlord and Protestant/Catholic to forms less gross; (4)
the new ground that Agitation opened up for Evangelical missionary re-
vivalism; (5) the rapprochement of Orange and Green on the notoriously

sectarian Ulster frontier; and (6) the expansion of the politics of gender as Agitation spread. For the purposes of this volume, the latter consequence is of particular significance, especially when gender is connected with the historically specific configurations of class and religion in the region. The local perspective offered here sheds light on connections among: (1) the construction of gender ideologies at the level of quotidian life—in families, domestic groups, neighborhoods, and communities; (2) the motivations for involvement in Agitation by men—how and why men appealed to other men through particular representations of their womenfolk; and (3) the forms of political participation by women in Land League Agitation and in counter-movements.

All unintended consequences are by nature circumstantial, and all the attention in the world to Agitation and the counter-currents among which it moved cannot disguise in Fermanagh the coercive power of militarism and wealth, both British and diasporic. Maybe the *Fermanagh Times* was right to perceive the threat of Land League Agitation bringing down the Empire. Maybe the Lisbellaw flower lovers had it right when they exerted womanpower on home ground. Nevertheless, in several respects "the Land League generation travelled further in historical time than all previous generations in Irish history."[63]

NOTES

1. Hugh Patrick Owens, quoted in Henry Glassie, *Passing the Time in Bally-menone: Culture and History of an Ulster Community* (Philadelphia: University of Pennsylvania Press, 1982), 260. The "three F's" the tenants demanded were fair rents, fixity of tenure, and free sale of their holdings.

2. *Freeman's Journal,* 17 Sept. 1881.

3. Samuel Clark, *Social Origins of the Irish Land War* (Princeton: Princeton University Press), 282.

4. Brian M. Walker, "The Land Question and Elections in Ulster 1868–86," in *Irish Peasants,* ed. Samuel Clark and James S. Donnelly, Jr. (Dublin: Gill and Macmillan, 1978), 230–268; Paul Bew, *Land and the National Question in Ireland 1858–82* (Atlantic Highland, NJ: Humanities Press, 1979); Clark, *Social Origins;* R. W. Kirkpatrick, "Origins and Development of the Land War in Mid-Ulster, 1879–85," in *Ireland Under the Union: Varieties of Tension: Essays in Honour of T. W. Moody,* ed. F. S. L. Lyons and R. A. J. Hawkins (Oxford: Oxford University Press, 1980), 201–235.

5. Fermanagh's population in 1881 was 55.8 percent (47,359) Roman Catholic; 34.4 percent (30,874) Episcopalian; 5.7 percent (4,863) Methodist; and 2.0 percent (1,708) Presbyterian. (House of Commons [H. C.], "The Census of Ireland for the Year 1881, part I, vol. 3, Ulster," *Parliamentary Papers,* 1882, vol. 78).

6. Emmet Larkin, "Church, State, and Nation in Modern Ireland," *American Historical Review* 80 (1975): 1,245.

7. Joyce Marlowe, *Captain Boycott and the Irish* (London: Andre Deutsch, 1973); T. W. Moody, *Davitt and Irish Revolution 1846–82* (Oxford: Clarendon Press, 1981), 271–327; Donald E. Jordan, "Merchants, 'Strong Farmers' and Fenians: The Post-Famine Political Elite and the Irish Land War," in *Nationalism and Popular Protest in Ireland,* ed. C. H. E. Philpin (Cambridge: Cambridge University Press, 1987), 320–348; idem., *Land and Popular Politics in Ireland* (Cambridge: Cambridge University Press, 1994).

8. See, e.g., Raymond Crotty, *Ireland in Crisis. A Study in Capitalist Colonial Undevelopment* (Dingle, Co. Kerry: Brandon, 1986), 37–39; Ania Loomba, *Gender, Race, Renaissance Drama* (Manchester: Manchester University Press, 1989); Ania Loomba and Suvir Kaul, "Introduction: Location, Culture, Post-Coloniality," *Oxford Literary Review* 16 (1989): 3–30.

9. Mary Poovey, *Uneven Developments: The Ideological Work of Gender in Mid-Victorian England* (Chicago: University of Chicago Press, 1988).

10. Thomas O'Neill, "From Famine to Near-Famine, 1845–1879," *Studia Hibernica* 1 (1961): 161–171.

11. Glassie, *Passing the Time,* 96, 260.

12. H. C., "Preliminary Report of the Assistant Commissioners for Ireland," *Parliamentary Papers,* Cmnd. 2951, 1881, vol. 16, p. 841, 1.

13. *Reporter,* 22 Jan. 1880.

14. The *New York Herald* reached the Fermanagh homes of several young applicants for passage money and 40 acres of land in Kansas or Nebraska, including young men and women from Kiltyclogher.

15. *Freeman's Journal,* 22 Dec. 1879; *Reporter,* 22 Jan. 1880; Bew, *Land and the National Question,* 76; William O'Brien and Desmond Ryan, *Devoy's Post Bag 1871–1928* (Dublin: C. J. Fallon, 1948), 475–516.

16. T. W. Moody, "The New Departure in Irish Politics, 1878–9," in *Essays in British and Irish History in Honour of James Eadie Todd,* ed. H. A. Cronne, T. W. Moody and D. B. Quinn (London: F. Muller, 1949), 303–333.

17. *Reporter,* 11 Jan. 1881.

18. Ibid.

19. Parnell was, by this time, president of the Irish National Land League; Dillon was staunchly anti-Fenian and constitutionalist; O'Sullivan represented the Fenian wing.

20. *Reporter,* 26 Aug. 1880; *Fermanagh Times,* 26 Aug. 1880; *People's Advocate,* 28 Aug. 1880; Bew, *Land and the National Question,* 123.

21. *Reporter,* 29 Sept 1881. The note read: "NOTIS. To Soupers, ould Grey Ned and all Servants who helped to put up the tent. You will all go your Quarters even in daylight. Signed Captain Moonlight. Com. 43rd Gang. I.R.B." Lisnaskea, in the southeast, saw little overt league activity: Ould Ned was landowner Edward Archdall, but note that laborers were also being intimidated. Neither Davitt nor Parnell was in control of the agrarian secret societies metamorphosized as "Captain Moonlight" (Moody,

Davitt and Irish Revolution, 536); Joseph Lee, *The Modernization of Irish Society, 1848–1918* (Dublin: Gill and Macmillan, 1973), 86.

22. Jordan first achieved prominence as chairman of the Enniskillen town commissioners and then as an elected guardian in the Enniskillen Poor Law union. An admirer of Isaac Butt, he initially tried to commit the league to the objectives of the tenants' rights movement avoiding illegal action. As a Fermanagh representative, Jordan was defeated on this issue at a Dublin conference on the land question in April 1880 (Moody, *Davitt,* 375).

23. *Fermanagh Mail,* 7 Apr. 1881. By 1890 boards of guardians were as important as grand juries; see William L. Feingold, "The Tenants' Movement to Capture the Irish Poor Law Boards, 1877–1886," *Albion* 7 (1975): 219.

24. Emmet Larkin, *The Catholic Church and the Creation of the Modern Irish State 1878–1886* (Philadelphia: University of Pennsylvania Press, 1975).

25. Joanna Bourke, *Husbandry to Housewifery: Women, Economic Change and Housework in Ireland, 1890–1914* (Oxford: Clarendon Press, 1993); David Fitzpatrick, "The Modernisation of the Irish Female," in *Rural Ireland 1600–1900: Modernisation and Change,* ed. Patrick O'Flanagan and Kevin Whelan (Cork: Cork University Press, 1987). Only 25.75 percent (20,232) of Fermanagh's total population of 84,879 was engaged in agriculture in 1881 and of these only 157 were women. They predominated in domestic service (5,386) and nearly equaled men in the industrial sector (3,657 cf. 3,714). Most telling was the 55.45 percent (47,065) of the population described as "indefinite and non-productive." Of these, 31,425 were women.

26. David Hempton and Myrtle Hill, *Evangelical Protestantism in Ulster Society, 1740–1890* (London: Routledge, 1992), 30–44, 129–144.

27. Anthony Trollope wrote *The Landleaguers* in 1882 after two visits to Ireland to research the political background. He writes of "a feminine weakness" being mistakenly bartered away for "women's rights," a common theme also in his Barchester novels (*The Landleaguers,* ed. R. H. Super [Ann Arbor: University of Michigan Press, 1992], 115).

28. O'Kelly, who represented Roscommon, was a frequent speaker at Fermanagh meetings. He had been at Belleek and was later to figure in the *Illustrated London News* for his confrontation with the resident magistrate at Brookeborough.

29. Manifesto of the Grand Orange Lodge of Ireland, 3 November 1880 (*Freeman's Journal,* 9 Nov. 1880).

30. *Fermanagh Times,* 9 Dec. 1880.

31. *Reporter,* 9 Dec. 1880.

32. *Reporter,* 24 Dec. 1880.

33. *Reporter,* 24 Dec. 1880; Peadar Livingstone, *The Fermanagh Story* (Enniskillen: Cumann Seanchais Chlochair, 1969), 260.

34. In the analysis that follows I am indebted to the work of Gary Owens, who has rescued mass demonstrations and public assemblies from the margins of Irish history. Gary Owens, "Nationalism without Words: Symbolism and

Ritual Behavior in the Repeal 'Monster Meetings' of 1843–5," in *Irish Popular Culture, 1650–1850,* ed. J. S. Donnelly, Jr. and Kerby A. Miller (Dublin: Irish Academic Press, 1998), 242–270.

35. Anna Parnell, "How They Do It in the House of Commons: Notes from the Ladies' Cage," in *Celtic Monthly* 3 (May 1880): 469–72; 3 (June 1880), 537–41; 3 (July 1880), 17–21. For commentary, see Niamh O'Sullivan, "The Iron Cage of Femininity: Visual Representation of Women in the 1880s Land Agitation," in *Ideology and Ireland in the Nineteenth Century,* ed. Tadhg Foley and Sean Ryder (Dublin: Four Courts, 1998), 181–196.

36. *Fermanagh Times,* 11 Nov. 1880. Wishful thinking, perhaps, led Livingstone to place the demonstration at Gaol Square in the center of town (Livingstone, *Fermanagh Story,* 260).

37. Ideally I should address not simply the inception of these texts but their subsequent deployments in particular institutional spaces and in relation to particular audiences, but this is hardly possible given the nature of the record. Cf. Glassie, *Passing the Time* with Michel-Rolph Trouillot, *Silencing the Past* (Boston: Beacon Press, 1996) for two relevant anthropological approaches to this problem.

38. *Reporter,* 8 Jan. 1881.

39. Ibid.

40. Ibid. Emphasis added.

41. Michael Davitt, *The Fall of Feudalism in Ireland, or The Story of the Land League Revolution* (New York: Harper & Brothers, 1904), 299.

42. Margaret Ward, *Unmanageable Revolutionaries: Women and Irish Nationalism* (London: Pluto Press, 1983), 4.

43. This reflects on the silencing of women's agency in contemporary narratives, where print capitalism, to coin a phrase, disseminates public knowledge selectively. Paradoxically, the memoir of the Ladies' Land League's most famous member, Anna Parnell, also silences the part played by ordinary women in the Irish National Land League. See Anna Parnell, *The Tale of a Great Sham,* ed. with an introduction by Dana Hearne (Dublin: Arlen House, 1986).

44. Janet K. TeBrake, "Irish Peasant Women in Revolt: the Land League Years," *Irish Historical Studies* 28 (1992): 67–68.

45. For the general principle, see particularly L. J. Jordanova, "Natural facts: A historical perspective on science and sexuality," in *Nature, Culture and Gender,* ed. Carol MacCormack and Marilyn Strathern (Cambridge: Cambridge University Press, 1980), 42–69.

46. Katherine Tynan, *Twenty-five Years: Reminiscences* (London: Smith & Elder, 1913), 75; quoted in Ward, *Unmanageable Revolutionaries,* 15.

47. Jenny Wise Power, "The Political Influence of Women in Modern Ireland," in *The Voice of Ireland,* ed. W. Fitzgerald (Dublin and London: Virtue Press, 1924), 158–61; quoted in Ward, *Unmanageable Revolutionaries,* 15.

48. *Reporter,* 24 Feb. 1881.

49. Its main function was teaching Irish history. O'Sullivan, "Iron Cage," 187–188.

50. *Reporter,* 25 Aug 1881. The term "man-on-the-spot" is used advisedly. Shortly after Agitation began, Trimble announced that he was employing local correspondents to cover Land League branch activities.

51. *Belfast News-Letter,* 18 Mar. 1881; quoted in Ward, *Unmanageable Revolutionaries,* 23.

52. *Reporter,* 7 Nov. 1881.

53. On the rhetoric of "good" and "bad" landowners during the Land War, see Lee, *Modernisation,* 95.

54. Joan Vincent, "Rural Industrialization in Nineteenth-Century Fermanagh: A Case Study." Paper presented at a symposium on Industrialization and Social Change in Peripheral Europe: the Case of Western Ireland. American Anthropological Association meetings, Los Angeles, November 1978.

55. Livingstone, *Fermanagh Story,* 262. He concludes his account of Porter's long career: "Men like Porter make the history of Fermanagh edifying, but their influence was too small to make it different."

56. O'Sullivan, "Iron Cage," 184.

57. *Lisbellaw Gazette,* 17 Feb. 1880.

58. *Reporter,* 25 Nov. 1880.

59. *Reporter,* 26 Aug. 1880.

60. *Freeman's Journal,* 10 Nov. 1880; *Fermanagh Times,* 11 Nov 1880; *Reporter,* 11 Nov. 1880. Only the *Reporter* covers Jordan's attack on Porter at that meeting, reading and tearing up a placard Porter had posted in Enniskillen protesting the "invasion," an action that might be read as a public challenge to the man who had once been a candidate for the House of Commons from the man who wished to be.

61. The first Young Women's Improvement Society was founded in Enniskillen in 1885.

62. Wilfrid Scawen Blunt, quoted by Declan Kiberd, *Inventing Ireland: The Literature of the Modern Nation* (London: Vintage, 1996), 88.

63. Lee, *Modernisation,* 93.

Chapter Thirteen

Between Mater and Matter: Radical Novels by Republican Women ▣

Heather Zwicker

Perhaps the most incisive moment in the feminist video *Mother Ireland* occurs when Mairead Farrell, remembering the tenor of Armagh conversations, comments that Republican women prisoners used to say, "Mother Ireland, get off our back!"[1] The command succinctly denounces the asphyxiating bond between "Mother" and "Ireland" that often emerges in Irish independence struggles. Although balanced by the video's careful history of the trope and its importance, Farrell's recollection testifies to the fact that feminist nationalists in 1980s Northern Ireland sought ways to move beyond the colluding limitations of a nation allegorized as a woman and a woman figured as nation. The allegory itself is ubiquitous in anti-colonial nationalisms. "Mother Ireland," like "Mother India" or "Mother Africa," offers the unmappable dark continent of Woman as metaphor for all the tantalizing and dangerous utopian possibilities of the unrealized nation, carefully reigned in by the twinned notions of heteronormativity and natality. Because the metaphor can give shape to, or "embody," the idea of nation even in the absence of a territorial expression of the nation as a state, it is especially useful for mobilizing popular sentiment in the struggle for a nation-state.[2]

The nation-state, as material realization of the dreams of territorial nationalism, necessarily moves somewhat away from the abstractions of allegory. The quotidian problems of existing people, laws, policies, and economies tend to push aside abstractions like "Woman" and "Nation" and to loosen the tautological bond between them; the nation, once materialized as a state, turns out to be more complex than its abstraction ever supposed, just as women, being varied social subjects and varied in their demands on the state, spill over the contours of the figure of Woman. I am not suggesting that "Woman" and "Nation" or "Mother Ireland" entirely disappear from national rhetoric or national consciousness, nor that these abstractions cease to serve as fodder in ideological battles over patriotism and policy. However, I am contending that they figure *differently* after statutory independence has been achieved, that the event of national independence precipitates a reorientation in the sense of what a woman is or could be. The *Mother Ireland* video evinces this difference. While the early part of the documentary, which details the history of the trope, features talking heads from both the Republic of Ireland and Northern Ireland, the latter segments, discussing the problems and possibilities of the "Mother Ireland" figure today, increasingly feature feminists from the North, where nation and nation-state are disjointed. The implication is that the realization of a viable nation-state makes the need for an abstraction like "Mother Ireland" less pressing.

Although one might expect a loosening of the bond between Woman and Nation to be salutary for women, it is not in fact clear that such a shift is necessarily progressive; women can be named in all sorts of ways in the service of the state.[3] Juridical descriptions of women as concrete material subjects can limit the range of acceptable ways for women to occupy both their gendered and their national subjectivity. Irish history confirms that when women were constitutionally produced as concrete material subjects in the Republic, it was to delimit severely both of these social scripts. When nation begat nation-state, women found their roles naturalized and codified in de Valera's 1937 Constitution, which states that "by her life within the home, woman gives to the State a support without which the common good cannot be achieved." Not only rendering the family the basic building block of society, in Gerardine Meaney's terms, establishing and policing "a particular construction of sexual and familial roles [that] became the very substance of what it meant to be Irish," de Valera's wording also establishes and polices what it means to be a woman and what it means for a woman to be a national subject.[4] As Geraldine Heng argues, a state policy like this does particular cultural and ideological work. It

> legislate[s] a description of female identity by establishing legal responses to
> a wide-ranging set of presumptive questions (What is a woman? What does
> she need? What is the nature/what are the conditions of her sexuality? What
> is her place? What is the place of her relationships to others?)[5]

The Irish Constitution answers such questions summarily by producing women as subjects of the state through their role as mothers, a move that restricts the range of both gendered subjectivity (all women are mothers) and national subjectivity (mothering is basic to Ireland's "common good"). Put simply, the trope of Mother Ireland gets recast in the concrete, material bodies of women produced as mothers, who move in domesticated spaces in order to direct their energies toward the nation-state.[6]

Although these particular historical referents speak to the Republic of Ireland, the strictly gendered patriotism reinforced by de Valera's constitution spills over into the republicanism of Northern Ireland. In settling the question of the nation for the Republic of Ireland, the 1916 Rising and the ensuing partition of 1920–21 inflamed the national question in the North. One result of this is that republicans in Northern Ireland must contend with both the romantic, utopian ideal of a united Ireland and the actual nation-state of the Irish Republic. But another result of this historical development of Irish nationalism is that, at least in the most widely circulating image of anti-colonial Irish nationalism—"Republicanism"—women are enjoined to mother and oversee familial spaces, while men are expected to fight and govern. Republicanism, in this way, maps gender dichotomy neatly onto the *binary* opposition of private versus public spaces; its public face relies on a masculine heroism figured by staunch and sometimes secret brotherhoods, technological expertise and self-sacrifice backed by the obscured contributions of domesticated women. As Begoña Aretxaga puts it in her excellent anthropological study *Shattering Silence: Women, Nationalism, and Political Subjectivity in Northern Ireland*: "Republican historical myth contains powerful gender models of historical action, models that erase the historical agency of women in favor of individual male heroes."[7]

I do not want to suggest that women do not participate in republican struggles, military or political; they have done so throughout the twentieth century.[8] But the respective publicity of men's versus women's participation in republicanism has been uneven, and this unevenness became particularly acute in the early 1980s. One measure of the inequity might be taken from the relative obscurity of the Dirty Protest in relation to the 1981 hunger strikes, but factors like the formation (1978) and quick demise (1981) of the group Women Against Imperialism, the establishment of Sinn Féin's Women's Department in 1980, and the controversy surrounding the 1983 abortion referendum in the Republic of Ireland, also suggest that the need to reconcile republicanism and feminism became especially pressing in the early 1980s.[9] The difficulty of such a reconciliation covers ground familiar to postcolonial feminists; while republican women saw feminism as a class-blind and British colonial importation, feminists were "quite unanimous in [their] contempt for republicanism, which they perceived as a militaristic and male-dominated ideology and movement that had given rise in the South to a patriarchal, conservative government."[10] A Northern Irish feminism that would be sympathetic to the goals of republicanism, then, finds itself in the difficult position of criticizing *both* British colonial domination *and* its republican nationalist opposition, all in the context of a nation still in the making.

The concept of citizenship offers one promising way out of such a bind. By citizenship I do not mean individual statutory rights such as voting or carrying a passport; I use the term rather in the broader, more materialist, sense in which feminist critics like Nira Yuval-Davis and Ruth Lister use it.[11] Citizenship in this formulation refers to the economic and social enfranchisement necessary for all members of a nation-state to participate fully in social polity. In paying attention to the material conditions that make identities intelligible, the concept of citizenship gives us a way of focusing on communities and collectivities within a nation, and not just the citizen's individual relationship to the state. Feminist organizations can become discernible this way, as can residents' associations and ethnic affiliations, to cite just a few examples. Citizenship requires that subjects negotiate with the nation-state on a quotidian basis, but it never imagines the public sphere as being limited to the state alone; it thus holds onto a sense of both private and public spaces as politically charged arenas for articulating belonging to a nation-state. This has obvious advantages for women who are constrained in domestic spaces. In a more discursive sense, the notion of citizenship can help to articulate an Irish political platform that does not intervene solely in either the too-reified (for women) concept of the nation and its utopian telos or the limitations of de Valeran state policy. As Lister points out, active citizenship, "one which creates [people] as subjects rather than objects," has been extremely useful in mobilizing feminists in Northern Ireland.[12]

Such active feminist citizenship finds discursive expression in Northern Irish novels that focus on working-class women with republican sympathies. Written during the late 1970s and early 1980s, when the need to reconcile feminism and republicanism was acute, Jennifer Johnston's *Shadows on Our Skin* (1977), Mary Beckett's *Give Them Stones* (1987), and Linda Anderson's *We Can't All Be Heroes, You Know* (1985) articulate latent social criticism written from the perspective of Catholic working-class women in Northern Ireland.[13] These texts are not well known and not always well written, two factors that undoubtedly contribute to their critical neglect. Yet I think it is important to read such minor texts because they serve as a significant location for articulating an oblique critique of nation and nation-state by describing and condemning masculinist narratives of heroism that obscure the everyday lives of women. My argument is that the concept of active feminist citizenship can give us a way of understanding the cultural work these novels perform.

The novelists themselves are diverse. Johnston is the best-known writer, having published nine novels and several plays over the last two and a half decades. Protestant and bourgeois by birth, Johnston often uses her fiction to revisit key moments in early twentieth-century Irish history. *Shadows* stands out from the rest of her novels because it deals with the contemporary Troubles; it has been discussed in print only in passing.[14] Beckett, Belfast-born and working class, has written two collections of short stories in addition to *Give Them Stones*.[15] The bulk of her fiction deals with working-class women in Belfast, although her latest collection, *A Literary Woman,* sets some stories in Dublin. Her critical neglect is baffling: apart from book reviews, no literary criticism has been published on any of her fiction.[16] Anderson is the most politically outspoken of the three. She is far better known as a feminist and cultural critic than as a novelist. *Heroes* is her first novel. It has never been critically discussed; her second novel, *Cuckoo,* is even more obscure and deals with the Troubles only as a backdrop to the novel's more overtly feminist concerns.[17]

Despite the differences among their authors, these three texts, read in tandem for the continuity of their subjects and styles, suggest a radical feminist nationalist tradition in formation. In seeing the novels this way, I disagree with Aretxaga's claim that "Northern Ireland women writers . . . tend to represent women as trapped victims." Aretxaga continues:

> When women struggle to establish an independent existence within a male-dominated universe of violence, they are either defeated as in Jennifer Johnston's *Shadows on Our Skins* (1978), or their defiance is composed of solitary and self-contained gestures, as in Mary Beckett's stories *A Belfast Woman* (1980).[18]

While Aretxaga's description of the fiction is accurate, her analysis falls short. The closely plotted novels do take place in narrow, domestic spaces; triumphs are tiny and misery is constant. However, I would argue that such settings serve not to corroborate or approve the division of spaces into public/masculine and private/feminine, but to critique it, and, at the same time, to decry the collusions of patriarchy and colonialism. The ways in which patriarchy asserts itself in domestic settings needs no comment, but Aretxaga's later observation explains how the household becomes an equally significant setting for colonialism: "In nationalist culture, state violence perpetrated in the space of the house is interpreted as the epitome of English violence to the Irish nation."[19] Domestic settings, then, offer the most efficient site for critiquing patriarchy and colonialism simultaneously.

Female characters may, as Aretxaga claims, be "defeated" when they try "to establish an independent existence within a male-dominated universe of violence," but this failure is not without broader social implications. The novels imply utopian potential rather than explicitly stating it: given the material, social, and political conditions of Northern Ireland's decolonization, these novels argue, the romantic ideal of a united Ireland is not enough. Insistently, Johnston, Beckett, and Anderson point to the cultural nationalist rhetoric of IRA-headed resistance, especially its homogenization of Irish people and ideals, as one of the forces that perpetuate systemic social inequities. The critique embodied in their novels directs itself not simply against British imperialism, then, but against discourses of romantic heroism wherever they are found. The novels call instead for meaningful citizenship and full enfranchisement in the project of nation building. They are not simply anti-colonialist and nationalist, but materialist and feminist as well.

Johnston's *Shadows on Our Skins* makes its critique of heroism and its demands for citizenship relatively explicit. The novel chronicles the friendship of Joe Logan, an adolescent boy from working-class Derry, with Kathleen Doherty, a teacher. The friendship, which coincides with the return of Joe's brother Brendan from England, functions in the novel as a foiled alternative to the bleakness of Joe's everyday life. His mother works at a cafe and governs the family with a tough competence that admits no tenderness, while Joe's father lies incapacitated in an upstairs bedroom as a result of his war injuries, or so he represents himself. In fact, his incapacity turns out to be capricious, never disabling him from going out drinking, even though he is petty, demanding, and self-pitying at home. Before Joe is all the way in the house after school his father is banging on the floor with his stick, ordering Joe to bring him tea, buy him beer, or listen to his stories. Meanwhile, Joe's mother is concerned primarily for Joe's safety in the troubled streets and his life chances in the troubled society of Northern Ireland, so her relationship to Joe consists largely of admonitions to come straight home from school, do his homework, and clean his shoes.

Joe's parents, neither of whom is ever named, establish the poles of debate between romantic idealism and everyday material realities. The father lives in a fantasy world of his heroic exploits in the past. The details of his stories mutate endlessly, leading Joe's mother to call them "fairy tales."[20] Although the mother means the term as a synonym for lies, it has a self-conscious generic resonance, suggesting set stories with a clear moral point and a happy ending. The stories, history mythologized, are siren songs: their promise of turning ordinary men into heroes seduces the older brother, Brendan, into involvement with the IRA.

> Brendan knew those names as well as he knew his own: Liam Lynch, Ernie O'Malley, Liam Mellows, Sean Russell, the Joes, the Eamons, the Charles, all

heroes, dead heroes, living heroes, men of principle, men of action. Heroes. The world was peopled with heroes, with patrols and flying columns and sad songs that used to drift down through the floor to Joe below, songs about death and traitors and freedom and more heroes.[21]

The mother's criticism of such stories is that their enchanting abstractions, "death and traitors and freedom and more heroes," obscure the contemporary backdrop of endless work and inescapable poverty.[22] While Brendan sits at the kitchen table strategizing IRA tactics in the company of his father's reminiscences, the mother works at a cafe, buys and prepares food for the family, cleans the house and supervises Joe's education. Although the republicanism of Brendan and his father articulates an important critique of colonialism that can account for poverty on a macrological level, it refuses to deal with the micrological effects of nationalist revolution, particularly the disproportionate exhaustion of women. This critique is acted out most poignantly in the novel when the British army conducts house-to-house searches after two of its soldiers are killed. After the patrol tears apart the Logans' house in the middle of the night, the men of the household have a drink and go back to bed, while the mother stays up all night putting things back in drawers, scrubbing black boot marks off the kitchen floor, and sweeping up broken glass. The next day she goes to work while the father stays at home nursing his war wounds along with his impotence and his hangover.

The ideological difference between Joe's parents is not about the value of republicanism *per se*—the novel assumes a critique of British imperialism—but a contest over the meaning of its ideals. When the father boasts of how he fought for freedom, the mother asks, "What's freedom?" The father's answer appeals to a tautological abstraction beyond material referentiality: "Don't be a fool, woman. You know well what freedom is. Didn't I fight for freedom? What did Pearse, God rest him, say about freedom?"[23] Patrick Pearse, of course, says that freedom is not just material, but importantly discursive too; his cultural nationalism emphasizes Celtic mythological heroes and the Irish language. Pearse's historical double is James Connolly, the radical labor organizer. If Pearse justifies the father's heroism in the service of the ideals of 1916, Connolly stands behind the mother's retort, which criticizes the freedom that actually exists in the Republic of Ireland:

Is there a job for every man? And a home for everyone? Have all the children got shoes on their feet? Are there women down there scrubbing floors to keep the home together because stupid, useless old men are sitting round gassing about freedom? Singing their songs about heroes?[24]

To the father she appears hopelessly small-minded: "I talk about freedom. You talk about shoes and pensions," he says in disgust.[25] But Johnston stands behind the mother's insistence that the ideals of revolution be made concrete. Her vision is materialist rather than cultural nationalist; whereas the father's version of nationalism relies on a romantic, masculine heroism voiced and enacted in public spaces, the kind of social revolution envisioned by the mother would start with the material amelioration of private domestic spaces in order to bring about a decent life for everybody. In other words, meaningful citizenship, "full enfranchisement in social polity," cannot be brought about through rhetorical assertion, however forceful. It demands rather a close attention to the material minutiae of everyday life.

A similar insistence runs through Mary Beckett's *Give Them Stones*. Although the novel starts out with republican sympathy, it ends with its defeat by everyday life in urban Northern Ireland. A fictional autobiography, the novel charts the life of Martha Murtagh, the working-class, Catholic, republican daughter of a seamstress and her IRA-sympathetic husband. Born during the General Strike of 1926, Martha is evacuated from Belfast during the air raids of World War II and spends a couple of years with two aunts in the country. Returning to Belfast after the aunts die, Martha marries, bears four sons, and starts a small home-baking business that is destroyed and rebuilt three times.

If *Shadows* is resolutely materialist in its resistance to national dreams, *Stones* holds on to utopian ideals, the nation among them, as a way of recognizing the desire for something beyond the Troubles, but without ever losing sight of the material conditions of everyday Belfast life that work against that vision. The relentlessness of Martha's labor, which constitutes the novel's plot, takes place against a number of tropes that Beckett critiques as fairy tale ideologies: the pull-yourself-up-by-your-own-bootstraps rhetoric of capitalism, here cast in the context of English occupation; Christian mythology; romantic love; and Irish cultural nationalism. These ideologies promise too easy a transcendence from the everyday, the novel argues; it is only when an emancipatory ideology finds expression in everyday life that it becomes meaningful.

Capitalism and colonialism find articulation in the classroom, through stories that attempt to tame Ireland and render it invisible. Martha's first lesson in school is a story about Fergus, a boy who owns a rabbit that escapes from its cage, thinking it wants to be a wild rabbit; however, when it gets lost in the snow the rabbit realizes it is better off being caged. The maxim here is fairly explicit, as it is in other school lessons. The sadistic schoolmistress teaches her students Shakespeare, English hunting songs, and obscure vocabulary, while geography lessons focus on the Balkans rather than Northern Ireland. Although they pretend to be nonpartisan, such class-room lessons value abstractions that devalue local realities and hence mystify the relationship between colonialism and Northern Irish students. Shakespeare exemplifies a concept of literary excellence that obliterates indigenous cultural production; English hunting songs promote aristocratic culture; vocabulary dehistoricizes language, ignoring dialects; and studying the Balkans suggests that the international is more significant than the regional. The disjuncture between the classroom and students' everyday lives becomes clearest when a school inspector from the Republic of Ireland visits a class that Martha's sister is teaching to Catholics in Belfast. The inspector interrupts Mary Brigid's geography lesson about the Six Counties with his progressive pedagogy, by which he promises to demonstrate how the students can teach her. The topic he chooses is shipbuilding:

> "How many girls have fathers or brothers working in the shipyard?" Some of them said their daddies were dockers but he said he wanted to hear about shipbuilding and they looked at one another without saying anything. He turned to Mary Brigid and asked, "Do they not understand my accent?" and she said that was no trouble to them only none of them had anybody working in the shipyard except now and again when there was a rush of work. Suddenly it dawned on him that he'd heard Catholics didn't get these jobs and he went pink and embarrassed so that Mary Brigid felt for him and began talking about the rocks in the Cave Hill that belong to everybody.[26]

The final lie of colonial pedagogy hinges on the capitalist promise of work for all who want it, a mythology of heroic effort that denies the material reality of discrimination in the workplace, not to mention the difficulty of finding work in an economy where unemployment is rampant. The implicit universality of classroom pedagogy works against an understanding of working-class Belfast life.

Although Mary Brigid appeals to Cave Hill as the site of democracy—its rocks "belong to everybody"—her statement is undercut by the story that follows this scene. Martha describes a trip to Cave Hill that she and Mary Brigid took one Easter Sunday when they were young. Near the top of the hill, they see a young man lying below the caves. Afraid, apparently, that he is hurt, the girls run down the hill to find a police officer to help the man. However, the police accuse the girls of acting as decoys for a sniper and, while one officer holds Martha at the bottom of the hill, another takes Mary Brigid back to where the girls saw the man, who has disappeared by the time they arrive. The story not only allows Martha to dispute the notion of democratically owned space (the police officers are clearly defending the space *against* the girls and the man), but also metacritically figures the way Christian mythology is thwarted in Northern Ireland. The story, taking place as it does on Easter Sunday, re-calls the New Testament account of Christ's resurrection, where Jesus' women disciples visit his tomb, only to discover his resurrection. In Beck-ett's version the man at Cave Hill has an ambiguous identity. Is he the angel entrusted with the tidings of Christ's resurrection, or perhaps Christ himself? Or, given the significance of Easter Sunday in republican Irish history, does he figure Wolfe Tone, Parnell, Pearse? Whatever heroic ca-pacity he has as a figure collapses, because he goes unrecognized. The New Testament with all its promises of supercession and transcendence finds expression in everyday life only as a backdrop to police repression.

Nor does romance offer any greater hope in the novel. Martha falls in love once, with a man named Hugh, but with tuberculosis in his family her aunts force her to stop seeing him. Eventually Martha marries a man named Dermot Hughes for the most dispassionate and pragmatic of rea-sons: his kitchen appliances. Martha says on her first visit to Dermot's "or-dinary wee house," where he lives with his mother:

> Then Dermot opened what I thought was the back door but it was into an extension they'd built. They called it "the back kitchen." There was a gas cooker with four rings and a grill, and below, an oven. Beside it there was a sink with hot and cold chromium taps. I knew then I wanted to marry Dermot.[27]

Stones nullifies the bourgeois myth of connubial bliss by pointing out that a woman's economic position gives her a particular relationship to the prospect of marrying. Martha's marriage is bland and predictable; she bears four children and then her sex life ends. When her husband accuses her of being hard, Martha says, "maybe I am. I just feel a terrible deep sadness that there is no life in Belfast for our children. Soft words do nothing for that kind of deprivation."[28] In other words, her hardness is not a maternal de-fect, but rather produced by the conditions of working-class life in Belfast. In this moment Beckett skillfully puts mothering into a historical context, not merely the juridical context of de Valera's constitution, and her appeal to history, rather than abstract idealized nation or the legislative strictures of the nation-state, suggests an avenue for articulating a version of citizen-ship that can be collapsed into neither.

While the novel's dismissal of romantic love is brief and brutal, Martha's disavowal of the IRA comes about slowly and painfully. As a working-class Catholic whose father is imprisoned for involvement in the IRA, Martha assumes IRA sympathy; she repeatedly condemns British imperialism and pays the IRA to protect her shop—at least initially. As the novel proceeds, however, Martha's respect for the IRA declines. Her dispute with republi-

canism concerns its blinding romanticism, which causes it to neglect the
conditions of people's everyday lives. Beckett makes this point obliquely by
way of an attack on cultural nationalism. When her niece is named after a
Celtic hero, Martha has this to say:

> I didn't think much of Cuchulain. I didn't believe all this "honour" stuff that
> made him kill his friend and then his own son. I didn't like the way he
> treated Emer, his wife, and I was sorry my wee godchild was called after her
> even though I liked the sound of the name.[29]

Romantic idealism is attractive in one sense, but the narrative it calls forth
can only wreak havoc. Cultural nationalism, like imperialism, religion, and
romance, is finally critiqued as another ideology of heroism.

What Martha does rely on, once the myths of capitalism, democracy,
Christianity, romance, and Irish cultural nationalism have failed, is labor.
She sets up shop as a home baker in the back kitchen and works from early
morning to late evening every day for years. Her bakery is destroyed three
times, once by a flood, once by British soldiers, and finally by the IRA.
Each time, Martha rebuilds her shop from nothing and resumes baking. Although her efforts are Herculean (or perhaps Sisyphean?), Martha eschews
any heroic interpretation of her actions. Prior to ransacking the shop, a
British soldier interrogates her about her political sympathies. To his question, "Are you a Republican?" Martha responds, "I was going to be a heroine but instead I said, 'I am a home baker.'"[30] In thus aligning her
subjectivity with her trade rather than her politics, Martha carves out a discursive space between British imperialism and republican revolution, all
the while keeping in the forefront the inconsequentiality of mere verbal
acts; no matter what answer she might give to the soldier, the result would
be the same. Significantly, even while she critiques both imperialism and
republicanism, Martha does not abandon nationalist longing, as the following conversation with her sister evinces:

> "Maybe the border will just fade away with people wearing clothes and eat-
> ing food from one part to the other."
>   All Mary Brigid said was, "You and your united Ireland! Are you always
> thinking about it?"
>   "No," I said. "I'm always thinking of baking bread and selling it and feed-
> ing my family and what they'll be when they grow up but the thought of
> the border's like a nail sticking up in my shoe. I've got used to it but it's
> never comfortable."[31]

The idea of a united Ireland is tantalizing, but rendered distant by the consistent material demands of everyday life. Like the mother in *Shadows,*

Martha cannot afford the utopian dream of the unrealized nation; at the same time, she rails against the restrictions of the actually existing nation-state. In positioning herself between nation and nation-state, republicanism and imperialism, Martha suggests the need for an alternative discursive space.

Beckett emphasizes the importance of such an alternative discursive space in the novel's title and epigraph, a biblical proverb translated through Nathanael West's *Miss Lonelyhearts:* "When they ask for bread don't give them crackers as does the Church, and don't, like the State, tell them to eat cake. Explain that man cannot live by bread alone and give them stones."[32] The obvious gloss on the epigraph is that it supports violence as the inevitable result of injustice. But Martha does not stand wholeheartedly behind this position. The terms of the epigraph ironically recall the French Revolution in its full narrative unfolding: the triumvirate ideals of liberty, equality, fraternity; their subversion by the Terror; and, eventually, Napoleon's dictatorship. Martha interrupts exactly this narrative telos: when people ask for bread, she gives them bread. Inasmuch as she casts her sympathy with ordinary people who live in ordinary houses and try to lead ordinary lives despite the Troubles, Martha's critique of romantic revolutionary struggle, and, by extension, Beckett's, espouses a complex view of citizenship that IRA revolutionary actions do not.

Linda Anderson's *We Can't All Be Heroes, You Know* similarly emphasizes the everyday and, as its title announces, has an anti-heroic bias. Like both Johnston and Beckett, Anderson conveys her critique through both plot and rhetoric. The novel involves three main characters in a fairly tight storyline. Rosaleen and Daniel Keenan are married to one another. A working-class Catholic couple, their perennial poverty determines their lives. A series of misfortunes is catalogued in the first few pages of the novel: Rosaleen's best friend, Aidan, has been killed by a sectarian group (probably the Provos); Rosaleen's pregnancy, out of wedlock, has interrupted her university career; and somebody has just shot their dog. When the added expense of a new baby drives Dan to approach the local pub owner, McGuire, for a loan, McGuire suggests that Dan do medical work for the Provos; shortly afterward, and despite Dan's avowed lack of interest, a substantial packet of money turns up, obliging him to the IRA. Dan fails on his first IRA mission, but a volunteer named Brendan McCartney spares his life. After Brendan is found dead in his H-Block cell, near the end of the novel, Dan decides he will volunteer after all. However, the IRA refuses to accept him and, to crown an irony, Dan is arrested and interned upon leaving the IRA safe house.

While all of this is going on, the third main character in the novel, an enlisted British soldier named Gerry, has fallen in love with Rosaleen from her picture in British intelligence files. They eventually meet and have sex with each other, secretly, twice. Besotted by Rosaleen and disenchanted with military life, Gerry eventually deserts. The story lines intersect in a catastrophic ending that sees the British soldier renouncing British occupation, the young couple who has tried to claw its way out of working-class penury slapped back into the Falls Road, and the husband marked for life by British authorities as a subversive, leaving the wife and child nothing to depend on or look forward to. The plot is typical of Northern Irish fiction; such is life in the "necropolis" of Belfast.[33]

No less typical than this plot is its rhetoric. As in *Shadows on Our Skin,* the stock character of the old IRA activist appears, this time as a neighbor's grandfather. When Rosaleen despairs about the Troubles, asking rhetorically, "Do you think it will ever end?" the old man holds forth:

> I'd love to be out there with the best of them. This time it will end! We were the lads would have finished it in '21. Betrayed! After all we did, sacrificed. I filled in every murdering Black and Tan crossed my path. Scum of the earth they were! Set loose out of English jails to come slaying and looting over here. . . . It's for you, you impudent female person, that good men are laying down their lives.[34]

Anderson's position is clear from Rosaleen's curt response: "I don't require it, I assure you."[35] The old man's statement has even greater impact if we take into account the allegorical implications of Rosaleen's name. An allegorical trope for Ireland since at least James Clarence Mangan's nineteenth-century poem, which figures Ireland as a woman for whom men voluntarily die, Anderson's character Rosaleen playfully materializes the abstraction that has fueled the discourse of Irish nationalism for so long, to the detriment, Anderson insists, of actual women.

If the stock character of the old IRA volunteer is reminiscent of *Shadows,* Rosaleen's ideological trajectory could be the basis for Martha's in *Stones.* Although Rosaleen starts from a position of relative sympathy for the Provos (albeit a weaker sympathy than Martha's), she ultimately decides "to cut out her own lingering instinctive loyalty to the Provisionals" because "there was nothing to choose between armies."[36] Like Martha she rejects both imperial and republican discourses; unlike Martha, though, Rosaleen does not identify herself by her labor. Also unlike *Stones, Heroes* counters Rosaleen's loss of faith with Dan's growing acceptance of the IRA. While Rosaleen increasingly questions the point of IRA politics, "the 'H' in 'hero' is the 'H' in 'H-block,'" she observes dryly," Dan grows into revolutionary commitment to the Provos.[37] By making the plot chiastic in this way, Anderson suggests that republicanism is a gendered ideology with different effects on and appeals to women and men. The IRA provides an ideology of masculine heroism in a society of chronic unemployment: given the impossibility of labor-based subjectivity, every man is "only interested in becoming a hero."[38] Working-class women, on the other hand, are already gendered differently, as *Shadows* goes to great lengths to document, and republicanism does nothing to alter that. Importantly for an argument in favor of inclusive citizenship, Anderson criticizes not just Republicanism's effects on women, but the ubiquity and rigidity of gender dichotomy. After Rosaleen's brother Leo has been punished by the IRA for moral degeneracy, he spits bitterly at Rosaleen, "I'd rather be expected to learn how to make tea and cakes than petrol bombs!"[39]

Even more formulaic than the plot chiasmus that has Dan join and Rosaleen renounce the Provos is their forced reunion at the end of the novel. After having spent the entire narrative bickering, they reach a reconciliation in the last twelve lines of the novel. Dan has just found out about Rosaleen's affair with Gerry:

> Ridiculous to imagine he could have a better life.
>   Suddenly [Dan] remembered Mrs Dwyer. No, he decided. No, I won't give in. He looked at Rosaleen out of the corner of his eye. How unhappy she was! You have to be alive to feel pain, he thought.
>   He stood. "I'm going to get some food."
>   "We could sell the house."
>   "Why?"
>   "Everything's ruined. You think I don't love you."
>   Everything is not ruined, he thought. I'm alive. She's alive. He walked forward and stood beside her. She was to the right of him, not looking, breathing fast.
>   "Which half of the baby would you prefer?" he said at last.[40]

The novel closes on an apparently conventional note: the marital couple is held together by a child, symbolizing continuity of life. But the tableau's classically comedic reconciliation calls attention to its artificiality, not just because it is so obviously forced, but also because the child's identity is so very overdetermined. When Dan learns that Rosaleen is pregnant, he dreams of having a daughter to name after an Irish heroine; when their son is born, they bizarrely name him Louis. In late 1979, the explicit setting of the novel, the name "Louis" cannot help but refer to Louis Mountbatten, the World War II general and British admiral killed by an IRA bomb earlier that year. The baby thus keeps before them always the omnipresence of the Troubles, not great Irish heroines. Bereft of comedic resolution, the narrative moves inexorably to its ironic conclusion.

The child's identity also stands against the utopian dream of the novel. Against Louis' overdetermined name and function, characters dream of being "no one in particular," being "nowhere in particular."[41] Gerry, ironically enough, puts it most clearly:

> He wanted to be outside, out there. To have a house no one dared enter
> without invitation. To feed, drink, make love, and be left in peace. To walk
> out free to meet her, her face, her voice, her body. He wanted to be full and
> glutted with natural happiness.[42]

His dream, and the dream of the novel, is that of ordinary personhood. Leaving unsettled the question of nation (Rosaleen exits the novel tempered in her nationalism, Dan more committed to it), Anderson considers instead the conditions necessary for happiness. *Heroes* suggests that Northern Irish society needs to imagine and nurture multiple identities, untrammeled by the ubiquity of sectarian violence created by colonialism and nationalist resistance to it. It is only through undoing, or ending, the violence of the Troubles that meaningful citizenship for ordinary persons can be achieved, and it is in this sense that Anderson's novel can be read as a contribution to the agitation for active, feminist citizenship.

All three of the novels I have discussed put forward a strong critique of both republican nationalism and British colonialism. While holding on to the utopian dream of the nation, these writers insist on the materialization of nationalist promises for all members of society, especially women. And while doing so, they resist the newly material but no less restrictive interpretation of women as maternal subjects that de Valera's constitution concretizes. Although the women protagonists of all three novels are mothers, their mothering is described in resolutely materialist detail. Furthermore, they act on a diverse range of fronts: the mother in *Shadows* attacks idealism head on; Martha identifies herself by her labor; and the baby that ought to cement Rosaleen's identity as a mother merely points to other intransigent barriers to meaningful citizenship. Such insistence on the complexity of women and their concerns is continuous with the history of feminism, and feminist nationalism, in Northern Ireland. It matters, after all, that the Troubles sparked in 1968 came about largely as a result of women's agitation for a decent standard of living for their communities. And although the grass-roots feminist concerns that have developed in Northern Ireland sometimes appear surprisingly tangential to what have come to be known as feminist issues in North America, this is because gender, as a set of social relations, is to some extent locally constructed. Since Irish gender under British colonialism is produced in part through the chronic unemployment and imprisonment of men, the women's movement is structured in response. Women in the North have organized around debt counseling, housing shortages, and prison visiting rights as well as around childcare, women's health, abortion, and the national question. Just as feminist praxis emerges out of the material crises in women's lives, so too do Johnston, Beckett, and Anderson ground their texts in women's everyday lives, describing the intimate effects of imperialism and republicanism, critiquing the utopian ideologies that sustain such practices, and implicitly condemning existing state policies for not adequately addressing women's concerns.

Such a response may not break down gender dichotomy, but it represents a viable third position in the dogged conflict between republicanism and British colonialism. In asserting a discursive space that criticizes both ideologies, the women writers I have discussed insist upon seeing Northern Ireland as neither Irish nor British, but necessarily contaminated by both; consequently, their dream of a nation cannot be absorbed into one ideology or the other. Nor is their vision a matter of class identification in the last instance; the gender-specificity of their critique of heroism ensures that. Finally, their dream is not post-national; they insist on imagining *some* nation of Ireland. They call instead for a formulation of citizenship that avoids the pitfalls of the utopian allegorization of nation implicit in tropes like Mother Ireland, and they neatly sidestep the insistent limitations entailed by the Republic of Ireland's production of women as mothers in order to call for an inclusive citizenship that enfranchises all citizens, providing everybody with the means to participate fully in social polity.

NOTES

I would like to acknowledge generous readings of this article by Maureen Engel, Kim Gillespie, Mark Simpson, and Teresa Zackodnik. Thanks too to Dave Watt for research assistance and Kathryn Conrad for stimulating conversations.
1. *Mother Ireland,* dir. Anne Crilly (prod. Derry Film and Video, 1988).
2. While Irish nationalism, especially when taken to be synonymous with anti-colonialism, may need no comment, the literature on nation and nation-states in general is vast. For the purposes of this essay, I assume "nation" to refer to the idea of a people as being more or less homogeneous and belonging to a place, "nationalism" to refer to the aspiration and political struggle for self-government over a sovereign, recognized territory; and "nation-state" to refer to the juridical apparatus that both realizes and regulates the idea of nation. On nation and nation-state generally, see M. Jacqui Alexander, "Erotic Autonomy as a Politics of Decolonization: An Anatomy of Feminist and State Practice in the Bahamas Tourist

Economy," in *Feminist Genealogies, Colonial Legacies, Democratic Futures,* ed. M. Jacqui Alexander and Chandra Talpade Mohanty (New York/London: Routledge, 1997), 63–100; Benedict Anderson, *Imagined Communities* (London: Verso, 1992); Homi K. Bhabha, "DissemiNation: Time, Narrative, and the Margins of the Modern Nation," in *Nation and Narration,* ed. Homi Bhabha (London: Routledge, 1990: 291–321); Partha Chatterjee, *Nationalist Thought and the Colonial World: A Derivative Discourse* (Minneapolis: University of Minnesota Press, 1986); idem., *The Nation and Its Fragments* (Princeton: Princeton University Press, 1993); Eric Hobsbawm, *Nations and Nationalisms Since 1780* (Cambridge: Cambridge University Press, 1990); and Tom Nairn, *The Break-Up of Britain* (London: Verso, 1981).

3. Geraldine Heng, in a very useful essay on feminism and nationalism in Singapore, reminds us to be wary of the putative connection between nationalism and feminism, even when the nation-state sees women as concrete material subjects and not merely as abstractions. Nationalism, she cautions, might make common cause with feminism in part because nationalism needs to represent itself as an inclusive category of political struggle, and addressing women's concerns (or at least appearing to) is one of the easiest ways to move away from the limitations of a so-called traditional past into modernity. See Geraldine Heng, "'A Great Way to Fly': Nationalism, the State, and the Varieties of Third-World Feminism," in Alexander and Mohanty, *Feminist Genealogies,* 30–45.

4. Gerardine Meaney, *Sex and Nation: Women in Irish Culture and Politics* (Dublin: Attic Press, 1991), 6.

5. Heng also adds, tellingly, "No comparable legislation exists that describes the configuration or borders of masculine identity under the law" (Heng, "'A Great Way to Fly,'" 37).

6. In an article focused on Mother India, an analogous figure to Mother Ireland, Sandhya Shetty makes a point very similar to this, arguing that the historical transition from an idealized figure (in the context of nation) to a material figure (in the context of the state) fails to overcome the limitations imposed on women. See Sandhya Shetty, "(Dis)figuring the Nation: Mother, Metaphor, Metonymy" *differences* 7 (1995): 50–79.

7. Begoña Aretxaga, *Shattering Silence: Women, Nationalism, and Political Subjectivity in Northern Ireland* (Princeton: Princeton University Press, 1997), 80.

8. For two examples of research on the relationship between feminism and republicanism, see Carol Coulter, *The Hidden Tradition: Feminism, Women and Nationalism in Ireland* (Cork: Cork University Press, 1993) and Margaret Ward, *Unmanageable Revolutionaries: Women and Irish Nationalism* (London: Pluto Press, 1983).

9. On the Dirty Protest by women prisoners in Armagh, see Christina Loughran, "Armagh and Feminist Strategy: Campaigns Around Republican Women Prisoners in Armagh Jail," *Feminist Review* 23 (1986): 59–80; Laura Lyons, "Feminist Articulations of the Nation: The 'Dirty'

Women of Armagh and the Discourse of Mother Ireland," *Genders* 24 (1996): 110–149.

10. Aretxaga, *Shattering Silence,* 156.

11. Ruth Lister, "Citizenship: Towards a Feminist Synthesis," *Feminist Review* 54 (Autumn 1997): 28–48; Nira Yuval-Davis, "Women, Citizenship and Difference," *Feminist Review* 57 (Autumn 1997): 4–27.

12. Lister, "Citizenship," 32. On the importance of active feminist citizenship in Northern Ireland, see Cynthia Cockburn, "Different Together: Women in Belfast," *Soundings* 2 (1996): 32–47; Eileen Evason, *Against the Grain: The Contemporary Women's Movement in Northern Ireland* (Cork: Cork University Press, 1993); Eileen Fairweather, Roisin McDonough, and Melanie Mc-Fadyean, *Only the Rivers Run Free* (London: Pluto Press, 1984); and Kate Fearon, ed., *Power, Politics, Positionings: Women in Northern Ireland* (Belfast: Democratic Dialogue, 1996).

13. Jennifer Johnston, *Shadows on Our Skin* (London: Heinemann, 1977); Mary Beckett, *Give Them Stones* (New York: Viking, 1987); Linda Anderson, *We Can't All Be Heroes, You Know* (New York: Ticknor & Fields, 1985 [orig. pub. *To Stay Alive* (London: Bodley Head, 1984)]).

14. See Joseph Connely, "Legend and Lyric as Structure in the Selected Fiction of Jennifer Johnston," *Eire-Ireland* 21 (Fall 1986): 119–124.

15. Mary Beckett, *A Belfast Woman* (Swords, Co Dublin: Poolbeg, 1980) and *A Literary Woman* (London: Bloomsbury, 1990).

16. I do discuss Beckett's fiction briefly in one essay. See Heather Zwicker, "A Gendered Troubles: Writing 'Woman' in Northern Ireland," *Genders* 19 (1994): 198–222.

17. Linda Anderson, *Cuckoo* (Dingle, Co. Kerry: Brandon Books, 1988).

18. Aretxaga, *Shattering Silence,* 9–10.

19. Ibid., 52.

20. Johnston, *Shadows,* 18.

21. Ibid., 20–21.

22. Ibid., 21.

23. Ibid., 153.

24. Ibid., 154.

25. Ibid.

26. Beckett, *Stones,* 69.

27. Ibid., 76.

28. Ibid., 138.

29. Ibid., 73.

30. Ibid., 123.

31. Ibid., 118.

32. Nathanael West, *Miss Lonelyhearts* (New York: Avon Books, 1964).

33. Anderson, *Heroes,* 7.

34. Ibid., 103–104.

35. Ibid., 104.

36. Ibid., 186.

37. Ibid., 71.
38. Ibid., 68.
39. Ibid., 102.
40. Ibid., 196.
41. Ibid., 108.
42. Ibid., 181.

Chapter Fourteen

Racializing the Irish in England: Gender, Class, and Ethnicity ▨

Mary J. Hickman and Bronwen Walter

INTRODUCTION

When asked to contribute to this volume, we were pleased to avail ourselves of the opportunity to explore further the complex interplay among gender, class, and ethnicity for Irish women and men in England.[1] Books about modern Ireland aimed at Gender Studies, Irish Studies and beyond, which include "the diaspora" in their subject matter, remain the exception rather than the rule. This book originated in North America, which in part explains why the diaspora figures in its contents. This nonterritorial definition of what constitutes the proper ambit of discussions of Irish identities is very welcome. England has been the major destination of Irish emigrants for most of the twentieth century. In 1991 over three quarters of a million Irish-born people were recorded in the British census as living in England, equivalent to more than one-sixth of the population currently living in the island of Ireland.[2]

The book is also an occasion for us to share more widely our conclusion that examining class, gender, and ethnicity for Irish women and men produces a critique of the constant conflation of "color" and ethnicity which pervades discussion of ethnic minorities in England. For example, in the early stages of the women's movement in England the pressing political objectives were those of gender, but as the 1970s progressed the articulation of gender and class became an important locus. However, from the early 1980s the dominant voice of English feminism, seen as belonging to young, white, and middle-class women, was challenged by black and other ethnic minority women who insisted that white women must recognize the specificities and limitations of their own experiences and the existence of difference.[3] Subsequently, there has been a considerable body of work produced examining questions of gender, "race," ethnicity and difference. Much of the work, however, has, in its turn, conflated the notion of ethnic minority with that of black; ethnic differentiation has, therefore, in England, chiefly been assumed to revolve around "color."

It is becoming more commonplace in England today to read analyses of how racism, imperialism, and colonialism have shaped the histories and identities of white women and men. This is part of a focus in the 1990s on "whiteness," representing a deliberate shift from the examination of black communities as the mainstay of studies of racism. This welcome reorientation in understanding the embeddedness of racism is, however, in danger of homogenizing whiteness in the way that "blackness" was once so homogenized.[4] Current attempts to "deconstruct whiteness" are challenging this black/white dualism.

Attempts are also being made in the late 1990s to de-couple English/British as a viable representation of an "homogenous" nation. Historically the Englishness of a particular class, the nineteenth-century middle class, was able to represent itself as Britishness by its marginalization and subordination of other ethnicities, in particular those of the Scots, Welsh, and Irish.[5] The assumptions about "others" upon which Englishness was based were not necessarily shared by the significant Irish population in Britain (especially the Catholics among them), even if they were middle-class, because their experiences of racism, imperialism, and colonialism were different. Claims are sometimes made about Irish collaboration in the British empire.[6] However, it is hard to sustain the argument that the average Irish domestic servant in nineteenth-century London, Manchester, or Glasgow, a far more typical Irish migrant of the period (both numerically and in class background) than either Irish officers in the British army or Irish civil servants in colonial administrations, was a collaborator in the British empire.

Our attempt to chart some of the interplay among gender, class, and ethnicity for Irish women and men in contemporary England is part of an exploration of the legacies of these different experiences of racism, imperialism, and colonialism. We are drawing attention to the specific context in which Irish migrants and their descendents have found themselves in England. In migrating to England, Irish people are going to live in the territory of the former colonizing power, with which there remains much "unfinished business," both evident and much more deepseated. The past colonial relationship therefore continues to play a profoundly important role in the experiences of Irish people living in England. This is significant for the Irish diaspora, because historically and currently many Irish people on leaving Ireland first arrive in England, but later move on. Their experiences of racism and colonialism, their notions of England, or their understandings of such phenomena, are not therefore limited to those acquired during the period of their lives spent in Ireland.

The particular experiences or understandings gained while living in England can have a decisive impact on their decision to migrate onward or return to Ireland, or they can significantly shape the manner of their settlement in England. These experiences are structured by gender in ways that are largely unacknowledged. Representations of both Irishness and Englishness are deeply gendered constructions, and the material conditions of migrant women's and men's lives are far from identical. Other positionalities, most notably social class in a labor migrant context, articulate with gender. Age, generation, sexuality, religion, and educational background all contribute to complexly structured identities.[7]

Ethnic identification is the process whereby one group seeks to distinguish itself and mark its distinctiveness from another, drawing upon a variety of historically variable criteria. Inevitably this process of boundary formation is grounded in the socio-economic and political circumstances of the moment.[8] We explore ways in which Irish migrants to England experience English constructions of their ethnicity that are racialized, gendered, and classed and that carry implicit messages about Englishness. The English constructions of Irishness form the context in which a range of Irish identities is produced. Irish ethnicity is of course also produced by a positive sense of shared "roots," which become apparent to migrants after they have left "home" or to individuals of Irish descent as they grow up. In this chapter, however, we focus on English stereotypes of the Irish as a significant element in English constructions of what it is to be "Irish" and the impact they have on the daily lives of Irish-born women and men in England.

We begin with an examination of the principal ways in which English constructions of Irish racialized identities rely on gendered and classed stereotypes of Irish migrants. Although the images we examine reproduce important elements of the more general stereotypes of the Irish that have long characterized Anglo-Irish relations, there is a specificity to those produced about Irish migrants over the past 200 years. We then present a range of socio-economic data to elucidate the gender composition and class patterns of Irish migrants to England. Finally, we explore some experiences of racial harassment recounted by Irish migrants and their gendered responses to racist treatment.

ENGLISH CONSTRUCTIONS OF
IRISH RACIALIZED IDENTITIES

Englishness has been constructed through the pathologization of "others," and these "others" provide its boundaries. The positive qualities of Englishness do not need to be stated, but are understood to be the binary opposites of those openly attributed to subordinated collectivities. By focusing on these inferiorized groups, Englishness can remain the "absent center" while the racialization of its own national identity is denied. The Irish are the longest-standing "others" in this process, constituting an "internal" model for subsequent "external" racializations that accompanied British imperial expansion outside Europe.[9]

The process of stereotyping plays a key role in the othering of Irish people. Stuart Hall argues that stereotyping has three main features. One is the reduction of a person's characteristics to a few, simple, easily recognized traits that are regarded as unchanging, fixed by Nature. The second is its function in the maintenance of symbolic order. It works to set up a symbolic frontier between the normal and the deviant, excluding those who are defined as not belonging.

> Stereotyping . . . facilitates the "binding" or bonding together of all of Us who are "normal" into one "imagined community"; and it sends into symbolic exile all of Them—"the Others"—who are in some way different— "beyond the pale."[10]

Tellingly, in elaborating this part of the definition, Hall draws on a description of the Irish ("beyond the pale") which has become so integrated into the English language that its origins have largely been forgotten. In fact, the phrase derives directly from the name given to the area around Dublin, which was fortified by the English crown in the statute of 1488 to protect its toehold in Ireland.[11] Thus the name came to symbolize the "civilized" population under English control, those within the Pale, in contrast to the "uncivilized" Irish in the rest of Ireland. It is now extended unthinkingly to any excluded social group.

An important extension of this rejection of "abnormal" others is their association with pollution, dirt, and impurity. In psychoanalytic terms they represent the split-off parts of the dominant group that cannot be acknowledged. One element of this disavowed part of dominant selves, which resonated particularly strongly in the English national identity, is that of dependence. Englishness is unusually constructed around a middle-class core, in contrast to nationalisms that have a revolutionary origin in which "the people" have been mobilized. Independence became a key characteristic of the dominant group, fostered in the English "public school" system, which removed boys as young as seven from their homes for education to become "manly" in homosocial school environments.[12] Women, the working classes, and colonized peoples represented the dependence that this class of English men had to deny in themselves, and therefore must subordinate and control in others.

In the nineteenth century "dirty Irish" was a common stereotype, used colloquially as a term of abuse but also incorporated into official reports on living conditions in industrial cities. Irish settlement was seen as a cause of decay and ill health, rather than a symptom of the failure of the economic system to provide adequate housing for the labor force. Writing in 1845 Engels linked the Irish with "dirt" in explicitly racial terms:

> One may depend upon seeing many Celtic faces, if ever one penetrates into a district which is particularly noted for its filth and decay. These faces are quite different from those of the Anglo-Saxon population and are easily recognisable.[13]

The epithet is still used in verbal abuse of Irish people in the 1990s.[14]

Thirdly, stereotyping involves violent power relationships. It is not associated simply with difference, but with "gross inequalities of power." However, Hall goes on to point out that this is a symbolic power exercised through control of representational practices. These practices have a wide range of effects, including social positioning and economic exploitation, as well as physical coercion.

There is not, however, a simple, one-way relationship between the dominant and dominated groups. The line between them is less sharply drawn than the stereotype suggests. On the one hand, the dominant group has ambivalent feelings, mirroring the splitting process, and thus also exhibits envy and desire.[15] On the other hand, the dominated group becomes part of the hegemony; as Ashis Nandy points out, colonialism "includes codes which both the rulers and ruled can share."[16]

Anti-Irish racism in England constructs gendered and classed stereotypes of Irish people that are then drawn on in discriminatory practices. This chapter explores the specificity of such stereotyping and the material effects it has on the gendered and classed Irish population in Britain. Negative stereotyping of ethnic groups works to homogenize diverse populations and essentialize a limited number of characteristics. There is likely therefore to be a mismatch between myth and reality, and also diversity in the ways in which different members of the collectivity are exposed, and react, to racist treatment. In the following sections each of these aspects of

Irish experience in England will be juxtaposed with the central stereotype of the male, working-class "Paddy."

ENGLISH STEREOTYPING OF THE IRISH: MALE AND WORKING CLASS

English stereotypes of Irish people continue to draw on nineteenth-century images of "navvies," working-class males in outdoor manual occupations that require "brawn" rather than "brain." These workplaces also associate Irish people with "dirt," reinforcing the image associated with their residential environments. As with other negatively racialized groups the stereotypes invoke the body/reason dualism.[17] Irish workers are engaged in physical labor that is of lower prestige than professional or clerical occupations. This "highly visible urban physicality" has parallels with black male bodies in Britain and the United States, and contrasts with the relative invisibility of Irish female bodies.[18]

An important aspect of Irish men's uncontrolled and uncivilized bodies produced in the stereotype is their proneness to physical violence. Often this is associated with excessive drinking, which reduces reasoning powers and leads to bodily clumsiness. Violence is linked with irrationality, doubly reinforcing its place on the bodily side of the dualism. By contrast the violence of British imperialism is described as necessary military force, a rational response to uncivilized behavior in "others."

The opposite side of the body/reason dualism highlights Irish "stupidity." This is most strongly reproduced in the "Irish joke," a pervasive form of humor in the English media as well as in workplace, neighborhood, and leisure sites. There is strong resistance amongst English people to defining these "jokes" as racist. Those who attempt to do so are told that they "have no sense of humor," a quality that is positively evaluated in the English stereotype of themselves. School playgrounds are places where anti-Irish "jokes" are implanted in succeeding English generations.

Stupidity is easily associated with different use of the English language, elite uses of which are associated with superior reasoning powers. Thus Irish accents are often sufficient to trigger this stereotype. The establishment of a standard dialect of English was itself a by-product of the "public school" education system and remains strongly associated with the middle-class Establishment, as its labeling as "The Queen's English" and "BBC English" indicates.[19] National and regional variations in pronunciation, syntax, and vocabulary are used to signify class difference, with very little reference to the objective socio-economic status of speakers.

Anti-Catholicism is a central strand to the "Paddy" image that has been both feared and mocked. On the one hand, it represents the danger of

Illustration 14.1

foreign invasion, and on the other, "mindless" dependence on Papal regulation in contrast to Protestant individual rationalism. Although anti-
Catholicism in England long predated the mid-nineteenth century peak
period of emigration, navvies were drawn from the rural working classes
in Ireland, who were overwhelmingly Catholic by religion. Catholicism
has thus readily been identified as synonymous with Irish origins, masking
the existence of the Protestant minority amongst Irish migrants. The threat
to political stability and public order posed by the Irish both outside and
inside Britain is thus an ongoing theme that is built on the foundation of
the male, Catholic, working-class stereotype. Clear elements of continuity
can be traced from the "Fenian menace" of the nineteenth century to the
IRA in the late twentieth century.[20]

The limited view of Irish migrants conjured up by this stereotype is
summed up in both language and visual representation. The Irish are collectively labeled "Paddies" and are still displayed in cartoons wearing construction workers' "donkey jackets" and carrying hods of bricks. Their working
lives are spent on building sites and their leisure hours in pubs (Illustration
14.1). An ape-like twist is given to their facial features, signaling subhuman
intelligence and belligerence. These images were developed during periods of
anti-British agitation in Ireland during the second half of the nineteenth century and given wide circulation through English media such as *Punch* maga-
zine (Illustration 14.2). Although they lost currency in the early twentieth
century, they have lingered on not far below the surface and could readily be
understood again in the late 1960s when they appeared in almost identical
form in British newspaper representations of the war in Northern Ireland.[21]

Through the homogenizing "Paddy" stereotype, therefore, men have
been made to stand in for the Irish population as a whole and have taken
the brunt of the racializing discourses. There has been remarkable continuity in this gendering. Music hall sketches in Manchester in the late nineteenth century, for example, depicted Irish men as small and weak figures,
heading households where domineering wives overshadowed them.
Rather than acknowledge the dangerous possibility that Irish women
might be the prime household providers, and recognize the precarious
earning power of male migrant workers, audiences were invited to laugh
at the congenital weakness of Irish men in contrast to the patriarchal
strength of Victorian English husbands.[22]

The importance of women, however, cannot be entirely hidden and
emerges in another sphere—through their prime roles in the processes of
reproduction. But although the "excessive" fertility of women's bodies is the
subtext to the debate, the rhetoric focuses on families and their threat to the
English way of life both biologically and culturally. Anti-Catholicism is implicit in these representations. In fact the domesticity of Irish women is

THE FENIAN-PEST.

Hibernia. "O MY DEAR SISTER, WHAT *ARE* WE TO DO WITH THESE TROUBLESOME PEOPLE?"
Britannia. "TRY ISOLATION FIRST, MY DEAR, AND THEN———"

Illustration 14.2

congruent with English ideas about women's place, but their larger than average family sizes become the focus of a range of fears. These include "swamping" and racial degeneration, the weakening of Protestantism, unfair demand for resources and lack of control over bodies, both their own and those of unruly, dirty, and over-numerous children.

The fears projected onto Irish families have long been in evidence in England and continue to resonate. For example, in the 1930s English racial anxieties were heightened by the sharp decline in births and were accompanied by hostile comments about Irish family sizes. In 1941 the social scientist R. S. Walshaw investigated the perceived problem, exacerbated by the need for additional labor for the war effort, of continuing emigration from Britain to the "Dominions" against a background of falling population at home.

> We have already noted that the United Kingdom is faced with a decline in population. Also we have seen that the policy of the United Kingdom Government is to use public money to help English, Scotch and Welsh to emigrate to the Dominions. At the same time Southern Irish enter Great Britain literally by the thousand. Would not these three facts taken together seem to suggest that the United Kingdom has not only decided to become peopled from Eire but is determined to bring about the change as quickly as possible?[23]

Following a period of sustained immigration from Ireland in the 1950s, often directed toward towns in southeast England that had little previous experience of Irish settlement, new Catholic schools were needed to educate the rapidly-expanding second generation. One such town was Luton, 30 miles north of London, where the number of Irish-born people rose from less than 2,000 in 1951 to over 7,000 in 1961. In 1961 there was a lengthy correspondence in the Luton News from English people complaining about taxes being used for state contributions to the provision of Catholic schools.[24] The theme of excessive demands continues to echo in the labeling of Irish benefits claimants as "scroungers," implying that they are taking resources which rightfully belong to the indigenous population.[25]

Harassment of Irish families often draws attention to their deviance in having more children than the Protestant English norm. A recent front page article in the London *Evening Standard* was headlined "Family from hell ruin £180,000 house" and subtitled "Single mother and 10 children turn home into 'human pig sty.'" According to the report:

> The family, which claimed more than £400 a week in state benefits, punched holes in the walls, ripped out electric cables, covered wallpaper with graffiti and defecated on the carpets in the £180,000 house. However Mrs S—was defiant today. She said: Yes, I am on benefits, but some people only think about money. My family are all that matters to me, not money. The problem with England is they treat dogs better than they treat the Irish. They just don't like big families.[26]

The overall effect of stereotyping is to construct a limited image of the Irish community in Britain whose public face is male and working class. Lurking in the shadows are the mothers of their over-large families, reminders of the alienness of Catholicism and its threatening material implication of invasion from within.

Although these representations focus attention onto the pathologized Irish, their prime function is the construction of a positive national identity for the English. Reiteration of negative stereotypes of the Irish allows the equally racialized stereotype of the English as rational, sober, peace-loving, and moderate to be taken for granted without needing to be spelled out.

IRISH POPULATION IN ENGLAND IN 1991: GENDER AND CLASS PATTERNS

We now turn to the gendered and classed profile of the Irish-born population in contemporary England, drawing on statistical data from the 1991 census.[27] Two issues need to be examined. The first is the gender composition of the Irish population in Britain. Stereotypes highlight men, placing women in more shadowy positions as reproducers of the next generation but hidden from national public gaze. Whereas men feature in cartoons commenting on the political relationship between Britain and Ireland, most notably in the conflict in Northern Ireland, women's stereotyped representations are largely confined to their roles as mothers. These images are therefore largely salient at more local levels, featured in exchanges in benefits offices, and in neighborhood gossip.

The second issue is that of the class composition of the Irish migrant workforce. The extent to which "working class" describes the economic situation of Irish women and men will be examined. Here there is also a distinct gender dimension. While women and men share some positions, on others their situations differ sharply.

Since 1921 censuses have recorded more Irish-born women than men in England. In the nineteenth century men slightly outnumbered women in census counts, but the higher out-migration of women from Ireland began to be reflected in Britain when emigration to the United States fell dramatically in the 1920s (see Illustration 14.3). Women have always comprised a very substantial section of the Irish population in England, but this has been overlooked in popular understandings. This invisibility has spilled over into academic writing. Even in the most recent period, when attention has been drawn to the gap and accurate information has been published quite widely, the misrepresentation continues outside Irish studies. For example, Scully draws attention to two sets of theorists who

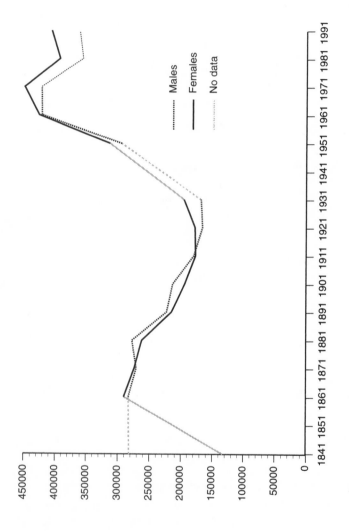

450000
400000
350000
300000
250000
200000
150000
100000
50000
0

1841 1851 1861 1871 1881 1891 1901 1911 1921 1931 1941 1951 1961 1971 1981 1991

········· Males

———— Females

··········· No data

Source: Census of G.B 1841, Vol. II, Preface pp. 14-16; 1851 Pop Tables II, Vol. 1, Tables XXXIX, XL; Census of England and
Wales, 1921. Gen. Tables, Table 52; 1951, Gen. Tables, Table 39;1961 Birthplace and Nationality Tables, Table1;
G.B. Country of Births, Table 3; Census 1981, Country of Birth Tables, Table 1; Census 1991, Ethnic Group and Country
of Birth Table 1.

Illustartion 14.1

perpetuate the idea that Irish males predominate in migration and settlement patterns.[28]

In 1991 Irish-born women comprised 53.6 percent of the population originating in the Republic and 51.0 percent of those coming from Northern Ireland. Gender ratios of Irish-born women per 1,000 men were thus 1,157 and 1,042 respectively. These ratios varied regionally in Britain, some parts having fewer women than men and some more. The southeast region, which includes Greater London, has by far the largest proportion of all Irish-born people in England (58.1 percent) and also a higher than average gender ratio of Republic Irish-born women (1,207 per 1,000 men).

The British census uses the Registrar-General's Social Class categories to group occupations according to their level of professional training and "skill." Although deficient in many respects, this provides a convenient shorthand for considering the broad occupational hierarchy in England. If occupations defined as manual are used to define working-class, then three categories can be considered—Social Class III (Manual), which includes occupations defined as "skilled," and Social Classes IV ("semi-skilled") and V ("unskilled").

The pattern shows that Irish Republic-born men are substantially more likely to be in working-class occupations (Table 14.1). Two-thirds (65.9 percent) are in these three categories compared with only half (53.7 percent) of "white" English-born men.[29] The proportion of Irish-Republic men is only slightly lower than that of the highest group, Black Caribbean men (68.2 percent). The next highest percentage is that of Pakistani men (60.9 percent). There is a striking similarity in these proportions, and a marked difference from that of the majority population.

The contrast between the occupational distribution of the Republic Irish-born and that of other migrant ethnic "white" groups living in England is even stronger. Scottish- and Welsh-born men have well under half their male working populations in manual occupation categories, 43.0 percent and 35.7 percent respectively. Even the Northern Irish-born (48.7 percent) have a lower proportion than the English-born (53.7 percent).

Clustering of Republic Irishborn men in the least-skilled and poorest-paid occupational categories is most clearly brought out when the lowest social class category is considered. They have by far the largest representation in Social Class V, the "unskilled" category, which accounts for 12.0 percent of the total, compared with 5.45 percent for the white English-born. The Black Caribbean proportion (8.4 percent) is lower than that of the Republic Irish-born, and the Northern Irish-born proportion is also substantially smaller (7.3 percent).

Republic Irish-born men, therefore, have a distinctively working-class occupational profile that is a direct reflection of their migrant status. They

280

Table 14.1   Registrar General's Social Class by Birthplace/Ethnic Group and Gender, England, 1991 (2% Individual SARS)

	Eng	Sco	Wa	NI	Ir Rep	Bl Car	Ind	Pak	Bl Afr
Women									
I	3,328	148	107	55	68	30	149	16	24
	1.5	3.1	3.1	3.8	1.9	1.0	4.2	2.6	2.9
II	55,209	1,614	1,295	508	1,082	880	717	122	255
	24.6	34.1	37.9	35.5	31.0	29.3	20.0	20.1	30.5
IIIN	89,363	1,578	1,131	420	884	978	1,214	193	246
	39.9	33.4	33.1	29.3	25.3	32.6	33.9	31.8	29.5
IIIM	16,987	260	185	69	233	202	225	39	44
	7.6	5.5	5.4	4.8	6.7	6.7	6.3	6.4	5.3
IV	39,742	748	450	237	663	566	1,023	191	136
	17.7	15.8	11.7	16.6	19.0	18.9	28.6	31.5	16.3
V	16,727	302	200	118	492	249	144	15	96
	7.5	6.4	5.8	8.2	14.1	8.3	4.0	2.5	11.5
Total	224,084	4,731	3,419	1,432	3,490	3,002	3,581	606	835
Men									
I	16,585	571	486	162	193	62	505	106	119
	6.3	9.2	11.9	9.9	11.8	2.2	10.7	5.7	13.3
II	71,128	1,967	1,508	449	815	384	1,245	324	204
	27.2	31.7	37.1	27.5	20.3	13.7	26.4	17.4	22.7
IIIN	29,991	675	429	152	266	327	709	240	149
	11.5	10.9	10.5	9.3	6.6	11.7	15.0	12.9	16.6
IIIM	84,551	1,488	817	443	1,462	1,048	1,099	565	147
	32.4	24.0	20.1	27.1	36.4	37.4	23.3	30.3	16.4
IV	41,458	875	494	233	705	629	835	450	148
	15.9	14.1	12.1	14.3	17.5	22.4	17.7	24.2	16.5
V	14,114	307	144	119	484	236	185	120	74
	5.4	4.9	3.5	7.3	12.0	8.4	3.9	6.4	8.2
Total	261,314	6,208	4,068	1,635	4,022	2,803	4,711	1,863	897

Source: Crown Copyright ONS. Samples of Anonymised Records.
Key:

Eng	England	Bl Car	Black Caribbean
Sco	Scotland	Ind	Indian
Wa	Wales	Pak	Pakistani
NI	Northern Ireland	Bl Afr	Black African
IrRep	Irish Republic		

continue to be recruited into the British economy to fill the least desirable jobs, as has been the case throughout the nineteenth and twentieth centuries.

They share this position with nonwhite migrant groups and their descendents. However, the continuation of labor migration from Ireland means that there is a replenishment of Irish workers, while the supply from other postwar sources, such as the Caribbean and the Indian subcontinent, has been halted by restrictive immigration policies based on criteria of "race."

The Irish pattern diverges, however, from that of Black Caribbean men at the other end of the social class spectrum. Although still below the white English-born averages, proportions in Social Classes I and II are higher for Republic-born Irish men than for other immigrant groups. Taken together these groups account for 33.5 percent of the white English-born, 25.1 percent of the Republic Irish-born, but only 15.9 percent of Black Caribbean men. Thus one quarter of Republic Irish-born men in England are in professional and managerial jobs, a proportion that grew substantially during the 1980s when there was an outpouring of Irish graduates, many of whom were drawn to London by an urgent shortage of financial and computer skills. Amongst Irish-born men in Britain aged 25–29 in 1991, 31.5 percent had higher-level qualifications (post-A-level) compared with 19.8 percent of the total population (Table 14.2). It is important to note that this more favorable profile derives from the characteristics of recent migrants, not from social mobility of earlier arrivals, whose upward rates are below the average for the population as a whole.[30]

Among Northern Irish-born men the proportion in higher-paid "white-collar" professions and managerial positions is substantially greater at 37.4 percent. This is close to that of immigrants from Scotland (40.9 percent), while those from Wales (49.0 percent) are clustered even more strongly in these categories.

There is thus a bi-modal pattern to the occupational groupings of male Irish migrants in England, though the overall profile is still weighted toward those in the manual working classes. Irish-born men are most underrepresented in lower-paid clerical work, included in Social Class III (non-manual). In these occupations, men from the Republic (6.6 percent) and from Northern Ireland (9.3 percent) are represented at levels well below the white English-born proportion (11.5 percent), which is matched by that of Black Caribbean men (11.7 percent). This is not a category that recruits migrants, since English-based workers easily fill the work.

The stereotype of Irish men as working class thus continues to resonate with the occupation structure of the Irish in England, which meets the ongoing need of the economy for low-paid casual work. However, a significant proportion of the Irish-born male population lies outside this category. The large, and growing, middle-class population of professional and managerial status is often overlooked. Moreover, the migrant population from

Table 14.2 Higher-Level Qualifications by Age and Gender, Total and Irish-Born Populations, Great Britain, 1991 (10% Sample)

	Women		Men	
	Total Population	Irish-Born	Total Population	Irish-Born
18–24% qualified	7.4	18.2	7.8	18.4
level a1.4	2.9	2.4	4.6	
level b	55.2	55.3	56.5	67.7
level c43.4	41.8	41.1	27.6	
25–9% qualified	18.4	34.2	19.8	31.5
level a3.9	6.7	7.2	11.4	
level b	52.7	54.2	57.8	66.5
level c	43.3	39.1	35.0	22.1
30–44% qualified	17.8	23.1	21.7	20.7
level a	5.5	6.6	11.3	18.7
level b	40.9	32.6	53.0	55.0
level c	53.6	60.7	35.7	26.3
45–59% qualified	11.8	14.5	16.5	8.3
level a3.9	3.6	10.5	16.3	
level b25.8	15.2	47.1	45.1	
level c70.3	81.2	42.4	38.6	
60–4% qualified	8.1	10.9	12.6	6.1
level a	2.6	2.9	7.5	15.1
level b	23.3	11.4	51.8	51.6
level c	74.1	85.6	40.7	33.3
65+% qualified	4.7	9.3	8.9	6.8
level a2.2	2.3	6.8	18.8	
level b22.5	12.6	55.5	54.9	
level c75.4	85.1	37.7	26.3	

Source: Crown Copyright ONS. House of Commons, "Census for 1991, Ethnic Group and Country of Birth tables, Table 17," (London: Her Majesty's Stationary Office, 1993).

Northern Ireland is particularly misrepresented, since its class profile is generally of higher status than the white English-born majority.

The class structure of Irish-born women in England is also bi-modal but differs from that of men in important ways. In part this reflects the structure of women's employment overall, but there are also specific features of Irish migration that explain the variation. Like men, Irish-born women originating in the Republic are clustered in the three manual class groupings (39.8 percent) to a greater extent than white English-born women (32.6 percent), with a lower than average proportion recorded for women from Northern Ireland (29.6 percent) (Table 14.1). Again they are most strikingly over-represented in the lowest grouping, the "unskilled" Social Class V, which accounts for 14.1 percent of all Republic-born women in paid work, compared with only 7.5 percent of white English-born women. Non-English United Kingdom-born groups again have lower rates (Scotland 6.4 percent, Wales 5.8 percent, and Northern Ireland 8.2 percent). As with the positioning of men by ethnic group, Black Caribbean women had above-average proportions in Social Class V but at a substantially lower rate than the Republic Irish-born (8.3 percent), similar in fact to the Northern Irish-born figure.

An important difference lies in the high proportions of Irish-born women located in Social Class II, which includes the professional category. Thirty-one percent of Irish-born women from the Republic fall into this grouping, significantly higher than white English-born women (24.6 percent). The proportion is higher still for those born in Northern Ireland (35.5 percent). This clustering reflects the migrant niche of nursing and to a lesser extent teaching. It suggests that the migration flow from Ireland contains a distinctive sector of highly educated women, traditionally from the middle classes, who make up nearly a third of the total. Although there was a marked increase in this proportion during the 1980s, so that 34.2 percent of Irish-born women in Britain had post-A-level equivalent qualifications in 1991 (compared with 18.4 percent of the total female population), unlike that of men, this pattern extends throughout all generations (Table 14.2). Again, in contrast to Irish men, Irish women share this clustering with Black Caribbean women (29.3 percent in Social Class II) who have also been recruited to fill the shortfall in the nursing labor force.

Under-representation of women from both parts of Ireland is marked in the intermediate levels of "white-blouse" clerical work. Whereas this is the largest category of employment for white English-born women (39.9 percent), it includes only a quarter of Republic-born women (25.3 percent) and a slightly larger proportion of those from Northern Ireland (29.3 percent). Again jobs in this area are considered more desirable by those educated in England and have fewer vacancies to be filled by migrants. Nursing and personal service jobs on the other hand cannot recruit enough women within Britain and rely on migrant labor.

A substantial proportion of Irish women therefore can also be classified as belonging to the manual working classes, but this characterization omits a long-standing and major middle-class presence. Irish women's role as nurses is publicly acknowledged, producing a strongly positive image of women who conform to the feminine stereotype of selfless caring for others. But other Irish women in the workforce are largely invisible, although occasional negative stereotypes from an earlier era are invoked, such as "Irish washerwoman."[31]

EXPERIENCES OF DISCRIMINATION: RACIAL HARASSMENT OF IRISH PEOPLE

In this section we draw on the findings of a report produced for the Commission for Racial Equality (CRE), entitled "Discrimination and the Irish Community in Britain."[32] This was the first publicly funded research project on the issue of anti-Irish racism and its consequences, although the Race Relations Act of 1976 defined "colour, race, nationality or ethnic or national origins" as "racial grounds" for discrimination. In 1971 the House of Lords confirmed that "national origin" included differences among people defining themselves as English, Irish, Scottish, and Welsh.

Press reactions to the announcement of the research in 1994 illustrate the paradox of British constructions of the Irish "with a strange combination of invisibility and exclusion."[33] Claims that it was unnecessary were accompanied by a torrent of anti-Irish "jokes."[34] Soon afterward the story of the £6,000 compensation awarded to an Irish man who was forced to leave his job in a Derbyshire foundry because racial harassment seriously affected his health was greeted with derision.

Scorn turned to outrage a year later when compensation to a college lecturer, also on sick leave because of harassment, was awarded at an increased rate. On 23 September 1995 headlines read:

An insult to common sense[35]
Justice gone mad? £30,000 for being called Gerry Adams[36]
£30,000 damages for Irish insult? stupidly high?[37]

It is ironic that these two cases were brought by Northern Irish Protestant men who were being racially harassed at work because of their "Irishness." Many Northern Irish Protestants would define themselves as British, both as a preferred identity because of the oppositional definitions of nationalism and unionism within Northern Ireland and because of their legal status as British citizens. Moreover, the stereotype linking Irish identity and Catholicism relies on understandings of irrational and childlike acceptance of religious dogma as an essential strand of "otherness." The lecturer was labeled "Gerry Adams" in a remarkable display of ignorance of his likely political support. Apparently anyone from Northern Ireland could automatically be branded as a supporter of, or substitute for, the demonized IRA. Irish origins alone were sufficient to invoke the full force of the stereotype.

Social class variations within the Irish-born population are also over-ridden by the stereotype, as the compensation cases illustrate. The strength of the working-class component of the Irish stereotype means that in England all Irish accents may be interpreted as working class. Mary Kells, in a social anthropological study, describes the experience of one of her respondents in London: "Alan, an accountant, was frequently assumed to be a builder, as a number of Irish builders were working locally."[38]

In another set of interviews, focusing on Irish women's lives, Rachel Harbron, a Protestant woman from Dublin whose father was a technical college lecturer, described her early months in England:

> I was half afraid to open my mouth in front of people in case they'd say, "Well, she's Irish and she's thick." I was afraid to make a mistake in my new job, afraid people would think, "Typical Irish." . . . It's a feeling I have, especially among upper middle-class English people, that they don't regard you in the same light as themselves. We are sort of second-class citizens, which you feel strongly. They might make jokes ragging your accent or whatever but the thought is still there, that in a general way they regard themselves as better.[39]

These blanket stereotypes, however, are experienced differently by women and men because their patterns of activity place them in different relationships to members of the majority English society and because of differently gendered patterns of social interaction. Women's occupations involve more personal contact with the majority society. In the "caring" professions of nursing and teaching, Irish women work face-to-face with English people using their verbal skills so that their accents are constantly on display. Although their perceived qualities may be thought to accord with positive feminine stereotypes, Irish women may be particularly exposed at times of heightened hostility. In the CRE survey nurses reported such treatment: "Sometimes even from clients, especially after something happened in Northern Ireland. Comments about the Irish—they should be shot and things." (Female nurse, London)

Office workers, largely women, also reported harassment from colleagues. This partly reflects their under-representation in clerical work (Table 14.1), which means they are often the only Irish people present. "White collar/blouse" workplaces also place emphasis on the use of standard English so that Irish accents appear more strongly deviant.[40] Respondents to the CRE survey described the atmosphere in places they had worked:

They think the Irish are thick and stupid. I was made to feel I had come out of a mud hut with pigs and chickens. Derogatory remarks—I was made to feel lower than the rest. (Female clerical worker, civil service)

They can be petty about things and make snide remarks: "Is that the Irish way of doing things?" (Female accounts assistant)

You look forward to 5:30 and hate 9:30 in the mornings. . . . I'd prefer another Irish person in there. It does help. (Female office worker)

Ironically, men in the most negatively stereotyped occupations in the construction industry may be more protected from direct harassment by working in an Irish environment.

Sound—no problems—you don't have them on the buildings. (Male construction worker)

Great on the site—the Irish are kings on the site, everyone respects them. Three to four months in a garage—bad, definitely because I was Irish. (Male laborer)

[Good atmosphere at work] The majority were Irish and we laughed the comments/jokes off. (Male construction worker)

Women who are mothers are also more exposed to neighbor harassment than men are, because they spend more time in the local area and have responsibility for children. A greater number of instances of anti-Irish abuse by neighbors was reported in areas with small Irish populations.

We were getting Irish abuse from our neighbors. My wife was called an "Irish cow," "fucking Irish bastards" etc. They threw glass in the baby's swimming pool. The council sent officers out and the abuse has since stopped. (Irish Republic-born man, London)

My previous neighbors didn't like me. I think it was because I was Irish. They didn't like my kids playing out in the garden. They complained about the noise. They expected me to muzzle my kids. (Irish Republic-born woman, London)

Gender differences can also be discerned in Irish people's responses to racist treatment, though much hostility is directed in very similar ways at both women and men. Overall about a third of the respondents said that they had no objection to Irish "jokes," while a further third felt ambivalent about them and said that their response depended on a range of factors including content, the manner in which they were recounted, and their own mood at the time. The final third always felt angered by these "jokes" and often challenged them.

Men were much more highly represented than women amongst the first group, who saw jokes as "simply a bit of fun." This may reflect gender differences in joking behavior.[41] Men are more orientated toward jokes and isolated pieces of humor and engage in aggressive and competitive forms of humor. "Irish jokes" fall into both these masculine categories of joking interaction. But men's apparent acceptance of "joking" may also mask the threat to their self-esteem posed by acknowledging this form of harassment. In the CRE survey women were also somewhat less likely to report hearing anti-Irish comments, possibly reflecting the masculinity of "banter" interactions in the workplace.

Irish responses to racist treatment have contributed to its invisibility and are also gendered. Nearly one fifth of the respondents in the CRE survey said that they had adopted the strategy of "keeping their heads down" at some time. Women were much more likely than men to admit to hiding their accents.

> At the beginning, because of people's reaction to my accent, taking the mickey out of the way you say words and you don't want to be seen as stupid. So I changed how I spoke, but not now. (Irish Republic-born woman in her twenties, London)
>
> When I came over at seventeen, I think you did because there was a lot of trouble. Didn't talk out loud in case it triggered it off. But then I decided I didn't care. (Irish Republic-born woman in her thirties, London)
>
> Often it would have been better not to have my accent. (Irish Republic-born woman in her sixties, London)

Speech is a key area of social evaluation in Britain, through which class identifications are made.[42] Linguistic analyses often comment on women's greater use of prestige forms of English in England.[43] This suggests that women are more conscious than men of social labeling by speech, and perhaps more liable to be judged in this way. Those at risk seek to protect themselves from the negative consequences of using undervalued speech patterns.[44] Irish women's attempts to disguise their accents can thus be understood as a form of protection from abuse. Silence ensures that attention is not drawn to one of the prime identifiers of Irishness.

CONCLUSION

Social classes comprise different groupings defined in terms of "race," ethnicity, and gender, just as ethnic groups consist not only of women and men but of people with a range of class positions.[45] Trying to discuss the interplay of racism, ethnicity, gender, and class involves a constant struggle against the urge to oversimplify and generalize without overstressing particularity.[46] The attempt to capture the complexity of the interplay is worthwhile, because all of us are more than whatever "race" or ethnicity we are taken to belong to, or identify with, and also more than whatever gendered or sexual identities we may possess. We have explored this complexity by examining how anti-Irish racism in England constructs gendered and classed stereotypes of Irish people, which then have specific impacts on, and evoke specific responses from, the gendered and classed Irish population in Britain.

Negative stereotypes of the Irish in Britain have a long history. There is a remarkably persistent core that continues to be drawn on: the male, working-class Catholic, likely to display the inherent characteristics of violence, drunkenness, stupidity, and duplicity. The vehemence with which it can be employed can partly be explained by English reactions to the open conflict in Northern Ireland since 1968, but shows strong elements of continuity with the 1950s and earlier periods, when "No Irish" signs were displayed in English cities.

These stereotypes place men at the forefront of the migrant population, depicting them "on the buildings" or in Irish pubs (Illustration 14.1). Ironically these locations afford some measure of protection to Irish men, who can restrict their interactions with the majority English population by their enclosure in Irish worlds. Irish women, in general, are more exposed to the effects of anti-Irish discrimination in their daily lives; and it is notable that many show a greater preference for adopting a low public profile. This is particularly the case in "white-blouse" work, where women are underrepresented and may often be the lone Irish person in the office.

There is not space here to draw out the full implications for the range of Irish identities that are produced in England. Previous research has indicated that second-generation Irish girls and boys in England, who grow up listening to anti-Irish jokes in the school playground, respond either with hostility or treat them as "a joke" in direct relation to the extent of their identification with their Irish background. The inferiorization of Irishness compared with Englishness means that they have to be in possession of a strong sense of themselves as Irish in order to resist these stereotypes.[47] Their parents, who mostly emigrated from the Republic of Ireland when its national identity was still constructed in opposition to but in terms derived from Britain, the ex-colonial oppressor, encounter these stereotypes from a different perspective. The "gaze" of the former colonial "other" positions Irish migrants in terms of hostile and exclusionary stereotypes. This is recognized, negotiated, resisted, accepted, or transformed daily, often in unconscious ways.

Recent migrants, who left in their tens of thousands in the 1980s, came from an Ireland that was already debating a postcolonial identity. They have settled in England during a period when the hegemony of Englishness is under sustained critique. Perhaps because of this there has been no decline in anti-Irish jokes, even while the global commodification of "Irishness" as sociability has apparently projected more positive representations of Irishness. Despite this changing context, most of the gendered and classed responses of Irish women and men to negative English stereotypes accounted for here are as representative of these new migrants as they are of earlier generations.

Gender permeates representations of the Irish in England at many levels, reflecting unequal power relations between the two nations. Although the stereotype that homogenizes Irish people is a predominantly masculine one, Ireland has occupied a feminized position of dependence in relation to Britain that continues to reverberate despite growing economic separation. This colonial legacy underlies the specificity of the experiences of the Irish diaspora in England, which remain much more hidden than those across the Atlantic.

NOTES

1. See also Mary J. Hickman and Bronwen Walter, "Deconstructing Whiteness: Irish Women in Britain," *Feminist Review* 50 (1995): 5–19.
2. Office for Population Censuses and Surveys (OPCS), *1991 Census Report for Great Britain. Ethnic Group and Country of Birth,* vol. 1 (London: Office for Population Censuses and Surveys, 1993).
3. See Catherine Hall, *White, Male and Middle-Class: Explorations in Feminism and History* (Cambridge: Polity Press, 1992) for an excellent account of the trajectory of debates within English feminism.
4. See Tariq Modood, Richard Berthoud, et al., *Ethnic Minorities in Britain: Diversity and Disadvantage* (London: Policy Studies Institute, 1997) for interesting discussions of the category "black" while maintaining a rigid black/white divide.
5. See Hall, *White, Male and Middle Class;* Philip Dodd, "Englishness and the National Culture," in *Englishness: Politics and Culture 1880–1920,* ed. Robert Colls and Philip Dodd (London: Croom Helm, 1986), 1–28; Philip Cohen, "The Perversions of Inheritance: Studies in the Making of Multi-Racist Britain," in *Multi-racist Britain,* ed. Philip Cohen and Harwant S. Bains (London: Macmillan, 1988), 9–118, on this process.
6. For example see Donald Akenson, *The Irish Diaspora. A Primer* (Belfast: Institute of Irish Studies, 1996).
7. Bronwen Walter, "Irishness, Gender and Place," *Environment and Planning D: Society and Space* 13 (1995): 35–50.
8. Avtah Brah, *Cartographies of Diaspora: Contesting Identities* (London: Routledge, 1996).
9. Robert Miles, *Racism after 'Race Relations'* (London: Routledge, 1993).
10. Stuart Hall, ed., *Representation: Cultural Representations and Signifying Practices* (London: Sage, 1997), 258.

11. Katharine Simms, "The Norman Invasion and the Gaelic Recovery," in *The Oxford Illustrated History of Ireland,* ed. Roy Foster (Oxford: Oxford University Press, 1989).

12. Dodd, *Englishness.* English "public schools" are private institutions charging substantial fees. Most have a large proportion of boarding pupils and serve a national market. Only selected fee-paying schools are included in the category.

13. Frederick Engels, *The Condition of the Working Class in England,* 105, quoted in Mervyn Busteed, Robert Hodgson, and Thomas Kennedy, "The Myth and Reality of Irish Migrants in mid-Nineteenth-century Manchester: A Preliminary Study," in *The Irish in the New Communities,* vol. 2, *The Irish World Wide,* ed. Patrick O'Sullivan (Leicester: Leicester University Press, 1992), 26–51.

14. Mary J. Hickman and Bronwen Walter, *Discrimination and the Irish Community in Britain* (London: Commission for Racial Equality, 1997).

15. Claire Pajaczkowska and Lola Young, "Racism, Representation, Psychoanalysis," in '*Race,' Culture, and Difference,* ed. James Donald and Ali Rattansi Ali (London: Sage, 1992).

16. Ashis Nandy, *The Intimate Enemy: Loss and Recovery of Self Under Colonialism* (Oxford: Oxford University Press, 1983), 2.

17. Iris Marion Young, *Justice and the Politics of Difference* (Princeton: Princeton University Press, 1989).

18. Mariella Buckley, "Sitting on Your Politics: The Irish Among the British and the Women Among the Irish," in *Location and Dislocation in Contemporary Irish Society: Emigration and Irish Identities,* ed. Jim MacLaughlin (Cork: Cork University Press, 1997), 105.

19. Tom Nairn, *The Enchanted Glass* (London: Radius Press, 1988).

20. Mary J. Hickman, *Religion, Class and Identity: The State, the Catholic Church and the Education of the Irish in Britain* (Aldershot: Avebury, 1995); Sarah Morgan, "The Contemporary Racialization of the Irish in Britain: An Investigation into Media Representations and the Everyday Experience of Being Irish in Britain" (Ph.D. diss., University of North London, 1997).

21. John Kirkaldy, "English Newspaper Images of Northern Ireland 1968–73: An Historical Study in Stereotypes and Prejudices" (Ph.D. diss., University of New South Wales, Australia, 1979); Roy Douglas, Liam Harte, and Jim O'Hara, *Drawing Conclusions: A Cartoon History of Anglo-Irish Relations 1798–1998* (Belfast: Blackstaff Press, 1998).

22. Melanie Tebbutt, "The Evolution of Ethnic Stereotypes: An Examination of Stereotyping with Particular Reference to the Irish (and to a lesser extent the Scots) in Manchester During the Late Nineteenth and Early Twentieth Centuries." (M.Phil. thesis, University of Manchester, 1983).

23. Ronald Walshaw, *Migration to and from the British Isles* (London: Jonathan Cape, 1941), 75.

24. Bronwen Walter, "Ethnicity and Irish Residential Distribution," *Transactions Institute of British Geographers* 11 (1986): 131–146.

25. Joan O'Flynn, *Identity Crisis: Access to Social Security and ID Checks* (London: Action Group for Irish Youth, 1993).

26. *London Evening Standard,* 4 Mar. 1998.

27. In the 1991 British Census the Irish were included as having two birthplace groups, those from the Republic being enumerated separately from people born in Northern Ireland. The Irish were not categorized as an "ethnic group," which was in practice defined by "whiteness" and "nonwhiteness" rather than according to ethnic origins. However, in the published Ethnic Group Tables, the two Irish birthplace categories were amalgamated into one entitled "Born in Ireland," which was added as a final column in many, but not all, tables. See Bronwen Walter, "Challenging the Black/White Binary: The Need for an Irish Category in the 2001 Census," *Patterns of Prejudice* 32 (1998): 73–86.

28. Judy Scully, "The Irish Diaspora as Bar Entrepreneurs: A Comparative Study Between Birmingham (UK) and Chicago (US)" (Ph.D. diss., University of Warwick, 1994); Stephen Castles and Mark Miller, *The Age of Migration* (London: Macmillan, 1993); Gerald Mars and Robin Ward, "Ethnic Business Development in Britain: Opportunities and Resources" in Ward Robin and Jenkins Richard, ed. *Ethnic Communities in Britain* (Cambridge: Cambridge University Press, 1984).

29. The "ethnic" labels used in this section are those adopted by the 1991 Census, which included white and a range of non-white categories, including Black Caribbean, Black African, Black other, Indian, Pakistani, Bangladeshi, Chinese.

30. Michael Hornsby-Smith and Angela Dale, "The Assimilation of Irish Immigrants in Britain," *British Journal of Sociology* 39 (1988): 519–543; Hickman and Walter, *Discrimination.*

31. Hickman and Walter, *Discrimination.*

32. Ibid.

33. Floya Anthias and Nira Yuval-Davis, *Racialized Boundaries. Race, Nation, Gender, Colour and Class the Anti-Racist Struggle* (London: Routledge, 1992).

34. *The Sun,* 22 Jan. 1994.

35. *Daily Mail,* 23 Sept. 1995.

36. *The Sun,* 23 Sept. 1995.

37. *Daily Telegraph,* 23 Sept. 1995.

38. Mary Kells, *Ethnic Identity Amongst Young Middle Class Irish Migrants in London* (London: Irish Studies Center Occasional Papers Series 6, 1995), 30.

39. Mary Lennon, Marie McAdam, and Joanne O'Brien, *Across the Water: Irish Women's Lives in Britain* (London: Virago, 1988), 208.

40. Jennifer Longman Coates and Deborah Cameron, ed., *Women in Their Speech Communities* (London: Longman, 1988).

41. Jerry Palmer, *Taking Humour Seriously* (London: Routledge, 1994).

42. John Osmond, *The Divided Kingdom* (London: Constable, 1988).

43. Martin Montgomery, *An Introduction to Language and Society* (London: Routledge, 1986).

44. Spender Dale, *Man-made Language* (London: Routledge and Kegan Paul, 1980).

45. Anthias and Yuval-Davis, *Racialized Boundaries.*

46. Vron Ware, *Beyond the Pale: White Women, Racism and History* (London: Verso, 1992).

47. Mary Hickman, "A Study of the Incorporation of the Irish in Britain with Special Reference to Catholic State Education: Involving a Comparison of the Attitudes of Pupils and Teachers in Selected Secondary Schools in London and Liverpool" (Ph.D. diss., University of London Institute of Education, 1990).

Index